Measuring ESG Effects in Systematic Investing

Founded in 1807, John Wiley & Sons is the oldest independent publishing company in the United States. With offices in North America, Europe, Australia, and Asia, Wiley is globally committed to developing and marketing print and electronic products and services for our customers' professional and personal knowledge and understanding.

The Wiley Finance series contains books written specifically for finance and investment professionals as well as sophisticated individual investors and their financial advisors. Book topics range from portfolio management to e-commerce, risk management, financial engineering, valuation, and financial instrument analysis, as well as much more.

For a list of available titles, visit our Web site at www.WileyFinance.com.

Measuring ESG Effects in Systematic Investing

ARIK BEN DOR, ALBERT
DESCLÉE, LEV DYNKIN,
JINGLING GUAN, JAY HYMAN
SIMON POLBENNIKOV

WILEY

This edition first published 2024

Arik Ben Dor, Albert Desclée, Lev Dynkin, Jingling Guan, Jay Hyman, and Simon Polbennikov ©2024

Registered Offices
John Wiley & Sons, Inc., 111 River Street, Hoboken, NJ 07030, USA

John Wiley & Sons Ltd, The Atrium, Southern Gate, Chichester, West Sussex, PO19 8SQ, UK

Editorial Office
The Atrium, Southern Gate, Chichester, West Sussex, PO19 8SQ, UK

For details of our global editorial offices, customer services, and more information about Wiley products visit us at www.wiley.com.

Library of Congress Cataloging-in-Publication Data is Available:

ISBN 9781394214785 (Cloth)
ISBN 9781394214792 (ePDF)
ISBN 9781394214808 (ePub)

Cover Design: Wiley
Cover Image: © fantasyform/Shutterstock

SKY10068736_030124

To my parents, Lya and Ron, for their lifelong dedication, love, and sacrifice, my wife Melina for her support and encouragement throughout, my brother Oren for always being there for me, and my biggest pride and achievement, my children Shiraz, Shelly, Tamir, and Nili

–ABD

To my wife, Anne-Louise, for her patience and support

–AD

To my wife Alina for her unwavering support and to my children David, Aryeh, Joseph, and Rachel who inspire all my work

–LD

To my mother Zuohua Yu and my father Xiaogang Guan for their unconditional love, support, and encouragement

–JG

To my dear wife Ella, who continually inspires and empowers me with her indomitable creative spirit

–JH

To my colleagues

–SP

Contents

Many investors choose to integrate ESG considerations into their portfolios, either through negative screening or using a best-in-class approach, in which top ESG-rated companies are selected to represent each market segment. These decisions might affect other portfolio attributes. We demonstrate the linkages of ESG scores to credit ratings and corporate bond spreads, and show that E, S, and G scores can be intercorrelated. Integrating ESG considerations into portfolios can potentially introduce biases if not properly controlled. We can measure the effect of ESG on security valuation and its changes over time. The ideas presented in this chapter form the motivation for much of the work in the book.

We present a methodology for measuring the effect of ESG on returns by constructing highly diversified index-tracking portfolios that maximize or minimize ESG score while matching the index in all other systematic risk exposures. Both portfolios are also constrained to be sufficiently diversified to avoid security-specific risk exposures. This "exposure-matched" approach ensures that these two portfolios differ only in their ESG scores. The performance difference between such Max-ESG and Min-ESG portfolios represents the return due purely to ESG. We apply this technique to track this ESG return premium in credit markets.

Using an exposure-matched approach similar to that of Chapter 2, we measure the ESG return premium in three equity markets: the US, Europe, and China. We show that these exposure-matched return premia can be very different than those measured by simple comparison of an ESG-constrained index with a standard benchmark.

As in corporate markets, ESG criteria tend to favour higher-quality sovereign issuers. ESG-tilted sovereign bond portfolios, if unconstrained, will therefore exhibit higher credit quality and lower spreads. Once we control for credit quality in portfolio construction, ESG attributes do not have a statistically significant effect on portfolio returns.

Almost all ESG-labelled credit funds employ negative screening to exclude issuers involved in certain non-compliant activities. We introduce a methodology to measure the performance of excluded issuers, relative to relevant peers, while controlling for differences in systematic risk exposures. The performance effect of negative screening is evaluated from both a bottom-up and a top-down perspective.

We investigate the effect of ESG constraints on performance in the context of a systematic bond selection strategy. The unconstrained strategy uses signals based on value, momentum, and sentiment to generate consistent outperformance of the target index. We show how ESG-based exclusions from the allowable bond universe can affect the strategy's ability to generate active returns.

CHAPTER 7
Incorporating ESG Considerations in Equity Factor Construction

The construction of factor portfolios has become a standard way to capture the key drivers of performance in equity markets, such as size, value, growth, and momentum. We impose ESG constraints of various types on factor portfolios to measure the extent to which such constraints can cause ESG-constrained factor returns to deviate from their unconstrained counterparts.

PART THREE: PERFORMANCE IMPLICATIONS OF COMPANIES' ESG POLICIES
Introduction to Part III

CHAPTER 8
ESG Rating Improvement and Subsequent Portfolio Performance

Some investors seek to invest in companies with an improving ESG profile. We examine whether changes in firms' ESG scores ('ESG momentum') generate a unique return premium distinct from the 'level premium' identified previously. We study equity and credit markets in parallel and find that ESG momentum generated a positive and economically significant return premium. Bonds and stocks of US firms with larger improvement in their ESG scores earned higher returns, even after controlling for the ESG level effect.

CHAPTER 9
Predicting Companies' ESG Rating Changes Using Job-posting Data

We employ a novel dataset of job postings by US firms, as well as natural language processing, to identify ESG-related openings of firms in our sample. We find that firms with higher ESG posting intensity than their peers were more likely to experience improvements in ESG ratings and higher subsequent stock returns.

ESG ratings from different providers may vary due to differences in
methodology. We examine whether the dispersion in firms' ESG rankings
among providers is informative in its own right, beyond what is reflected in
the average level of their ESG ratings. We find that firms with higher
dispersion in their ESG rankings have experienced larger rating revisions in
the following year. We also document that dispersion has been negatively
related to subsequent performance in both stock and bond portfolios.

Foreword

There are many ways in which the financial industry can facilitate the path to a sustainable economy. These include financing relevant companies and projects, developing themed investment products, contributing to the development of regulatory guidelines, and influencing corporate disclosure in related areas. One of the key tasks in motivating the efforts in all of these directions is the quantification of the impact of ESG investing on the performance and valuation of financial assets. While financial performance is not the only decision variable in shaping the integration of sustainability principles into corporate practice and investment management, it is certainly an important consideration, given the fiduciary responsibilities of corporate boards to shareholders and portfolio managers to their investors.

Has an ESG tilt been additive, all else equal, to performance of credit and equity portfolios? Have investments by corporations in improving their ESG ratings paid off in improved valuation of their bonds and stock? Objective, data-driven answers to such questions have only recently become feasible because they require, in addition to quantitative research expertise, sufficient accumulation of historical data. The authors took full advantage of such data to develop innovative methodologies of quantifying ESG effects on financial assets.

The authors of this book are part of the top-ranked Quantitative Portfolio Strategy (QPS) team within Barclays Research.[1] They do not seek to present their views on ESG investing. Rather, they approach ESG investing from a purely quantitative perspective. They offer important methodologies for measuring ESG factor returns and quantifying their effects on portfolio performance. ESG is a firm-level attribute. Its impact on performance of financial assets must be analysed in a consistent fashion across the debt and equity securities of a company. An integrated approach not only provides the reader an opportunity to understand ESG effects more broadly, but also to demonstrate how robust these effects are. By drawing on their experience across bond and equity markets, as well as ESG-related expertise across Barclays Research, the authors of this book are uniquely positioned to offer readers a map for consistently navigating ESG implications in both credit and equity investing.

This work represents yet another successful installment in the research efforts of the QPS team.

C.S. Venkatakrishnan
Group Chief Executive Officer, Barclays

NOTE

1. The QPS team was ranked number 1 in quantitative analysis in the Fixed Income Institutional Investor Survey in 2023.

Preface

This book views the sustainability aspect of institutional investing—a topic often debated based on convictions and opinions—through a purely quantitative, objective lens. The authors are members of the Quantitative Portfolio Strategy (QPS) Group, which has been a part of Barclays' research for over 15 years. The group's mandate includes advising the largest institutional investors around the globe on any quantitative aspects of portfolio management across asset classes including fixed income and equity.

As a result, all of the research from this team, this book included, addresses practical issues of the investment process. The group enjoys a strong reputation in the industry as evidenced by its long-standing high ranking in the Institutional Investor Fixed Income research survey for the past 15 years and the readership of its prior four books—all on different aspects of quantitative portfolio management. The group's dual focus on equity and fixed income portfolio management allows it to apply consistent methodologies across asset classes and perform additional verification of their robustness. QPS research on ESG investing is informed by the focus of the larger Barclays' Research on various related topics—from the evolution of the regulatory landscape to natural language processing of ESG-related text.

This book doesn't take sides in the debate on the merits of ESG investing but rather informs it by providing data-driven evidence of the impact of the sustainability tilt on portfolio performance and valuation. Quantifying this impact requires controlling all other systematic exposures in an ESG-compliant portfolio. The authors propose a comprehensive approach to isolating ESG-related effects on investment performance and valuation, apply it consistently to both credit and equity portfolios, and track these effects historically in both markets. The authors also address one of the main challenges of ESG research: the lack of an industry standard for what aspects of corporate activity should be measured as part of the evaluation of ESG compliance, how to measure them, and how to summarize the complex set of disparate activities undertaken across the breadth of a large corporation. The authors not only present a mechanism for normalizing diverse scores across providers to make them comparable, but also show that the extent of their dispersion itself has implications for future portfolio performance.[1]

The authors investigate the impact of an ESG tilt on characteristics of traditional equity style factors and on systematic credit style factors such as value and momentum.

In addition to a detailed presentation of the issues facing ESG investors, the book discusses the implications for corporations of the investments they make to improve their ESG footprint.

The methodologies and findings described in this book are relevant to all investment practitioners active in sustainable investing in either equity or credit as well as to researchers, risk managers, and academics in this field.

Jeff Meli

Global Head of Research, Barclays

NOTE

1. *This book is published for academic purposes. The information provided in this book does not constitute 'investment research' or a 'research report' and should not be relied on as such. This book does not contain investment advice or recommendations and it should not be used to make investment decisions. Information in this book does not constitute a financial benchmark. Information in this book may not be accurate or complete and may be sourced from third parties. Any past or simulated past performance including back-testing, modelling or scenario analysis contained herein is no indication as to future performance or results.*

   Environmental, Social, and Governance ('ESG') Related Information: *There is currently no globally accepted framework or definition (legal, regulatory or otherwise) of, nor market consensus as to what constitutes, an 'ESG', 'green', 'sustainable', 'climate-friendly' or an equivalent company, investment, strategy or consideration or what precise attributes are required to be eligible to be categorized by such terms. This means there are different ways to evaluate a company or an investment and so different values may be placed on certain ESG credentials as well as adverse ESG-related impacts of companies and ESG controversies. The evolving nature of ESG considerations, models and methodologies means it can be challenging to definitively and universally classify a company or investment under an ESG label and there may be areas where such companies and investments could improve or where adverse ESG-related impacts or ESG controversies exist. The evolving nature of sustainable finance related regulations and the development of jurisdiction-specific regulatory criteria also means that there is likely to be a degree of divergence as to the interpretation of such terms in the market. It is expected that industry guidance, market practice, and regulations in this field will continue to evolve. Any references to 'sustainable', 'sustainability', 'green', 'social', 'ESG', 'ESG considerations', 'ESG factors', 'ESG issues' or other similar or related terms in this book are not references to any jurisdiction-specific regulatory definition or other interpretation of these terms, unless specified otherwise.*

Acknowledgements

The authors would like to thank their colleagues from the Quantitative Portfolio Strategy (QPS) team at Barclays Research—Mathieu Dubois, Stephan Florig, Felix Kempf, Vadim Konstantinovsky, Hugues Langlois, Alberto Pellicioli, Yunpeng Sun and Xiaming Zeng—for their contributions to this book and their help in preparing and reviewing the manuscript.

We would also like to thank our colleagues from other parts of Barclays Research: Maggie O'Neal for valuable discussions of ESG-related topics and for writing the introduction to Part IV; Ryan Preclaw and Adam Kelleher for their partnership in analyzing some of the large data sets used in this book; and Valerie Monchi and Amy Pompliano for their guidance on compliance aspects of the production of this book.

The authors are grateful to Jeff Meli, Global Head of Barclays Research, for his continued support of the group's work.

Finally, the authors would like to thank their families for bearing over the years the sacrifices of family time necessary to produce the research in this book and prepare the book for publication.

Introduction

The ongoing debate about the merits of ESG (Environment, Social, Governance) investing in financial markets requires careful measurement of its effect on portfolio performance. Investors may choose to integrate ESG tilts in their portfolios for different reasons, based on sustainability considerations and/or because they believe that ESG ratings reflect material risks and corresponding performance opportunities. These considerations may be reflected in the investment policy in different ways, ranging from strict exclusion of companies and sectors involved in non-compliant activities to a more nuanced best-in-class approach that selects the companies with the best ESG rankings within each peer group.

A simple comparison between the returns of a sustainability index and the standard underlying index, whether in equities or in credit, can result in a distorted view of the ESG effect on performance. Two such indices could differ in sector allocations, average issue size, and credit ratings—all sources of performance with risk premia of their own. How should we measure the effect of ESG investing on portfolio performance? Do traditional risk factors in both equity and credit markets retain their properties when subjected to ESG constraints? Do measures taken by corporate issuers to improve their ESG profile help their subsequent ratings and the performance of their debt and equity securities? How should investors handle the lack of uniformity in ESG definitions? Addressing all these issues requires a quantitative framework aligned with the systematic approach to investing.

We pursue a consistent parallel analysis of the ESG effect on systematic strategies in equity and bond markets. Applied to security selection these strategies involve the systematic use of financial models for all securities within the investment universe, and the construction of highly diversified portfolios that reflect a number of investment themes, or factors, in a risk-efficient manner. While systematic investing has been in the mainstream of equity investing for decades, it has recently started gaining popularity among bond investors as well. There are several reasons for these past differences and for the recent convergence in acceptance of algorithmic investing between the two markets. Most equities are exchange traded and more liquid than bonds. Equity market data have been broadly available to researchers in academia and the financial industry for many years. As a result, all aspects of quantitative investing in equities—from definition of the factors driving stock returns, to selection signals predictive of future security or sector performance, to portfolio optimization methodologies—have been well researched, exploited by investors, and widely accepted alongside the traditional fundamental, discretionary investment style. In the past few years fixed-income investors also saw increased availability of bond market data from vendors, improved price transparency, increased liquidity due to regulatory reporting requirements to shared databases such as TRACE, and a rise in e-trading, ETFs, and portfolio trading. All of these developments, coupled with the influence of established quantitative insights from the equity markets, enabled the expansion of systematic investing to fixed income, as we discussed in our book, *Systematic Investing in Credit* (Wiley, 2021). In the current volume, we focus on the intersection of systematic investing with the trend towards ESG integration, particularly on the impact of an ESG ratings tilt ('positive screening') or of ESG-related exclusions ('negative screening') on the performance of systematic strategies in credit and equities and on the valuation of securities. Our objectives are to offer consistent methodologies for measuring the effects of ESG on the performance of equity and fixed income portfolios, to document the historical magnitude of these effects and the related valuation trends, to quantify the impact of ESG constraints on the performance of systematic strategies and style factors, and to measure the efficacy of corporate actions in the sustainability area.

The book is purely methodological and relies on historical analysis of market data,[1] offering no subjective views on the merits of ESG investing. This is in line with the long-standing mandate of our research group. The authors are members of the Quantitative Portfolio Strategy (QPS) group, which has been a part of Barclays (and previously Lehman Brothers) Research for over three decades. The group has a unique focus on working with major institutional investors across the globe on any issues of portfolio management that are quantitative in nature. As a result of this focus, research produced by the group tends to be practical and implementable. The group's publications target portfolio managers and other investment practitioners, as well as research analysts and academics. The group's past involvement in the creation of fixed-income indices and expertise in quantitative research in both equities and bonds further helped it develop consistent methodologies across the two markets. To enable parallel analysis in equity and bond markets, we rely on a proprietary issuer-level historical mapping (that accounts for corporate events) between corporate bonds and equity of a given company. The approach taken in this book is fully objective and free of any views or opinions. Rather, we 'let the data speak'.

The conventional definition of systematic strategies includes fully rule-based algorithmic methodologies aimed at improving portfolio performance by generating alpha. Some of them fall into the 'smart beta' category and take advantage of inefficiencies in the design of traditional market indices. Others harvest risk premia associated with risk factors, both traditional and new. In this book, we take a more expansive view of systematic investing to include any aspects of portfolio construction that are quantitative in nature. For example, we will include in this expanded definition methodologies for isolating the ESG risk premium from other unrelated systematic exposures. In the language of systematic investing, a risk factor is a source of portfolio risk independent of other established risk factors, which is priced in the market and is expected to be compensated by extra portfolio return—the risk premium. Is ESG a risk factor? Do bonds issued by firms that have strong ESG ratings have fundamentally different risk profiles than those with low ESG ratings? On the one hand, many proponents of ESG investing hold the view that stronger governance is associated with management quality, and hence corporate decisions that lead to higher investor cash flows. Stronger credentials on the Environmental and Social dimensions may reduce exposure to adverse corporate developments such as litigation, changes in regulation, or changes in customer acceptance. On the other hand, there has been insufficient empirical evidence so far that ESG ratings are indeed associated with systematic risk. In this book, although we use the term 'ESG risk premium' to refer to the isolated ESG-related return (free of any other risk factor exposures and idiosyncratic risk), we are not taking a view on whether ESG exposure is a risk factor that should be expected to carry a risk premium. (In fact, in Chapter 4 we show that for sovereign bonds the ESG-related return is subsumed by the credit rating.) We hope that our work to document the relationships between ESG characteristics will help inform this discussion going forward.

All the materials included in the book reflect original QPS research as it was first published. With few exceptions where an update was essential, we decided against going back and updating the data analysis in individual chapters to avoid any possibility of hindsight tainting the results.

This book is structured in four parts.

In Part I, we address the seemingly simple question of how to measure the returns associated with an ESG tilt in a portfolio or an index. Most sustainable versions of broad market indices in both equity and credit are defined by exclusion of non-compliant issuers or industries. However, the difference in performance between these sustainable indices and the original index cannot be interpreted as return due to ESG, as the two indices differ in sector allocations, credit quality, issuer size, and a number of other characteristics that also affect security returns. Even if sector allocations are constrained to match the broad index, tilting a portfolio within sectors towards high ESG issuers will simultaneously tilt it towards higher rated, large-cap companies, which tend to be more compliant. We propose a methodology for isolating the performance effect of ESG while matching the underlying index in all other risk dimensions, and we document the behaviour of this premium in equities and bonds over time. The ESG risk premium obtained in this exposure-matched way, free of all systematic biases, can differ from the simple performance differential between a sustainable and standard index not only in magnitude, but also in sign. Separately we study the ESG effect on the pricing and performance of sovereign bond portfolios. In addition to our methodology for measuring the performance of 'best-in-class' ESG investing, we also study the effect of the exclusionary approach of Socially Responsible Investing (SRI) on credit portfolio performance. The negative screening of entire industry groups makes it difficult to exactly match index risk characteristics; we therefore introduce a new technique for measuring the performance effect of such constraints.

In Part II, we measure the impact of ESG constraints on the performance of a systematic credit strategy that utilizes three of our proprietary signals—value, momentum, and sentiment. The key question addressed is whether the ESG constraints interfere with the strategy's ability to generate alpha. We follow this up with a study of the ESG effect on the return profile of equity style factors introduced by our group. These include, among others, well-established factors such as momentum, value, growth, quality, yield, low volatility, and size (some of them with proprietary changes in definition), which our group publishes across global equity markets. We test whether the return profile associated with each factor is preserved after applying ESG constraints of different types.

In Part III, we switch our focus from studies of ESG-related choices made by investors to the implications of ESG-related activities of the issuers. Does the market reward corporations with improving ESG scores by raising the valuations of their debt and equity? Do ratings providers reward companies that hire for ESG-related positions at a greater rate than their peers by raising their ESG ratings? Does improved corporate governance as measured by the G in the ESG ratings lead to higher company profitability?

In Part IV, we analyse the investment implications of the dispersion in ESG scores across different providers and of ESG labelling of mutual funds. Sustainable investing is still a young field and convergence to standards is not yet complete. This applies both to ESG rating methodologies and to the scale on which these ratings are assigned. This dispersion complicates score comparison across vendors. We show how to properly calculate a consensus score among multiple providers despite these difficulties by first normalizing the scores. Even after this normalization, there can be significant disagreement among score providers. Does such disagreement have implications for future ESG returns? A similar lack of clarity can be found in the labelling of mutual funds, particularly in the United States. Do ESG-labelled funds indeed invest in issuers with above-average ESG ratings? How does this label influence fund performance, fund flows, and AUM?

This book could not have been written until a sufficient history of ESG scores became available across multiple vendors utilizing comparable (even if different) methodologies. Some of the ESG-related effects discussed in Parts III and IV had persistent implications for performance of equities and bonds over the period of the respective studies. We find that both equity and credit securities of issuers with improving ESG ratings outperformed their peers with unchanged or declining ESG scores on an all-else-equal basis. Securities of issuers with significant dispersion of ESG scores across rating providers underperformed their risk-matched peers with more consensus on their ratings. Firms with an above-average rate of ESG-related hiring saw their ratings subsequently improve and their equity outperform risk-matched peers. We document these predictive relationships between ESG attributes and subsequent performance, but hesitate to label them as persistent alpha sources since these relationships may change according to investor interest in ESG investing. In fact, all of our numeric findings are subject to change—ESG-related returns that were positive over one period of history can turn negative in another. The evolving regulatory landscape can change the dynamics of ESG ratings produced by different vendors or the rules of ESG fund labelling. However, it is our hope that the methodologies outlined here will remain applicable throughout changing markets and regulations and will help investors navigate ESG-related decisions in their bond and equity portfolios.

We would like to thank our clients for the stimulating questions and continual dialogue that led to many of the results covered in this book, our colleagues who provided invaluable help with the analysis and preparation of the manuscript, and the senior management of Barclays for their unwavering support and encouragement of our work. We hope that portfolio managers, research analysts, and academics in the field of systematic investing, in both fixed income and equities, will find these chapters useful. As always, we welcome inquiries and challenges to our work.

Lev Dynkin
Global Head of Quantitative Portfolio Strategy, Barclays Research

NOTE:

Notes on Data Providers:

"MSCI" refers to MSCI ESG Research.

"Compustat" refers to S&P Global Market Intelligence Compustat®.

"CSI" refers to the China Securities Index Company. All rights in the CSI 800 ("Index") vest in China Securities Index Company ("CSI"). CSI does not make any warranties, express or implied, regarding the accuracy or completeness of any data related to the Index. CSI is not liable to any person for any error of the Index (whether due to negligence or otherwise), nor shall it be under any obligation to advise any person of any error therein.

One

Effect of ESG Constraints on Portfolio Performance and Valuation

INTRODUCTION TO PART I

The very first question to address in discussing ESG-related investing is the effect an ESG tilt has on portfolio performance and the valuation of securities. Has ESG compliance been a benefit or a cost to portfolio returns? Have investors who elected to introduce an ESG tilt been rewarded by superior performance compared with ones that ignored this tilt or even took a contrarian view on its return impact? In markets and time periods when the ESG tilt benefited the portfolio performance, has it been achieved by an increase in valuation of high-ESG securities, which should at some point stop, mean-revert, and generate future underperformance? Given the fact that ESG ratings are formed at the issuer level, has the ESG risk premium been consistent across the equity and bonds of an issuer? With European asset managers leading the United States in ESG adoption, has this risk premium been consistent across the two geographies?

This seemingly simple question of what part of a portfolio return is related to ESG is often answered incorrectly. One approach to computing this risk premium is to sort the universe of securities by ESG scores and measure the performance difference between the highly rated and low-rated parts of this universe. Another common approach is to compare the return of a standard

1

index describing a given market segment to its sustainable version, often built by excluding non-ESG-compliant sectors and issuers. In Part I we argue that both of these approaches are misleading. As we show in Chapter 1, securities with high ESG ratings tend to be issued by large, highly rated companies which are able to fund ESG compliance initiatives and related reporting. They also tend to be concentrated in compliant market sectors which can perform differently from the broad market. So a simple difference between the performance of a high-ESG-rated portfolio and one with low ESG scores can reflect a size risk premium, a quality premium, or sector timing mixed in with the ESG risk premium.

In Chapters 2 and 3, we propose a consistent approach across credit and equity markets to computing a pure ESG risk premium (or the ESG part of the return) in isolation, controlling for all other risk factors. For a given market segment (e.g. S&P 500, investment grade credit, high yield) we create portfolios that are risk-matched to the corresponding index in every risk exposure except the ESG rating. We first seek to maximize this rating subject to constraints on all other systematic risk exposures and to a diversification constraint (to avoid impact of issuer-specific risk). We then we similarly find the low-ESG risk-matched portfolio. These two portfolios match in all risk attributes that affect performance (average issue size, credit rating, sector distribution, etc.) and differ only in their ESG exposure. We suggest that the difference in returns between these max-ESG and min-ESG portfolios represents a pure ESG risk premium and can be used to evaluate the effect of an ESG tilt on portfolio performance. We apply this risk-matched approach consistently across credit, high yield, and equities in different geographies and document the trajectory of this pure ESG risk premium in all these markets over the study period. Interestingly, results obtained using this risk-matched methodology can differ from the naïve measures of the ESG risk premium described earlier not only in magnitude but also in sign.

In Chapter 4, we study the effect of ESG on the pricing and performance of sovereign bonds. As in corporate markets, we find that ESG criteria tend to favour higher-quality sovereign issuers. ESG-tilted sovereign bond portfolios, if unconstrained, will therefore have higher credit quality and lower spreads. However, once we control for credit quality, we find that ESG attributes do not have a statistically significant effect on either spreads or portfolio returns. This is established using both a statistical approach and using our risk-matched portfolio construction methodology.

The risk-matched methodology featured in Chapters 2 to 4 is aligned with the 'best-in-class' approach, in which each market sector is represented in the portfolio by the issuers with the highest ESG ratings in the sector. However, many ESG-labelled credit funds employ a negative screening approach, in which they exclude issuers whose business activities conflict with certain values or social norms. The negative screening approach can lead to a very different effect on portfolio performance, as the systematic risk premium of the excluded sectors may fluctuate with market regimes and result in unintended portfolio volatility. In Chapter 5, we analyse the effect of such negative screening strategies, often referred to as Socially Responsible Investing (SRI), on the performance of credit portfolios, from both a bottom-up and a top-down perspective.

CHAPTER 1

How Do ESG Criteria Relate to Other Portfolio Attributes?

Sustainable investing, in which Environmental, Social, and Governance (ESG) issues are incorporated into the investment process, has become widespread in financial markets. While the primary focus of this movement was originally in equity markets, concerned investors have sought to extend these principles to their bond portfolios as well. The extent to which these considerations should be incorporated into investment guidelines is now very much a part of the discussion in both markets.

For some of the most committed investors, the knowledge that their funds are being invested to support the values in which they believe is so important that they would accept a lower return on their investments. A much larger group would be happy to support these values, but only once they are convinced that there is limited negative return effect. Finally, if consideration of ESG principles can actually help to improve portfolio performance – as many adherents claim – then it would be hard to justify any resistance to their adoption. The relationship between ESG characteristics and performance is therefore of primary importance.

Our first investigation of the effect of ESG on portfolio performance focused on the credit markets for several reasons. First, an increasingly large number of bond investors are interested in ESG investing. Second, credit investing is dominated by institutional investors, including pension funds, which are leading the trend for sustainable returns; bonds represent a substantial percentage of their assets. Finally, corporate bonds are complex: they combine exposure to interest rates and credit spread, so allocations along both dimensions influence risk and performance. Unintended biases can therefore easily appear when overweighting one bond relative to another. To aid bond managers in evaluating the potential performance effect of integrating ESG data into their portfolio construction, we must carefully control any systematic risk exposures.

In this chapter, we first introduce the ESG ratings that form the basis for much of the analysis in this book, and show how these ratings relate to other portfolio characteristics. What exactly do these scores measure and how are they constructed? We describe in general the approach followed by the major ESG providers. Next, we investigate the relationships among different metrics. How do these scores relate to more traditional credit ratings, or to corporate bond spreads? How stable are the scores over time? Are E, S, and G scores linked to each other? We investigate these questions in the context of the US investment grade (IG) credit market, using ESG ratings from MSCI ESG Research. Finally, we try to measure whether there is a detectable ESG spread premium: have bonds with better ESG scores been able to command higher prices and tighter spreads? How has this spread premium changed over time? In addition to the US IG market, we evaluate these spread premia for Euro IG corporates and for US high-yield (HY) bonds as well.

HOW ARE ESG RATINGS FORMED?

Each firm that provides independent ESG research and ratings has its own methodology for ratings formation. As there are naturally many similarities among the different approaches used, we begin with some general statements about the process. ESG ratings are based on a multicriteria scoring of individual corporations based on a large set of factors or metrics across all three E, S, and G dimensions. Environmental scores consider issues connected to global warming, energy usage, pollution, and the like. Social rankings deal with things like how a company treats its workers, health and safety considerations, data privacy, and community outreach. Corporate governance focuses on topics such as business ethics, board structure and independence, executive compensation policies, and accounting.

Global warming may be the most widely recognized 'poster child' of sustainable investing, but it is far from being the only issue considered. In fact, ESG ratings reflect a broad range of considerations within each of the three categories. Each ratings provider has a detailed hierarchy of sub-categories and specific issues that are used to arrive at numeric scores for each company. Table 1.1 offers a small sampling of the more detailed sets of issues examined by ESG ratings providers to form their E, S, and G scores.

The ranking process begins in a bottom-up manner. Within each of the three main dimensions, dozens of specific categories of risk are assessed, and each company is scored on its exposure to that category of risk and the steps it has taken to mitigate that risk. ESG score providers use information gleaned from a combination of sources, including both public information and company disclosures. These fine-grained scores on individual metrics are calculated on an absolute basis. These are then aggregated up to overall scores for each of the three pillars, or themes (E, S, and G), and from there to an overall ESG score, as weighted averages of the granular scores. An important component of the scoring process is the assignment of weights in this aggregation

TABLE 1.1 Sample issues considered in forming ESG scores.

Environment	Social	Governance
Carbon Emissions	Labour Management	Corporate Governance
Energy Efficiency	Diversity and Discrimination	Business Ethics
Natural Resource Use	Working Conditions	Anti-Competitive Practices
Hazardous Waste Management	Employee Safety	Corruption and Instability
Recycled Material Use	Product Safety	Anti-Bribery Policy
Clean Technology	Fair Trade Products	Anti-Money Laundering Policy
Green Buildings	Advertising Ethics	Compensation Disclosure
Biodiversity Programmes	Human Rights Policy	Gender Diversity of Board

Source: MSCI, Sustainalytics, Barclays Research.

process. A given corporation may be involved in many different businesses and geographies, each bringing a different set of ESG exposures. Similarly, the relative importance of each metric may vary substantially by industry or country. To meet this challenge, each ESG ranking firm has developed a scheme for assigning different sets of weights to underlying risk factors for each industry and company. Thus, while an overall Environment ranking will be provided for every firm, be it a bank, a pharmaceutical firm, or an oil company, the three scores will represent very different things, and the Environment score will form a different percentage of the overall ESG score. For example, the Environment pillar score has a relatively small weight in the combined ESG score of banks, but a large weight in the ESG rating of energy companies.

Both the selection of the underlying metrics that are evaluated and the weights assigned to these metrics change over time, reflecting industry developments and evolving beliefs regarding corporate 'best practice'. ESG assessments are based largely on a systematic multicriteria scoring approach, but this is supplemented by analyst research. Committee reviews of various issues that may arise in the ranking process leave room for subjective judgement. ESG ratings are reviewed periodically, and as needed, based on specific events. All of the major providers have in recent years increased the frequency of ESG monitoring, and now claim to follow corporations on a continuous basis.

We note that the research produced by the ESG rating firms contains two different kinds of rankings: relative and absolute. The most fine-grained metrics are typically absolute scores, or raw scores, for which scores can be compared between any two companies across the board. Conversely, the highest-level ESG ratings are based on relative rankings relative to a peer group of firms in the same industry. The precise definition of peer groups varies among ratings providers, often by sector but potentially also by geography. Comparisons of these ratings are most useful for comparing two firms within the same peer group; a comparison of the overall ESG scores of two firms in very different industries is much less meaningful. In this sense, ESG ratings are very different to credit ratings, which are meant to rank the creditworthiness of firms in all industries on a common scale.

The services provided by independent vendors of ESG research extend far beyond publishing ratings. They offer complete in-depth reports with analysts' insights on the key ESG issues facing each covered company, as well as special reports on key research themes. They may also provide advice on engagement, proxy voting, and governance issues, and monitor reputational risk and controversies.

Each ratings provider has developed their own unique approach to aggregating a multidimensional information set up to a set of high-level ratings. Although there are many commonalities in the process, as described earlier, each provider emphasizes a different set of characteristics when translating their analysis into numeric scores. The details of these calculations can be quite complex; each provider offers subscribers a lengthy document describing their rating methodology in detail.

Investment managers who wish to integrate ESG information into their investment processes thus have a large set of available data sources that they can draw upon. They can subscribe to the ranking services from one or more ESG ratings providers of the type described earlier. Alternatively, or in addition, they can obtain the raw data reported by corporations in their regulatory reports. The high dimensionality of this data, the lack of clear standards for evaluating them, and the potential for disagreement among the various data sources, raise a number of issues that we will address in Part IV of this book.

PROPERTIES OF ESG SCORES

How are ESG Scores Related to Corporate Bond Spreads and Credit Ratings?

Although using non-financial information, ESG scoring aims to discriminate among firms based on risk and opportunities on a long horizon. It may therefore have similarities with credit analysis, which aims to measure a corporation's risk of default. If that is the case, issuers that have high ESG scores are more likely to also have a high credit quality and trade at a lower spread to government bonds as the market demands a lower compensation for risk.

TABLE 1.2 Average characteristics of bonds in different tiers of ESG scores (August 2009 to April 2016).

	Low	Medium	High	High − Low
Average ESG Score	2.6	4.9	7.7	5.1
Spread over Treasury Bonds (bp)	172	154	134	−38
Rating Quality	A3	A3	A2	
Rating Quality Number	8.2	8.0	7.3	−0.9

Source: MSCI, Barclays Research.

This would also mean that filtering an investment or index universe to simply exclude low ESG bonds could automatically translate into a systematic bias to lower yield, and might therefore lead to inferior performance over time.

To find out whether ESG constraints can give rise to a quality or spread bias, we consider a broad universe of corporate bonds and investigate whether different sets of bonds, grouped by ESG scores, have different properties. Our universe is the Bloomberg US Corporate investment grade index, a popular benchmark for institutional asset managers investing in the US credit market.

We sort index bonds by their ESG scores and group them into three equal size buckets: low, medium, and high ESG. We report the average characteristics of the three portfolios in Table 1.2. We find that spreads decrease steadily with increasing ESG score; the average spread of high-ESG bonds was 38 basis points (bp) lower than that of the low-ESG group.

To measure the difference in quality, we transform the traditional letter ratings from credit rating agencies into a number (higher for lower quality and lower for higher quality) and then average the numeric ratings.[1] The difference in average rating between high and low ESG buckets corresponds to a one-notch change in credit rating.

We repeat this analysis for individual E, S, and G scores and for different points in time. The time-averaged results are shown in Figure 1.1. Investing in top tier ESG bonds comes with roughly a one-notch uptick in average credit quality. The effect is persistent, is more pronounced for the Environment pillar, and is almost absent for the Governance pillar. This might indicate that issuers with higher credit quality might generally be better able to comply with environmental constraints than those with lower credit quality, likely higher leverage and tighter financial constraints. A stronger balance sheet might indirectly help score well on Environmental metrics. From these results, it is

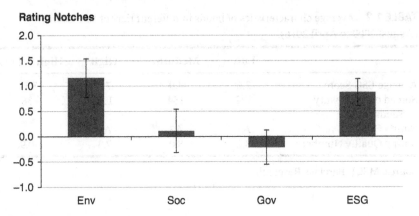

FIGURE 1.1   Average difference in credit rating between top and bottom tier of MSCI ESG rating (August 2009–February 2016).
Note: Error bars indicate one standard deviation around the mean.
Source: MSCI, Bloomberg; Barclays Research.

clear that investors should be careful when integrating ESG data in portfolio construction to avoid unintentional biases in allocation and in risk profile. Just overweighting better ESG companies can easily result in lower yields and, consequently, lower returns.

Individual E, S, and G scores can all have implications for the performance and risk of underlying companies. For example, a change in regulation in response to environmental challenges can affect corporate profitability and even survival, making a high Environmental score a desirable characteristic for a corporate issuer. Similarly, the Social score can indirectly reflect a better ability to attract and retain skilled workers. Finally, good corporate Governance not only ensures that management incentives are aligned with shareholder interests, but also that high-level risk controls are effectively implemented. ESG considerations may not be fully incorporated into credit ratings, leaving room for ESG providers to bring relevant incremental information to investors. A low correlation between credit rating and ESG scores could be a sign of such complementarities.

Figure 1.2 reports the average correlations[2] between ESG scores and credit ratings. Correlations with the composite ESG scores are positive but small – about 17%. The correlation between Governance and credit ratings is effectively zero, while the highest correlations are observed for the Environmental factor. When extending the analysis to individual industry sectors, we found that the highest correlation between ESG score and credit rating was observed in the banking sector.

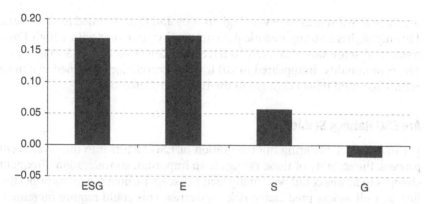

FIGURE 1.2　Average correlation between credit rating and MSCI ESG scores (August 2009–February 2016).
Source: MSCI, Bloomberg; Barclays Research.

How Correlated are the Individual Pillar Scores?

To what extent are individual E, S, and G scores from a single provider correlated with each other? For example, is a company that scores highly in terms of Governance also likely to have high Environment or Social scores? To address this question, Figure 1.3 shows monthly cross-sectional correlations between E, S, and G scores of individual issuers. The exercise is repeated every month to plot the evolution of correlations over time. The correlations among

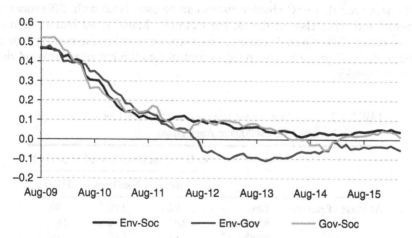

FIGURE 1.3　Correlations among MSCI E, S, and G scores.
Source: MSCI, Barclays Research.

the three MSCI scores were very high in 2009 and then declined to about zero. This highlights a strong historical commonality: an issuer with a high Environmental score was also likely to have high Governance and Social scores. The commonality disappeared in 2011, when correlations declined to almost zero. This could reflect changes in the ESG rating methodology.

Are ESG Ratings Stable?

For investors considering full integration of ESG factors into the investment process, the stability of these ratings is an important consideration. Frequent changes in scores could potentially lead to excess turnover in investor portfolios, as well as less predictable risk exposures. This could require incremental portfolio rebalancing and generate additional transaction costs, thereby reducing net performance.

Our data analysis reveals that MSCI ESG scores have been stable. A company that has a high ESG rating is likely to retain a high ESG rating on a one-year horizon. Similarly, a low ESG rating today is a strong predictor of a low ESG rating one year forward. For example, Table 1.3 shows that a top tier ESG company has more than an 80% probability of remaining in the top tier a year later. Thus, there is little reason to fear that the adoption of ESG criteria would become a cause of excessive portfolio turnover.

THE EFFECT OF ESG ON BOND VALUATION

We have seen that ESG characteristics can be associated with differences in spread and other risk attributes. For example, higher-rated issuers tend to have better ESG scores. Therefore, to determine whether the market is pricing in an 'ESG premium', we need to control for all other relevant bond risk characteristics.

TABLE 1.3 Transition frequencies across MSCI ESG tiers on a one-year horizon (August 2009 to April 2016).

		ESG rating level at end of period		
		Low	Medium	High
At start of period	Low	73%	24%	3%
	Medium	22%	60%	18%
	High	2%	17%	81%

Source: MSCI, Barclays Research.

To isolate the effect of ESG ratings on bond valuation, we run a regression analysis in which we explain the spread of all bonds in our study universe at a particular point in time using the ESG score of their respective issuer while controlling for systematic sources of risk such as credit rating, sector, and duration. This analysis provides an attribution of issuer spread, including the component due to the ESG factor.

Table 1.4 provides a sample result of such a regression in the US IG market using MSCI ESG scores, as of the end of March 2018. The regression has a high R-squared (72%), meaning that the full set of bond attributes used (industry, credit rating, option adjusted spread duration [OASD], and ESG score) explains much of the spread of any given bond at this time. Most of the control variables are highly significant, economically (large coefficient) and statistically (t-stats well in excess of 2 in most cases). The factor that we are interested in, the ESG spread premium, is negative, meaning that high ESG bonds tend to trade at slightly tighter spreads than low ESG bonds. The coefficient of −0.6 means that for a one-standard deviation increase in the ESG score of an issuer, the spread of its bonds decreases by 0.6 bp, making them marginally more expensive than comparable bonds of other issuers. The statistical significance of this coefficient is low (t-stat of −0.5), as there is substantial uncertainty around that estimate.

By repeating this analysis every month, we can chart the evolution of the ESG spread premium over time. Any significant changes in the ESG spread premium can point to a change in valuation of bonds resulting from their ESG characteristics. For example, if the spread difference between high and low ESG bonds decreases (or becomes more negative), meaning that high ESG bonds become more expensive relative to low ESG ones, one could assume that high ESG bonds benefit from increasing investor appetite. However, such re-pricing is typically limited in time, as high ESG bonds cannot continue to become increasingly expensive forever. Therefore, any performance based on such transient phenomenon should not be expected to be sustained but could be exposed to the risk of a reversal.

Figure 1.4 presents the time series of results for the ESG factor for the regression in Table 1.4.[3] The solid line in the plot shows the coefficient obtained for the ESG factor each month; a negative result means that high ESG bonds trade at tighter spreads than low ESG peers. The shaded region around each plot represents the 95% confidence interval; if a value of 0 is included in this region, then the result for that month is not statistically significant. We find that the results of the regression over the past few years have been consistent with that shown in Table 1.4. There is a slight indication of an ESG spread premium in US credit, but it is not often statistically significant.

We have carried out a similar analysis in the Euro IG credit market. In this case, in addition to credit rating, sector, and duration, we also control for

TABLE 1.4 Example spread attribution to ESG attributes in the US IG market at the end of March 2018 (using MSCI ESG data).

| | ESG | Duration | Credit Rating | | | | | | Industry Sector | | | | | | | |
	Score	OASD	A1	A2	A3	BAA1	BAA2	BAA3	BAS	CYC	NCY	COT	TRE	UTI	BAB	FIO
Coefficient	−0.6	8.4	2.3	8.8	18.9	35.7	51.2	77.6	62.8	64.9	57.3	72.2	77.0	77.1	87.0	76.0
t-stat	−0.5	22.7	0.4	1.7	3.8	7.3	10.6	14.6	12.2	11.1	12.1	14.3	14.3	12.9	18.5	14.4
R-Squared	71.8%															

Source: Bloomberg, MSCI, Barclays Research.
Note: Industry sector dummy variables have been added by partitioning the corporate universe into eight industry groups: basic industry, consumer cyclicals, consumer non-cyclicals, communications and technology, transportation and energy, utilities, banking and brokerage, and other financials.

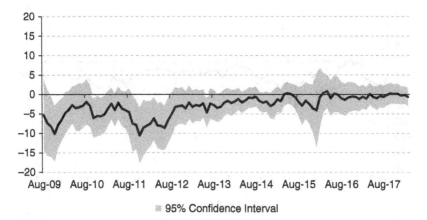

FIGURE 1.4 Historical ESG spread premium in the US IG market (bp per one standard deviation in ESG score).
Source: Bloomberg, MSCI, Barclays Research.

geography, as issuers from peripheral Europe are likely to have been affected by the high volatility of sovereign spreads observed from 2010 to 2012.

Figure 1.5 shows the ESG spread premium for the Euro IG market. We see that in Europe, high ESG bonds have traded at lower spreads than their low ESG peers. The magnitude of the spread factor in the latter part of the sample period is small (approximately −5 bp per standard deviation of ESG score) but significant. This could indicate different attitudes to ESG investing in the two markets: European investors might be more prepared to give up some income in favour of desirable ESG characteristics. This might also be a reflection of investor guidelines mandating a focus on high ESG issuers.

One might have expected that increased interest in sustainable investing would have driven up the prices (thus reducing spreads) of high ESG bonds. This hypothesis, which could explain why high-ESG portfolios have outperformed over this period (as we will show in Chapter 2), is not supported by the data in Figures 1.4 and 1.5. We do not observe a downward trend in ESG-related spreads in IG markets; if anything, they seem to have increased, becoming less negative in both US and Euro IG.

Can this analysis tell us which pillar score has been most valued by investors? To address this, we repeat our analysis with two changes: we substitute either the E, S, or G score alone for the overall ESG score in the above analysis; and we pool together the results for all months of the study. Table 1.5 summarizes the results of this pooled analysis for the US IG and Euro IG markets.

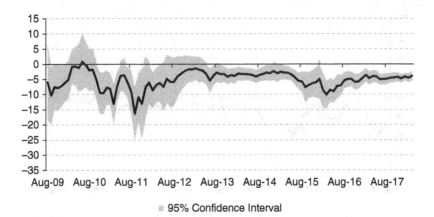

■ 95% Confidence Interval

FIGURE 1.5   Historical ESG spread premium in the Euro IG market
(bp per one standard deviation in ESG score).
Source: Bloomberg, MSCI, Barclays Research.

TABLE 1.5   Average spread premium, by ESG pillar, in US IG
and Euro IG markets (2009–2018).

	US IG	Euro IG
ESG Score (bp per std)	−3.0	−5.1
Env. Score (bp per std)	−2.2	−2.3
Soc. Score (bp per std)	0.0	−2.9
Gov. Score (bp per std)	−4.2	−5.0

Source: Bloomberg, MSCI, Barclays Research.

All three pillars of ESG are found to have a significant effect[4] on bond
valuations in Euro IG credit: a higher ESG rating corresponds to tighter
spreads, and a cheaper cost of debt. Governance has the largest and most significant effect. The same analysis performed in the US IG market is less conclusive: the coefficients are generally smaller in magnitude, and their signs
vary depending on the pillar considered.

We carried out a similar monthly analysis to assess the ESG spread premium in the US HY market as well. Estimated spread premia and corresponding 95% confidence intervals (shaded areas) are shown in Figure 1.6.
We find that the overall results are similar to those for IG credit: the indication is that the spread premium has been consistently negative, meaning that
issuers with high ESG scores command tighter spreads, but there is a lot of
uncertainty around these results. This spread premium has not followed a
clear trend during the time window considered: starting and ending premia

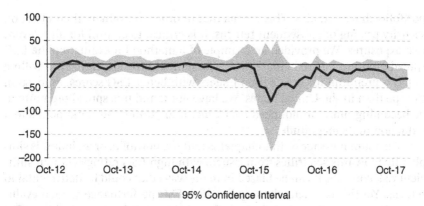

FIGURE 1.6 Historical ESG spread premium in the US HY market (bp).
Source: Bloomberg, MSCI, Barclays Research.

are not significantly different from each other. There was a clear increase in the magnitude of the spread premium (and the confidence intervals) during the energy crisis of 2015–16, which was characterized by elevated spread volatility, as well as spread dispersion across issuers and sectors.

Spread premium analysis reveals differences in appetite for ESG attributes between the US and Euro markets. These differences are not very large and did not follow a very clear trend or pattern during the time of our analysis, but they have been significant in recent years. From the perspective of Euro issuers, high ESG attributes have been rewarded with lower credit spreads and, hence, a lower cost of funding. On the other hand, investors favouring high ESG bonds have received slightly lower income returns. This effect was not as prominent in the US market. Could this mean that that an investment style that systematically favours high ESG bonds would perform differently in Europe than in the United States? This is one of the issues we will explore in the next chapter.

CONCLUSION

One way of viewing ESG ratings is that they measure aspects of a company's activities that had previously been overlooked by standard financial analysis and that are expected to be material to financial performance over a long horizon. Nevertheless, as we have illustrated in this chapter, ESG ratings are indeed correlated with traditional risk measures like spreads and credit ratings. These illustrations, although drawn from credit market data, highlight a more universal issue that applies to equity portfolios as well. ESG scores do not exist in a vacuum, and they can be closely related to other portfolio characteristics. This means that in order to evaluate their effect on security pricing or subsequent returns, it is critical to control for all relevant risk exposures. We provided an example of a method for evaluating the ESG spread premium in credit markets. We found that investors have been willing to pay a premium for bonds from issuers with better ESG scores, more so in Europe than in the United States. We have not found this spread premium to be becoming more pronounced over time; if anything, the trend points to a reduction in its magnitude.

The main message of this chapter is that if a portfolio, or an index, is simply tilted towards securities from issuers with high ESG ratings without sufficient risk controls, it can be biased in many ways that could be detrimental to returns. Yet this is exactly the way in which ESG performance is often evaluated. Many index providers, in both fixed income and equity markets, offer ESG-constrained versions of their flagship benchmark indices, formed by filtering the benchmark universe to exclude some companies based on ESG-related criteria. The difference between the returns of the ESG-constrained benchmark and the standard one is often quoted as the most easily accessible metric for the performance due to the ESG constraint. However, due to the biases we have highlighted, this is a flawed measure. In the next two chapters, we present a methodology for evaluating ESG effects on portfolio performance that corrects for these biases and gives a more balanced assessment of ESG-related performance. Chapter 2 presents this analysis for credit portfolios in both the United States and Europe, and Chapter 3 applies this methodology to equity markets in the United States, Europe, and China.

NOTES

1. The credit ratings used throughout this chapter are the index ratings from Bloomberg, which incorporate credit rating data from three agencies: Moody's, S&P, and Fitch. In case of split ratings, the index rating is defined as the median of the ratings from the three agencies. This is also converted to a numeric 'quality' ranking in which higher numbers correspond to lower ratings, with an increment of one corresponding to a single ratings notch.
2. The cross-sectional rank correlation between credit rating and ESG score is measured every month and then averaged over time, over the whole period of the analysis.
3. For conciseness, neither the charts in Figures 1.4 through 1.6 nor the data in Table 1.5 include results for the (highly significant) control variables related to duration, credit rating, and sectors. They are all key drivers of spread, but our interest is on the incremental effect of ESG rating on spread after controlling for these.
4. We base this conclusion on the prevalence of significant monthly results. t-statistics are not shown for the time-averaged coefficients in Figures 1.4 through 1.6 and Table 1.5. In this setting, the standard interpretation of t-statistics is not applicable since the results of the spread regression exhibit trends and are highly correlated over time.

CHAPTER 2

Measuring the ESG Risk Premium: Credit Markets

ESG has become an important part of the decision-making process for many credit investors. It is therefore essential to understand the impact of ESG investing on portfolio performance. One approach used frequently to measure ESG returns is to compare the returns of an ESG-constrained index with those of an unconstrained index. However, such analysis can be contaminated by non-ESG effects due to differences in systematic risk exposures between the two indices. Indeed, in Chapter 1, we found that high ESG ratings are often associated with higher credit quality and tighter spreads.

In this chapter, we first review a detailed example illustrating how systematic risk exposures can dominate the performance differences between a standard benchmark index and its ESG-constrained variation. Next, we introduce a methodology for measuring ESG returns while neutralizing systematic risk. Our approach is based on the construction of highly diversified exposure-matched portfolios with positive or negative ESG tilts. We demonstrate that the risk profile achieved by this approach is much less subject to systematic risk than the simpler approach of comparing an ESG-constrained benchmark to an unconstrained one. Next, using our exposure-matched approach, we review the historical effect on portfolio returns that has been associated with an ESG tilt in both the US IG and Euro IG markets, for each market as a whole and separately by industry. We find that the high-ESG portfolios have tended to outperform historically. We also illustrate how this method can be used to measure the effect of individual E, S, and G pillar scores on corporate bond returns. Finally, after ascertaining that there was no systematic increase in the magnitude of the ESG spread premium that could have explained the observed outperformance of ESG-tilted portfolios, we seek to understand its source. One possible hint is found in a pattern of reduced downgrade rates for US IG issuers with high governance pillar scores.

COMPARISON TO AN ESG-CONSTRAINED INDEX: A BIASED APPROACH

In Table 2.1 we compare the market structures of a traditional unconstrained index, the Bloomberg US Corporate Index, to that of an ESG-constrained index, the Bloomberg MSCI US Corporate Sustainability Index, which excludes issuers with an MSCI ESG rating below BBB.[1] We observe several significant differences in terms of risk profile and sector allocation. Indeed, the spread and DTS[2] of the Sustainability index are lower (by 9 bp and 0.94 respectively) as the lower ESG-rated issuers excluded from the index tend to have a lower credit quality and trade at wider spreads than the corporate index average. The sustainability index has a lower DTS than the corporate index in almost all industry sectors except for technology and insurance. The two indices also have different sector allocations. Indeed, the sustainability index overweights the non-cyclical, technology, utility, and banking and brokerage sectors and underweights cyclical, energy, industrial other (e.g. transportation), insurance, and financial other.

Table 2.2 shows a similar pattern in the euro credit market. The Bloomberg MSCI Euro Sustainability index has a lower DTS than the Euro Corporate IG index from which it is derived, although the difference is smaller than in the United States (−0.21 vs −0.94 in the United States).

Are the differences in allocations and DTS exposures reported in Tables 2.1 and 2.2 likely to overwhelm ESG effects in the relative performance of the two indices? We answer this question by estimating the projected tracking error volatility (TEV) of the US and Euro Sustainability indices over their conventional counterparts using the Bloomberg Global Risk Model (GRM).

The risk model separates projected TEV into systematic and idiosyncratic components. Systematic TEV results from mismatches in systematic risk exposures between the two indices and is measured using common risk factors that affect multiple securities. Figure 2.1 provides an attribution of TEV to yield curve reshaping (Curve), changes in swap spreads (Swp Sprd), rates volatility (Vol), and credit spreads (Crd & EMG). Idiosyncratic TEV (Idio) represents the residual portion of the total TEV, which is attributed to security and name selection as opposed to systematic effects. If systematic risk exposures of the two indices are identical, TEV is fully attributed to idiosyncratic effects. If, however, there are significant differences in systematic risk exposures, as shown in Figure 2.1, systematic TEV dominates. Bloomberg's Global Risk Model[3] does not have a systematic ESG risk factor. Therefore, all ESG effects are attributed to the idiosyncratic portion of TEV.

Panel A of Figure 2.1 shows components of the TEV between the US Corporate Sustainability and US Corporate IG indices as of 31 December 2020. The largest TEV component (10.5 bp/month) is attributed to systematic

TABLE 2.1   US Corp. Sustainability vs US Corp. indices, 31 December 2020.

Sector	US Corp. Sustainability Index				US Corp. Index				Difference: Sustainability - US Corp.			
	% MV	OASD	OAS	DTS	% MV	OASD	OAS	DTS	% MV	OASD	OAS	DTS
Basic	2.9	9.5	110	12.5	2.9	9.4	121	13.0	-0.01	0.16	-10	-0.48
Capital Goods	6.2	8.5	78	8.4	5.7	8.8	98	10.7	0.51	-0.28	-20	-2.29
Cyclical	6.1	8.4	68	7.2	7.2	7.9	82	7.8	-1.07	0.43	-14	-0.56
Non-cyclical	8.0	9.4	93	11.1	6.2	9.3	96	11.4	1.82	0.08	-3	-0.31
Healthcare	10.9	9.2	82	9.7	10.3	9.9	86	10.7	0.62	-0.67	-5	-1.03
Energy	6.7	8.3	127	13.2	8.0	8.5	137	14.3	-1.27	-0.19	-10	-1.11
Technology	10.7	8.9	72	8.2	8.8	8.5	75	7.9	1.89	0.42	-3	0.28
Industrial Other	6.1	10.2	104	12.6	9.5	10.8	120	15.2	-3.30	-0.64	-15	-2.61
Communication	2.7	11.4	97	13.2	3.0	11.8	112	13.8	-0.29	-0.37	-15	-0.59
Utility	10.1	11.0	101	12.7	8.1	10.8	106	13.0	2.00	0.18	-5	-0.35
Banks/Brokerage	23.7	5.6	70	5.2	22.0	5.8	72	5.6	1.72	-0.25	-2	-0.42
Financial Other	2.5	6.3	105	7.4	3.8	6.3	119	8.2	-1.27	0.01	-14	-0.81
Insurance	3.2	9.8	107	11.8	4.5	9.9	105	11.7	-1.33	-0.14	2	0.07
Total	**100**	**8.4**	**87**	**9.2**	**100**	**8.6**	**96**	**10.2**	**0.00**	**-0.16**	**-9**	**-0.94**

Source: Bloomberg, MSCI, Barclays Research.

TABLE 2.2 Euro Corp. Sustainability vs Euro Corp. indices, 31 December 2020.

Sector	Euro Corp. Sustainability Index				Euro Corp. Index				Difference: Sustainability - US Corp.			
	% MV	OASD	OAS	DTS	% MV	OASD	OAS	DTS	% MV	OASD	OAS	DTS
Basic	3.2	5.3	77	4.4	3.0	5.3	79	4.5	0.2	-0.05	-2	-0.14
Capital Goods	5.1	5.2	74	4.0	5.2	5.5	80	4.8	0.0	-0.25	-6	-0.79
Cyclical	6.9	4.9	81	4.2	9.4	4.7	100	5.2	-2.4	0.14	-19	-0.98
Healthcare	6.2	6.9	75	6.0	7.2	6.7	83	6.3	-1.0	0.19	-8	-0.26
Non-cyclical	8.9	6.3	78	5.5	8.1	6.3	82	5.8	0.8	0.02	-3	-0.23
Technology	3.8	5.5	73	4.4	3.2	5.5	74	4.4	0.6	0.00	-1	-0.05
Communication	7.8	6.2	88	6.0	8.3	6.2	91	6.3	-0.4	-0.08	-3	-0.34
Transportation	3.3	5.7	93	5.6	3.0	5.6	99	5.7	0.3	0.14	-5	-0.09
Energy	5.0	6.1	107	6.8	5.1	6.1	99	6.4	-0.1	-0.04	8	0.39
Utility	8.0	5.5	84	5.1	7.1	5.4	87	5.1	0.8	0.07	-2	-0.03
Banks/Brokerage	31.3	4.2	82	3.8	29.2	4.2	83	3.8	2.1	-0.02	-1	-0.06
Insurance	5.3	5.4	141	8.1	5.2	5.3	134	7.6	0.1	0.09	7	0.47
Financial Other	5.2	5.9	128	8.1	6.1	5.6	127	7.7	-1.0	0.22	1	0.36
Total	100	5.3	88	5.1	100	5.3	92	5.3	0.0	0.00	-4	-0.21

Source: Bloomberg, MSCI, Barclays Research.

Panel A: US Corporate Sustainability over US Corporate IG index

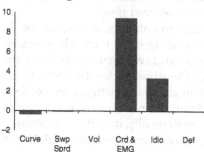

Panel B: Euro Corporate Sustainability over Euro Corporate IG

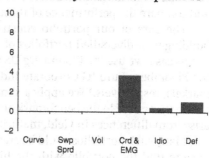

TEV Summary	
Total TEV	12.4
Systematic TEV	10.5
Idiosyncratic TEV	6.5
Default TEV	0.1

TEV Summary	
Total TEV	5.0
Systematic TEV	4.2
Idiosyncratic TEV	1.5
Default TEV	2.3

FIGURE 2.1 Contributions to TEVs of US and Euro Corp. Sustainability indices over the US and Euro Corp IG indices, 31 December 2020.
Source: Bloomberg

spread effects and results essentially from the DTS mismatch between the two indices[4] highlighted in Table 2.1.

Panel B reports components of the TEV between the Euro Corporate Sustainability and Euro Corporate IG indices, which is again dominated by systematic risk resulting mostly from the difference in DTS between the two indices. Idiosyncratic TEV, which captures ESG effects, is comparatively very small.

The results reported in Figure 2.1 imply that the relative returns of the Sustainability indices over ESG-unconstrained market indices are likely to be dominated by differences in sector allocation and DTS as opposed to ESG effects. How can we control systematic risk to isolate and measure ESG-specific returns?

BUILDING ESG-TILTED EXPOSURE-MATCHED PORTFOLIOS

To measure the effect of ESG investing on credit portfolio performance in an objective manner, it is important to isolate the ESG effect from all other possible sources of risk. To do this, we construct pairs of portfolios that differ drastically in their ESG scores, but whose risk profiles are nearly identical across all important dimensions of risk for corporate bonds. We then measure and compare the performance of these portfolios over time.[5]

The core of our portfolio construction technique is a mechanism for building well-diversified portfolios of bonds designed to track a benchmark. In this case, we use the Bloomberg US Corporate Investment Grade Index and the Bloomberg Euro IG Corporate Index as benchmarks for the US and Euro markets, respectively.[6] We apply a simple model that constrains the portfolio to remain neutral to the benchmark along multiple risk dimensions that could arise from differences in yield, maturity, credit quality, or sector allocation.

Many such portfolios could be created; in our procedure, the model is run once to find the portfolio with the highest possible average ESG score that meets these constraints and once to find the one with the lowest ESG score. The two tracking portfolios are reconstructed on a monthly basis, coordinated with the monthly index rebalancing, to ensure that they keep pace with any changes in the structure of the corporate bond market. Both are expected to track the index, experiencing the same broad rallies and declines as the benchmark, so that monthly tracking error volatility should be low. The key question is whether substantial differences arise over time between the average returns of the two portfolios.

The difference between the high and low ESG tracking portfolios can be interpreted as the return contribution associated with systematically favouring high ESG corporate bonds over low ESG ones while keeping everything else equal. This approach does not automatically exclude any issuer or any industry sector, no matter how controversial they might be.

In addition to pairs of portfolios with the minimum and maximum overall ESG rating, we also create portfolio pairs that accentuate the differences in individual E, S, and G scores, to try to observe which one of these three pillars is most related to performance.

Table 2.3 outlines the methodology applied to build ESG-tilted exposure-matched portfolios in the US and Euro Corporate IG markets. The problem is defined as a linear program (LP) that maximizes or minimizes the average ESG scores of a portfolio in each sector subject to exposure and issuer concentration constraints. Both Max and Min ESG portfolios are rebalanced every month to make sure their allocations and systematic risk exposures match those of a broad corporate bond index and reflect the structure of the market. Replicating the structure of the corporate bond market represented by the unconstrained indices ensures the analysis is relevant to a broad set of investors, including those benchmarked to market indices.

Table 2.3 details the exposure constraints applied to Max and Min ESG portfolios in order to ensure they match the underlying indices. Portfolios are required to match the option-adjusted spread (OAS), duration times spread

TABLE 2.3 Building max and min ESG exposure-matched portfolios by sector.

Building ESG Exposure-Matched Portfolios	Details
Objective	Maximize (minimize) portfolio ESG scores (can also be applied to individual E, S, and G pillars)
Index Exposure Constraints by Sector	Match index aggregate exposures: ■ Portfolio sector allocation by market weight ■ Portfolio OAS, DTS, OASD relative to index sector exposure ■ Portfolio avg. amount outstanding relative to index ■ Portfolio avg. bond age relative to index sector bond age
Sub-sector Exposure Constraints	Target index exposures by sub-sector: ■ Target index sub-sector weights ■ Target sub-sector DTS contributions ■ Target sub-sector OASD contributions
Rating Constraints by Sector	Target index weights by rating
Seniority Constraints	Target index exposures to subordinated bonds: ■ Target index weight in subordinated bonds ■ Target index DTS contribution from subordinated bonds ■ Target index OASD contribution from subordinated bonds
Geography Constraints (for Euro credit only)	Target index exposures to core and peripheral markets in Europe: ■ Target index weight by geography ■ Target index DTS contribution by geography ■ Target index OASD contribution by geography
Issuer Concentration Constraints	■ Limit maximum issuer overweight over index weight ■ Limit maximum excess issuer DTS contribution
Investment Universe	Constituents of the Bloomberg US Corporate Index / Bloomberg Euro Corporate Index
Benchmark	Bloomberg US Corporate Index / Bloomberg Euro Corporate Index
Rebalancing Frequency	Each month-end

Source: Barclays Research.

(DTS), and spread duration (OASD) of the index in each sector. In addition, we match the index average amount outstanding and bond age (time since issuance) by sector to mimic the liquidity profile of the index.

ESG-tilted portfolios are required to match sub-sector weights as well as their OASD and DTS contributions in the index. Similar exposure constraints are applied to subordinated bonds in sectors where they represent a significant proportion of the overall amount outstanding.

In addition to DTS contributions, we also introduce an explicit constraint on the rating allocation within each sector by allowing only minimal deviations from the index allocation across rating buckets within each industry sector. Finally, we apply issuer concentration constraints to ensure ESG-tilted portfolios are well diversified.

ESG-tilted portfolios follow index rules concerning the eligible bond universe and the rebalancing schedule. All index bonds are eligible to be included into our ESG-tilted portfolios,[7] and they are rebalanced monthly on the last business day of each month.

Table 2.4 shows that ESG-tilted portfolios match the aggregate characteristics of underlying indices very well. Both Max and Min ESG portfolios are highly diversified as they contain over 700 bonds in the United States and over 450 bonds in Europe. This means that, except for the ESG component induced by the ESG tilt, idiosyncratic (or issuer-specific) excess returns of ESG-tilted

TABLE 2.4 Characteristics of max and min ESG exposure-matched portfolios in US and Euro IG.

		US Corporate IG				Euro Corporate IG			
		2017	**2018**	**2019**	**2020**	**2017**	**2018**	**2019**	**2020**
Avg. # bonds	Index	5540	5721	5975	6435	2098	2334	2659	2946
	Max ESG	735	732	745	737	461	472	480	493
	Min ESG	697	699	705	707	452	462	461	482
	Max-Min	**38**	**33**	**41**	**30**	**10**	**10**	**19**	**11**
Avg. OAS,	Index	109	111	116	150	104	109	115	149
bp	Max ESG	109	111	116	150	104	109	115	149
	Min ESG	109	111	117	151	104	110	115	150
	Max-Min	**0**	**0**	**−1**	**−1**	**0**	**−1**	**0**	**−1**
Avg. DTS,	Index	9.6	9.8	10.6	14.0	6.1	6.5	6.7	8.6
yrs x %	Max ESG	9.5	9.7	10.6	14.0	6.1	6.4	6.7	8.6
	Min ESG	9.5	9.8	10.6	14.0	6.1	6.4	6.7	8.6
	Max-Min	**0.0**	**−0.1**	**0.0**	**0.0**	**0.0**	**0.0**	**0.0**	**0.0**
Avg. Amt.	Index	1.46	1.47	1.44	1.47	0.97	0.96	0.93	0.92
Outstanding,	Max ESG	1.45	1.47	1.44	1.47	0.97	0.95	0.93	0.92
$/€ bn	Min ESG	1.45	1.47	1.44	1.47	0.97	0.95	0.93	0.92
	Max-Min	**0.00**	**0.00**	**0.00**	**0.00**	**0.00**	**0.00**	**0.00**	**0.00**

Source: Bloomberg, Barclays Research.

portfolios should be small. Moreover, ESG-tilted portfolios and benchmark indices have identical OAS and DTS exposures so that the spread carry and the systematic credit risk exposures of the two portfolios are exactly the same. The portfolios also emulate the liquidity of the underlying indices by matching average amounts outstanding and average bond age (not shown in the table).

While not reported in Table 2.4, the ESG-tilted portfolios also match indices in other aspects required by the optimization constraints, including sector allocation, DTS, OAS, and OASD by sector, rating allocation, allocation, and DTS contributions by sub-sectors. This can allow for a measurement of the performance effect of ESG at sector level in addition to overall index level, as illustrated in the following section.

Panel A of Figure 2.2 reports the breakdown of the expected TEV of the Max ESG portfolio over the US Corporate index according to Bloomberg's Global Risk Model. We find that almost the entire TEV can be attributed to idiosyncratic (issuer-specific) risk which, as discussed previously, is the risk representation of the ESG tilt. The systematic portion of the TEV is negligible because the portfolio matches the index risk profile. In contrast, Panel B

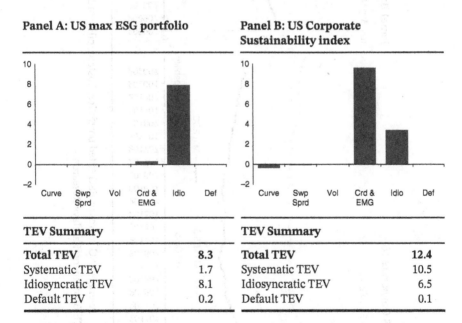

Panel A: US max ESG portfolio

Panel B: US Corporate Sustainability index

TEV Summary	
Total TEV	**8.3**
Systematic TEV	1.7
Idiosyncratic TEV	8.1
Default TEV	0.2

TEV Summary	
Total TEV	**12.4**
Systematic TEV	10.5
Idiosyncratic TEV	6.5
Default TEV	0.1

FIGURE 2.2 Contributions to TEV of US max ESG portfolio and the US Corp. Sustainability Index over the US Corp. Index, 31 December 2020.
Source: Bloomberg; Barclays Research.

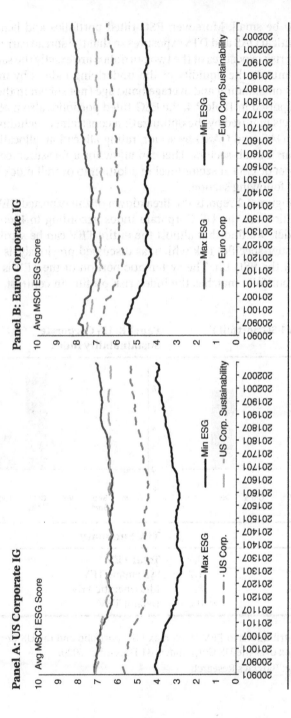

FIGURE 2.3 Average ESG scores of ESG-tilted portfolios, Sustainability indices, and broad corporate indices in US and Euro IG.
Source: MSCI, Bloomberg, Barclays Research.

(repeated from Panel A of Figure 2.1) shows that the TEV of the US Corporate Sustainability index over the US Corporate index is predominantly *systematic* because of the mismatches in sector allocation and credit spread exposures shown in Table 2.1.

Figure 2.2 indicates that our construction methodology neutralizes any systematic non-ESG effects on the expected tracking errors of the Max ESG portfolio. Similar results are obtained for the Min ESG portfolio. The difference between these two portfolio returns should therefore provide a pure measurement of the ESG return premium for a given month, free of any systematic bias.

Given that our portfolios are subject to significant constraints and must be highly diversified, can they possibly implement positive or negative ESG tilts of significant magnitude? Figure 2.3 shows that the ESG scores achieved by our Max ESG portfolios for IG corporates in both the US and euro markets compare favourably with those of the associated Sustainability index. For each market, we plot the average MSCI ESG score (which ranges from 0 to 10) for the standard benchmark index, the associated Sustainability index, and our Max and Min ESG portfolios. Panel A of Figure 2.3 shows that the average ESG score of the Max ESG portfolio in the United States is comparable to that of the Corporate Sustainability index. The negative tilt of the Min ESG portfolio is of similar magnitude, and the resulting difference between the average ESG scores of Max and Min ESG portfolios has recently been greater than 3. In Europe, as seen in Panel B, we similarly find a symmetric pattern of positive ESG tilt for the Max ESG portfolio and negative tilt for the Min ESG one, which has also grown to 3 in the most recent observations. Here, we actually find that the ESG tilt of the Max ESG portfolio has become significantly stronger than that achieved by the Sustainability index. This decline in the ESG tilt of the Euro Sustainability index is linked to the fact that ESG scores of European issuers are generally higher than those of their US peers. Therefore, relatively few issuers qualify for exclusion from the Euro Corporate Sustainability index, which results in its relatively small ESG tilt relative to the unconstrained market index.

MEASURING ESG RETURNS IN CREDIT

ESG-tilted exposure-matched portfolios can be used to measure ESG returns in credit as the excess returns of the Max ESG portfolio over the index or over the corresponding Min ESG portfolio.

Figure 2.4 compares the cumulative excess returns (or realized tracking errors) of Max ESG portfolios and Sustainability indices over market indices in the United States and Europe, using MSCI ESG ratings. It shows

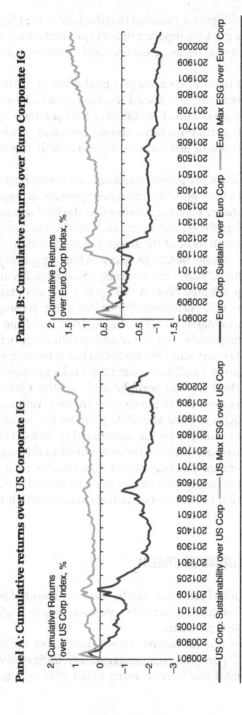

FIGURE 2.4 Cumulative excess returns of max ESG portfolios and Sustainability indices over corporate benchmarks.

Source: MSCI, Bloomberg, Barclays Research.

that ESG-specific returns, measured as return differences between Max ESG portfolios and benchmark indices, have been positive between 2009 and 2020 both in the United States and Europe.

In contrast, ESG returns measured as the difference between Sustainability and market indices are negative over the same period, as they are contaminated by differences in risk exposures. Indeed, Sustainability indices generally have lower DTS exposures than corresponding market indices. Their relative performance is therefore directional on the market: they tend to underperform in benign or bullish environments and outperform during credit down-cycles. Figure 2.4 illustrates this pattern well and shows that Sustainability indices have performed better in credit market downturns: the 2011 sovereign crisis, the energy crisis of 2015 and the recent Covid-19 crisis. This pattern is more pronounced in the United States than in Europe as the difference in DTS between Sustainability and standard indices is larger in the former than in the latter.

Figure 2.5 reports cumulative ESG returns in the US and Euro IG markets. The ESG return premium has been persistently positive in both markets since 2009. ESG returns have also been larger in the United States than in Europe. Figure 2.5 shows that avoiding low ESG issuers accounts for a larger part of the return premium, as indicated by the outperformance of the index over the Min ESG portfolios. The strategy of favouring high ESG-rated issuers, while also positive, has delivered a smaller cumulative return over the past decade.

We should note that the reported ESG returns are unlikely to be achievable in practice, because they represent returns of a long-short portfolio in credit and ignore rebalancing costs associated with portfolio turnover.

ESG-tilted exposure-matched portfolios are well diversified and designed to carefully mimic index exposures within every broad sector. Consequently, we can measure ESG returns in individual industry sectors by analysing the relative performance of sector-specific portions of Max and Min ESG portfolios. These sector-specific ESG returns can help monitor the performance impact of ESG investing at a more granular level.

Table 2.5 provides ESG returns in the US IG market from 2009 to 2020 for broad industry sectors as well as for the entire market (0.64 %/yr on average, with an information ratio of 1.3). The first two columns report the average number of bonds and issuers across industry sectors in the Max ESG portfolio,[8] while the third column provides the number of issuers across industry sectors in the Bloomberg US Corporate Index. The last three columns provide performance data by sector. Sector-level ESG returns are calculated as differences in returns between sector-specific Max and Min ESG portfolios.

Table 2.5 shows that ESG returns have been positive in 2009–2020 across most industry sectors of the US IG corporate bond market. The average ESG

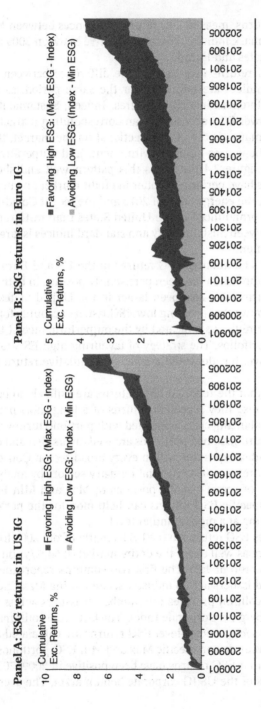

FIGURE 2.5 Cumulative ESG returns (max over min ESG portfolios) in US and Euro IG credit.

Source: MSCI, Bloomberg, Barclays Research.

TABLE 2.5 US IG: ESG returns (returns of max over min ESG portfolios) by sector, February 2009–December 2020.

	US Max ESG	US Max ESG	US Corp Index	ESG Returns (Max ESG - Min ESG)		
	Avg. #bonds	Avg. #issuers	Avg. #issuers	Avg Ret, %/yr	Vol, %/yr	IR
Basic	35	19	48	0.94	1.69	0.6
Capital Goods	40	18	57	0.47	1.16	0.4
Cyclical	52	26	51	0.62	0.79	0.8
Non-cyclical	51	21	48	0.99	0.87	1.1
Healthcare	57	24	60	0.69	0.72	1.0
Energy	60	27	54	1.37	1.43	1.0
Technology	44	17	47	0.07	1.13	0.1
Industrial Other	24	12	37	2.12	1.78	1.2
Communication	61	22	34	−0.02	0.99	0.0
Utility	71	29	71	0.50	0.88	0.6
Banks/Brokerage	142	53	80	0.56	0.84	0.7
Financial Other	35	16	59	1.30	1.42	0.9
Insurance	39	21	62	0.12	2.50	0.0
Total	*709*	*302*	*700*	*0.64*	*0.48*	*1.3*
Total ex Covid (Mar 20–Dec 20)	*706*	*300*	*695*	*0.46*	*0.30*	*1.5*

Source: MSCI, Bloomberg, Barclays Research.

premium is 0.64 %/yr, while the largest average ESG returns are realized in the industrial other (+2.12 %/yr), energy (+1.37 %/yr), and financial other (+1.30 %/yr) sectors, followed by the non-cyclical (+0.99 %/yr) and basic (+0.94 %/yr) sectors. Communications (−0.02 %/yr), technology (+0.07 %/yr), and insurance (+0.12 %/yr) exhibit the lowest returns over the course of the study period. The volatility of ESG returns at the overall index level (or the TEV of Max over Min ESG portfolios) is relatively high (0.48 %/yr) considering that the Max and Min ESG portfolios are well diversified and have identical exposures to systematic credit risk. This high volatility of ESG returns can partly be attributed to the Covid-19 crisis. Indeed, the ESG return volatility drops to 0.30 %/yr when we exclude the period between March (when the Covid-19 crisis began to unfold) and December 2020 from the sample. Excluding the Covid period has the effect of increasing the information ratio from 1.3 to 1.5.

Table 2.6 reports ESG returns in the Euro IG universe by industry sector as well as for the whole market. Similarly to Table 2.5, individual sectors are

TABLE 2.6 Euro IG: ESG returns (returns of max over min ESG portfolios) by sector, February 2009–December 2020.

	Euro Max ESG	Euro Max ESG	Euro Corp Index	ESG Returns (Max ESG - Min ESG)		
	Avg. #bonds	Avg. #issuers	Avg. #issuers	Avg Ret, %/yr	Vol, %/yr	IR
Basic/Capital Goods	42	23	62	0.68	0.91	0.7
Cyclical	38	21	44	0.09	0.71	0.1
Non-cyclical	51	26	57	0.22	0.44	0.5
Communication/ Technology	47	21	43	0.03	0.70	0.0
Energy/Transportation/ Utility	68	32	67	0.22	0.56	0.4
Banks/Brokerage	144	59	97	0.42	0.69	0.6
Insurance/Financial Other	46	21	71	0.31	0.87	0.4
Total	*437*	*201*	*437*	*0.33*	*0.30*	*1.1*
Total ex Covid (Mar 20–Dec 20)	*433*	*198*	*426*	*0.29*	*0.29*	*1.0*

Source: MSCI, Bloomberg, Barclays Research.

derived from the Level 3 classification utilized by Bloomberg bond indices. We use broader sector definitions in Euro IG than in US IG because the population of bonds in the Euro Corporate index is smaller. We require each sector in the partition to be sufficiently populated to achieve a meaningful ESG tilt between Max and Min ESG portfolios in each sector while maintaining issuer diversification. The results in Table 2.6 are broadly consistent with those for the United States. ESG returns have been positive across all sectors between 2009 and 2020, but significantly smaller in magnitude than in the United States (0.33 %/yr in Euro IG versus 0.64 %/yr in US IG).

The largest ESG returns in Euro IG are observed in the enlarged basic/ capital goods (+0.68 %/yr), banks & brokerage (+0.42 %/yr), and insurance/ financial other (+0.31 %/yr) sectors; while the lowest average ESG return is found in the communication/technology sector (+0.03 %/yr), which is consistent with the pattern seen in the US market.

The volatility of ESG returns is lower in the Euro IG than in the US IG: 0.30 %/yr versus 0.48 %/yr respectively. Volatilities become comparable when excluding the Covid period of 2020: 0.29 %/yr in Europe versus 0.30 %/yr in the United States. We also observe that excluding the Covid period makes the

TABLE 2.7 ESG return premium for E, S, and G pillar scores, US and EUR IG, 2009–2018.

	US IG Exposure-Matched Portfolios			EUR IG Exposure-Matched Portfolios		
	Average (%/yr)	Volat. (%/yr)	Inf. Ratio	Average (%/yr)	Volat. (%/yr)	Inf. Ratio
Max - Min ESG	0.60	0.30	2.0	0.35	0.26	1.4
Max - Min Env	0.45	0.26	1.8	0.09	0.30	0.3
Max - Min Soc	0.11	0.24	0.5	0.07	0.27	0.3
Max - Min Gov	0.37	0.24	1.6	0.17	0.31	0.6

Source: MSCI, Bloomberg, Barclays Research.

average ESG returns in the two markets closer to each other: 0.29 %/yr in Euro IG versus 0.46 %/yr in US IG. We find that ESG returns through the Covid episode were stronger in the United States than in Europe.

These results measure the returns due to overall ESG scores. We can carry out a similar analysis to separately measure returns due to E, S, and G pillar scores. To do this, we simply repeat the optimization process used to construct the Max ESG and Min ESG portfolios using the same constraints,[9] but modify the objective function to maximize or minimize a single pillar score, as described in the first row of Table 2.3. The results of this analysis are shown in Table 2.7. In the US IG market, we find that environment pillar scores were associated with the largest risk premia. In EUR IG, the magnitudes of the ESG-related returns were smaller across the board, but the pillar with the largest risk premium was governance.

To gain more insight into the key drivers of outperformance, we can also check which leg of our tracking pairs generates the most performance: is it that the high ESG names outperform the index, or that the low ESG names underperform? We expand the analysis shown in Figure 2.5 to individual pillar scores and obtain different results to this question in the two markets. As shown in Table 2.8, if we look only at the performance of our Max ESG portfolios relative to the index, we find a different story than in the Max ESG versus Min ESG numbers shown in Table 2.7. For this long-only variation, performance is generally better in Europe than in the United States, both overall and for both the social and governance pillars. In the United States, the environment pillar produces a healthy risk premium, but the portfolios tilted to maximize social or governance scores perform roughly in line with the index.

Table 2.9 shows the other side of the coin: low ESG portfolios underperformed relative to the index. This effect seems to be much stronger in the US

TABLE 2.8 Max ESG portfolios separately for E, S, and G pillar scores, US and EUR IG, 2009–2018.

	US IG Exposure-Matched Portfolios			EUR IG Exposure-Matched Portfolios		
	Average (%/yr)	Volat. (%/yr)	Inf. Ratio	Average (%/yr)	Volat. (%/yr)	Inf. Ratio
Max ESG - Index	0.22	0.34	0.6	0.29	0.24	1.2
Max Env - Index	0.22	0.30	0.7	0.15	0.27	0.6
Max Soc - Index	−0.04	0.32	−0.1	0.17	0.21	0.8
Max Gov - Index	0.06	0.29	0.2	0.18	0.29	0.6

Source: MSCI, Bloomberg, Barclays Research.

TABLE 2.9 Min ESG portfolios vs index, separately for E, S, and G pillar scores, US and EUR IG, 2009–2018.

	US IG Exposure-Matched Portfolios			EUR IG Exposure-Matched Portfolios		
	Average (%/yr)	Volat. (%/yr)	Inf. Ratio	Average (%/yr)	Volat. (%/yr)	Inf. Ratio
Min ESG - Index	−0.38	0.22	−1.7	−0.06	0.20	−0.3
Min Env - Index	−0.24	0.27	−0.9	0.07	0.21	0.3
Min Soc - Index	−0.16	0.21	−0.8	0.10	0.28	0.3
Min Gov - Index	−0.32	0.20	−1.6	0.00	0.18	0.0

Source: MSCI, Bloomberg, Barclays Research.

market than in Europe. It appears that the US strategy of choice during this time period was 'avoid poor ESG ratings', while in Europe it was 'seek the best ESG ratings'.

We applied the same approach to evaluate the ESG risk premium in the US HY corporate market. The detailed parameters of the optimization were by necessity slightly different than that described previously, due to the different structure of the HY and IG markets; the results are shown in Table 2.10. We once again find that positive performance was associated on average with a pro-ESG tilt, but with greater volatility than in US IG. In this case, the best single-pillar results were observed for governance, while a pro-environment tilt produced mildly negative returns.

An ESG tilt is seldom the only active bias in a portfolio but more often part of a set of active strategies that can be fundamental or quantitative.

TABLE 2.10 Portfolios of high ESG issuers have outperformed low ESG portfolios in the US HY market (2012–2018).

	Average (%/yr)	Volatility (%/yr)	Information Ratio
Max - Min ESG	0.45	0.97	0.5
Max - Min Env	−0.28	1.34	−0.2
Max - Min Soc	0.28	1.07	0.3
Max - Min Gov	1.23	1.11	1.1

Source: MSCI, Bloomberg, Barclays Research.

For example, credit portfolios can integrate ESG scores in the management process by combining them with security-level quantitative scorecards that provide momentum or relative value signals and correspond to thematic style factors.[10] Such ESG integration into the portfolio management process can be implemented in different ways. For example, an ESG filter can help screen out securities with weak ESG attributes, at the risk of reducing the investment universe and, hence, the potential for generating alpha. On the other hand, portfolios can be constructed with the aim of achieving a high average ESG score without a priori excluding any securities (as in the simulations presented earlier) and at the same time choosing from securities that have desirable characteristics, such as relative value or momentum. In that case, it might be acceptable to include a low ESG issuer in a portfolio considering the trade-off between ESG and purely financial characteristics.

The Effect of ESG on Downgrade Rates

We have found that imposing an ESG tilt on a portfolio, while controlling for all other risk exposures, has produced a small but positive return premium over time in all markets that we studied. One potential explanation of this effect is that a steady increase in the magnitude of the 'greenium', the price premium (or negative spread premium) that investors are willing to pay for bonds with high ESG scores, has caused valuations to increase for early adopters of pro-ESG investment guidelines. However, as we showed at the end of Chapter 1, we have not found this to be the case. We have not detected a steady trend towards an increasingly negative spread premium over the period studied; if anything it has tended to become less negative over the period of our analysis.

If there was no systematic enrichment of bonds with good ESG rankings, what has made them outperform? One interpretation could be that poor ESG rankings relate to risks of various types of adverse events that could negatively affect companies' fortunes and that even over the relatively short time period we have investigated, our high-ESG portfolios experienced fewer such events than the low-ESG portfolios. Unfortunately, we do not have sufficient data to document such an effect with regard to ESG-specific events. However, we know that in bond markets, negative changes to a company's outlook are often associated with a downgrade in credit ratings, as well as negative returns. Do we find that high ESG scores are associated with a lower rate of subsequent downgrades?

To test this, we partitioned our bond universe into two groups – above and below the median ESG scores – and observed the number and magnitude of downgrades in each set. This allowed us to report an annual 'downgrade notch rate' capturing both the frequency and intensity of downgrades. (For example, if 10% of the issuers in a given group experience one-notch downgrades and another 3% have two-notch downgrades, the downgrade notch rate for the year would be 16%.) We compared these downgrade rates for bonds scoring high and low in different ESG categories; the most striking difference between the two groups was observed using Governance scores. As shown in Figure 2.6, bonds with low governance scores experienced a consistently higher rate of subsequent downgrades than those with high scores throughout most of our study period.[11]

We extended this analysis to other ESG scores and to other markets and found that other ESG metrics exhibited a similar pattern, but none were statistically significant, neither in the United States nor in Europe.

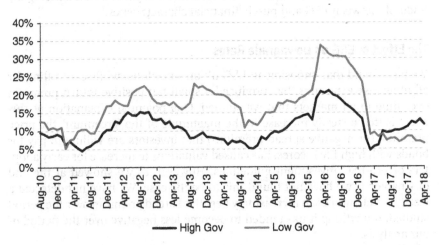

FIGURE 2.6 Rolling average number of downgrade notches per issuer and per year (US IG market).

Source: Bloomberg Indices, MSCI, Barclays Research.

CONCLUSION

Performance attribution to ESG investing is often done by observing the relative returns of an ESG-constrained index over a conventional unconstrained one. However, non-ESG effects, such as differences in systematic risk exposures between the two indices, can significantly contaminate such an analysis.

In this chapter, we introduce a simple and precise approach to measuring the effect of ESG investing in credit. We explain the methodology for constructing ESG-tilted exposure-matched portfolios to isolate ESG from other systematic effects. Portfolios with positive (Max ESG) and negative (Min ESG) tilts have identical risk profiles but very different ESG characteristics. The return difference between Max and Min ESG portfolios can therefore represent the ESG-specific return premium. Our methodology can help monitor the performance effect of ESG investing in corporate bond markets at the level of industry sectors as well as for the overall market.

This analysis shows that tilting a portfolio systematically to companies with better ESG ratings has been beneficial to performance. Avoiding issuers with poor ESG ratings had a larger effect on performance than favouring issuers with high ESG scores.

We found the effect of ESG on performance varied by ESG pillar – Governance and Environment had a stronger impact than the Social pillar. We also found differences according to the market – US vs Euro credit – and to the industry sector considered, with the general conclusion being that ESG was associated with a positive return premium.

This chapter provides evidence that ESG had a positive effect on credit portfolio performance. However, it still leaves us with a bit of a puzzle: if there has been no systematic change in the ESG valuation premium, as explained in Chapter 1, then what has driven the outperformance of high ESG portfolios? Our hypothesis is that companies that are better prepared to face the broad range of non-financial risks covered by ESG scores might be less likely to have negative surprises. One finding that supports this is that in the United States, bonds with lower corporate governance scores experienced higher frequencies of downgrades in credit ratings. More generally, the ESG return benefit may take the form of idiosyncratic (issuer-specific) returns. Low ESG companies may be more likely to suddenly experience a problem during a month of otherwise calm markets (e.g. an environmental disaster or a labour conflict), while high ESG ones might be better positioned than their peers to weather some market turmoil. The benefits of a systematic tilt towards higher ESG scores might, thus, be hard to identify as a market-wide ESG factor, but still accrue slowly and steadily towards better long-term performance.

REFERENCES

Ben Dor, A., Desclée, A., Dynkin, L., Hyman, J., and Polbennikov, S. (2021). *Systematic Investing in Credit*. Wiley.

Ben Dor, A., Dynkin, L., Hyman, J., Houweling, P., van Leeuwen, E., and Penninga, O. (2007). DTS (Duration Times Spread). *Journal of Portfolio Management*, 33 (2), pp. 77–100.

Dynkin, L., Desclée, A., Dubois, M., Hyman, J., and Polbennikov, S. (2018). ESG Investing in Credit: A Broader and Deeper Look, *Barclays Research*, 22 October.

NOTES

1. MSCI ESG Research produces a number of different types of rankings. They produce numeric scores for many different aspects of ESG categories, which roll up to numeric scores for the three pillars as well as an overall numeric score. This is then converted to an alphanumeric rating, similar to those used by credit rating agencies. We typically use numeric scores in our analysis, but Bloomberg indices are defined based on the alphanumeric ratings. In our writing, we use the terms 'scores' and 'rankings' interchangeably.

2. DTS stands for Duration Times Spread, which is our favored measure of credit exposure. The DTS approach to credit risk management is based on the empirical observation that systematic changes in spread tend to follow a pattern of relative spread change, in which bonds with wide spreads widen (or tighten) by more than those with tight spreads. This makes the price risk of credit securities proportional to spread as well as duration. See Ben Dor et al. (2007) for details.

3. The Bloomberg Global Risk Model is a factor-based model that originated as the Barclays POINT Global Risk Model. In credit, the model includes a number of systematic risk factors associated with relative spread changes at the industry level. Additional risk factors capture systematic risks related to maturity, geography, and seniority.

4. While net DTS exposure is usually the major contributor to systematic TEV in credit, there can be other sources of systematic risk.

5. We could have considered a different approach to measure ESG returns, using statistical analysis as opposed to portfolio simulations. In that case, we would perform cross-sectional regression analysis on monthly excess returns of individual bonds, taking bond characteristics such as OASD, OAS, and sector into account with a view to control systematic risk. This approach allows us to isolate the ESG effect from other factors and is similar to the Fama–MacBeth regression technique often applied to attribute returns in equity markets. However, results of such regression analysis might not be very intuitive or appealing to investors. Regression analysis implicitly gives the same weight to all observations, while portfolio simulations are anchored to the structure of the market capitalization-weighted index, which can be unevenly distributed across issuers. The results of statistical analysis can be heavily influenced by model specifications such as, for example, the nature of the

relationship (linear or not), the weighting of individual observations, or the choice of control variables. We find portfolio simulations more practical and intuitive. Exposure-matched portfolios are built to represent the broad market, which makes them relevant to a large group of investors. The resulting ESG premium, measured as the return difference between ESG-tilted portfolios, also reflects the structure of the market. In earlier research, we found that portfolio simulations and regression analysis provide consistent results.

6. To ensure consistency, the universe of bonds considered for portfolio construction was not the entire index, but limited to those for which ESG ratings were available from ESG rating agencies.

7. The ESG-tilted portfolios described in this chapter are built to measure ESG effects in corporate bond returns rather than as investable portfolios. They do not control turnover. Investors who would like to deploy ESG-tilted portfolios in practice would also need to ensure high liquidity and low turnover in their portfolios. These two issues are discussed in the context of style factor investing in credit in Ben Dor et al. (2021).

8. The numbers in the Min ESG portfolio are comparable.

9. Actually, the results shown in Tables 2.7 to 2.10 are taken from an earlier version of this analysis in Dynkin et al. (2018), which used a slightly different approach to setting the diversification constraints by sector.

10. For an overview of systematic investing in credit markets, see Ben Dor et al. (2021).

11. Figure 2.6 demonstrates a link between governance scores and future *changes* in credit ratings. Note that this does not contradict Figure 1.2, which shows low correlation between governance scores and contemporaneous *levels* of credit rating.

CHAPTER 3

Measuring the ESG Risk Premium: Equity Markets

ESG considerations have become increasingly central to the investment process for many equity investors. To make an informed decision about ESG investing in equities, one key question that investors need to answer is whether it is costly or beneficial for stock performance. One commonly used approach to address the question is to compare the returns of an ESG-focused stock index with its generic and broader parent index (henceforth 'the index approach'). However, using the index approach to measure ESG returns can be inaccurate because the ESG versions usually differ from their parent indices in terms of risk characteristics and/or sector allocations. When a mismatch in risk characteristics arises, differences in systematic risk could contaminate ESG returns: the tracking error between the ESG version and its parent index could be substantial in months when the risk factors have large return realizations. Furthermore, the mismatch of risk characteristics is not random: previous studies have shown that ESG scores are correlated with firm characteristics such as quality and size, and such correlations create systematic biases in the index approach.[1] In addition, the sector allocations of an ESG index could differ from its parent index, because of either no sector match at construction or infrequent rebalancing. Consequently, measuring ESG returns using the index approach is inaccurate: any return difference between the two indices could be driven by the differences in sector allocation and risk exposures and not necessarily attributable to the differences in their ESG characteristics. In the next section, we illustrate these differences using the MSCI USA index[2] and its ESG version (MSCI USA ESG Leaders index), which is a benchmark widely used by ESG funds, as an example.

Given the limitation of the index approach, we apply the 'exposure-matched' approach discussed in Chapter 2 to measure ESG equity risk premium. This approach builds a pair of diversified risk-matched sector-neutral stock portfolios while maximizing and minimizing ESG scores, respectively. We implement risk-matching and sector-neutral construction on a monthly basis to isolate the effects of ESG. Because the two portfolios differ only in their ESG attributes, their return difference is fully attributable to ESG investing.

Next, we describe the dynamics of the ESG return premium measured using the exposure-matched approach applied to several key US equity indices using MSCI ESG scores. Once we match the risk exposures properly, the conclusion of how ESG investing affects returns is different from that found using the index approach: the index approach suggests that ESG investing has hurt performance between 2009 and 2020 in the United States, whereas the exposure-matched approach indicates that ESG investing would have improved performance in the United States. This result is consistent with the findings in Chapter 2 for credit markets, which document considerable discrepancies in ESG return premium dynamics between the exposure-matched and index approaches. The consistent differences in ESG returns using the exposure-matched and index approaches in both equities and credit underline the importance of using the appropriate measurement technique.[3]

We further illustrate how the exposure-matched approach can be used to measure the ESG return premium in each sector and for each pillar. This allows investors to zoom in on the detailed dynamics of the ESG return effect in their specialized universes to monitor trends in a timely and accurate fashion.

We conclude the chapter by discussing the advantages of the exposure-matched approach over an alternative regression-based approach that is popular in academic studies to assess the significance of ESG alpha. The alternative approach starts with sorting stocks into buckets based on their ESG scores. It then forms a long-short strategy by buying stocks with high ESG scores and selling short stocks with low ESG scores. The L-S returns are regressed on a host of risk factors to evaluate the magnitude of ESG alpha. Compared to this approach, the exposure-matched approach is able to capture month-to-month ESG returns as opposed to the average effect. In addition, we argue that the exposure-matched approach is more investable, practical, and scalable, which would be especially useful for investors interested in building a portfolio to gain pure ESG exposures.

THE DRAWBACKS OF DERIVING ESG RETURNS USING INDICES

An ESG index and its underlying parent index usually differ in their risk characteristics and sector weights, which could explain their performance differences. In this section, we use the MSCI USA ESG Leaders index as an example to illustrate such differences. The construction process of the MSCI USA ESG index does not involve matching its key risk characteristics with those of its parent index (MSCI USA Index): it starts with the constituents of the parent index and selects the names with top MSCI ESG scores within each sector until reaching 50% of the cumulative market cap of that sector

(MSCI 2020).[4] Figure 3.1 compares the ESG index with its parent index in terms of key risk characteristics (market beta, size, book-to-market ratio, profitability, and investment rate) on a monthly basis.[5] As shown in Panels A–C, the ESG version had lower betas, larger size,[6] and lower book-to-market ratios over most of the sample period compared with its parent index. Because beta and book-to-market ratios have positive return premia and size has a negative return premium (Fama and French 1995, 1996), the differences in characteristics could lead to return differences between the ESG index and its parent. Panels D and E compare the quality characteristics in terms of profitability and investment rate and highlight that some mismatches are time varying. For example, the ESG index had lower profitability than its parent index earlier in the sample period, but higher profitability in the latter part of the sample period. Although such mismatches in characteristics may not have an effect on the performance difference between the ESG and parent index over the entire period, they would still result in inaccurate measurement on a monthly basis.

Another difference between the ESG index and its parent index is sector allocation. The MSCI ESG Leaders index is designed to track the sector allocations of its parent index,[7] but still exhibits sector biases since rebalancing is done only at an annual frequency. Figure 3.2 lists the differences in sector weights between the ESG version (MSCI USA ESG Leaders index) and its parent (MSCI USA index) at year-end from 2014 to 2020 with two-year increments. Most of the sector weight differences were smaller than 1%, but there were still occasionally large deviations. For example, the ESG index overweighted the information technology sector by more than 3% at the end of 2018. These sector differences could confound the returns attributed to ESG investing.

When we applied the index approach to the MSCI USA index and its ESG version, the overall ESG return measured using this approach was positive in 2009 and became negative after 2010, as shown in Figure 3.3.[8] Does this mean that investing in stocks with high ESG scores has been hurting portfolio performance since 2010? Based on the characteristics and sector weight differences shown in Figures 3.1 and 3.2, the index approach cannot provide an accurate answer, because the factor and sector realized returns, instead of ESG returns, could drive the return differences between the ESG version and its parent.

Note that we are only arguing that using the return difference between an ESG index and its parent index is not appropriate for the purpose of measuring ESG returns. We are not claiming that ESG indices should not be used as benchmarks. The ESG indices reflect mandate constraints of ESG investors in terms of their exclusion rules, eligible universes, security selection procedures, and rebalancing frequencies and therefore serve as good practical

Panel A: Market beta

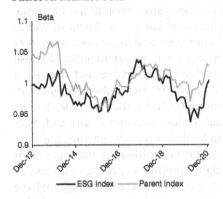

Panel B: Market cap ($bn, median)

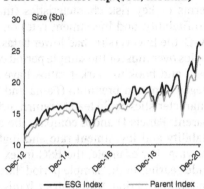

Panel C: B/M ratio

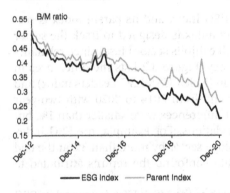

Panel D: Profitability

Panel E: Investment rate

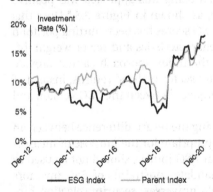

FIGURE 3.1 Comparison of average key risk characteristics between MSCI USA ESG leaders index and MSCI USA index. *Note:* See note 5 for the definition of risk characteristics. The number reported for size is median instead of average because the median size is more representative of the overall distributions. The difference between the two indices in monthly average size was skewed by a few disproportionally large firms that were in the underlying parent index but not in the ESG index. *Source:* Compustat, Bloomberg, MSCI, Barclays Research.

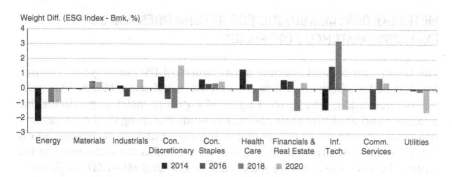

FIGURE 3.2 Sector weight difference of MSCI USA ESG leaders index over MSCI USA index.
Note: The sector allocations reported are as of end of December in each year.
Source: Bloomberg, Compustat, MSCI, Barclays Research.

Source: Bloomberg, Compustat, MSCI, Barclays Research

FIGURE 3.3 Cumulative return difference of the MSCI ESG index over its parent index.
Source: Bloomberg, Compustat, MSCI, Barclays Research.

performance benchmarks for investors with similar limitations in their mandates. However, when one takes a step back from those limitations and thinks about ESG investing from a more general perspective (for example, investors who have more flexibility with their mandates or asset owners who design the mandates), the index approach may provide misleading answers regarding the performance effects of ESG investing.

METHODOLOGY: MEASURING ESG RETURN PREMIUM USING EXPOSURE-MATCHED PORTFOLIOS

The key to a proper and accurate measurement of ESG returns is to neutralize return effects from other firm characteristics and sector biases. To achieve risk neutralization, we construct a pair of exposure-matched portfolios that maximize and minimize their ESG scores while matching the key systematic risk exposures and sector allocations to those of an underlying generic equity index. The ESG return premium is then measured as the differences in the returns[9] between the exposure-matched Max-ESG and Min-ESG portfolios:

$$\text{ESG Return Premium} = \text{Ret}\big(\text{Max-ESG Portfolio}\big) - \text{Ret}\big(\text{Min-ESG Portfolio}\big)$$

Returns associated with other systematic exposures cancel out because the two portfolios have identical sector allocations and key risk characteristics. Specifically, we match the indices' sector weights and five key risk characteristics (market beta, size, book-to-market, profitability, and investment) based on Fama and French (2015) on a monthly basis.[10] The details are outlined in Table 3.1.

TABLE 3.1 Construction details of exposure-matched Max- and Min-ESG stock portfolios.

	Max-ESG Portfolio	**Min-ESG Portfolio**
Objectives	Maximize portfolio's weighted-average ESG score	Minimize portfolio's weighted-average ESG score
Sector Neutral Constraint	Matching sector weights of the index (Sector = 2 digit GICS code)	
Key Risk Exposure Constraints	Portfolio risk characteristics are matched with the index ■ Market Beta ■ Size ■ Book to Market Value ■ Operating Profit (Operating Profit/Book Equity) ■ Investment Rate (% change in total assets)	
Issuer Over/Underweight Constraint	Allow 0.5% stock over/underweight compared to index weight [A stock has a minimum weight of 0% and maximum weight of 10%]	
Universe	Index constituent stocks with available ESG ratings	
Index benchmark	Corresponding Index (e.g. S&P 500, MSCI USA)	
Rebalance frequency	Month end	

Source: Barclays Research.

We illustrate our approach using the MSCI ESG scores, since they have a long history and good cross-sectional coverage. MSCI rates the E, S, and G pillars separately for each firm, on a scale of 0 to 10, and then aggregates the individual scores using a weighted sum to form a composite ESG score (also on a scale of 0 to 10). The scores take into consideration the key ESG-related risk exposures of each firm and how well those have been addressed, with 0 and 10 indicating the maximum and minimum level of risk, respectively. Our analysis focuses mostly on the dynamics of the composite ESG scores since they represent a more comprehensive picture of firms' ESG practices, but we also present results for the individual pillars.

The main analysis is conducted for two universes: the S&P 500 and the MSCI USA indices. The MSCI USA universe is included in addition to the S&P 500 for two reasons. First, using both the MSCI universe and the MSCI ESG scores allows us to compare the dynamics of the ESG return premium from the exposure-matched approach with the ESG returns from the index approach examined in the previous section. Because the two ESG return time series are constructed using the same underlying universe and the same ESG scores, any difference in ESG returns is driven by the difference in the respective approaches. The second reason for using two universes is to make sure that the ESG return premium dynamics identified are not specific to the index we choose. Since the methodology is general and can be applied to any index, we also expand the analysis later in the chapter to the Russell 1000 and 2000 indices. Based on the ESG score coverage, the sample period is from January 2009 to December 2020. The coverage of ESG scores, as shown in Table 3.2, is comprehensive for both the S&P 500 and MSCI USA universes, from around 95% (in terms of market cap) at the beginning of the sample to more than 99% at the end.

TABLE 3.2 MSCI ESG score coverage of US equity indices.

	Coverage (Number of Stocks)				Coverage (Market Cap)			
	S&P 500 (%)	MSCI USA (%)	RS1000 (%)	RS2000 (%)	S&P 500 (%)	MSCI USA (%)	RS1000 (%)	RS2000 (%)
2009	87	86	56	1	96	95	89	2
2013	99	99	95	74	100	100	99	88
2017	100	99	98	72	100	100	99	91
2020	100	99	96	66	100	100	99	87

Note: All coverage ratios reported are as of the end of December of each year.
Source: Bloomberg, Compustat, MSCI, Barclays Research.

TABLE 3.3   Average number of stocks in the Max- and Min-ESG portfolios.

	S&P 500 Universe			MSCI USA Universe		
Year	Max-ESG	Min-ESG	Index constituents with ESG ratings	Max-ESG	Min-ESG	Index constituents with ESG ratings
2014	138	137	498	141	142	616
2017	129	135	498	138	142	620
2020	127	120	499	135	135	606

Note: All numbers are reported as of December of each year.
Source: Bloomberg, Compustat, MSCI, Barclays Research.

The risk exposure matching approach guarantees that returns are not driven by unintended factor tilts, but it does not guarantee that the portfolios are sufficiently diversified and returns are not driven by idiosyncratic risk. Therefore, in addition to matching the risk exposures, we also use a weight constraint to ensure that the portfolios are well diversified. In the main analysis, we implement an over/underweight constraint of 0.5% for each stock relative to the underlying index. For example, if Apple's weight in the S&P 500 is 6%, its weight in the exposure-matched portfolio has to be within the [5.5%, 6.5%] range.[11] Table 3.3 reports the number of stocks in the Max- and Min-ESG portfolios at the end of 2014, 2017, and 2020 using this constraint. The results indicate that the number of stocks in each portfolio was over 100, far superseding what is sufficient for diversification.[12] To make sure that the ESG return premium measured is not specific to the choice of over/underweight constraint, we repeat the analysis with different over/underweight constraints and find similar ESG return premium dynamics.

To show how much ESG tilt the Max- and Min-ESG portfolios were able to achieve with all the constraints, Table 3.4 reports the average ESG scores (scale 0–10) of the Max- and Min-ESG portfolios and their differences from the S&P 500 and MSCI USA universes at the ends of 2014, 2017, and 2020. Despite the risk and sector weight matching, as well as the over/underweight constraints, the Max-ESG portfolio still had more ESG exposures than the ESG index: the average ESG score of the Max-ESG portfolio in the MSCI universe (column 5) was larger than that of the MSCI ESG index (column 8). In the MSCI USA universe, the Max-ESG portfolio's ESG score was 2.09, 1.60, and 1.31 higher than that of the Min-ESG portfolio in 2014, 2017, and 2020, respectively (column 7). To put the magnitude in perspective, these score differences between the Max- and Min-ESG portfolios were larger than the cross-sectional standard deviation of scores in the MSCI USA universe

TABLE 3.4 Average MSCI ESG scores (Scale 0–10) of exposure-matched portfolios, and ESG score distribution among MSCI USA index constituents.

	Avg. ESG Scores of the Exposure-Matched Portfolios						ESG Score Distribution among MSCI USA Index Constituents					
	S&P 500 Universe			MSCI USA Universe			Average ESG Score			ESG Score Distribution		
1	2	3	4	5	6	7	8	9	10	11	12	13
Year	Max-ESG	Min-ESG	(2)–(3)	Max-ESG	Min-ESG	(5)–(6)	ESG Index	Parent Index	(8)–(9)	Std. Dev.	Q3	Q1
2014	5.72	3.82	1.89	5.81	3.72	2.09	5.17	4.73	0.44	1.2	5.4	3.9
2017	5.43	3.97	1.46	5.48	3.88	1.60	5.17	4.65	0.52	1.0	5.2	4.0
2020	5.43	4.26	1.17	5.48	4.16	1.31	5.24	4.79	0.45	0.8	5.4	4.3

Note: All numbers are reported as of December of each year.
Source: Bloomberg, Compustat, MSCI, Barclays Research.

(column 11) at each point in time. The ESG score differences (column 7) were also almost three times the size of the score differences between the ESG index and its parent index (column 10). The score differences between the Max- and Min-ESG portfolios decreased over the years, mostly because of the increase in Min-ESG scores. One possible reason is that more firms have been spending considerable effort on improving their ESG scores, which brought up the scores near the lower bound of the universe. For example, we show in Chapter 9 that the fraction of ESG-related job postings increased since 2014 for S&P 500 firms, and that firms with higher abnormal ESG posting intensity were more likely to experience subsequent ESG rating improvements than peers with lower ESG posting intensity. The distribution of ESG scores in the cross-section is consistent with this explanation: the range of the scores had become narrower, driven mostly by improvement from the lower end of the distribution: the first quartile of ESG scores increased (column 13), but the third quartile remained relatively stable (column 12).

DYNAMICS OF ESG RETURN PREMIUM

Once we control for characteristic and sector differences, our exposure-matched approach paints a starkly different picture about the return effects of ESG investing compared with the index approach. Table 3.5 reports the

TABLE 3.5   Performance statistics of ESG return premia and ESG returns from the index approach using MSCI USA indices (January 2009–December 2020).

	S&P 500 Universe			MSCI USA Universe			Index Approach (MSCI USA ESG Leaders over MSCI USA)
	ESG Return Premium	Max-ESG over S&P 500	Min-ESG over S&P 500	ESG Return Premium	Max-ESG over MSCI USA	Min-ESG over MSCI USA	
Avg. Ret (%/Yr)	0.96	0.60	−0.35	1.00	0.54	−0.46	−0.20
Vol (%/Yr)	2.21	1.29	1.28	2.31	1.46	1.36	1.90
Inf. Ratio (ann.)	0.43	0.47	−0.28	0.43	0.37	−0.34	−0.11
Worst Monthly Ret (%)	−1.67	−0.92	−0.95	−1.82	−1.06	−1.26	−1.82
Max Drawdown (%)	−6.13	−3.03	−7.59	−5.63	−3.11	−8.01	−9.86

Source: Bloomberg, Compustat, MSCI, Barclays Research.

performance statistics of ESG return premia and ESG returns using the index approach. ESG return premia were positive for both the S&P 500 (0.96%/year) and MSCI USA (1.00%/year), suggesting that investing in stocks with high ESG scores actually had a positive effect on performance after controlling for risk characteristics and sector allocation. This is opposite to the conclusion from the index approach to measure ESG effects on returns: the average annual return of the ESG version over its parent index was negative for the MSCI USA index (−0.20%/year) during the same period. In addition, the contributions from both the Max- and Min-ESG portfolios to the ESG return premium were similar: the Max-(Min-)ESG portfolios outperformed (underperformed) the corresponding benchmark index by 0.60% (−0.35%) for S&P 500. Similar results were obtained for the MSCI index.

In addition, the Max-ESG over benchmark returns have lower volatility (1.46%/year in the MSCI USA universe) than the ESG returns from the index approach (1.90%/year), even though the former had more ESG tilt, as shown in Table 3.4. This is because part of the ESG returns from the index approach are driven by differences in systematic factor exposures, while the exposure-matched approach neutralizes such biases, leading to a more accurate and less noisy measure of the ESG return premium.

To take a closer look at the time series dynamics of the ESG return premia, Figure 3.4 plots cumulative returns from the S&P 500 and MSCI USA universes and compares them with the ESG returns using the index approach (ESG version over parent index). It is clear that the positive performance of ESG return premium reported in Table 3.5 came from the latter years of the sample period. In both universes, the ESG premia were hovering around zero before 2016 and started to exhibit an upward trend after 2016. The ESG

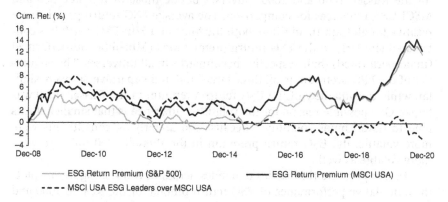

FIGURE 3.4 Cumulative performance of ESG return premium (January 2009–December 2020).
Source: Bloomberg, Compustat, MSCI, Barclays Research.

returns using the index approach, however, exhibited a consistent downward trend since 2010.

Not only were the general trends of ESG returns from the exposure-matched and index approaches different, their month-to-month dynamics were also different. Figure 3.5 plots the monthly ESG returns using the exposure-matched approach (Max-ESG-over-benchmark, x-axis) against the contemporaneous ESG returns using the index approach (ESG version over its parent index with the MSCI USA indices, y-axis). The exposure-matched ESG returns showed low correlations with their index-approach counterparts (0.30).

Figure 3.6 plots the ESG monthly returns using the exposure-matched approach for the MSCI USA universe (x-axis) against the contemporaneous counterparts from the S&P 500 universe (y-axis). As a contrast to the low correlations between the exposure-matched and index approach returns, the ESG returns using the exposure-matched methodology from two different universes had a high correlation of 0.87.[13]

ESG Return Premia in Russell 1000 and 2000 Universes

In addition to large-cap universes (S&P 500 and MSCI USA indices), we expand our analysis to mid- and small-cap universes in the United States (Russell 1000 and 2000). The sample periods start from January 2009 for the Russell 1000 (the same as for S&P 500 and MSCI USA) and from December 2012 for the Russell 2000 because of limited coverage of ESG scores at the beginning of the sample (Table 3.2).

Table 3.6 reports the performance statistics of the ESG return premia for the Russell 1000 and 2000 universes beside those of the S&P 500 and MSCI USA universes for comparison. The average ESG return premia were positive for all four. In addition, both the Max- and Min-ESG portfolios contributed similarly to the ESG return premia: Max-(Min-)ESG outperformed (underperformed) their respective benchmarks in all universes. The volatilities of the ESG premium in all three large- and mid-cap universes were similar, while the volatility of the ESG return premium in the Russell 2000 was larger. One possible reason for the volatility difference is that smaller stocks tend to have higher volatility.[14] Because the underlying constituents were more volatile, the ESG return premium in the Russell 2000 universe were more volatile as well.

To compare the time series dynamics across universes, Figure 3.7 plots the cumulative performance of ESG return premia for the Russell 1000 and Russell 2000 universes, together with the S&P 500 and MSCI USA as a comparison. The ESG return premia in all four universes showed upward trends in the latter years of the sample period, coinciding with a period during which ESG investing gained popularity. Among the four, the ESG return premia for

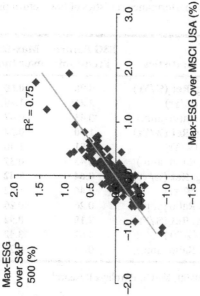

FIGURE 3.6 Scatter plot of Max-ESG-over-benchmark monthly returns in S&P 500 and MSCI USA universes (January 2009–December 2020).
Source: Bloomberg, Compustat, MSCI, Barclays Research.

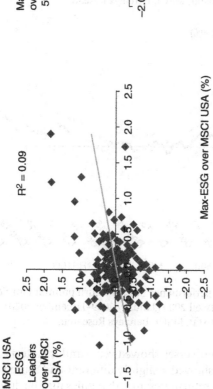

FIGURE 3.5 Scatter plot of Max-ESG over benchmark vs ESG returns from the index approach (ESG version over parent index with MSCI USA indices, January 2009–December 2020).
Source: Bloomberg, Compustat, MSCI, Barclays Research.

TABLE 3.6 Comparison of performance statistics of ESG return premia for different universes.

Universe and Sample Period	Statistics	ESG Return Premium	Max-ESG over Index	Min-ESG over Index
S&P 500	**Avg. Ret (%/Yr)**	**0.96**	**0.60**	**−0.35**
(01/2009–12/2020)	Vol (%/Yr)	2.21	1.29	1.28
	Inf. Ratio (ann.)	0.43	0.47	−0.28
MSCI USA	**Avg. Ret (%/Yr)**	**1.00**	**0.54**	**−0.46**
(01/2009–12/2020)	Vol (%/Yr)	2.31	1.46	1.36
	Inf. Ratio (ann.)	0.43	0.37	−0.34
Russell 1000	**Avg. Ret (%/Yr)**	**0.64**	**0.42**	**−0.22**
(01/2009–12/2020)	Vol (%/Yr)	2.46	1.62	1.58
	Inf. Ratio (ann.)	0.26	0.26	−0.14
Russell 2000	**Avg. Ret (%/Yr)**	**2.19**	**0.92**	**−1.27**
(12/2012–12/2020)	Vol (%/Yr)	4.62	3.42	2.72
	Inf. Ratio (ann.)	0.47	0.27	−0.47

Source: Bloomberg, Compustat, MSCI, Barclays Research.

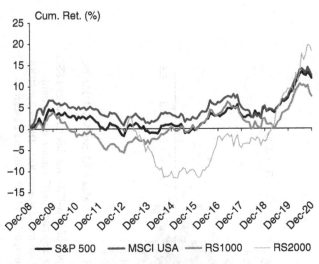

FIGURE 3.7 Cumulative performance of ESG return premium for S&P 500, MSCI USA, Russell 1000, and Russell 2000 (January 2009–December 2020).
Source: Bloomberg, Compustat, MSCI, Barclays Research.

the large- and mid-cap universes showed very similar patterns, while the premium for Russell 2000 showed a slightly different and more volatile pattern, suggesting that the ESG return premium dynamics may be different for small-cap stocks.

TABLE 3.7 ESG return premium correlations for S&P 500, MSCI USA, Russell 1000, and Russell 2000 by periods.

Time Span		S&P 500 and MSCI USA	S&P 500 and RS1000	MSCI USA and RS1000	S&P 500 and RS2000	MSCI USA and RS2000	RS1000 and RS2000
Whole Period	01/2009–12/2020	0.87	0.81	0.82			
	12/2012–12/2020	0.90	0.82	0.85	0.31	0.26	0.22
Sub-Periods	01/2009–12/2012	0.80	0.78	0.76			
	01/2013–12/2015	0.89	0.85	0.84	0.33	0.22	0.40
	01/2016–12/2020	0.91	0.82	0.86	0.28	0.22	0.16

Source: Bloomberg, Compustat, MSCI, Barclays Research.

To further examine how different the ESG return dynamics were across the universes, Table 3.7 reports the correlations of the ESG return premia in the four universes for different periods. The correlations of ESG return premia were relatively high among the large- and mid-cap universes (above 0.75 between S&P 500, MSCI USA, and Russell 1000 in all periods). On the other hand, the ESG return premium for the Russell 2000 had lower correlations with those in the large- and mid-cap universes, ranging from 0.16 to 0.40. These low correlations again highlight the different dynamics for the small-cap universe relative to the large- and mid-cap universes.

The Effect of Over/Underweight Constraints on the ESG Return Premium

As described in the construction details in Table 3.1, the weights of stocks in the exposure-matched portfolios are allowed to deviate by an absolute amount of 0.5% from the benchmark index weight. To analyse the effect of different weight constraints, we construct the exposure-matched portfolios using different over/underweight constraints. Figure 3.8 Panel A reports the average ESG return premium, and Panel B plots the time series of ESG return premium by different over/underweight constraints. The ESG return premia demonstrated consistent dynamics: the averages were all positive as in Panel A, and the time series all showed a positive upward trend since 2016 in Panel B. The consistency of the dynamics is further verified

Panel A: ESG return premium by over/underweight constraints (S&P 500 universe, January 2009–December 2020)

	Stock Over/Underweight Constraint			
	0.5% (original)	1%	2%	5%
Avg. Ret (%/Yr)	0.96	0.92	1.54	2.79
Vol. (%/Yr)	2.21	3.17	4.19	5.50
Inf. Ratio (ann.)	0.43	0.29	0.37	0.51
Avg. # of Stocks in Max-ESG or Min-ESG	131	84	51	31

Note: the 'Avg. # of stocks in Max-ESG or Min-ESG' numbers were first calculated as the average number of stocks across the Max- and Min-ESG portfolios each month, then averaged over the time series.

Panel B: ESG return premium cumulative performance by over/underweight constraint (S&P 500 universe, January 2009–December 2020)

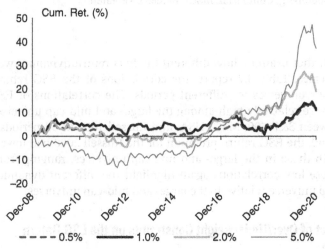

Panel C: Correlation between ESG return premium with different over/ underweight constraints (S&P 500 universe, January 2009–December 2020)

	1%	2%	5%
0.5%	0.88	0.75	0.53
1%		0.84	0.59
2%			0.74

FIGURE 3.8   Max- and Min-ESG portfolios with alternative weight constraints.
Source: Bloomberg, Compustat, MSCI, Barclays Research.

in Panel C, which reports the fairly high correlations among ESG return premia under different over/underweight constraints. For example, ESG return premia with 0.5% and 1.0% constraints had a correlation of 0.88. Even for the highly concentrated 5%-constraint portfolio, its ESG return premium still had a correlation of 0.53 with that of the well-diversified 0.5% constraint portfolio.

Despite the similarity in return dynamics, the magnitude of the weight constraint did have an effect on the dynamics of the portfolios and the ESG return premium. The direct mechanical effect is that a more lenient over/underweight constraint leads to a more concentrated portfolio with fewer stocks and higher returns volatility. The indirect effect is that a more lenient constraint gives the Max-(Min-)ESG portfolios more room to maximize (minimize) their ESG scores, such that the Max-over-Min-ESG portfolios will have a larger ESG difference and a magnified ESG return premium. For example, Panel A of Figure 3.8 shows that when we increase the over/underweight constraint from 0.5% to 5.0%, the average number of stocks in the Max-ESG or Min-ESG portfolios decreases from 131 to 31, the volatility of the ESG returns more than doubles, and the average ESG return premium increases from 0.96%/year to 2.79%/year. In practice, investors could customize the over/underweight constraint for their desired level of diversification when measuring the ESG return premium or constructing their ESG portfolios.

ESG RETURN PREMIUM BY SECTOR, PILLAR, AND IN OTHER GEOGRAPHIES

This section illustrates how we can use the exposure-matched approach to measure ESG return premia in each sector and for each individual E, S, and G pillar. We outline how the general approach should be modified in each case to capture the granular ESG return premium accurately. We also examine the ESG return premium in the European and Chinese equity markets using the same exposure-matched approach.

ESG Return Premium by Sector

To measure the ESG return premium accurately for each sector, we first implement a more granular risk matching at the sector level. For example, to ensure that the ESG return premium for the energy sector is not contaminated by risk exposures, we construct the Max- and Min-ESG portfolios using energy stocks while matching the portfolio's weighted average risk characteristics to those of the energy sector in the benchmark. We repeat the same procedure for each sector in the portfolio. In addition, to ensure sufficient diversification, we apply the over/underweight constraint to individual stocks' weights within their respective sectors, rather than at the index level, with a constraint of 2%.[15] For example, if a stock's market cap weight is 5% within its sector, its weight range in the sector portfolio is set to [3%, 7%]. Table 3.8 shows the average number of stocks in the exposure-matched portfolios by sector with the two modifications. Each sector had around 20–30 stocks so that the estimated sector premia are not driven by individual names. For brevity, we show the results only for the S&P 500 and Russell 1000 universes. The results for the other two universes were similar.

Figure 3.9 reports the average annualized ESG return premia by sector for the S&P 500 and Russell 1000 universes, both for the whole sample period (January 2009–December 2020) and for a latter part of the period (January 2016–December 2020). There are three observations worth noting. First, the ESG return premia were positive for most sectors. In the latter part of the sample period, only energy, materials, and communication services showed negative ESG return premia for both universes. Second, the performances in the two universes were very similar. For instance, the ESG return premia of industrials were the largest among all sectors in both universes between 2016 and 2020; and in consumer staples, the ESG return premium was negative in the whole sample, but turned positive between 2016 and 2020 in both universes. Third, the dynamics of ESG return premia at the sector level could

TABLE 3.8 Average number of stocks in Max-ESG or Min-ESG portfolios (January 2009–December 2020).

	S&P 500	RS1000
Energy	22	26
Materials	22	30
Industrials	32	36
Con. Discretionary	29	34
Con. Staples	23	25
Health Care	30	34
Financials	28	33
Info. Tech.	26	30
Comm. Services	15	19
Utilities	25	30
Real Estate	21	33
Total	*274*	*332*

Note: The number of stocks is first averaged across the Max- and Min-ESG portfolios each month and then averaged across the time series.
Source: Bloomberg, Compustat, MSCI, Barclays Research.

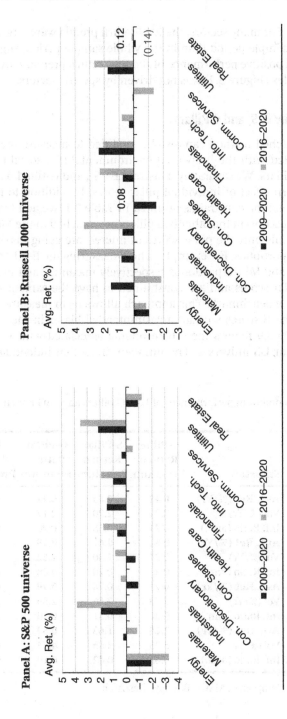

FIGURE 3.9 ESG return premium performances by sector.
Source: Bloomberg, Compustat, MSCI, Barclays Research.

change over time. For many sectors, the ESG return premia were larger in the latter part of the sample period than in the whole sample period, suggesting that the increased positive performance of the ESG return premium over time in the broader index (Figure 3.7) was not driven by specific sectors.

Return Premium by E, S, and G Pillars

The exposure-matched method can also be modified to measure the return premium associated with the individual environmental (E), social (S), and governance (G) pillars. We separately construct E-, S-, and G-tilted portfolios to assess the return effect of individual pillar scores. In addition to the risk characteristics-matching constraints outlined in Table 3.1, we add two other constraints so that scores in the other two pillars are matched in the Max- and Min- portfolios while only the pillar scores of interest are being maximized/ minimized in the portfolios. For example, when measuring the E-pillar return premium, Max-E and Min-E portfolios respectively maximize and minimize the average E pillar scores and are constrained to have the same average S and G scores as the benchmark. This approach allows us to measure returns associated with the E scores without any unintended biases in the S and G pillar scores. Table 3.9 reports the return premia associated with E, S, and G pillars in all four US universes. The numbers show that individual pillar

TABLE 3.9 Return premium performances of E, S, G pillars and ESG return premium.

Universe and Sample Period	Statistics	E-Pillar Return Premium	S-Pillar Return Premium	G-Pillar Return Premium	ESG Return Premium
S&P 500	**Avg. Ret (%/Yr)**	**0.48**	**0.83**	**0.44**	**0.96**
(01/2009–12/2020)	Vol (%/Yr)	2.29	2.20	2.17	2.21
	Inf. Ratio (ann.)	0.21	0.38	0.20	0.43
MSCI USA	**Avg. Ret (%/Yr)**	**0.88**	**0.47**	**0.19**	**1.00**
(01/2009–12/2020)	Vol (%/Yr)	2.32	2.30	2.52	2.31
	Inf. Ratio (ann.)	0.38	0.20	0.08	0.43
Russell 1000	**Avg. Ret (%/Yr)**	**0.77**	**0.78**	**0.79**	**0.64**
(01/2009–12/2020)	Vol (%/Yr)	2.53	2.56	2.59	2.46
	Inf. Ratio (ann.)	0.30	0.31	0.30	0.26
Russell 2000	**Avg. Ret (%/Yr)**	**2.25**	**1.63**	**0.84**	**2.19**
(12/2012–12/2020)	Vol (%/Yr)	5.35	3.85	4.34	4.62
	Inf. Ratio (ann.)	0.42	0.42	0.19	0.47

Source: Bloomberg, Compustat, MSCI, Barclays Research.

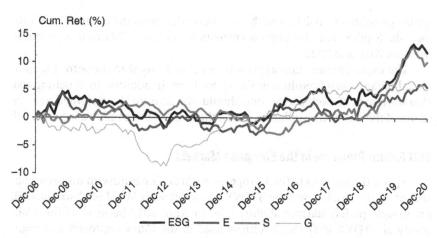

FIGURE 3.10 Cumulative return of return premia of E, S, and G pillars and ESG (S&P 500, January 2009–December 2020).
Source: Bloomberg, Compustat, MSCI, Barclays Research.

return premia were all positive during the sample period in all four universes. For S&P 500 and MSCI USA, ESG return premia were higher than the return premia associated with individual pillars, suggesting that the aggregate ESG scores may have a stronger return effect in these two universes.

To compare the time series dynamics, Figure 3.10 plots the cumulative returns for the separate pillar premia for the S&P 500 index. All return premia showed an upward trend from the middle of the sample period, with the G pillar starting the earliest. The G-pillar return premium started to increase steadily in 2013, indicating that investors may have adopted corporate governance into decision making before environmental (E) and social (S) considerations. After 2016, though, the S pillar displayed the strongest trend and the highest similarity with the ESG return premium. To better illustrate the relation between individual pillar premia and the overall ESG premium, Table 3.10 shows the correlations between the E, S, and G return premia and the ESG

TABLE 3.10 Correlation between ESG return premium and individual pillar return premium.

	ESG and E	ESG and S	ESG and G
Whole Sample Period (01/2009–12/2020)	0.43	0.42	0.19
Subsample (01/2016–12/2020)	0.39	0.51	0.26

Source: Bloomberg, Compustat, MSCI, Barclays Research

return premium. Consistent with the observation from the cumulative return plot, the S pillar had the highest correlation with the ESG return premium between 2016 and 2020.

The exposure-matched approach can also be used to measure the individual pillar return premium at the sector level. In addition to matching risk characteristics of each sector, one should also require the weighted average scores of the non-tilting pillars to match those of the benchmark at sector level.

ESG Return Premium in the European Markets

We expand the analysis to the European markets. The European universe consists of all the stocks from the STOXX 600 index with MSCI ESG scores, with the sample period starting slightly later in April 2012 because of the availability of STOXX ESG index returns used in the index approach as a comparison. We apply the same exposure-matched approach and the same set of constraints/parameters to the European universe.

We find similar results in the European markets. Figure 3.11 reports the performance of the ESG return premium in Europe, with Panel A showing the average performance statistics and Panel B plotting the cumulative returns. The numbers in Panel A suggest that the average ESG premium in European markets was also positive (2.75%/year). As a comparison, the average ESG returns using the index approach in Europe (STOXX 600 ESG index over STOXX 600)[16] was around zero in the sample period. The correlations between ESG returns measured using the exposure-matched approach (Max-ESG over benchmark) and those measured using the index approach were very low (0.09).[17]

Panel B shows the cumulative returns of the European ESG return premium versus the return difference from the index approach. The ESG return premium in Europe showed a more consistent upward trend since 2012 than in the United States, where the ESG return premium was mostly flat before 2016. This pattern is consistent with European investors adopting ESG considerations into their investment process earlier and more widely than US investors.

ESG Return Premium in China A-share Market

We also expand the analysis to the China A-share market. Due to its role in global supply chains, China has long been suffering from environmental issues such as water shortages, air pollution, and soil contamination. As a result, the country has sought to play an active role in the Paris Agreement – it has submitted pledges to the UN with ambitious goals of achieving a CO_2 emissions peak before 2030 and carbon neutrality before 2060. China's transformation from an industrialized economy to a service-based

Panel A: Performance of ESG return premium in European markets (April 2012–December 2020)

	Stoxx 600 Universe (Apr. 2012–Dec. 2020)				MSCI USA Universe (Apr. 2012–Dec. 2020)	
	ESG Return Premium	Max-ESG over Benchmark	Min-ESG over Benchmark	ESG version over Parent Index	ESG Return Premium	ESG Version over Parent Index
Avg. Ret (%/Yr)	2.75	1.67	−1.08	0.05	1.03	−0.60
Vol (%/Yr)	2.59	1.31	1.81	0.48	2.35	1.67
Inf. Ratio (ann.)	1.06	1.28	−0.59	0.10	0.44	−0.36
Worst Monthly Ret (%)	−1.43	−1.05	−1.46	−0.36	−1.82	−1.82
Max Drawdown (%)	−4.30	−2.13	−10.48	−1.84	−5.22	−6.68

Panel B: Cumulative returns of ESG return premium vs STOXX 600 ESG over STOXX 600

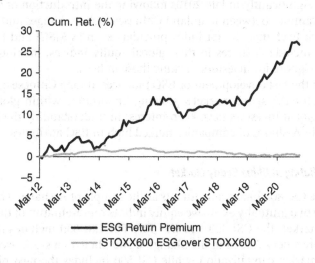

FIGURE 3.11   ESG return premium in European markets.
Source: Bloomberg, Compustat, MSCI, Barclays Research.

economy also brings many social challenges, such as widening inequality and a declining birth rate. In addition, although the corporate governance of many Chinese companies is improving, it is believed many structural issues still remain.[18] Facing such problems, China began to implement rapid changes in its policies related to ESG issues, and consequently ESG awareness is growing at the firm level. A 2019 study by UNEP FI/PRI (United Nations Environment Programme Finance Initiative/Principles for Responsible Investment) found the percentage of the largest 300 listed firms in the China A-share market that provided some form of voluntary ESG data disclosure through annual sustainability reports nearly doubled between 2009 and 2018 (UN PRI 2019).

This new change in ESG practices has been happening concurrent with China's decision to continue opening up A-share markets to foreign investors. Chinese companies issue two separate classes of shares in mainland Chinese stock exchanges to foreign and domestic investors. A-shares are issued to domestic investors and traded in Chinese yuan. B-shares are issued to foreign investors and traded in US dollars for those listed on the Shanghai Stock Exchange and in Hong Kong dollars for those listed on the Shenzhen Stock Exchange. A-shares were initially exclusive to domestic investors, which means a significant part of the Chinese stock market was inaccessible to foreign investors because an overwhelming majority of Chinese companies only issue A-shares. However, since 2002, China has started to open up its stock market to allow foreign investors to invest in A-shares. Foreign access improved significantly in late 2010s following the introduction of stock connect programmes between mainland Chinese stock exchanges and the Hong Kong Stock Exchange. Major index providers such as MSCI and FTSE have started to include A-shares in their global equity indices, making A-shares difficult to ignore for investors tracking these indices.

Given the fast development of ESG practices among Chinese companies, and the China A-share market's growing importance within global equity markets, global investors have keen interest in understanding the impact of investing in A-shares of companies ranked high in ESG attributes.

MSCI ESG Rating in China Equity Market

We use the CSI 800 index constituents as the sample of A-shares. The index is formed by two mutually exclusive equity indices representative of the Chinese A-share market: the CSI 300 and CSI 500. The CSI 300 includes the largest 300 A-share stocks traded in the Shanghai and Shenzhen stock exchanges in terms of market capitalization, while CSI 500 includes the next biggest 500 A-share stocks traded on the two exchanges. We focus on CSI 800 constituents because they represent the most liquid segment of China's A-share market.

Figure 3.12 reports the MSCI ESG score coverage on the CSI 800 stock universe in terms of number of stocks and market cap. In May 2018, MSCI initiated a China A-share ESG rating on all the constituents in the MSCI China A International index. As shown in Figure 3.12, the coverage on CSI 800 has

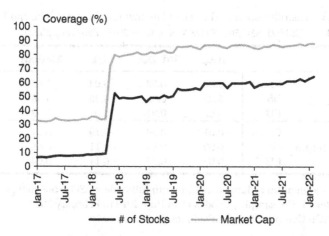

FIGURE 3.12 Coverage of ESG data in China A-share market (CSI 800 index, January 2017–February 2022).
Source: MSCI, Compustat, Refinitiv, Barclays Research.

grown steadily ever since. In terms of market cap, coverage has been staying above 80% since mid 2018. However, in terms of number of stocks, coverage is moderate, around 50%.

There is no major difference in MSCI's rating methodology for China stocks compared to stocks in major developed markets. MSCI ESG adopts an industry-neutral approach and compares a company's ability to mitigate key ESG risks with its global industry peers. As a result, the ESG scores for the China A-share market are directly comparable to those in the United States and Europe. The key difference lies in the data sources used in their assessment. Voluntary self-disclosure on companies' ESG policies and performance metrics are extremely low in China (as of May 2018, 2% of Chinese companies disclose ESG data compared to 34% of MSCI ACWI constituents, MSCI 2018). To address the lack of voluntary ESG disclosure, for Chinese listed firms, MSCI seeks information from local publicly available data, which includes 11,000 local media sources and over 40 local norms and regulations to identify ESG controversies, such as corruption allegations, and business ethics concerns. For companies in the United States and the European Union, MSCI is able to rely more on company-disclosed information.

MSCI ESG scores indicate that despite the growing ESG awareness among Chinese companies and regulators, the China A-share market is still not at the same stage as the United States and Europe as of February 2022 in terms of its ESG development. As shown in Table 3.11, companies in the China A-share market had much lower ESG scores compared to the US and

TABLE 3.11   Distribution of ESG level and momentum in China, US, and European stock markets (CSI800, S&P500, STOXX 600, June 2019–February 2022).

		Avg.	Std. Dev.	Q1	Median	Q3
ESG Level	China	3.60	0.88	3.03	3.65	4.20
	US	5.02	0.85	4.46	4.98	5.57
	EU	5.62	0.91	5.03	5.58	6.23
ESG Momentum	China	−0.01	0.39	−0.19	−0.01	0.17
	US	0.09	0.39	−0.11	0.05	0.31
	EU	0.07	0.37	−0.11	0.04	0.28

Note: ESG momentum is defined as 12-month full-review ESG score changes (see Chapter 8). The sample period is from June 2019 to February 2022.
Source: MSCI, Compustat, Refinitiv, Barclays Research.

European markets (Q1, median, Q3 numbers were all much lower than for the United States and the European Union). Moreover, the companies were not on improving paths either. ESG momentum[19] for Chinese companies was lower compared to US and EU companies. While in the United States and Europe, companies had positive ESG score changes on average (0.09 for US companies and 0.07 for EU ones), companies in China even experienced a negative average score change (-0.01) over the same period. The differences in the distributions of ESG scores and score changes match the overall development status of the Chinese economy and ESG adoption stage in China. For instance, approximately one-third of the Chinese companies under coverage are in industrial and materials sectors. They lag behind in adopting stricter environmental policies, as similar companies in developed economies have been dealing with consistent regulatory scrutiny on such issues from a much earlier time. It is also worth pointing out that MSCI does not automatically assign lower governance scores to state-owned-enterprises (SOE) – a significant portion of listed companies in China. They only become an area of concern for cases in which controlling ownership leads to governance risks, such as lack of board independence and unequal voting rights (MSCI 2018).

Exposure-Matched ESG Return Premium in China A-share Market

Using our exposure-matched approach, we calculated the ESG return premium for the China A-share market. Table 3.12 reports the performance statistics for the period from July 2019 to March 2022. It shows that investing in companies with high ESG scores had positive effects on performance: Max-over-Min-ESG portfolios delivered positive returns on average, with an information ratio of 0.63.

TABLE 3.12 ESG return premia in China A-share, US, and European equity markets (CSI800, S&P500, STOXX 600, July 2019–March 2022).

			China			US	EU
	Max	**Min**	**Max over Min**	**Max over Bmk**	**Bmk over Min**	**Max over Min**	**Max over Min**
Avg. Ret (%/Yr)	9.63	4.95	4.68	2.54	2.14	1.16	3.06
Vol (%/Yr)	15.46	15.90	7.43	3.49	4.41	3.24	6.27
SR/IR (ann.)	0.46	0.15	0.63	0.73	0.49	0.36	0.49
Worst Monthly Ret (%)	−7.76	−8.25	−3.91	−1.77	−2.26	−2.64	−2.83
Max Drawdown (%)	−15.25	−12.05	−6.63	−2.29	−4.59	−4.98	−6.90

Source: MSCI, Compustat, Refinitiv, Barclays Research.

The ESG return premium was much larger in China than in the United States and comparable with its European counterpart (4.68% annualized average return for China, 1.16% for the United States, and 3.06% for Europe). The ESG return premium is larger for China even though it had lower average ESG ratings than in the United States and the European Union as shown in Table 3.11. But the ESG score dispersion in China (0.88, measured by score standard deviation), which partly determines the size of the ESG return premium, is similar in magnitude to those in the United States (0.85) and Europe (0.91).

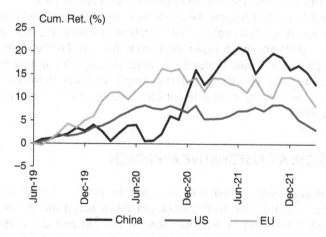

FIGURE 3.13 Cumulative returns of ESG premia in China A-share, US, and European equity markets (CSI800, S&P500, STOXX 600, July 2019–March 2022). *Source*: MSCI, Compustat, Refinitiv, Barclays Research.

TABLE 3.13 Correlations among China A-share, US, and European stock markets, for index returns and ESG return premia (CSI800, S&P500, STOXX 600, July 2019–March 2022).

	Index	ESG Return Premium
China – US	0.48	0.27
China – Europe	0.36	−0.22
US – Europe	0.90	0.42

Source: MSCI, Compustat, Refinitiv, Barclays Research.

Table 3.12 also shows that the effects were of similar magnitude from both the Max- and Min- sides, as both 'Max over Bmk' and 'Bmk over Min' returns were positive. Another noticeable pattern of the return dynamics, as shown in the cumulative return chart in Figure 3.13, is that the ESG return premium was close to zero in the earliest part of the sample, and became steadily positive around September 2020. The change followed almost immediately China's announcement that it would peak CO_2 emissions before 2030, and achieve 'carbon neutrality' before 2060, which highlights the significant amount of influence government policies have on China's equity markets.

Figure 3.13 also compares the cumulative returns of the ESG premia in China, the United States, and Europe. Overall, the ESG cumulative return in China exhibits a steep pattern after September 2020, while ESG premia show a similar and smoother pattern in the United States and Europe.

Table 3.13 further reports the correlations of ESG monthly premia in the three regions. It is worth noting that correlations among the ESG premia of the three regions are much lower than the index correlations, reflecting different stages of ESG awareness and ESG practice adoptions among companies in the three regions. This shows that investing in China A-shares could potentially bring diversification benefits for ESG investors in the new era of global asset allocation.

DISCUSSION: AN ALTERNATIVE APPROACH

A popular academic approach to studying the effects of ESG attributes is to construct quintile (or decile) stock portfolios based on ESG scores and regress the differences in returns between the top and the bottom quintile portfolios on a host of equity risk factors[20] (henceforth 'the regression approach'). The intercept from the regression measures the unique returns coming from ESG attributes (ESG alpha). For example, a recent study by Bruno et al. (2021) uses the regression approach to examine ESG returns.

While this approach is popular in academic research because of its simplicity, we discuss three drawbacks that make this method inferior to the exposure matched approach.[21]

Month-to-Month Measure of ESG Returns

First, the regression approach only generates an average alpha estimate (intercept), but does not accurately measure the ESG returns on a month-to-month basis, as it assumes that the return time series have constant exposures to the risk factors. In reality, the risk exposures of ESG portfolios may change from month to month, especially because ESG is a relatively new metric and ESG investing is still evolving. For example, Figure 3.1 Panel D shows that the MSCI USA ESG Leaders index had lower profitability than its parent index from December 2012 to December 2013, but consistently higher profitability than its parent index after December 2016. Because a time series regression only estimates the average exposure, the negative and positive profitability biases will partially cancel out when averaged across the whole sample period. Moreover, if there is some correlation between the monthly risk exposure and the factor returns, the average results from the factor regression will also be misleading (see Jagannathan and Wang [1996] for an example in the CAPM framework). As a comparison, the exposure-matched approach addresses the time-varying risk exposure issue by matching risk characteristics between the long and the short at each rebalancing date to neutralize the time-varying risk effects and, thus, measures the ESG returns accurately on a month-to-month basis.

Investability

Second, the regression approach is designed to measure the average ESG alpha, but not to invest in it. In contrast, investors can use the exposure-matched portfolios directly to capture the ESG return premium from investable portfolios. A linear regression decomposes the returns from the L-S ESG portfolios into a combination of the ESG alpha plus a weighted average of the factor portfolios. In theory, to capture the ESG alpha, an investor would go long the L-S ESG portfolios and sell short the weighted average of the factor portfolios. There are a couple of problems with implementation. First, the factor portfolios may not be tradable, either because microcap stocks with low liquidity are included in the factor portfolios or because an investor's mandate prohibits shorting. The exposure-matched approach, on the other hand, starts with a liquid universe of mid- and large-cap stocks, and an investor with a shorting constraint can simply invest in the Max-ESG portfolio to gain ESG exposure. More importantly, in the regression approach, the coefficients (weights) of each risk factor are estimated ex post using the whole sample period with hindsight. In real time, investors would not be able to estimate factor weights to neutralize portfolio risk. In contrast, the exposure-matched approach is implementable each month, as it requires data that are readily available at each point in time.[22]

Practicality and Scalability

Finally, the setup of the exposure-matched approach corresponds with the practice of many portfolio managers – anchoring to a market cap-weighted generic index while enhancing certain attributes. One reason for this practice is that many investors face strict mandates to benchmark to an index. Given its construction, the exposure-matched approach can be easily implemented by portfolio managers to access ESG returns given their mandates. In addition, one advantage of anchoring to a market cap-weighted index is that the portfolios are easily scalable, as the weights are roughly proportional to each stock's market cap. By construction, a small stock would not receive an overly large weight and become hard to trade in large portfolios. In contrast, the ESG L-S portfolios from the regression approach are equally weighted and their capacity may be very limited, as the positions on small and illiquid stocks are hard to implement in a large portfolio.

To put our findings in the context of the regression approach, we regress the ESG return premium from our exposure-matched approach on the Fama–French 5 factors. Table 3.14 reports the regression results. A few observations

TABLE 3.14 Ex post regression of ESG return premium (exposure-matched approach) on Fama–French five factors, January 2009–December 2020.

	Universe			
	S&P 500	**MSCI USA**	**Russell 1000**	**Russell 2000**
Constant (%/m)	**0.08**	**0.10**	**0.06**	**0.12**
Mkt-RF	0.00	−0.01	−0.01	0.06
SMB (size)	−0.02	−0.02	−0.03	0.01
HML (value)	0.00	0.02	0.01	0.02
RMW (profitability)	0.02	0.01	0.03	−0.04
CMA (investment)	−0.02	−0.05	−0.02	0.02
R^2	1%	2%	2%	5%

Note: *, **, *** represent significance at the levels of 0.1, 0.05, and 0.01, respectively. Statistical significance is based on the null hypothesis that coefficients equal zero. None of the results in this table are significant even at the 0.1 level.
Source: Bloomberg, Compustat, Ken French Data Library, MSCI, Barclays Research.

are worth mentioning. First, the ESG return premia in all four major US equity universes have no significant exposures to any of the five Fama–French risk factors, and the regressions had small R^2s, indicating that the exposure-matched approach neutralizes the risk in the long and the short. Second, the intercepts in all four universes are positive but not statistically significant, indicating that the exposure-matched portfolios do not contain significant ESG alphas after accounting for the risk factors. These results are qualitatively similar to the findings in Bruno et al. (2021). They use the regression approach on a custom-defined large- and mid-cap equity universe and find that the exposures to profitability and investment factors were significant (their approach did not neutralize the factor exposures at construction like the exposure-matched approach). After accounting for the risk exposures, the intercept of their ESG L-S regression was insignificant, and they conclude that there was no significant alpha associated with ESG investing.

CONCLUSIONS

Performance attribution to ESG characteristics is a key component in decision making about ESG investing. Return attribution is often done using a simple approach, by taking the difference between the returns of an ESG index and that of its parent index. However, many ESG indices do not match the systematic risk exposures of their parent indices. Moreover, these ESG indices are usually rebalanced at an annual frequency, so their sector weights may deviate substantially from their parent indices between rebalancing dates, even if the ESG indices were constructed to be sector-neutral to their parent indices at rebalancing. Therefore, the differences in systematic risk exposures and in sector weights could contribute to the return difference between the ESG version and its parent index, thus contaminating the return attribution to ESG characteristics.

In this chapter, we use an exposure-matched approach to measure the return premium related to ESG investing. We construct a pair of exposure-matched portfolios with positive (Max-ESG) and negative (Min-ESG) tilts to firms' ESG attributes while matching key risk characteristics and sector weights on a monthly basis. Therefore, the return difference between the Max-ESG and Min-ESG portfolios measures the ESG return premium accurately, since the differences in risk and sectors weights in the two portfolios have been neutralized.

We find that the average ESG return premia in the major US equity indices (S&P500, MSCI USA, Russell 1000 and 2000), the STOXX 600 index in Europe and the CSI 800 index in China were positive. Once we control for risk and sector, investing in firms with better ESG scores actually would have improved performance, especially after 2016. Using the index approach, one would have come to the incorrect conclusion that ESG investing hurt performance in the US market and had a limited performance effect in Europe.

Overall, the exposure-matched approach is able to measure ESG returns accurately, and investors can use it to monitor the time-varying effects of ESG investing in the equity markets at the aggregate or more granular levels.

REFERENCES

Asness, C., Frazzini, A., and Pedersen, L. (2018). Quality minus Junk. *Review of Accounting Studies*, 24, pp. 34–112.

Breedt, A., Ciliberti, S., Gualdi, S., and Seager, P. (2019). Is ESG an Equity Factor or Just an Investment Guide? *The Journal of Investing*, 28 (2), pp. 32–42.

Bruno, G., Esakia, M., and Goltz, F. (2021). 'Honey, I Shrunk the ESG Alpha': Risk-adjusting ESG Portfolio Returns. *Scientific Beta*, April.

Fama, E. and French, K. (1995). Size and Book-to-market Factors in Earnings and Returns. *Journal of Finance*, 50, pp. 131–155.

Fama, E. and French, K. (1996). Multifactor Explanations of Asset Pricing Anomalies. *Journal of Finance*, 51, pp. 55–84.

Fama, E. and French, K. (2015). A Five-Factor Asset Pricing Model. *Journal of Financial Economics*, 116 (1), pp. 1–22.

Giese, G., Lee, L. E., Melas, D., Nagy, Z., and Nishikawa, L. (2019). Foundations of ESG Investing: How ESG Affects Equity Valuation, Risk, and Performance. *The Journal of Portfolio Management*, 45 (5), pp. 69–83.

Jagannathan, R. and Wang, Z. (1996). The Conditional CAPM and the Cross-section of Expected Returns. *The Journal of Finance*, 51 (1), pp. 3–53.

MSCI (2018). China A Shares: MSCI ESG Ratings Overview. *MSCI ESG Research*, June.

MSCI (2020). MSCI ESG Leaders Indexes Methodology. MSCI, November.

Statman, M. (1987). How Many Stocks Make a Diversified Portfolio? *Journal of Financial and Quantitative Analysis*, 22 (3), pp. 353–363.

UN PRI (United Nations Principles for Responsible Investment) (2019). ESG Data in China: Recommendations for Primary ESG Indicators. June.

NOTES

1. For example, our prior studies found that firms with higher ESG ratings tend to have better quality (lower investment rate, higher operating profits, and better ratings on their bonds), as well as larger size (see Chapters 2 and 13). Existing studies have also documented that highly rated ESG companies tend to be larger in market capitalization (Breedt et al. 2019, Giese et al. 2019).

2. The MSCI USA index is designed to measure the performance of the large and mid-cap segments of the US market. The index covers approximately 85% of

the free float-adjusted market capitalization in the United States, with around 600 constituents.

3. The pitfalls involved in using the index approach may explain the results in Chapter 11, which find no significant differences in performance and risk exposures between ESG-focused and regular equity US mutual funds. The differences are also small for the same fund before and after it switched its classification as ESG-focused. Many ESG-focused mutual funds use ESG indices as benchmarks, which may expose investors to unintended risk factors. To offer purer ESG exposure, ESG mutual funds would need to construct a benchmark that neutralizes the risk and sector differences from the broad generic index, such as an exposure-matched portfolio.

4. There are additional filters such as controversies and business involvement. For details, please refer to MSCI ESG leader index methodology.

5. The risk characteristic captures the exposures to the five key risk factors in the widely used Fama–French 5-Factor model (Fama and French 2015). Market beta is the slope estimate from a trailing five-year regression of monthly stock excess returns (over 1m Libor) on the market excess returns (S&P 500 return over 1m Libor). Size is measured as the market capitalization of each company. Book-to-market (B/M) ratio is a company's most recent book equity over its current-month market cap. Operating profit is a company's annualized revenues minus cost of goods sold, interest expenses, and selling, general, and administrative expenses divided by book equity from the previous year. Investment rate is measured as the change in a firm's most recent total assets from the previous year.

6. The number reported for size is median instead of average because monthly averages were not representative of the distributions, as a few disproportionally large firms were in the underlying MSCI index but not in the ESG version.

7. The MSCI USA ESG Leaders index aims to cover the top 50% of market cap in each sector of the underlying MSCI USA index at index rebalancing of each May.

8. This analysis uses total returns. The ticker for the MSCI USA index is M2US Index, and the ticker for the ESG version (MSCI USA ESG Leaders index) is TUSSLMU Index.

9. Stocks' total returns are used to calculate portfolio returns.

10. See note 5 for definition of risk characteristics. The investment and profitability factors are similar in concept to the QMJ (quality-minus-junk) factor proposed by AQR (Asness et al. 2018). The QMJ factor captures three components: profitability, growth, and safety. The operating profitability in FF captures a concept similar to the profitability component in QMJ, although the latter includes several profitability measures, rather than just one in FF. The investment factor in FF is similar to the safety factor in QMJ: the investment factor finds that firms expanding too quickly on average have lower returns. The safety factor measures this aspect from another angle by focusing on firms' betas (already captured in our beta factor), leverage (taking on too much debt to expand), and volatility.

11. An alternative to ensure diversification is to implement an absolute weight cap, say 1%. This approach will produce a portfolio that is more similar to equal weighting and deviate more from the existing index weights. We choose the current approach because it represents more of a tilt from the index within some reasonable range and is closer to what is done in practice.

12. Based on the general guideline of 30–40 stocks outlined in Statman (1987)
13. A simple regression between the two ESG return time series has a significant slope close to one and an insignificant constant, confirming that they have similar ESG return dynamics.
14. The annualized volatility of the S&P 500, MSCI USA, and Russell 1000 indices were similar at around 15%/year from January 2009 to December 2020, whereas the volatility of the Russell 2000 index was 20%/year for the same period.
15. The target benchmark weight in this constraint is now each stock's market capitalization weight within its respective sector in the index, instead of its weight in the index as in the main specification.
16. We use total returns from both indices. The ticker for STOXX 600 ESG index is SXXWESGX, and the ticker for the STOXX600 index is SXXGR.
17. The STOXX600 ESG index is constructed using Sustainalytics ESG scores.
18. See, for example, https://www.unpri.org/pri-blog/corporate-governance-in-china-key-takeaways-for-investors/7398.article (accessed 4 August 2023).
19. ESG momentum is defined as 12-month full-review ESG score changes. The choice of look-back window balances the number of companies with non-zero ESG changes and the freshness of the changes. The relevant details can be found in Chapter 8.
20. For example the Fama–French five factors (Fama and French 2015).
21. Similar to the quintile sorting in the regression approach, one could also regress the time series returns from the index approach in a similar regression and examine the alpha, but it is subject to the first caveat discussed here.
22. Of course, an investor wishing to implement a pro-ESG tilt in a portfolio would be well advised to adjust the portfolio construction mechanism to limit transaction costs. This is beyond the scope of this chapter; we do present results for a turnover-constrained active credit strategy in Chapter 6.

CHAPTER 4

Performance Impact of an ESG Tilt in Sovereign Bond Markets

One of the key themes of this book is the relationship between ESG factors and financial performance in different markets. In the preceding chapters we have measured ESG effects in portfolios of corporate bonds and equities. We now turn our attention to sovereign bonds, and ask the same two questions we asked earlier about corporate bonds: to what extent are ESG characteristics priced into the spreads of different sovereign issuers, and do they have any predictive power regarding subsequent returns?

Forming assessments of the relative ranking of countries with regard to ESG characteristics is inherently different from comparing those of corporations. In fact, for this chapter we do not use sovereign ESG scores from a commercial ESG ratings provider; rather, we base our analysis on various rankings from a variety of publicly available sources. This approach, which is followed by many investors in this space, brings with it some additional challenges. Chief among these are that the rankings we rely on are published infrequently, often with a significant lag from the measurement date, and not synchronized with each other. In addition, there can be significant overlap or correlation among ESG signals and more traditional financial indicators. We will explore some of these relationships as well.

The chapter is organized as follows. First, we present the data used in our study, which includes three different categories of information: bond market data, ESG data, and fundamental data.

Second, we test to what extent ESG information is incorporated into market prices. We start with a market snapshot as of a single point in time to simplify the presentation, and then extend our analysis to a multi-year data panel. We find that while it is fairly simple to demonstrate that ESG rankings are related to credit spread levels, these relationships are no longer significant once we control for credit ratings.

Third, we explore the correlations among the various metrics in our dataset. We find that ESG characteristics can be correlated with each other, but also with some fundamental metrics, with credit ratings, and with spreads.

Next, we test the extent to which ESG characteristics can help predict future returns – either in terms of levels or volatilities. We test the connection between ESG characteristics and returns using two distinct approaches: a mathematical approach in which we regress country returns against ESG characteristics, and a portfolio-construction approach in which we backtest the performance of ESG-tilted portfolios carefully rebalanced to match all the other risk exposures of a selected benchmark. Our results are consistent with those of our analysis of spreads: taken alone, ESG characteristics have predictive power; but once we control for credit ratings and other risk characteristics, the results are no longer statistically significant. Having established that credit ratings subsume much of the material information available in ESG characteristics, we then check to what extent changes in credit ratings can be explained by changes in ESG exposures. We find that governance scores do have a significant contribution, while environmental and social scores do not.

Finally, we test ESG-tilted portfolios for unintended exposures in other dimensions that were not explicitly controlled for. We find that tilting a portfolio to maximize ESG scores, while controlling for credit ratings, can result in an overweight to countries with poor financial fundamentals, such as high debt levels.

DATA SOURCES

Market Data (USD-denominated Emerging Market Sovereign Bond Spreads)

For this study, we combine data of three different types: bond market data, ESG characteristics, and economic fundamentals by country. Our focus was emerging market (EM) bonds. Compared to developed country bond markets, which are fairly homogeneous, this segment offers a much wider variation across all of our metrics. We further limit ourselves to USD-denominated debt. This market is represented by a panel of data from the Bloomberg Emerging Market USD Sovereign Index, subdivided by country. For each country-specific sub-index, we track index characteristics and returns using monthly data from 2012 to 2021. We consider such index characteristics as average spread, duration, and the duration times spread (DTS), as well as the average Index Quality.[1]

We then line these up against a panel of additional country-level data, which can be divided into two categories: ESG factors and financial fundamentals. In each of these dimensions, we have chosen just a small sample of the available indicators. After some mild filtering of the data to keep only countries included in all the datasets selected for this study, our panel contains 65 countries and covers a wide range of credit spreads, credit ratings, and other characteristics.

ESG Data

The UN Principles for Responsible Investment (PRI) has published 'A Practical Guide to ESG Integration in Sovereign Debt'.[2] Among other things, this guide presents lists of publicly available data sources that rank countries on different aspects of E, S, and G issues. We have selected some of these rankings to represent each category.

Governance Factors

To measure governance, we use the set of *Worldwide Governance Indicators*[3] (WGI) produced by the World Bank, which ranks countries on six different dimensions:

- Voice and Accountability
- Political Stability / No Violence
- Government Effectiveness
- Regulatory Quality
- Rule of Law
- Control of Corruption

In addition to looking at these indicators one at a time, we also produce an overall governance score by taking a simple average of these six indicators. This approach helps to compress the amount of data we need to present when looking across multiple dimensions.

We have also included the *Freedom in the World* index, produced by Freedom House.[4] The main categories in this scoring system are: Political Rights, Political Pluralism and Participation, Functioning of Government, Freedom of Expression and Belief, Associational and Organizational Rights, Rule of Law, Personal Autonomy, and Individual Rights.

Social Factors

Under the category of social factors, we have examined two different measures, produced by different organizations. In each case, the overall country score is produced as an aggregate of scores relating to multiple subcategories. The two measures are:

The *Human Development Index*[5] (HDI) produced by the United Nations (UN). This index has subcomponents relating to life expectancy, education, and standard of living (GDP per capita).

The *Social Progress Index*[6] (SPI) produced by the Social Progress Imperative. This index is far from homogeneous, and although its name presents it as a social score, it covers a broad range of subjects, and actually contains components associated with governance and environmental factors. For the first part of our analysis, we use only the top-level SPI score. In addition to the overall SPI, we include 10 sub-components of the SPI for separate evaluation.

The SPI is organized hierarchically. The overall index is an average of three component scores, which in turn are averages of more granular subcomponents. We include the three top-level components, as well as the subcomponents highlighted below in italics:

- *Basic Human Needs* (*Nutrition and Basic Medical Care, Water and Sanitation*, Shelter, Personal Safety)
- *Foundations of Wellbeing* (Access to Knowledge, Access to Information and Communications, *Health and Wellness, Environmental Quality*)
- *Opportunity* (*Personal Rights, Personal Freedom and Choice*, Inclusiveness, *Access to Advanced Education*)

Environmental Factors

In the environment category, we have chosen to include the University of Notre Dame's *Global Adaptation Index*[7] (ND-GAIN). This index is designed to measure a country's current vulnerability to climate disruptions. It also assesses a country's readiness to leverage private and public sector investment for adaptive actions. It tracks over 74 variables divided into those that measure vulnerability to shocks concerning food, water, health, ecosystem services, human habitat, and infrastructure; and those that measure readiness to deal with such shocks, including economic readiness, governance readiness, and social readiness. We focus only on the overall ND-GAIN score.

However, the ND-GAIN index takes a somewhat unique approach to climate risk, and does not fully capture the metrics typically associated with E scores. To fill out our coverage of environmental issues, we also include a metric that more directly corresponds to a country's environmental profile: the SPI subcomponent score for Environmental Quality, listed above under social factors. This score is computed as a combination of four factors: deaths attributable to outdoor air pollution, greenhouse gas emissions, biome protection, and particulate matter.

Fundamental Data

A few basic data series summarizing the economic fundamentals of the included countries are obtained from the IMF World Economic Outlook[8] dataset. The indicators we selected are:

- Debt as a Percentage of Gross Domestic Product (GDP)
- Deficit as a Percentage of GDP
- Current Account Balance as a Percentage of GDP
- GDP (Purchasing Power Parity – PPP) per Capita

Public debt as a percentage of GDP is a direct measure of leverage for sovereign issuers, and perhaps the simplest measure of fiscal solvency. It is a long-term indicator that reflects not just borrowing over a short-term window, but also the net accumulation of debt over time.

Public deficit[9] (government revenue – expenditures, as a percentage of GDP) is a measure of budget shortfall in a given year and is a useful short-term indicator of the direction and rate of change of financial solvency. In a sense, total debt can be thought of as an accumulation of deficits over time; thus, this variable brings an element of momentum to the selection of financial solvency fundamentals.

Current account balance is another 'flow' indicator that measures the annual improvement or deterioration of a country's economic strength. The current account balance (exports – imports) as a percentage of GDP is representative of the dependence of an economy on external lending.

While the three above indicators are all normalized by the country's GDP, the raw level of GDP per capita is also useful as a broad indicator of the level of development.

Numeric Characteristics of the Data

The diversity of the data sources we have considered presented a number of challenges regarding how to analyse them. While market data is readily available on a monthly, or even daily, frequency, most of the ESG sources are published only annually, and some even less frequently. There is typically a certain publication lag, which also varies from one source to another. In addition, different metrics are published in different units, or use different numeric scales. Furthermore, even the directionality of the scoring can vary. For most of the ESG metrics, higher scores represent better rankings. However, for some risk metrics, such as spreads, numeric credit ratings, and gross debt, higher numbers represent greater risk, and should be associated with a lower level of credit-worthiness. All this needs to be kept in mind when interpreting some numeric results we present, including both regression analysis and correlations. Two metrics may agree with each other conceptually, but if their numerical representations have opposite signs, this agreement is indicated by a negative regression coefficient. An appendix to this chapter provides a table that details the numeric characteristics of each data source we use.

ARE ESG CHARACTERISTICS PRICED INTO SPREADS?

In a number of existing studies of ESG effects in sovereign bonds, researchers have demonstrated that sovereign bond spreads show clear relationships with ESG factors. This is borne out by our findings as well. For example, Figure 4.1 shows a scatter plot of log spreads vs the average level of the WGI Governance indicators as of October 2020. It is clear both visually and from the regression equation shown on the chart that there is a strong relationship between governance and credit spreads. Countries with better governance scores tend to have tighter spreads and vice versa.

However, this result is less remarkable if we consider it relative to a similar plot of the same spreads against their credit ratings as of the same date. For this, we use the Index Rating from the Bloomberg indices, which represents the median credit rating from the three major agencies. In the numeric

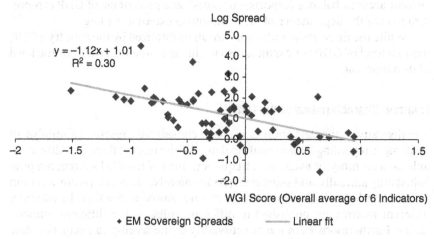

FIGURE 4.1   (Log) sovereign spreads vs WGI governance scores, October 2020.
Note: Spreads shown on a log scale (0.0 => 100 bp, 1.0 => 272 bp, 2.0 => 739 bp, 3.0 => 2009 bp).
Spreads as of 30 October 2020; WGI Governance scores for 2019, published October 2020.
Source: World Bank, Bloomberg, Barclays Research.

version of this index rating, 1 corresponds to AAA, and each increment of 1 represents one notch further down the scale, so that 2 means AA+ and so on, all the way to 23, which corresponds to C rating.

As Figure 4.2 demonstrates, the relationship between (log) spread and credit rating is much closer to linear than the one for governance scores shown in Figure 4.1.

The fact that both governance rankings and credit ratings are closely related to spreads suggests a positive correlation between them. We will explore and discuss this relationship later. (For instance, Table 4.5 shows a correlation of magnitude 0.67 between the WGI governance scores and credit ratings.[10])

One issue that might help explain why credit ratings do a better job of explaining spreads (R-squared of 0.84 vs 0.30 for governance scores) is the lag in the timing of the two datasets. The spreads and credit ratings in Figure 4.2 were obtained from index data as of the same date, but the spreads and the governance scores in Figure 4.1 were not.

Although the governance scores were published in October 2020, they were based on the state of affairs during 2019. As important as this issue is, it does not seem to explain the difference in fit. If we switch the timing of Figure 4.1 to use spreads as of December 2019, the fit actually deteriorates slightly, giving an R-squared of 0.28. Furthermore, if we switch the source of credit ratings in Figure 4.2, using ratings as of December 2019 to explain the spreads as of October 2020, the fit also becomes slightly worse, but still appears largely linear and has a high R-squared of 0.76 – still far better than the 0.30 achieved by the WGI overall governance score.

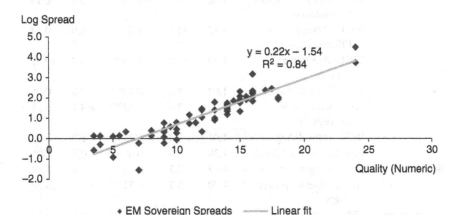

FIGURE 4.2 (Log) sovereign spreads vs credit rating, 30 October 2020.
Note: Spreads shown on a log scale (0.0 => 100 bp, 1.0 => 272 bp, 2.0 => 739 bp, 3.0 => 2009 bp).
Source: Bloomberg, Barclays Research.

Of course, simple scatter plots like these are not sufficient to resolve the question of whether ESG factors are priced in the EM sovereign market. Despite the very nice fit between spreads and credit ratings shown in Figure 4.2, there is still a considerable range of spreads left unexplained. For example, at a rating of B2 (numeric value 15), we find a set of sovereigns with spreads ranging from 379 bp for Mongolia to 1,003 bp for Tunisia.[11]

There is reason to believe that adding more factors might help explain why market spread levels are sometimes so different for countries with the same credit rating. To properly assess the extent to which ESG factors explain variation in credit spreads – either on their own or in conjunction with credit ratings or other fundamental factors – we carry out a set of regressions.

TABLE 4.1   Results of single-variable regressions for (log) EM sovereign spread.

		Intercept		Variable		
		Coeff	T-stat	Coeff	T-stat	R-sq
Credit Rating	Qual Num	−1.54	−9.7	0.22***	18.5	0.84
Fundamentals	Gross Debt	−0.08	−0.3	0.02***	5.1	0.30
	Deficit	0.80	2.5	−0.05	−1.5	0.03
	Curr Acct Bal	1.05	7.3	−0.04*	−2.6	0.10
	GDP per Capita	1.87	10.1	0.00***	−4.6	0.25
Governance	WGI - Voice and Accountability	1.19	8.5	−0.12	−0.7	0.01
	WGI - Political Stability No Violence	1.02	7.7	−0.62***	−3.8	0.19
	WGI - Government Effectiveness	1.15	11.3	−1.21***	−6.9	0.43
	WGI - Regulatory Quality	1.14	11.0	−1.22***	−6.7	0.41
	WGI - Rule of Law	1.02	8.3	−0.92***	−4.8	0.26
	WGI - Control of Corruption	1.00	7.6	−0.83***	−4.1	0.21
	WGI - OverallAvg	1.01	8.4	−1.12***	−5.2	0.30
	Freedom in the World	1.38	4.4	−0.003	−0.6	0.01
Social	Social Progress Index	4.57	5.1	−0.05***	−3.8	0.19
	Human Development Index	4.70	5.7	−4.71***	−4.3	0.22
Environment	ND_GAIN	5.61	7.7	−0.09***	−6.1	0.37

Note: * denotes statistical significance with $p<0.05$; ** denotes $p<0.01$; *** denotes $p<0.001$
Spreads as of 30 October 2020; other metrics are scores published as of October 2020.
Source: Barclays Research.

In the first round of regressions, we test each fundamental factor or ESG score on a standalone basis to see to what extent it explains the variation in EM sovereign spreads. The results, still based on a single, October 2020, snapshot of data, are in Table 4.1.

We find that, on a standalone basis, most of the factors we have investigated have a statistically significant relationship with sovereign spreads – with the notable exceptions of the WGI's measure of Voice and Accountability and the similarly themed Freedom in the World index. However, while many of these variables are statistically significant, some explain the variation in spreads much better than others, as indicated by the R-squared values of the regressions.

The best results among the ESG variables are for Government Effectiveness and Regulatory Quality, with each explaining more than 40% of the variance in spreads – more than any fundamental variable, but far less than credit ratings. The ND_GAIN ranking also performed quite well.

In a second round of regressions, we test whether the ESG variables remain significant in conjunction with fundamentals. We select gross debt as the fundamental variable that best explained credit spreads on a standalone basis (Table 4.1) and regress credit spread on two variables: gross debt and one additional ESG factor at a time. In this case, we test only the single average of the WGI scores rather than the six individual scores.

This analysis, presented in Table 4.2, shows that variables from all three ESG pillars give significant information well beyond what is contained in

TABLE 4.2 Regression coefficients for (log) EM sovereign spreads vs gross debt and one ESG factor.

Variable	WGI_Avg	SPI	HDI	ND_GAIN	Freedom
Intercept	−0.16	2.95	3.04	3.86	0.17
GrossDebt	0.02***	0.02***	0.02***	0.01***	0.02***
WGI - OverallAvg	−1.03***				
Social Progress Index		−0.04***			
Human Development Index			−4.04***		
ND_GAIN				−0.07***	
Freedom in the World					−0.01
R-Squared	0.54	0.44	0.46	0.53	0.31

Note: * denotes statistical significance with p<0.05; ** denotes p<0.01; *** denotes p<0.001.
Spreads as of 30 October 2020, WEO Gross Debt estimated for 2021 as published in Oct 2020, other indices are as of October 2020.
Source: Barclays Research.

TABLE 4.3 Regression coefficients for (log) EM sovereign spreads vs credit rating and one ESG factor.

Variable	WGI_Avg	SPI	HDI	ND_GAIN	Freedom
Intercept	−1.58	−1.67	−2.15	−1.68	−1.47
Index Credit Rating (Numeric)	0.23***	0.22***	0.23***	0.23***	0.22***
WGI - OverallAvg	0.06				
Social Progress Index		0.00			
Human Development Index			0.67		
ND_GAIN				0.00	
Freedom in the World					0.00
R-Squared	0.85	0.84	0.85	0.84	0.85

Note: * denotes statistical significance with p<0.05; ** denotes p<0.01; *** denotes p<0.001.
Spreads and credit ratings as of 30 October 2020, other indices are as of October 2020.
Source: Barclays Research.

basic fundamental data. Once again, all the scores are statistically significant, except for the Freedom in the World index.

Finally, we check whether ESG factors provide significant information beyond what is contained in credit ratings. We now regress credit spreads on two variables: numeric credit ratings and one additional ESG factor at a time. The results of this analysis are shown in Table 4.3.

These regressions show clearly that, once credit ratings are included as explanatory variables, the ESG factors no longer provide statistically significant information regarding sovereign spread levels.

We now expand this study in two ways. First, we use a longer time sample, from October 2012 to October 2021.[12] We also include a wider variety of scores. Specifically, we break out exposures into 10 sub-components of the SPI, described earlier. The results of this expanded regression analysis of country spreads, shown in Table 4.4, are in line with the previous results.

On the left side of the table in Table 4.4, we regress log country spreads against each single variable at a time. Almost all of them are highly statistically significant. The only exceptions are the Freedom score (consistent with Table 4.1), the closely related SPI component on Personal Rights, and the SPI score for Environmental Quality.

On the right side of Table 4.4, we regress log spreads against two explanatory variables: numeric credit quality (by far the strongest explanatory variable at the single-factor level) and one other variable at a time. We find that many ESG characteristics, the WGI scores for example, are no longer significant.

TABLE 4.4 Regression results for country-level log spreads, 2013–2020.

Selected Variable	Single-Variable Regressions			Two-Variable Regressions: Numeric Quality and Selected Variable			
	Constant Coeff	Variable Coeff	R^2	Constant Coeff	Quality Coeff	Variable Coeff	R^2
Quality (Numeric)	−0.99***	0.18***	0.81				
Gross Debt	0.29***	0.01***	0.19	−0.99***	0.18***	0.000	0.81
Deficit	0.61***	−0.07***	0.14	−0.99***	0.18***	−0.008	0.81
Curr Acct Bal	0.74***	−0.05***	0.24	−0.94***	0.17***	−0.009***	0.82
GDP	1.20***	0.00***	0.26	−1.30***	0.20***	0.000***	0.82
WGI_Avg	0.74***	−0.85***	0.36	−0.99***	0.18***	−0.005	0.81
WGI_Voice	0.85***	−0.17***	0.06	−0.99***	0.18***	−0.038	0.81
WGI_Stability	0.79***	−0.31***	0.13	−0.99***	0.18***	−0.001	0.81
WGI_Effective	0.82***	−0.90***	0.50	−0.96***	0.18***	−0.029	0.81
WGI_Regulate	0.85***	−0.89***	0.49	−0.93***	0.17***	−0.052	0.81
WGI_Law	0.73***	−0.74***	0.37	−1.03***	0.18***	0.045	0.81
WGI_Corrupt	0.73***	−0.64***	0.29	−1.06***	0.19***	0.082*	0.81
SPI	3.32***	−0.04***	0.30	−0.38**	0.17***	−0.008***	0.82
SPI_Basic Needs	3.02***	−0.03***	0.31	−0.47***	0.17***	−0.006***	0.82
SPI_Wellbeing	3.56***	−0.04***	0.30	−0.45**	0.17***	−0.007***	0.82
SPI_Opportunity	2.23***	−0.03***	0.16	−0.63***	0.17***	−0.006***	0.81
SPI_Nutrition	3.14***	−0.03***	0.23	−0.56***	0.17***	−0.005**	0.82
SPI_Water	2.32***	−0.02***	0.29	−0.63***	0.17***	−0.004***	0.82
SPI_Health	2.57***	−0.03***	0.23	−1.02***	0.18***	0.000	0.81
SPI_EnvQual	1.01***	0.00	0.03	−0.74***	0.18***	−0.004***	0.82
SPI_Personal Rights	1.06***	0.00	0.04	−0.83***	0.18***	−0.002**	0.81
SPI_Choice	2.94***	−0.04***	0.30	−0.82***	0.17***	−0.002	0.81
SPI_Education	2.12***	−0.03***	0.26	−0.68***	0.17***	−0.005***	0.82
HDI	3.39***	−3.91***	0.33	−0.62***	0.17***	−0.453**	0.81
ND-GAIN	3.76***	−0.07***	0.43	−0.56***	0.17***	−0.008**	0.81
Freedom	1.06***	0.00*	0.04	−0.92***	0.18***	−0.001*	0.81

Note: The analysis was done as a panel regression, including dummy variables for each calendar year (not shown) to control for market-wide changes in spread levels.
* denotes statistical significance with $p<0.05$; ** denotes $p<0.01$; *** denotes $p<0.001$.
Source: Barclays Research.

A few social scores, like the SPI index and some of its components, remain statistically significant, but the coefficients are just a small fraction of what they were in the uncontrolled case, and the total explanatory power (as indicated by the R-squared) is only marginally higher than that achievable by credit quality alone.

This expanded dataset thus supports the conclusion of the initial analysis based on a single snapshot of market data: the extent to which various measures of ESG characteristics are priced into sovereign bond spreads is largely captured by credit ratings. Hence, ESG rankings provide little additional information. However, this does not negate the possibility that beyond their relationship with spreads and credit ratings, ESG characteristics could have some predictive power regarding future returns (in terms of either level or volatility). We investigate this possibility in subsequent sections. First, though, we take a closer look at the correlations among the different metrics in our dataset.

EXAMINING THE RELATIONSHIPS AMONG THE DATA SETS

Some additional insight into what all these variables tell us and how they relate to each other can be gleaned from their cross-sectional correlations. The next two tables present two sets of correlations:

- The first examines the correlations of ESG indicators with market and fundamental variables (using just the average of the six WGI indicators).
- The second explores correlations among the ESG factors in greater detail, showing how the six individual WGI factors relate to the other ESG factors in the dataset.

Table 4.5 shows the big picture. For the most part, the selected variables tend to agree conceptually on the relative ranking of countries. The first three variables, which are measures of risk (and therefore oppositely signed, see Appendix for details), are positively correlated with each other, and negatively correlated with most other variables. All the others tend to have positive correlations among them.

In particular, we find high positive correlations among the four variables at the bottom right of Table 4.5: WGI (overall), SPI, HDI, and ND-GAIN. This is somewhat unexpected, since these represent the three distinct pillars of the ESG framework. One part of the explanation may be that the comprehensive nature of some of these scores does not really mirror the clean partition of E, S, and G factors. For example, as mentioned when we first introduced the data sources, SPI includes some components relating to Governance; and ND-GAIN, although counted as an E score, contains some S and G components

TABLE 4.5 Correlation matrix of market quantities, fundamental variables, and ESG factors.

	Log Spread	Qual Num	Gross Debt	Deficit	Curr Acct Bal	GDP	Freedom	WGI_Avg	SPI	HDI	ND-GAIN
Log Spread	1.00	0.88	0.37	-0.34	-0.46	-0.48	-0.16	-0.59	-0.53	-0.56	-0.63
Qual Num	0.88	1.00	0.44	-0.32	-0.44	-0.64	-0.13	-0.67	-0.51	-0.58	-0.67
Gross Debt	0.37	0.44	1.00	-0.41	-0.40	-0.14	0.06	-0.05	-0.01	-0.05	-0.12
Deficit	-0.34	-0.32	-0.41	1.00	0.42	0.25	-0.01	0.13	0.12	0.11	0.19
Curr Acct Bal	-0.46	-0.44	-0.40	0.42	1.00	0.39	-0.07	0.22	0.26	0.41	0.34
GDP	-0.48	-0.64	-0.14	0.25	0.39	1.00	-0.19	0.45	0.36	0.60	0.56
Freedom	-0.16	-0.13	0.06	-0.01	-0.07	-0.19	1.00	0.58	0.52	0.16	0.17
WGI_Avg	-0.59	-0.67	-0.05	0.13	0.22	0.45	0.58	1.00	0.73	0.60	0.72
SPI	-0.53	-0.51	-0.01	0.12	0.26	0.36	0.52	0.73	1.00	0.88	0.82
HDI	-0.56	-0.58	-0.05	0.11	0.41	0.60	0.16	0.60	0.88	1.00	0.87
ND-GAIN	-0.63	-0.67	-0.12	0.19	0.34	0.56	0.17	0.72	0.82	0.87	1.00

Note: Annual data, publication dates October 2013–October 2020.
Source: Barclays Research.

under its Readiness category. HDI, meanwhile, includes GDP per capita as part of its calculation.

It is interesting to note that GDP per capita is highly correlated not just with HDI, which includes it explicitly, but with all the top-level ESG variables except the Freedom in the World Index. It seems that even measures of very different dimensions of human experience often share a common dependence on the overall standard of living as measured by GDP per capita. Credit ratings are in agreement as well, as evidenced by the negative correlations between numeric credit quality and all ESG factors.

The Freedom in the World index merits a closer look. This metric stands out as uniquely distinct from financial factors, and largely from the other ESG metrics as well. A near-zero correlation with spreads confirms our regression findings and is echoed by similarly low correlations with credit ratings and fundamental variables. (Table 4.5)

The Freedom index's correlations with the other ESG indicators are somewhat enigmatic. It exhibits very low correlations with HDI and ND-GAIN, and moderately high positive correlations with the WGI average score and the SPI. How can its correlations with HDI and SPI be so different, when those two indices are so closely related to each other (with correlation of 0.88)?

The explanation is revealed by reviewing the construction of the various indices. The SPI contains a group of factors covering Basic Human Needs, which is largely aligned with the HDI; but it also contains a group of factors related to personal rights and personal freedom. These factors, which are conceptually within the purview of the Freedom Index, have sufficient weight in the SPI to create a correlation of about 0.5 between these two.[13] The HDI, though, has no exposure to these factors, and is therefore largely uncorrelated with the Freedom index.

Table 4.6 drills down into the six individual factors in the World Bank's WGI rankings. The last four WGI factors (government effectiveness, regulatory quality, rule of law, and control of corruption) are highly correlated. They also have moderately high positive correlations with the E and S factors, the strongest of these being between Government Effectiveness and ND-GAIN. This is also not surprising, as one of the components of ND-GAIN is government effectiveness in responding to various shocks.

Table 4.6 also provides additional information regarding Freedom and related factors. We find that the WGI factor on Voice and Accountability has a correlation of 0.98 with the Freedom in the World index, and a similar pattern of correlations with all other ESG factors. We also have included the SPI measure of Personal Rights,[14] which follows a similar pattern. In Table 4.7, we highlight the close relationship among these three metrics by showing both the contemporaneous correlations among them and the correlations among their year-over-year changes.

TABLE 4.6 Detailed correlation matrix of ESG factors, including all six individual WGI indicators.

	Voice	Stability	Effective	Regulate	Law	Corrupt	SPI	SPI_Personal Rights	HDI	ND-GAIN	Freedom
Voice	1.00	0.38	0.36	0.49	0.40	0.41	0.55	0.93	0.20	0.22	0.98
Stability	0.38	1.00	0.50	0.45	0.54	0.57	0.52	0.39	0.40	0.48	0.37
Effective	0.36	0.50	1.00	0.87	0.88	0.85	0.68	0.17	0.70	0.80	0.28
Regulate	0.49	0.45	0.87	1.00	0.85	0.77	0.66	0.31	0.62	0.74	0.42
Law	0.40	0.54	0.88	0.85	1.00	0.91	0.61	0.24	0.58	0.73	0.33
Corrupt	0.41	0.57	0.85	0.77	0.91	1.00	0.59	0.24	0.53	0.68	0.34
SPI	0.55	0.52	0.68	0.66	0.61	0.59	1.00	0.48	0.88	0.82	0.51
SPI_Personal Rights	0.93	0.39	0.17	0.31	0.24	0.24	0.48	1.00	0.09	0.12	0.94
HDI	0.20	0.40	0.70	0.62	0.58	0.53	0.88	0.09	1.00	0.87	0.15
ND-GAIN	0.22	0.48	0.80	0.74	0.73	0.68	0.82	0.12	0.87	1.00	0.17
Freedom	0.98	0.37	0.28	0.42	0.33	0.34	0.51	0.94	0.15	0.17	1.00

Note: Annual data, publication dates October 2013–October 2020.
Source: Barclays Research.

TABLE 4.7   Correlations among freedom-related scores from different organizations.

Cross-sectional correlations across contemporaneous rankings				Correlations among year-over-year changes in rankings			
	WGI Voice	SPI Personal Rights	Freedom		WGI Voice	SPI Personal Rights	Freedom
WGI Voice	1.00	0.93	0.98	WGI_Voice	1.00	0.36	0.59
SPI Personal Rights	0.93	1.00	0.94	SPI Personal Rights	0.36	1.00	0.47
Freedom	0.98	0.94	1.00	Freedom	0.59	0.47	1.00

Note: Annual data, publication dates October 2013–October 2020.
Source: Barclays Research.

Freedom was one dimension that stood out in our previous analysis as not strongly correlated with spreads or credit ratings. Thus, unlike with other ESG characteristics, it should be relatively easy to implement a pro-Freedom tilt without impacting spreads.

MEASURING ESG EFFECTS ON RETURNS

We now address the key question: are ESG characteristics associated with future returns? Can we expect that creating an ESG tilt in a portfolio of sovereign bonds will improve performance? To answer this question, we carried out two additional tests. The first is based on regression analysis, using a similar setup to the one used above for spreads. In the second, we take a portfolio construction approach, in the spirit of the methodology used in the previous two chapters, and carry out a historical backtest of risk-matched ESG-tilted portfolios.

Regressions of Forward-looking Returns on ESG Characteristics

After calculating the average monthly excess returns (over duration-matched Treasuries) for each country index for each annual observation period (from one end-of-October to the next), we regress these against the country characteristics that were observable at the beginning of the period. In each regression, we select a single ESG characteristic to test as an independent variable, and add controls for other beginning-of-period characteristics, as well as annual dummy variables to control for the overall trends in the market. The general form of the regression can be written as

$$R_{it} = \alpha_t + \beta^{ESG}(k) f_{it}^{ESG}(k) + \sum_j \beta(j) f_{it}(j) + \varepsilon_{it}$$

Where: R_{it} is the average excess return for bonds from country i during year t; α_t is a dummy variable which should pick up the average return (over all countries) during year t; $f_{it}(j)$ is the average value of characteristic j for country i as of the beginning of year t; and the betas are the sensitivities of returns to these characteristics as estimated by the regression. j spans the set of control variables used, and k indicates the single ESG variable being tested in each regression. The controls used were the beginning-of-year spread and numeric credit rating.[15] We repeat this regression for each ESG variable shown in Table 4.4 (WGI and components, SPI and components, HDI, ND-GAIN, and Freedom). We do not find a single variable that predicts returns in a statistically significant way, even at the 90% level.

We then reformulated the regression to predict return volatility (in this case, measured by the time-series standard deviation of the 12 monthly excess returns reported for each country index throughout each year). Here, instead of spread, we used DTS along with numeric quality and annual dummies as controls. Once again, we did not find significant results for any of the ESG characteristics tested. These results suggest that, if done in a risk-controlled manner, an ESG tilt along any of the investigated dimensions would not have materially affected either returns or return volatility over the course of our data sample.

Historical Backtest of ESG-tilted Portfolios

For completeness, and to be consistent with the methodology used in Chapters 2 and 3 to measure the ESG-related return premium in credit and equity markets, we also carried out a series of experiments based on the construction of ESG-tilted portfolios. For this exercise, we used data on individual bonds from the Bloomberg EM USD Sovereign Index. All the data on country-level economic fundamentals and ESG characteristics was considered to be available only annually,[16] with updates on 31 October of each year, as in our regression analysis. However, the portfolios were rebalanced on a monthly basis, using monthly updated bond data, including spreads, durations, and credit ratings.

We measured the potential impact of each ESG characteristic using the following procedure. We constructed a pair of portfolios at the start of each month, with both of them designed to track the benchmark as well as possible, but with one having the greatest possible value for the selected characteristic (the Max-ESG portfolio) and the other having the lowest (Min-ESG portfolio). We then recorded the performance of these portfolios over time, with a focus on the relative performance achievable by an ESG tilt either for long-only portfolios (outperformance of Max-ESG over the benchmark) or for long-short portfolios (outperformance of Max-ESG over Min-ESG). All return analysis was done using excess returns over duration-matched Treasuries to minimize the effect of any differences in rates exposures by country.

One difficulty in working with EM country allocations is the extreme differences in market weight between the largest and smallest countries within this universe. If we used a standard market-weighted index as a benchmark, it would be hard to express meaningful views on smaller countries without taking inordinately large amounts of risk. To avoid this, we used a customized index as the benchmark for our study, in which we first measured index market weight by whole-letter credit rating, then assigned equal weights to all countries within the same whole-letter rating bucket.

Our Max-ESG (and Min-ESG) portfolios were then formed by an optimization procedure that sought to maximize (minimize) the selected ESG characteristic while enforcing a number of constraints designed to reduce portfolio tracking error relative to the benchmark. The details of the linear programming optimization used to form the ESG-tilted portfolios are summarized in Table 4.8.

TABLE 4.8   Optimization procedure used to form ESG-tilted EM sovereign portfolios.

Optimization Feature	Details
Objective	Maximize (or minimize) selected ESG characteristic
Quality Allocation Constraint	Exactly match benchmark weight in each whole-letter quality cell
Spread Constraint	Exactly match benchmark OAS in each whole-letter quality cell
DTS Constraint	Exactly match benchmark DTS in each whole-letter quality cell
Long-only constraint	No short positions allowed; maximum underweight to any country or bond is negative of benchmark allocation
Concentration Constraint	Maximum overweight to any bond or country is 1% of overall portfolio

Source: Barclays Research.

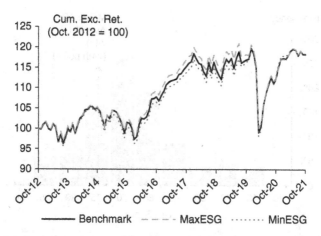

FIGURE 4.3 Cumulative returns of portfolios that maximize or minimize SPI score, relative to benchmark, October 2012–October 2021.
Source: Barclays Research

The formulation of the optimization using equality constraints (exact matching of some index characteristics) rather than setting an allowable range around each target may seem to run the risk of causing numerical difficulties in finding solutions. However, we did not find this to be the case.[17] As the optimization is carried out at the security level, the number of degrees of freedom is far greater than the relatively small number of constraints. Thus, even though we require the portfolio to exactly match a number of benchmark characteristics at the whole-letter quality level, this can be managed by adjusting the duration profile within each country allocation.

The optimization procedure performed nicely in designing portfolios that track the index well while imposing a significant tilt along the selected ESG dimension. For example, Figure 4.3 shows the cumulative excess returns of the Max-ESG and Min-ESG portfolios, alongside those of the benchmark, for the strategy designed to maximize/minimize the overall SPI score. We find that while the returns were rather volatile over the study period, both tracking portfolios matched the index returns quite closely. This is despite the fact that the average SPI score was substantially higher in the Max-ESG portfolio. As shown in Figure 4.4, the average SPI score of 74.0 for the Max-ESG portfolio was at about the 74th percentile of the cross-sectional distribution of these scores across countries, while the average score of 66.1 for the Min-ESG portfolios was at the 36th percentile. While the difference of 7.9 in the raw SPI scores may appear small at first glance, it is actually quite substantial once we factor in the relatively tight distribution of these scores.

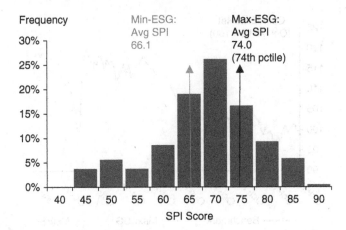

FIGURE 4.4   SPI Scores of Max-ESG and Min-ESG portfolios relative to SPI score distribution.
Source: Barclays Research.

As described earlier, this procedure was applied to produce a separate set of ESG-tilted portfolios based on each ESG-related characteristic. The back-tested performance of these portfolios is detailed in Table 4.9. For each selected ESG variable, or ranking characteristic, in turn, this table reports the performance that would have been achieved in either a long-only setting (the outperformance of the Max-ESG portfolio relative to the benchmark) or a long-short strategy (outperformance of the Max-ESG portfolio over the Min-ESG portfolio). In both cases, we report the average monthly outperformance, the volatility of this outperformance, and the resulting information ratio. We find that, as in the SPI example, the index tracking constraints succeeded in keeping tracking error volatility (TEV) under control. The TEV of the Max-ESG portfolios relative to the benchmark was about 20 bp/month.[18] Given that the excess return volatility of the benchmark over this period was about 200 bp/month, this TEV can be considered quite small. For the long-short strategy, we also report the size of the imposed tilt in percentile terms. This is calculated as the difference between the average values of the characteristic in the two portfolios, converted to percentiles.[19] (For example, for the portfolios based on the overall SPI score, as shown in Figure 4.4, the Max-ESG score is at the 74th percentile and the Min-ESG is at the 36th, so the percentile difference is 38.) These results show that our optimization procedure always manages to impose a significant bias along the selected dimension. However, the average relative returns show that a pro-ESG tilt has not produced a consistent meaningful return advantage. For both the long-only and long-short strategies, the magnitude of relative returns is quite small relative to the TEV, and the returns are fairly evenly split between positive and

TABLE 4.9 Historical performance of ESG-tilted tracking portfolios, October 2012–October 2021.

ESG Characteristic to Optimize	Long-Only Performance (Max-ESG vs Benchmark)				Long-Short Performance (Max-ESG vs Min-ESG)		
	Mean Excess Return (%/mo)	Excess Return Vol (%/mo)	Inf. Ratio (annual)	Pctile Tilt	Mean Excess Return (%/mo)	Excess Return Vol (%/mo)	Inf. Ratio (annual)
Gross Debt	0.00	0.19	0.00	−35	0.01	0.39	0.06
Deficit	0.03	0.20	0.54	38	0.04	0.38	0.36
Curr Acct Bal	0.00	0.19	−0.08	42	−0.01	0.39	−0.12
GDP	−0.02	0.17	−0.34	22	−0.04	0.33	−0.48
WGI_Avg	−0.02	0.21	−0.36	32	−0.03	0.37	−0.32
WGI_Voice	−0.01	0.22	−0.10	37	−0.03	0.39	−0.28
WGI_Stability	−0.02	0.20	−0.36	38	−0.05	0.40	−0.48
WGI_Effective	0.02	0.20	0.27	25	0.01	0.35	0.13
WGI_Regulate	0.02	0.23	0.23	19	0.03	0.40	0.26
WGI_Law	0.01	0.23	0.09	24	0.00	0.39	−0.01
WGI_Corrupt	0.00	0.23	0.03	31	−0.01	0.41	−0.11
SPI	0.00	0.18	−0.01	38	0.00	0.35	−0.01
SPI_Basic Needs	0.00	0.17	−0.05	40	−0.01	0.32	−0.09
SPI_Wellbeing	0.01	0.19	0.21	34	0.01	0.34	0.13
SPI_Opportunity	−0.02	0.18	−0.40	38	−0.05	0.32	−0.57
SPI_Nutrition	0.00	0.18	0.04	33	−0.01	0.35	−0.13
SPI_Water	−0.01	0.17	−0.12	33	−0.01	0.32	−0.15
SPI_Health	−0.01	0.19	−0.23	34	−0.03	0.33	−0.30
SPI_Env Qual	0.01	0.19	0.14	32	0.00	0.36	−0.04
SPI_Personal Rights	0.00	0.18	−0.06	35	−0.02	0.33	−0.18
SPI_Choice	−0.02	0.23	−0.23	34	−0.02	0.42	−0.16
SPI_Education	0.00	0.16	0.08	34	0.00	0.34	0.00
HDI	0.00	0.17	0.02	33	0.00	0.33	−0.03
ND-GAIN	0.02	0.21	0.36	26	0.02	0.37	0.15
Freedom	−0.02	0.21	−0.26	32	−0.05	0.38	−0.42

Source: Barclays Research

negative. Our overall impression is that these are random outcomes. We see no evidence that a pro-ESG tilt has any systematic effect on future returns, either positive or negative.

Importantly, the lack of positive performance impact of ESG tilts is not necessarily a setback. For many investors, financial performance is not the main motivation for introducing ESG criteria into the investment process. Supporting sustainability is a goal in itself for some. In other cases, investors are concerned that not paying sufficient attention to ESG may have regulatory or financial consequences. Our results should reassure the latter category that creating an ESG tilt in an EM sovereign bond portfolio can be accomplished without paying the price of an increased TEV or a drag on portfolio performance.

ESG SCORES AND CREDIT RATINGS

The regression results in Table 4.4 show that while many ESG characteristics taken alone seem to be closely related to bond spreads, they no longer show a statistically significant influence once we control for credit ratings. One possible explanation is that credit ratings already incorporate some ESG-related information relevant for predicting the default risk of a country. It is somewhat difficult to untangle the complex relationships among the various variables we have collected, as most of them are highly correlated. Typically, countries in better financial shape tend to have higher ESG rankings of all types. This can be clearly seen in the cross-sectional correlations among key variables shown in Table 4.5. To shed some light on the role played by ESG criteria in shaping country credit ratings, we focus on what happens when things change. We look at year-over-year changes in numeric credit quality, and test the extent to which these depend on the contemporaneous year-over-year changes in financial fundamentals[20] and ESG rankings. Table 4.10 shows both the correlations between credit quality and each individual variable, and the results of single-variable regressions, which provide us with a better measure of statistical significance.

Both the correlations and the regression results confirm a strong relationship between credit ratings and financial fundamentals. Not surprisingly, the strongest single factor associated with a credit downgrade is an increase in gross debt. Several WGI governance indicators are also highly significant. Overall, the four most significant variables are the annual deficit, changes in gross debt, and changes in the World Bank indicators on 'Regulatory Quality' and 'Political Stability and Absence of Violence/Terrorism'.

We ran a separate regression using all four of these variables, and found that, even when taken together, they all remain highly significant. These results are shown in Table 4.11. However, if added as a fifth variable in this model, no other ESG characteristic retained statistical significance. Social and environmental factors do not seem to have played a major role in driving changes in country credit ratings.

TABLE 4.10 Dependence of year-over-year ratings transitions on year-over-year changes in fundamentals and ESG scores.

Variable	Correlation	Regression Results	
		Coeff	R-Squared
GrossDebt	0.36	0.03***	0.13
Deficit	−0.28	−0.05***	0.08
CurrAcctBal	−0.16	−0.02***	0.03
LogGDP	−0.16	−0.89***	0.03
WGI_Avg	−0.26	−3.14***	0.07
WGI_Voice	−0.02	−0.20	0.00
WGI_Stability	−0.24	−1.05***	0.06
WGI_Effective	−0.14	−1.01**	0.02
WGI_Regulate	−0.23	−1.97***	0.05
WGI_Law	−0.09	−0.74*	0.01
WGI_Corrupt	−0.12	−0.94**	0.01
SPI	−0.03	−0.04	0.00
SPI_BasicNeeds	−0.01	−0.01	0.00
SPI_Wellbeing	0.02	0.02	0.00
SPI_Opportunity	−0.09	−0.08*	0.01
SPI_Nutrition	0.00	0.00	0.00
SPI_Water	0.06	0.08	0.00
SPI_Health	0.07	0.06	0.00
SPI_EnvQual	0.03	0.02	0.00
SPI_PersonalRights	−0.07	−0.02	0.01
SPI_Choice	−0.08	−0.09	0.01
SPI_Education	−0.08	−0.08	0.01
HDI	0.08	6.18	0.01
ND-GAIN	−0.10	−0.16*	0.01
Freedom	−0.01	0.00	0.00

Note: * denotes statistical significance with $p<0.05$; ** denotes $p<0.01$; *** denotes $p<0.001$.
Source: Barclays Research.

Unintended Tilts and Implications for Credit Ratings

We were able to shed additional light on the relationship between credit ratings and ESG characteristics by investigating unintended, secondary tilts in ESG-tilted portfolios. If a portfolio tries to maximize its social profile (say the SPI), subject to constraints on risk and credit quality, what unintended exposures

TABLE 4.11 Regression model for year-over-year (YoY) changes in credit ratings, 2013–2021.

Variable	Coeff	T-stat
Constant	−0.06	−1.40
Deficit	−0.02**	−2.65
Gross Debt (YoY chg)	0.03***	6.49
WGI Regulatory Quality (YoY change)	−1.63***	−4.63
WGI Political Stability (YoY change)	−0.69***	−3.90
R-squared	0.21	

Note: * denotes statistical significance with p<0.05; ** denotes p<0.01; *** denotes p<0.001.
Source: Barclays Research.

might be introduced along other dimensions – either other ESG rankings, or financial fundamentals, or both? What trade-offs must be achieved among competing preferences? To investigate, we checked some of the incidental exposures developed in our ESG-tilted portfolios. The results, reported in Table 4.12, are normalized as follows. First, having created a set of tilted portfolios that maximize and minimize each characteristic in turn, we record the level of the active exposure that we were able to create (the difference between the values of that characteristic in the Max-ESG and Min-ESG portfolios). Next, for the long/short portfolio pair that imposes an intentional tilt on each variable in turn (rows of Table 4.12), we calculate the unintended tilts[21] on several other variables (columns of Table 4.12). We then divide the magnitude of the unintentional tilt on a particular variable by the level achieved when we targeted that column, and report the result. For example, we constructed a pair of portfolios that impose a tilt on Gross Debt (targeting low-debt countries) and found that the difference between the Min and Max portfolios was −20.4. (The Max-ESG portfolio achieved an average debt as a percentage of GDP of 36.2, while the value for the Min-ESG portfolio was 56.6.) For the long/short portfolio pair targeting the WGI indicator for Regulatory Quality, the exposure to Gross Debt was 7.7 (a little less than half the magnitude, but with the opposite sign). We express the unintended exposure of 7.7 as a fraction of the −20.4 achieved when that variable was targeted; as a result, the number shown in the Gross Debt column of the WGI_Regulate row is −0.38. This procedure is followed throughout Table 4.12. We find that this negative result, which represents an unintended exposure to Gross Debt in the direction opposite to the desired one, is a common theme for many of our Pro-ESG portfolio tilts.

We can see that this analysis of unintended tilts is largely in line with the correlations discussed earlier. For the most part, we find that the various

TABLE 4.12 Unintended tilts in long/short portfolios as a fraction of the intended tilt.

	Dimension of unintended tilt							
Intended Tilt	Gross Debt	GDP	WGI Avg	SPI	SPI Env Qual	HDI	ND-GAIN	Freedom
Gross Debt	1.00	−0.21	−0.44	−0.22	0.05	−0.21	−0.21	−0.27
Deficit	0.28	−0.04	−0.19	−0.05	0.18	0.00	0.01	−0.04
Curr Acct Bal	0.15	0.12	−0.23	−0.03	−0.11	0.12	0.00	−0.25
GDP	−0.19	1.00	0.19	0.55	−0.34	0.85	0.66	−0.14
WGI_Avg	−0.33	0.00	1.00	0.57	0.41	0.34	0.47	0.74
WGI_Voice	−0.19	−0.35	0.80	0.53	0.69	0.14	0.15	0.99
WGI_Stability	−0.09	0.27	0.69	0.32	0.30	0.20	0.29	0.37
WGI_Effective	−0.39	0.17	0.78	0.57	0.12	0.46	0.52	0.34
WGI_Regulate	−0.38	0.12	0.79	0.61	0.31	0.47	0.49	0.56
WGI_Law	−0.36	0.11	0.88	0.49	0.17	0.28	0.45	0.45
WGI_Corrupt	−0.33	0.18	0.87	0.33	0.16	0.26	0.40	0.42
SPI	−0.33	0.14	0.64	1.00	0.39	0.84	0.76	0.58
SPI_Basic Needs	−0.45	0.36	0.41	0.84	0.03	0.88	0.81	0.21
SPI_Wellbeing	−0.34	0.16	0.59	0.86	0.49	0.78	0.64	0.54
SPI_Opportunity	−0.32	−0.15	0.73	0.91	0.48	0.57	0.57	0.78
SPI_Nutrition	−0.46	0.36	0.43	0.76	0.00	0.91	0.82	0.22
SPI_Water	−0.46	0.31	0.32	0.84	−0.01	0.83	0.72	0.17
SPI_Health	−0.41	0.42	0.45	0.69	0.19	0.76	0.59	0.29
SPI_Env Qual	−0.07	−0.47	0.45	0.30	1.00	−0.03	−0.10	0.67
SPI_Personal Rights	−0.10	−0.33	0.72	0.64	0.69	0.19	0.19	0.94
SPI_Choice	−0.50	0.46	0.65	0.60	−0.13	0.67	0.69	0.31
SPI_Education	−0.22	0.19	0.27	0.81	−0.15	0.83	0.81	0.14
HDI	−0.29	0.55	0.43	0.75	0.01	1.00	0.84	0.18
ND_GAIN	−0.30	0.32	0.47	0.80	−0.11	0.83	1.00	0.17
Freedom	−0.21	−0.24	0.77	0.57	0.71	0.18	0.16	1.00

Source: Barclays Research.

dimensions of ESG are positively correlated in this sense as well – a pro-ESG tilt in one dimension tends to bring with it a pro-ESG tilt in other dimensions. However, we find that the relationship between ESG characteristics and financial fundamentals tends to work in the opposite direction. In many cases, when we imposed a pro-ESG tilt on our portfolio, controlling for credit rating, it was accompanied by a tilt towards countries with weaker fundamentals, for example, with a higher average level of gross debt.

These findings imply that ESG characteristics are already factored into credit ratings, at least to some extent. The same rating might be given to a country with better financial fundamentals and worse governance, and to a country with the opposite combination. A tilt towards better governance, controlling for quality, might favour the high-governance countries at the expense of those with better fundamentals. To investigate whether this is indeed the case, we plot gross debt against the average WGI governance score for two whole-letter grade slices of our dataset as of October 2020. Countries with index ratings from BAA1 through BAA3 are shown in Figure 4.5, while those rated BA1 through BA3 are shown in Figure 4.6.

Both Figures 4.5 and 4.6 show a clear relationship between gross debt and governance score within each credit rating bracket. In both cases, the correlation between these two quantities is over 60%. Yet this correlation is only seen within a same-rating slice; across the whole dataset, the correlation between these two quantities is near zero. For rating purposes, it seems that a higher level of debt can be tolerated if a country is considered to have better governance. This explains why a tilt to better governance, with a control on allocations by credit rating, leads to a tilt to greater debt.

These results on unintended tilts are thus partially consistent with our findings relating to changes in credit ratings. We found that year-over-year changes in governance scores were strongly linked to contemporaneous changes in credit ratings. This provides strong evidence that at least some of the criteria used by the World Bank to form governance scores overlap significantly with those considered by credit rating agencies. This finding strengthens the hypothesis proposed earlier for why a pro-ESG tilt to a governance

FIGURE 4.5   Gross debt vs average WGI governance score, BBB-rated countries, October 2020.
Source: World Bank, IMF, Bloomberg, Barclays Research.

FIGURE 4.6 Gross debt vs average WGI governance score, BB-rated countries, October 2020.
Source: World Bank, IMF, Bloomberg, Barclays Research.

score should bring with it an unintended tilt towards more-indebted countries. However, this explanation is less convincing with regard to social and environmental characteristics: here, we find no statistically significant link between changes in ESG rankings and changes in credit ratings but we do find the same unintended tilt to high debt in our socially tilted portfolios. Perhaps the ratings agencies do indeed incorporate social and environmental considerations into their ratings assessment, but these characteristics tend to change more slowly than, say, political stability. A political upheaval can cause a huge change in the country's G rankings, and affect its credit rating at the same time. Environmental or social events of a similar magnitude are much less likely, and too rare to be present in our relatively short data sample.

DISCUSSION

We have established that, broadly speaking, country ESG rankings are positively correlated with sovereign credit spreads and credit ratings. Countries with better governance, higher standards of living, and lower risk of a climate-related catastrophe earn higher credit ratings and trade at tighter spreads.

Thus, in our set of single-factor regressions, almost all of the ESG factors we examined, considered in isolation, were shown statistically to be highly significant in explaining credit spreads. They remained significant when considered together with gross debt, the single most important fundamental factor we examined. However, when considered together with credit ratings, the ESG scores were no longer significant.

Several observations can explain these findings. First, the line between ESG analysis and fundamental credit analysis of sovereigns is rather blurred, leading to a significant overlap between ESG scores and traditional measures of credit risk.

As a case in point, consider our primary dataset of sovereign governance factors, the Worldwide Governance Indicators from the World Bank. These indicators were used by Barclays Economics Research as far back as 2010 in the construction of a Fiscal Vulnerability Index.[22] That work was not motivated by the drive to sustainable investing. Its purpose was to measure the fiscal health of sovereign issuers. In that context, the WGI scores were viewed just as useful supplements to fundamental data.

In general, it would be rather naïve to think that ESG scores now measure tangible dimensions of risk hitherto ignored by markets; the truth is more nuanced. The purview of the various metrics included under the ESG umbrella is quite broad. As we have seen, a single index like SPI, HDI, or ND-GAIN can include a mix of factors touching on E, S, and G issues, sometimes along with more fundamental economic variables such as GDP per capita.

ESG Factors and Credit Ratings

The role of credit rating agencies is to evaluate the overall risk of default for a given issuer, regardless of the underlying cause. To produce ratings for sovereign issuers, the agencies of course review the financial fundamentals reported by a country's central bank – but this has never been the full story.

Analysts evaluating a sovereign issuer study the country in depth, learning its particular strengths and weaknesses, challenges, and resources. There is no question that this could and should include factors relating to the environment, to social conditions, and to governance, with the amount of attention given to each factor tailored to the key risks facing that country.

In a country with a historical record of frequent earthquakes or hurricanes, the level of preparation for such events will be given greater weight. In a country with a poorly managed economy, financial crises are the key risk.

One factor deemed largely immaterial to credit risk is the level of personal freedom. Both the Freedom in the World index and the World Bank's WGI indicator for Voice and Accountability are generally uncorrelated with credit ratings, and have no significant relationship with sovereign credit spreads. It seems that as long as a country's economy is run efficiently, and the risk of default is low, this country attribute was not priced in the sovereign bond market during the time period covered by our study.

Thus, the ESG-related risk factors most material to credit risk are already incorporated into credit ratings. It is not clear whether this is a new state of affairs or a long-standing reality. This has possibly been the case since before formal ESG scoring became mainstream. Recently, with increasing

ESG awareness on the global investment scene, investors have sought greater transparency on how each dimension of risk contributes to the assignment of the credit rating. Credit rating agencies have responded by providing additional ESG-related information and analysis.

The integration of ESG rankings into the portfolio-management process, alongside traditional credit ratings, needs to be guided by a reasonable set of expectations. ESG scores are unlikely to reveal anything material that the rating agencies did not know already. Rather, the scores can help gain deeper understanding of specific country characteristics covered by each ranking category that cannot be backed out from spreads or credit ratings.

ESG vs Credit Ratings: Setting Investment Priorities

Our exploration of the relationship between ESG characteristics and credit ratings draws attention to a complex set of issues that investors must consider carefully. Bond investors have long relied on credit ratings as a cornerstone of their approach to risk management. Many mandates use ratings-based criteria to set risk limits. ESG considerations are often conceived as being outside this framework. Increasingly, however, credit rating agencies recognize that non-financial events can impact an issuer's creditworthiness, and incorporate ESG criteria into their methodologies.

Investors who wish to impose a pro-ESG tilt on their portfolios must carefully balance that desire against the levels of risk and return they are comfortable with. If a pro-ESG tilt is imposed without strict controls on credit rating, it is likely that the portfolio will drift towards higher ratings, and hence toward lower levels of spread, risk, and return. At the same time, if a tilt is imposed while controlling for credit ratings, much as we have done in this study, it could create unintended exposures to many other (non-ESG) risks factored into credit ratings.

Commercial Providers of ESG Scores

Market participants seeking more timely ESG information can turn to a number of commercial providers of ESG ratings. These vendors are not limited to annual publication schedules, but adjust country ratings whenever they detect a change in conditions. However, they may rely to some extent on periodic data releases from individual countries and supranational agencies. It will be interesting to see whether the proprietary scores from such vendors add sufficient value relative to the publicly available rankings tested here to retain explanatory power even after controlling for credit ratings.

Finally, there is a new category of data providers offering services based on natural language processing (NLP) of textual data from official documents, news feeds, and social media. Some of these use ESG-related keywords to associate these sources with sustainability themes and form measures of market sentiment that may provide investors with early warning of impending changes in the ESG characteristics of a particular issuer. Just as with the ESG rankings explored in this chapter (and maybe even more so), we expect the lines between NLP-based ESG signals and more general signals to be rather blurry. There is likely to be a significant overlap between the overall economic news flow about a country and the news flow flagged to specific ESG topics.

CONCLUSION

Broadly speaking, when proper risk controls are imposed, country ESG rankings are not closely linked with the financial performance of sovereign bonds. Although many ESG characteristics are highly correlated with sovereign spreads, regression analysis that controls for credit rating shows that their residual influence on sovereign spreads is either statistically insignificant or negligible.

Similarly, we find that, once credit ratings are taken into account, ESG rankings do not predict returns. Regression analysis (controlled for spread and credit quality) shows that, during the period studied, imposing an ESG tilt would have conferred no significant performance advantage – neither in terms of increased returns nor in terms of decreased return volatility. These results are confirmed by a comprehensive backtest of ESG-tilted portfolios constructed at the individual bond level subject to a comprehensive set of index-tracking constraints. Given the objective of maximizing the pro-ESG tilt to a single selected ESG characteristic, we are able to assemble portfolios of bonds that maintain a significant tilt in the desired dimension while matching the benchmark exposures to credit rating and other relevant risk measures. These portfolios succeeded in tracking the benchmark returns with low TEV – but did not provide any significant bias in the returns achieved.

For proponents of sustainable investing, these results show that, as long as proper risk controls are implemented, a pro-ESG tilt can be imposed on a sovereign bond portfolio without incurring any significant penalty in the form of reduced returns. However, we have not found any evidence to support claims that doing so would help investors outperform their benchmark in this market.

Lastly, we have explored the complex relationship between ESG characteristics and credit ratings. Most ESG characteristics (with the exception of Freedom and related metrics) are positively correlated with credit ratings: better-rated countries tend to earn higher ESG rankings. A regression study of changes in credit ratings shows that these have been closely related to changes in governance scores, but not to the other ESG metrics that we tested. Another perspective on this is our measurement of unintended tilts in ESG-tilted portfolios. Our portfolio construction technique, which imposes a pro-ESG tilt with strict controls on credit rating exposures, leads to portfolios with a bias towards more indebted countries. This raises important questions about how investors should think about integrating ESG goals within their existing risk-management frameworks.

REFERENCES

Georgieva, A. and Sloggett, J. (2019). A Practical Guide to ESG Integration in Sovereign Debt, UN Principles for Responsible Investment, November 2019. https://www.unpri.org/fixed-income/a-practical-guide-to-esg-integration-in-sovereign-debt/4781.article

Ghezzi, P., Keller, C., and Wynne, J. (2010). Our Measure of Fiscal Vulnerability: A Systematic Global Approach, Barclays Research, 9 September 2010. https://live.barcap.com/go/publications/link?contentPubID=FC1632712

Kaufmann, D., Kraay, A., and Mastruzzi, M. (2010). The Worldwide Governance Indicators: Methodology and Analytical Issues, The World Bank. https://doi.org/10.1596/1813-9450-5430

APPENDIX: SUMMARY OF DATA SOURCES

Table 4.A1 provides a detailed summary of all the key variables used in our study, including bond characteristics, country fundamentals, and country ESG rankings. The 'risk sign' column indicates the direction of the relative ranking. For variables marked with a negative sign, higher values of the variable represent a better assessment, and are associated with lower values of risk. This includes all of the ESG metrics. For variables marked as positive, increasing values correspond to greater risk. Numeric quality is in this group because the convention used in the Bloomberg family of indices to convert ratings to numeric values starts at 1 for AAA, and increases by one for each ratings notch downward. Likewise, Gross Debt, like OAS, is marked as positive, as increasing values are associated with greater credit risk. Deficit, in contrast, is marked as negative, because despite the name by which we refer to it, the quantity is actually defined as the surplus of revenues minus expenditures; we only refer to it as deficit because unfortunately it is negative more often than positive. The sign is useful in understanding the correlations among the variables. If two quantities are conceptually positively correlated to each other, but they are captured by metrics with opposite signs (like spread and GDP), we expect their correlation to be negative.

TABLE 4.A1 List of data sources used in this study, with frequency, sign and scaling information.

Short Name	Long Name	Source	Orig. Year	Freq. Publ.	Freq. Used	Units	Risk Sign	Average	Std Dev
OASD	Spread Duration	Bloomberg	2002	D, M	M, Y	years	+	6.6	2.1
OAS	Spread	Bloomberg	2002	D, M	M, Y	bp	+	389	505
DTS	Duration Times Spread	Bloomberg	2002	D, M	M, Y	years × bp	+	2,256	1,517
Qual Num	Index Rating – Numeric	Bloomberg	2002	D, M	M, Y	1 (AAA) – 20 (CCC)	+	11.9	3.7
Exc Ret	Excess Return	Bloomberg	2002	D, M	M, Y	percent/year		3.0	10.8
Gross Debt	General government gross debt	IMF World Economic Outlook	1999	S	Y	% of GDP	+	53.5	27.5
Deficit	General govt revenue – general govt total expenditure	IMF World Economic Outlook	1999	S	Y	% of GDP	–	−4.2	4.0
CurrAcctBal	Current account balance	IMF World Economic Outlook	1999	S	Y	% of GDP	–	−3.1	7.1
GDP	Gross domestic product per capita (PPP)	IMF World Economic Outlook	1999	S	Y	$ per capita	–	$17,239	$17,818
WGI_Avg	World Governance Indicators	World Bank	2004	Y	Y	Scale −2.5 to 2.5	–	−0.2	0.5

WGI_Voice	Voice and Accountability	World Bank	2004	Y	Scale −2.5 to 2.5	—	−0.2	0.7
WGI_Stability	Political Stability and Absence of Violence/Terrorism	World Bank	2004	Y	Scale −2.5 to 2.5	—	−0.3	0.8
WGI_Effective	Government Effectiveness	World Bank	2004	Y	Scale −2.5 to 2.5	—	−0.1	0.6
WGI_Regulate	Regulatory Quality	World Bank	2004	Y	Scale −2.5 to 2.5	—	0.0	0.6
WGI_Law	Rule of Law	World Bank	2004	Y	Scale −2.5 to 2.5	—	−0.3	0.6
WGI_Corrupt	Control of Corruption	World Bank	2004	Y	Scale −2.5 to 2.5	—	−0.3	0.6
SPI	Social Progress Index	Social Progress Imperative	2011	Y	Scale 0 to 100	—	68.2	9.8
SPI_BasicNeeds	Basic Human Needs	Social Progress Imperative	2011	Y	Scale 0 to 100	—	77.8	12.8
SPI_Wellbeing	Foundations of Well-being	Social Progress Imperative	2011	Y	Scale 0 to 100	—	69.0	9.5
SPI_Opportunity	Opportunity	Social Progress Imperative	2011	Y	Scale 0 to 100	—	57.8	10.2

(Continued)

TABLE 4.A1 (Continued)

Short Name	Long Name	Source	Orig. Year	Freq. Publ.	Freq. Used	Units	Risk Sign	Average	Std Dev
SPI_Nutrition	Nutrition and Basic Medical Care (subset of Basic Needs)	Social Progress Imperative	2011	Y	Y	Scale 0 to 100	–	85.9	11.8
SPI_Water	Water and Sanitation (subset of Basic Needs)	Social Progress Imperative	2011	Y	Y	Scale 0 to 100	–	78.6	19.1
SPI_Health	Health and Wellness (subset of Well-being)	Social Progress Imperative	2011	Y	Y	Scale 0 to 100	–	62.3	11.3
SPI_EnvQual	Environmental Quality (subset of Well-being)	Social Progress Imperative	2011	Y	Y	Scale 0 to 100	–	71.5	13.4
SPI_Personal Rights	Personal Rights (subset of Opportunity)	Social Progress Imperative	2011	Y	Y	Scale 0 to 100	–	71.2	17.3
SPI_Choice	Personal Freedom and Choice (subset of Opportunity)	Social Progress Imperative	2011	Y	Y	Scale 0 to 100	–	63.5	10.9

SPI_Education	Access to Advanced Education (subset of Opportunity)	Social Progress Imperative	2011	Y	Y	Scale 0 to 100	–	53.3	14.1
HDI	Human Development Index	United Nations	1990*	Y	Y	Scale 0 to 1	–	0.72	0.11
ND–GAIN	Global Adaptation Index	University of Notre Dame	1995	Y	Y	Scale 0 to 100	–	48.5	7.0
Freedom	Freedom in the World Index	Freedom House	2003	Y	Y	Scale 0 to 100	–	57.5	24.3

Note: Frequency codes for frequency published and frequency used columns: Y = yearly, S = semi-annually, M = monthly, D = daily. HDI index was published annually since 2017. Prior to that, there are scores for 1990, 2000, 2010, 2014 and 2015. For 2012 and 2013 we use the 2010 scores; for 2016 we use the 2015 scores.

Source: Barclays Research.

Setting up a coherent annual time series of all these metrics posed a number of challenges. At the most basic level is the availability of data. We tried to restrict ourselves to data that are published on an annual basis. Some potentially interesting metrics were excluded based on this constraint.[23] Nevertheless, we chose to include the UN HDI even though it was not published every year during the early part of our study, using the most recent score available at each point in time. Second, the data releases are not synchronized. All of the metrics we use are published with a lag,[24] and the length of the lag varies both across organizations and over time. Results for a given calendar year are typically posted between June and October of the following year,[25] but it is hard to ascertain the exact timing of a particular historical release. We chose a conservative approach, with our key concern being to ensure that our backtests do not use any data point before it was actually published. To do this, we line up the data by publication year, using the most recent available data point for each metric as of the end of October each year. Table 4.A1 shows both the frequency published and frequency used. For example, the IMF publishes estimates of economic fundamentals semi-annually, in April and October, but we prefer a synchronized switch to next year's forecasts on 31 October, and so ignore any April updates.

Similarly, index data is published on a daily basis but we use annual snapshots for our regression studies and monthly updates for our portfolio backtests.

The units used to express different metrics differ by several orders of magnitude. This makes it difficult to interpret the coefficients of the regression results shown in this chapter. We report here some basic statistics of their magnitudes.

NOTES

1. The Bloomberg indices incorporate credit rating data from three agencies: Moody's, S&P, and Fitch. In case of split ratings, the Index Rating is defined as the median of the ratings from the three agencies. This is also converted to a numeric 'Quality' ranking in which higher numbers correspond to lower ratings.
2. See Georgieva and Sloggett (2019).
3. See Kaufmann et al. (2010).
4. Freedom House produces an annual report on Freedom in the World, with accompanying data. See https://freedomhouse.org/report/freedom-world
5. See http://hdr.undp.org/en/content/human-development-index-hdi
6. An overview of the SPI methodology may be found at https://www.socialprogress.org/index/global/methodology
7. The ND-GAIN country index is described at https://gain.nd.edu/our-work/country-index/

8. The IMF produces its World Economic Outlook report twice a year, and makes available an accompanying database of global economic data. See https://www.imf.org/en/Publications/WEO

9. Technically, since we have defined this variable as revenue minus expenditures, it should be called surplus; it is only a deficit when it becomes negative. Unfortunately, this occurs quite frequently. When evaluating solvency, large negative values for this metric give rise for concern, and hence can be expected to be associated with wider credit spreads. Indeed, we shall see that the regression coefficient on this variable takes a negative sign.

10. The correlation shown in Table 4.5 actually appears as −0.67, but the negative sign is misleading. It reflects the fact that in the numeric scale used for credit quality, higher numbers represent lower levels of credit worthiness, while in the WGI scores higher numbers are better. The two measures tend to favor the same issuers.

11. The log scale used in these figures may make these differences appear smaller – but keep in mind that a difference of 1 between two countries on this log scale means that the spread of one is nearly three times that of the other.

12. The full nine years of the sample are used in our portfolio performance backtests; for much of the analysis of ESG characteristics, we use the eight annual snapshots of scores from 2013 to 2020.

13. In a separate cross-sectional regression, we found that the SPI score could be approximated quite well by a combination of HDI and the Freedom in the World index; this combination of two factors produced an R-squared of 0.91.

14. The SPI category for Opportunity actually contains two distinct metrics whose names seem to relate to freedom: Personal Rights (shown here), and Personal Freedom and Choice (not shown). However, the descriptions of the issues covered by these metrics makes it clear that Personal Rights is the one that belongs in this group. This represents political rights, freedom of expression, freedom of religion, access to justice, and property rights for women. The score for Personal Freedom and Choice, by contrast, covers vulnerable employment, early marriage, satisfied demand for contraception, and corruption. Correlations confirm that the Personal Freedom and Choice metric has much lower correlations with the freedom-related metrics shown earlier; we have therefore excluded it from this group.

15. We tried several variations, using different sets of control variables. In one variation, the controls were numeric quality, gross debt, deficit, current account balance, and GDP per capita. In another, they were numeric quality and log(GDP). Results were not materially different in either case.

16. Estimates of economic fundamentals are published semi-annually by the IMF, in April and October. We do not incorporate the April updates in our study. Similarly, each of the organizations that publish country ESG characteristics does so on its own schedule; we impose a synchronized switch to the next year's rankings each October 31 although some rankings may have been available sooner.

17. Technically, the implementation of equality constraints in the linear programming engine used to solve these optimizations involves constraining the targeted variable to be within a certain very small range (tolerance) of its target. What we mean by 'exactly match' is that we specify equality constraints to the solver, and rely on its choice or tolerance, which would be negligible in terms of financial impact.

18. The TEV of the Min-ESG portfolios relative to the benchmark were similar in magnitude; we do not report the detailed performance of these strategies separately due to space constraints.

19. This calculation is carried out on an overall basis for the full period, not cross-sectionally over time. The Max-ESG portfolio is represented by its average score over time, and the distribution of each score is estimated using all observed values for all countries over all years.

20. Generally speaking, the regression calculated in Table 4.10 is $\Delta y_{it} = \beta \cdot \Delta x_{it} + \varepsilon_{it}$, where Δy_{it} is the year-over-year change in numeric credit quality and Δx_{it} is the contemporaneous year-over-year change in the selected characteristic. However, for Current Account Balance and Deficit (revenues less expenditures), we do not take differences, as these metrics are intrinsically defined as single-year changes to a country's financial condition. For these quantities, we use $\Delta y_{it} = \beta \cdot x_{it} + \varepsilon_{it}$.

21. The tilts along each characteristic, both intended and unintended, are calculated in terms of the natural scoring range for that characteristic. However, given the big differences in scale among the different measures, these would be very difficult to interpret. Therefore, we do not show the raw tilt numbers themselves, but rather the ratio of the unintended tilt to an intended one, as described earlier.

22. See Ghezzi et al. (2010).

23. For example, Yale University produces an Environmental Performance Index that is published every two years, and the UN publishes scores on Sustainable Development Goals that have been published every two years since 2016.

24. The lagged nature of the publicly available ESG metrics makes it difficult to use them as trading signals. Unless the publication of the score itself has the power to move the market, it is very likely that the conditions flagged by any change in score were already known to market participants months earlier. In any case, though, most of these metrics are fairly stable and do not change dramatically from year to year.

25. The ND-GAIN index actually is lagged by over a year. The scores published in 2020, for example, correspond to calendar year 2018.

CHAPTER 5

Effect of SRI-Motivated Exclusion on Performance of Credit Portfolios

Negative screening is a popular strategy in Socially Responsible Investing (SRI). We introduce a methodology to measure the performance of excluded issuers, relative to relevant peers, while controlling for differences in systematic risk exposures. Our exposure-matched performance analysis of individual exclusions in the US corporate universe finds that the strategy has not had a material performance impact over the period from June 2013 to April 2022.

INTRODUCTION

Different approaches have been developed to implement SRI in portfolio management. For example, *best in class* investing aims to favour issuers with strong Environmental, Social, and Governance (ESG) ratings. In such an approach, investors can balance economic and ESG considerations to achieve both strong expected returns and desirable ESG characteristics at the same time. In this context, ESG ratings can influence portfolio allocation but do not necessarily narrow the investment universe. Indeed, many best in class ESG mandates retain broad market indices as benchmarks.

In contrast, SRI exclusions are used by many investors to build portfolios compliant with specific social and ethical values. This approach consists of excluding from the investment universe issuers with business activities that are controversial from an investor's point of view. For example, SRI screens can exclude companies involved in tobacco, alcohol, gambling, military weapons, or nuclear power from the eligible investment universe.

SRI screens are often customized to accommodate the values of different investors. The corresponding reduction in opportunity set is reflected in customized benchmarks. However, index providers have published various broad indices based on SRI exclusions as well. For example, Bloomberg and MSCI launched a suite of SRI bond indices, which apply exclusion criteria based on business involvement and controversies screening.

SRI exclusions and best in class ESG investing can view the same issuers in very different ways. For example, a utility company can be given a strong ESG rating, as it is perceived to outperform its sector peers in terms of management of ESG issues, but at the same time, the company can be excluded by the SRI filter because it uses nuclear power plants. The differences in such outcomes are likely to translate to differences in performance contributions.

In Chapter 2, we explained how to measure returns of corporate bond portfolios attributed to ESG. We introduced an approach based on diversified exposure-matched portfolios with significant ESG tilts and applied it to find the return premium associated with ESG at the index level. We apply a similar approach to study the effect of MSCI SRI exclusions at the sector or index level.

However, such a top-down approach is not suitable to analyse the performance of individual issuers excluded from the index. We therefore introduce a new methodology to analyse the performance of an excluded issuer relative to an optimized portfolio of SRI-eligible peers. The optimized peer portfolio seeks to match characteristics, such as rating and spread duration, of the excluded issuer. Our approach allows us to analyse individual issuers in isolation. By aggregating issuer-specific returns, we can also assess the performance contribution of SRI exclusions at the portfolio or index level.

Our bottom-up and top-down approaches lead to broadly consistent results: MSCI SRI exclusions had no significant performance impact over the period of our study. This outcome contrasts with Chapter 2, which showed that tilting a corporate bond portfolio in favour of high ESG-rated issuers has been associated with a positive return premium.

EFFECT OF SRI EXCLUSIONS ON INDEX ALLOCATION

Our analysis is based on SRI exclusions implemented in the Bloomberg MSCI US Corporate SRI Bond Index. This index is a subset of the Bloomberg US Corporate Bond Index, which represents a broad benchmark for the investment grade US corporate bond market. The SRI index is defined by excluding issuers according to the MSCI Business Involvement Screens and the MSCI ESG Controversies Screens. The SRI index was launched in May 2013, which represents the starting point of our analysis.

SRI exclusions apply to issuers involved in activities in conflict with global norms and values, seen as detrimental to the environment, or subject to sanctions or controversies.[1] Examples of activities excluded on ethical grounds are

TABLE 5.1 Percentage market value excluded by MSCI SRI screens from the Bloomberg US corporate bond index.

Sector	May 2013 to Apr 2022 (%)	May 2013 to Dec 2014 (%)	Jan 2015 to Dec 2017 (%)	Jan 2018 to Dec 2020 (%)	Jan 2021 to Apr 2022 (%)	End April 2022 (%)	Sector Market Capitalization ($, bn) End April 2022
Basic	37	46	47	29	21	26	165
Capital Goods	54	62	56	52	46	41	337
Healthcare	1	0	0	2	0	0	574
Non-cyclical	44	34	45	47	44	40	354
Cyclical	17	14	18	21	7	2	431
Communications	0	0	0	0	0	0	548
Technology	1	3	1	0	0	0	609
Energy	20	12	20	17	36	56	449
Industrial Other	12	17	17	9	1	0	174
Utility	65	62	70	63	63	70	494
Banks/Brokers	7	6	7	7	7	7	1,470
Insurance	7	8	8	7	6	6	268
Financial Other	0	0	0	0	0	0	263
Index	18	20	19	17	16	17	6,136

Source: Bloomberg, Barclays Research.

tobacco and gambling. Controversies may arise, for example, over toxic waste emissions, human rights violations, bribery, or fraud.

SRI exclusions can have a significant effect on the composition and market structure of the index. Table 5.1 shows that the market capitalization of the SRI index has been 16–20% lower than that of the broad market index.

The effect of SRI exclusions varies by sector. Utilities, Capital Goods, and Non-cyclicals are the most affected sectors: 70%, 41%, and 40% of their respective market capitalizations in the broad market index were excluded at the end of April 2022. These sectors are exposed to SRI exclusions because they include issuers seen as involved in controversial business activities, such as nuclear power, military weapons manufacturing, and tobacco. At the other end of the spectrum, we find sectors such as Healthcare, Communications, and Technology that have been mainly unaffected by SRI exclusions. Their market capitalization in the SRI index has remained practically the same as that in the broad corporate index.

SRI exclusion criteria have gradually evolved over time as business involvement and ESG controversies screens have been updated. For example, the share of excluded issuers in the Basic sector declined from 46% in the first period to 26% at the end of April 2022. On the other hand, the share of excluded names in the Energy sector increased from 17% in 2018–2020 to 56% at the end of April 2022.

Table 5.1 also shows that SRI exclusions significantly affect the universe of eligible corporate issuers and lead to large changes in the index market structure. Should one expect a significant systematic performance impact from these exclusions after controlling for changes in the market structure and systematic risk exposure? In the following analysis, we address this question, both at the individual issuer and at the overall sector or index levels.

MEASURING ISSUER-SPECIFIC RETURNS OF SRI EXCLUSIONS

How should we measure the relative performance of an issuer affected by the SRI screening process? The conventional approach is to compare the returns of that issuer with those of its sector. However, this approach implicitly assumes that an excluded issuer and its industry sector have similar risk exposure profiles. This assumption rarely holds in practice.

In Figure 5.1 we contrast the characteristics of a tobacco company which we call Issuer A with the SRI-eligible issuers in the non-cyclical sector,[2] to which it belongs. Panel A shows that the average rating of issuer A (A2) is significantly higher than that of the non-cyclical sector (Baa1). This difference in average credit quality can make the comparison of issuer and sector returns challenging because resulting relative returns are likely to remain directional. In addition, Panel B shows that the average spread duration of issuer A bonds has been different from that of the underlying non-cyclical sector. This mismatch in spread duration has changed over time, from +1.5 years in 2013 to −1 year in 2021–2022, as the sector average duration increased over time while issuer A's duration remained stable. Similar to the rating differences, the mismatch in spread duration between issuer A and its sector makes measuring issuer-specific returns difficult.

To address these challenges, we create a customized peer group for each excluded issuer with a view to replicate its risk profile. We do this in two steps. First, we identify 10 SRI-eligible sector peers with average ratings closest to the rating of the excluded issuer. Such issuers, in the case of issuer A, have ratings of A1, A2, or A3, indicated in light grey in Panel A of Figure 5.1. Initially, individual issuers are equally-weighted and, for any issuer, individual bonds are market-weighted to form a *reference portfolio*. Second, we customize the peer group portfolio by minimizing the sum of squared deviations from bond weights in the reference portfolio subject to matching the average rating and average duration of the excluded issuer. In this way, we obtain a peer group

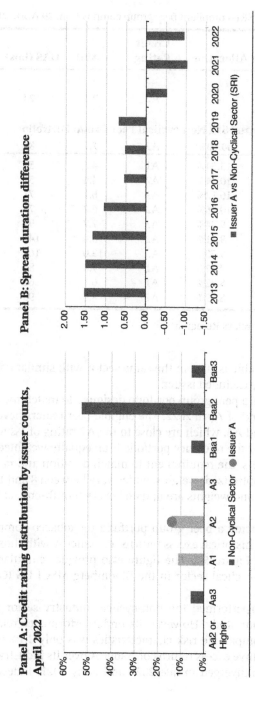

Panel A: Credit rating distribution by issuer counts, April 2022

Panel B: Spread duration difference

■ Issuer A vs Non-Cyclical Sector (SRI)

■ Non-Cyclical Sector ● Issuer A

FIGURE 5.1 An example tobacco company (Issuer A) vs SRI issuers in the non-cyclical sector.
Source: Bloomberg, Barclays Research.

TABLE 5.2   Example SRI–compliant peer group composition, 29 April 2022.

Issuer	Allocation	Credit Rating	OASD	OAS (bps)	DTS
Non SRI Issuer					
A tobacco company "Issuer A"	-	A2	7.1	128	12.2
Optimized SRI Non-cyclical Peer Group Portfolio					
Total	**100.00%**	**A2**	**7.1**	**89**	**8.1**
Issuer B	13.54%	A1	4.2	57	3.0
Issuer C	10.54%	A2	4.6	51	3.3
Issuer D	10.12%	A2	6.1	71	5.8
Issuer E	10.06%	A2	6.2	79	5.9
Issuer F	9.84%	A3	7.7	97	9.1
Issuer G	9.81%	A2	8.8	145	13.1
Issuer H	9.70%	A3	13.0	166	22.1
Issuer I	9.47%	A1	7.8	84	7.8
Issuer J	8.82%	A1	6.1	60	4.4
Issuer K	8.09%	A2	8.5	95	8.7

Source: Bloomberg, Barclays Research.

portfolio of comparable issuers in the same sector with similar credit ratings and durations to the excluded issuer.

Table 5.2 shows a peer group portfolio designed to match the risk profile of Issuer A at the end of April 2022. The eligible peer issuers have credit ratings between A1 and A3, which are close to the A2 rating of Issuer A. While the starting point for the reference portfolio is an equally-weighted allocation across eligible issuers, the requirement to match duration and rating quality results in uneven (optimized) weights, which vary between 8 and 13.5%.[3] Peer group composition and weights are updated every month-end, at the time of index rebalancing.

Having constructed a peer group portfolio for tobacco company Issuer A, we can compare historical excess returns[4] of Issuer A with those of its SRI peers, as shown in Figure 5.2. The figure also provides cumulative returns relative to the non-cyclical sector in the Bloomberg MSCI US IG Corporate SRI index.

Issuer A underperformed the non-cyclical industry sector by 5.2% in the nine years of our study. However, its underperformance relative to the peer group with comparable risk characteristics was only 3.1% in the same period. The cumulative excess returns of Issuer A over its industry sector and over its peer group diverged in late 2020 and early 2021. Indeed, Issuer A

FIGURE 5.2 Cumulative excess return (%) of Issuer A over its customized SRI peer group and over the SRI non-cyclical sector average.
Source: Bloomberg, Barclays Research.

outperformed its SRI peer group but underperformed its broad sector, which had lower credit quality and therefore benefitted more from the credit rally in that period. Choosing the appropriate customized peer group is essential when measuring issuer-specific returns if an excluded issuer has a very different risk profile from its broad sector.

In Figure 5.3 oil producer Issuer L provides a more striking example of the divergence between returns measured over the optimized peer group or the industry sector. Issuer L has been excluded as a non-SRI issuer for almost the entire period of our study. It has a high credit rating (Aa3) compared to other SRI-eligible issuers in the energy sector (Baa2 on average). As a result, its relative cumulative returns over the sector were volatile during the 2016 energy and the 2020 Covid-19 crises. Issuer L has underperformed the energy sector by 7.5% over the full sample period, which could suggest that excluding it would have been beneficial. However, its performance should be compared only to peers with similar characteristics (ratings and duration), rather than the overall energy sector. When measured over its optimized peer group, the excess returns of Issuer L have been persistently positive and with resulting cumulative outperformance of +7.1% in the overall sample period.

In Table 5.3 we report the performance of select SRI exclusions over the entire period of our analysis. The figure includes issuers with the largest positive or negative average returns over respective customized peer groups. The strongest issuer-specific performance (2.84%/y) has been recorded for Issuer M, a mining company, while the most negative one has come from aerospace company Issuer V (−1.68%/y). Interestingly, companies in the Electric utility sector appear as both outperformers and underperformers versus their peers.

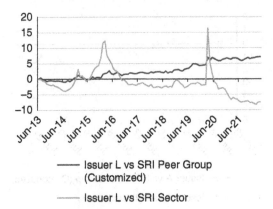

----- Issuer L vs SRI Peer Group
(Customized)

----- Issuer L vs SRI Sector

FIGURE 5.3 Cumulative excess return (%) of oil producer Issuer L over its customized SRI peer group and over the SRI energy sector average.
Source: Bloomberg, Barclays Research.

TABLE 5.3 Selected SRI exclusions with the strongest and weakest issuer-specific returns, June 2013–April 2022.

Issuer	Sector	Industry	Avg. TE (%/y)	TEV (%/y)	IR
Most positive average relative returns (vs customized peer group)					
Issuer M	BASIC	METALS AND MINING	2.84	7.39	0.38
Issuer N	UTILITY	ELECTRIC	1.94	3.62	0.53
Issuer O	UTILITY	ELECTRIC	0.64	3.45	0.19
Issuer P	UTILITY	ELECTRIC	0.52	1.18	0.44
Issuer Q	BASIC	CHEMICALS	0.50	5.29	0.10
Most negative average relative returns (vs customized peer group)					
Issuer R	UTILITY	ELECTRIC	−0.36	1.34	−0.27
Issuer S	INSURANCE	P&C	−0.53	1.64	−0.32
Issuer T	UTILITY	ELECTRIC	−0.60	3.34	−0.18
Issuer U	NON-CYCLICAL	TOBACCO	−0.92	3.09	−0.30
Issuer V	CAPITAL GOODS	AEROSPACE/ DEFENSE	−1.68	4.37	−0.38

Note: Issuers included in this table were both included in the standard index and excluded from the SRI index over the full period of our analysis.
Source: Barclays Research.

In all reported cases, information ratios attributed to issuer-specific returns are small as large average tracking errors relative to peers came with significant tracking error volatility.

Figure 5.4 plots the distributions of the average issuer-specific relative returns of all excluded issuers over three different periods. We find that, from June 2013 to April 2022, the median average issuer-specific relative return for all screened-out issuers was close to zero, meaning that SRI exclusions had little systematic effect on corporate bond returns in the period of our analysis.

Issuer-specific performance, however, can vary with the period, which is illustrated in Figure 5.4. For example, the median issuer-specific return across excluded issuers was −15 bp/month at the height of the Covid-19 crisis, from January to March 2020. The return distribution widened in that period, which was characterized by an extreme bearish market which reverted in subsequent months. On the other hand, the median performance of screened-out issuers was a positive +4 bp/month in the three months from February to April 2022, a period that corresponds to the onset of the war in Ukraine. In those three months, issuers excluded by the SRI screens slightly outperformed their SRI-eligible peers on average.

Table 5.4 shows some of the largest positive and negative tracking errors relative to optimized peer groups at the onset of the war in Ukraine (Feb–Apr 2022). Notable outperformers in these three months included defence companies, as well as issuers in the Mining and Energy sub-sectors. On the other hand, some Utility issuers significantly underperformed their peers.

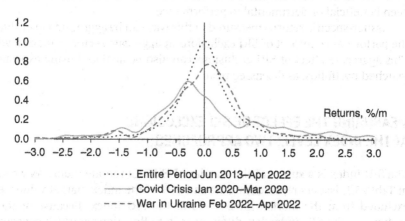

FIGURE 5.4 Distributions of average returns of SRI excluded issuers relative to their customized SRI peer groups.
Source: Bloomberg, Barclays Research.

TABLE 5.4 SRI excluded issuers with the largest positive or negative tracking error relative to their customized SRI peer groups at the onset of the war in Ukraine (February–April 2022).

Issuer	Sector	Industry	TE (%)
	Most positive tracking errors		
Issuer W	CAPITAL GOODS	AEROSPACE/DEFENCE	2.06
Issuer X	CAPITAL GOODS	AEROSPACE/DEFENCE	1.59
Issuer Y	NON-CYCLICAL	TOBACCO	1.48
Issuer Z	BASIC	METALS AND MINING	1.34
Issuer AA	ENERGY	INDEPENDENT	1.27
	Most negative tracking errors		
Issuer AB	UTILITY	ELECTRIC	−1.49
Issuer AC	CYCLICAL	GAMING	−1.95
Issuer AD	UTILITY	ELECTRIC	−2.08
Issuer AE	UTILITY	NATURAL GAS	−2.51
Issuer AF	UTILITY	ELECTRIC	−3.62

Source: Bloomberg, Barclays Research.

Our methodology of using optimized peer groups can help measure issuer-specific returns attributed to individual issuers affected by SRI exclusions. It can therefore help assess whether a particular exclusion decision has been beneficial or detrimental to performance.

Issuer-specific returns measured in this way can be aggregated to evaluate the performance impact of SRI exclusions at aggregate sector or index levels. This aggregate effect of SRI exclusions can also be analysed using exposure-matched portfolios, as discussed next.

MEASURING THE EFFECT OF SRI EXCLUSIONS AT THE INDEX LEVEL: TWO APPROACHES

The SRI index is a subset of the standard US IG Corporate index. As we saw in Table 5.1, issuers representing around 17% of the index market value were excluded from the market index to form the SRI index. Because of these exclusions, the SRI index has different sector allocations and risk exposures than the standard corporate index. This is illustrated in Table 5.5: the Basic, Capital Goods, Non-cyclical, and Utility sectors are underweighted relative to the standard market index, while the Healthcare, Communications, Technology, and Banks/Brokers sectors are overweighted. SRI exclusions also lead to

TABLE 5.5 Bloomberg MSCI US IG SRI Corp. index vs Bloomberg US IG Corp. index at the end of April 2022.

Sector	Bloomberg MSCI US IG SRI Corp Index				Bloomberg US IG Corp Index				Difference: US Corp SRI - US Corp			
	%MV	OASD	OAS	DTS	%MV	OASD	OAS	DTS	%MV	OASD	OAS	DTS
Basic	2.4	8.6	145	13.8	2.7	8.7	155	14.7	-0.3	-0.1	-10	-0.9
Capital Goods	3.9	7.2	113	9.7	5.5	7.5	124	11.1	-1.6	-0.4	-11	-1.4
Healthcare	11.3	9.1	119	12.6	9.3	9.1	119	12.6	2.0	0.0	0	0.0
Non-cyclical	4.2	8.1	111	10.7	5.8	8.5	139	13.9	-1.6	-0.4	-28	-3.2
Cyclical	8.3	7.2	113	9.8	7.0	7.1	118	9.9	1.3	0.1	-5	-0.1
Communications	10.8	9.7	165	18.0	8.9	9.7	165	18.0	1.9	0.0	0	0.0
Technology	12.0	7.8	118	11.0	9.9	7.8	118	11.0	2.0	0.0	0	0.0
Energy	3.9	7.9	169	15.4	7.3	7.9	151	14.1	-3.5	0.0	17	1.2
Industrial Other	3.4	10.8	133	15.5	2.8	10.8	133	15.5	0.6	0.0	0	0.0
Utility	2.9	10.1	129	14.3	8.1	9.6	141	14.9	-5.2	0.4	-12	-0.6
Banks/Brokers	26.9	5.4	127	8.0	24.0	5.5	128	8.3	2.9	-0.1	-1	-0.2
Insurance	4.9	9.0	140	13.8	4.4	9.2	138	13.9	0.6	-0.2	2	-0.1
Financial Other	5.2	5.6	157	9.2	4.3	5.6	157	9.2	0.9	0.0	0	0.0
Index	100.0	7.6	131	11.5	100.0	7.8	135	12.0	0.0	-0.2	-3	-0.5

Source: Bloomberg, Barclays Research.

differences in exposures: the spread duration of the SRI index is shorter by 0.2 years, while the DTS is lower by 0.5.

With a methodology similar to the one introduced in Chapter 2, we use exposure-matched portfolios to assess the performance effect of SRI investing while avoiding the effect of unintended risk exposures. We build diversified portfolios of SRI-eligible issuers that match the systematic risk exposures of the market index. The methodology is summarized in Table 5.6. To ensure diversification, the portfolio is anchored to the composition of the market index by minimizing deviations from bond weights in the broad index. Constraints include matching allocations across sectors and credit ratings, as well as matching OAS, DTS, and OASD within each sector. The analysis is repeated every month-end to ensure synchronization with the rebalancing of published bond indices.

This approach produces exposure-matched SRI portfolios that are highly diversified. They include the same bonds as the Bloomberg MSCI US Corp. SRI Index (5,828 bonds at the end of April 2022), but their weights depart from the market weights of the SRI index to ensure that sector allocations and risk exposures are aligned with those of the standard market index.

As opposed to the published SRI Index, the exposure-matched SRI portfolios do not exhibit any significant systematic risk relative to the standard market index. The contrast in risk profiles is illustrated in Figure 5.5, which reports the main sources of tracking error volatility (TEV) relative to the market index according to Bloomberg's multi-factor risk model. Panels A and

TABLE 5.6   Building exposure-matched SRI portfolios by sector.

Exposure-Matched SRI Portfolio by Sector	Details
Objective	Minimize the sum of squared deviations from bond weights in the market index
Index exposure constraints by sector	Match the exposures of the market index: ■ MV allocation across broad sectors ■ OAS, DTS, OASD of the standard market index within each sector
Rating constraints by sector	Match market index weights by rating
Investment universe	Constituents of the Bloomberg MSCI US IG Corporate SRI Index
Market index	Bloomberg US IG Corporate Index
Rebalancing frequency	Monthly, end-of-month

Source: Barclays Research.

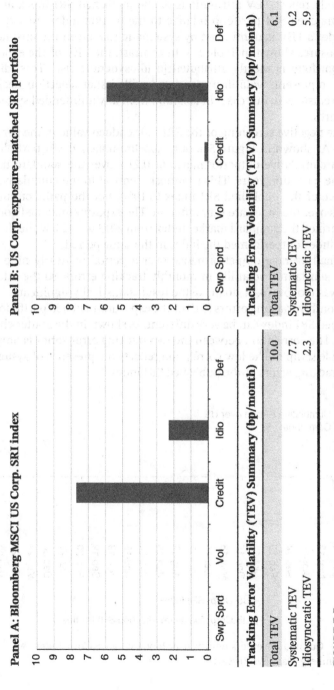

FIGURE 5.5 Contributions to tracking error volatility (TEV in bp/month) over the Bloomberg US corporate index, 29 April 2022.
Source: Bloomberg, Barclays Research.

B respectively report TEV attributions of the published SRI index and the exposure-matched SRI portfolio relative to the market index. As expected, the SRI index's TEV is dominated by systematic risk given the mismatches in risk exposures shown in Table 5.5. In contrast, the TEV of the exposure-matched portfolio is mostly attributed to idiosyncratic risk. This idiosyncratic TEV represents volatility associated with issuer selection decisions (i.e., SRI exclusions in our case) in isolation from any unintended systematic risk exposures.

Has the negative screening of the SRI index added value in the period of our study? As shown in Figure 5.6, our exposure-matched SRI portfolio has delivered a cumulative outperformance of 0.21% over the standard market index in the past nine years. This is almost identical to the cumulative outperformance of the published SRI index (0.19%), but the paths of cumulative returns over the index are very different. The exposure-matched portfolio underperformed the standard market index from 2013 to 2020, while the published SRI index outperformed the index in the same period.

The small average outperformance over a period of nearly nine years came with substantial volatility in monthly tracking errors, so the information ratio was too low (0.14) to make the result statistically significant.

The monthly tracking errors (TE) of the exposure-matched portfolios and the published SRI index can be very different, as shown in the scatter chart in Figure 5.7. The correlation between the two tracking error series is only 34% for the whole sample. The low correlation reflects the presence of systematic effects in tracking errors of the published SRI index.

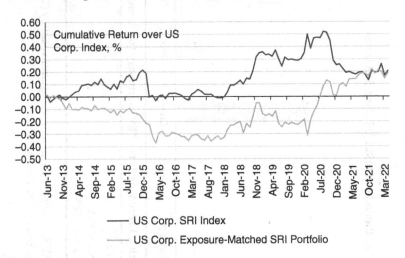

FIGURE 5.6 Cumulative excess returns over Bloomberg US Corp. index, %.
Source: Bloomberg, Barclays Research

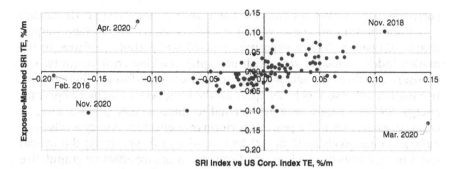

FIGURE 5.7 Monthly tracking errors of exposure-matched SRI portfolios and SRI index over Bloomberg US Corp. index, June 2013–April 2022.
Source: Bloomberg, Barclays Research.

As well as measuring the effect of SRI exclusions at the index level, Table 5.7 shows sector-level details: the average number of issuers in the standard market index, the average number of SRI exclusions, and tracking error statistics of sector-level exposure-matched SRI portfolios over

TABLE 5.7 Tracking errors of exposure-matched SRI portfolios by sector, June 2013–April 2022.

Sector	US Corp. Avg. # Issuers	Avg. # Excluded Issuers	Avg TE, %/y	TEV, %/y	IR
Basic	49	10	−0.29	0.90	−0.32
Capital Goods	62	15	0.22	1.04	0.21
Healthcare	78	0	−0.01	0.03	−0.33
Non-cyclical	47	9	0.41	0.67	0.61
Cyclical	59	3	−0.07	0.22	−0.32
Communications	33	0	–	–	–
Technology	56	2	0.00	0.02	0.00
Energy	59	5	−0.12	0.40	−0.30
Industrial Other	41	2	−0.11	0.27	−0.41
Utility	62	23	0.19	0.49	0.39
Banks/Brokers	89	1	0.02	0.08	0.25
Insurance	64	1	−0.03	0.11	−0.27
Financial Other	67	0	–	–	–
Index	*762*	*71*	*0.02*	*0.15*	*0.14*

Source: Bloomberg, Barclays Research.

corresponding market sub-indices. Some sectors, for example Healthcare and Communications, have very few exclusions, so the average outperformance (average TE) of exposure-matched SRI portfolios relative to the market index is close to zero, with negligible tracking error volatility. The exposure-matched SRI sector sub-portfolios underperformed their respective market index sectors by 29 bp/yr for the basic sector and by 12 bp/yr for energy: SRI exclusions were detrimental to these sectors' performance. In contrast, exclusions had a positive performance effect for non-cyclicals (+41 bp/yr), capital goods (+22 bp/yr) and utilities (+19 bp/yr). At the overall index level, exclusions had no significant performance effect on cumulative performance over the study period, which is qualitatively consistent with our issuer-level analysis.

Is our approach of measuring the effect of SRI exclusions using exposure-matched SRI portfolios consistent with the issuer-specific methodology presented in the previous section? Figure 5.8 compares the monthly returns attributed to SRI exclusions obtained using the issuer-level (bottom-up) approach to those obtained using the index-level (top-down) approach.

In the bottom-up approach, we aggregate returns of excluded issuers over their respective optimized peer groups to form a diversified portfolio of excluded names using market-capitalization weights. Monthly excess returns of the portfolio of excluded issuers are shown on the horizontal axis of the chart. These returns are contrasted with the monthly tracking errors of the exposure-matched SRI portfolios over the Bloomberg US Corp. Index, reported on the vertical axis.

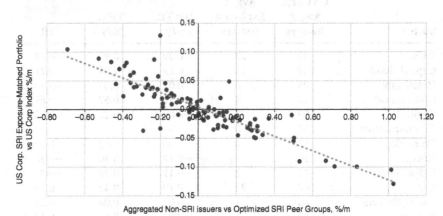

FIGURE 5.8   SRI exposure-matched portfolios outperform the Bloomberg US corp. index when screened-out issuers underperform their peers, June 2013–April 2022. *Source:* Bloomberg, Barclays Research.

We observe a strong negative relationship between the two series: whenever the exposure-matched portfolio outperforms the market index, the portfolio of excluded non-SRI issuers underperforms. The scales of the two axes are different because excluded issuers represent only a fraction of the overall index universe. Although the two approaches follow different methodologies, they appear to deliver broadly consistent results.

CONCLUSION

We introduce a methodology for measuring the performance effect of SRI exclusions. Issuer-specific performance impact is assessed relative to optimized peer groups in the same sector, where a portfolio of peer issuers is used to match the risk characteristics of an excluded issuer.

This new bottom-up approach helps quantify the relative performance of specific SRI exclusions, with examples drawn from tobacco and oil companies. This methodology has many potential applications beyond SRI screening. It can be applied to any situation in which issuer-specific returns need to be measured net of systematic effects. For example, one may want to assess the returns of individual ESG names with especially high or low rankings, or those of issuers recently involved in public controversy.

In the SRI context, we find that negative screening had no significant performance impact in the period of our analysis. The average issuer-specific return of excluded issuers was close to zero. While some excluded issuers underperformed their peers, others outperformed them.

We confirm our issuer-level results by constructing diversified portfolios of SRI issuers designed to match risk exposures of the standard market index. As systematic risk is neutralized, the tracking errors of these portfolios relative to the index are mainly associated with SRI exclusions. Using index- and sector-level exposure-matched SRI portfolios provides results broadly consistent with those of our issuer-level analysis: SRI exclusions have not affected index-level returns over the past nine years as different exclusion decisions have had offsetting performance effects.

SRI exclusions are driven by value alignment or by ethical considerations without consideration for materiality to financial performance. Therefore, there is no particular reason to expect a persistent underperformance or outperformance of non-SRI companies at either issuer or index level.

Finally, SRI criteria can be specific to certain groups of investors. SRI screens are in this respect very different from the ESG investing approach, which ranks issuers within each sector based on their exposures to environment, social, and corporate governance risks.

NOTES

1. Involvement is defined for each restricted activity and may be based on percentage of revenue, total revenue, or any tie regardless of revenue, see Bloomberg MSCI US Corporate SRI Bond Index prospectus.
2. Tobacco companies are subject to a different regulatory environment than most other issuers in the non-cyclical sector. This can make the performance of a tobacco company relative to its sector peers especially idiosyncratic.
3. We do not require the peer portfolio to match OAS and DTS of an excluded issuer. Indeed, such requirements could result in a peer group with high turnover and concentrated risk allocation.
4. All returns used in this chapter are excess returns over duration-matched Treasuries, as reported by the index provider. This ensures that our analysis relates only to credit spreads and is not affected by changes in Treasury yields.

Systematic Strategies and Factors Subject to ESG Constraints

INTRODUCTION TO PART II

As mentioned in the Introduction, systematic strategies employ models or rules-based algorithms to select securities, issuers, or sectors that are expected to outperform their peers and help generate portfolio alpha. They are often contrasted with fundamental or discretionary strategies, in which investment decisions are based on the subjective views of the portfolio manager. Systematic strategies often do not have the depth of a discretionary strategy when it comes to analysing a specific issuer, but they offer much higher breadth, frequent updates, and low correlation to the subjective views of managers. Financial theory suggests that high-breadth strategies, even with modest skill levels or signal efficacy, can risk-efficiently improve a portfolio's alpha.[1]

Systematic investing has gained broad acceptance in equities over the past few decades, often alongside discretionary mandates. One of the key reasons is the transparency and availability of equity market data from

133

the exchanges and company fundamental data from commercial vendors. This data abundance led to a rich body of research on predictive signals in equity markets and equity risk factors associated with distinct risk premia. In fact, there has been a high degree of standardization on the Fama and French (1993)[2] risk factors, to the point where an innovative equity market factor is described in terms of an incremental risk premium over these standard factors.

Until recently, the penetration of systematic investment styles into fixed income in general and credit in particular was low due to the opaque price discovery, lack of historical data, low and at times non-existent liquidity, and high transaction costs. Over the past few years, these strategies have been gaining acceptance as a result of a number of recent developments: the imposition of regulatory reporting requirements (in the United States—to the TRACE database) for most credit transactions, a shift of bond index development and data from investment banks to vendors resulting in increased data availability, and a rise in ETFs, e-trading, and portfolio trading in credit, contributing to improved liquidity. In addition, systematic strategies in fixed income can use equity market information and benefit from signals well established in the equity markets.

Many systematic strategies seek to achieve steady outperformance of a benchmark with low tracking error volatility, by taking highly diversified active positions that achieve a desired set of factor exposures. In this part of the book, we study the effect of an ESG tilt on the performance of systematic strategies and risk factors in credit and equity markets.

In Chapter 6, we analyse the extent to which the imposition of an ESG constraint can affect a systematic strategy in credit markets. For example, if an issuer with desirable factor exposures carries a low ESG score, or is subject to exclusion, the strategy will not be able to implement its preferred position. We measure the effect this can have on performance in the context of a specific and implementable credit strategy exploiting a set of three style factors—value, momentum, and sentiment—all introduced in our book, *Systematic Investing in Credit* (Wiley, 2021). We document the effect of different types of ESG constraints on the performance and risk of these strategies.

In Chapter 7, we address the same question as in Chapter 6, but in the context of seven commonly used style factors in the equity market, including size, value, momentum, and quality. We examine the performance effect on the characteristics of these factors, applying ESG constraints of different magnitudes, using both the positive screening and negative screening paradigms. As emphasized throughout the book, the ESG score of an issuer can be correlated to its other attributes, so that the extent to which an ESG tilt affects factor performance needs to be evaluated empirically.

NOTES

1. Grinold and Kahn (1999) proposed a 'fundamental theory of active management', in which the information ratio of an active portfolio is expressed as a function of its breadth and its information coefficient. The latter is a measure of skill, defined as the correlation between the signal, or security-specific return forecast, used to construct the portfolio, and the ultimately realized returns. Grinold, R.R. and Kahn, R.N. (1999). *Active Portfolio Management*, 2nd ed. McGraw-Hill.
2. Fama, E.F. and French, K.R. (1993). Common Risk Factors in the Returns on Stocks and Bonds. *Journal of Financial Economics*, 33 (1), pp. 3–56.

CHAPTER 6

Effect of ESG Constraints on Credit Active Returns

In Chapter 2, we demonstrated that a positive ESG tilt has generally improved the performance of credit portfolios designed to track a standard bond index as long as index risk exposures were carefully matched. Similarly, portfolios with negative ESG tilts have underperformed their benchmark, all else equal.

However, the imposition of an ESG constraint can have an additional type of effect on actively managed portfolios. ESG-related constraints generally reduce the set of corporate bonds available for investing, potentially decreasing a portfolio manager's ability to generate alpha via security selection.

We use numerical simulations to show how ESG constraints might affect active returns. We then use historical simulations to illustrate the effect of ESG and SRI-motivated constraints on the active returns of systematic strategies in the US IG corporate bond market. In our historical simulations, we base our strategies on three signals that we have found to generate outperformance in corporate bond markets: value, momentum, and sentiment. We first simulate the effect of ESG constraints on each strategy in isolation, with no consideration of transaction cost. We then conclude with a more realistic simulation that uses a combination of all three signals in a turnover-constrained setting.

IMPOSING ESG CONSTRAINTS ON CORPORATE BOND INDICES

The effect of ESG-related constraints on the performance of corporate bond portfolios is a key consideration for institutional investors. While many asset managers are required to incorporate ESG considerations into their portfolio management process, they also need to fulfil fiduciary duties to their clients and therefore maximize return.

In Chapter 2 we demonstrated that creating a positive ESG tilt while carefully matching risk exposures relative to a standard index has improved returns of index-tracking portfolios. Figure 6.1 updates our earlier results by reporting the cumulative returns of diversified US IG credit portfolios that implement positive or negative ESG tilts. The Max- and Min-ESG portfolios

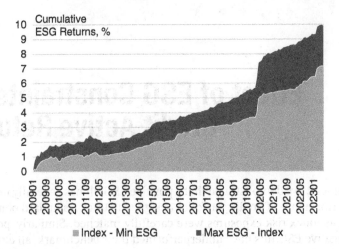

FIGURE 6.1   Cumulative excess returns associated with positive and negative ESG tilts relative to the Bloomberg US IG corporate bond index.
Source: Bloomberg, MSCI, Barclays Research.

are constructed to create maximum positive and negative tilts in the average ESG score relative to the index, while matching index exposure and allocation constraints. The tilted portfolios are diversified across 600–800 bonds to limit portfolio concentration. The portfolio with positive ESG tilt (Max-ESG portfolio) has outperformed the index by a cumulative 3% from January 2009 to July 2023. This result suggests that overweighting issuers with high ESG has on average benefited portfolio performance. Underweighting issuers with low ESG would have benefited performance as well because the corporate index has outperformed the portfolio with negative ESG tilt by 7% over the period.

Many institutional investors manage their credit portfolios actively with the aim of outperforming their benchmark index. For such investors, the positive effect of ESG, as reported in Figure 6.1, might be offset by the negative effect on active returns associated with a reduction in the opportunity set: a manager is less able to implement issuer selection strategies when the size of the universe is reduced because of ESG-related exclusions. This effect is likely to be larger when a larger portion of the investment universe is excluded due to ESG constraints.

Investors have taken a variety of different approaches to integrating ESG considerations into their portfolios. To accommodate this, index providers have created numerous ESG-based variations on popular benchmark indices. For example, Bloomberg offers three different ESG-constrained versions of their US IG Corporate Index, which are filtered in different ways based on data from MSCI ESG Research. The Bloomberg MSCI US Corporate SRI Index excludes issuers that are involved in activities deemed controversial. The Bloomberg MSCI Corporate ESG Sustainability indices take more of a best-in-class approach; rather than excluding entire industries, they exclude issuers with ESG ratings below a selected threshold. The Sustainability Index BB+ excludes issuers with MSCI ESG ratings below BB, while the Sustainability Index is more aggressive, excluding all issuers with ESG ratings below BB+.[1] Figures 6.2 and 6.3 report the reduction in the investment universe relative to the Bloomberg US IG corporate index for each of these ESG-filtered variants.

Figure 6.2 reports percentage reductions in the number of bonds in Bloomberg MSCI Sustainability and SRI indices relative to the conventional Bloomberg US IG Corporate index over time. The ESG and SRI constraints reflected in the Bloomberg MSCI indices result in considerable reductions of the original US IG investment universe. However, while the percentage of index bonds excluded by the SRI approach has remained relatively stable at about 20% over the past decade, there has been a marked decline in the percentage of index bonds excluded based on a fixed ESG ratings threshold. For the Sustainability Index, for example, the percent of bonds excluded has fallen from about 50% between 2011 and 2016 to about 15% in 2023. This result presents a challenge: how can we build forward-looking expectations based on a historical analysis? To help address this challenge, this chapter will use two different approaches to ESG-based filtering: one based on a fixed threshold on

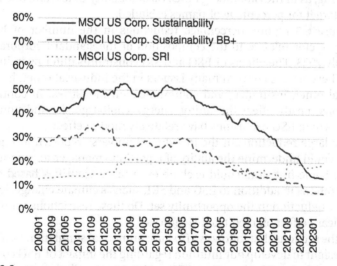

FIGURE 6.2 Percentage reduction in the number of bonds in the Bloomberg US IG corporate bond index resulting from ESG and SRI exclusions in Bloomberg MSCI bond indices.
Source: Bloomberg, MSCI, Barclays Research.

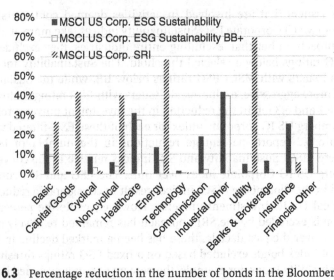

FIGURE 6.3 Percentage reduction in the number of bonds in the Bloomberg US IG corporate bond index by sector resulting from ESG and SRI exclusions in Bloomberg MSCI bond indices, July 2023.
Source: Bloomberg, MSCI, Barclays Research.

ESG rating, as in the Bloomberg MSCI Sustainability Index, and one based on a fixed target for percentage of names excluded.

Figure 6.3 reports percentage reductions in the number of bonds by industry sector relative to the composition of the standard corporate index as of July 2023. The effects of ESG and SRI constraints differ by industry sector. ESG exclusions concern many issuers in the industrial other, healthcare, financial other, insurance, and communication industries. In contrast, SRI exclusions mostly affect the utility, energy, capital goods, and non-cyclical sectors, where ESG exclusions have relatively modest effects.

The large reductions in the investment universe reported in Figures 6.2 and 6.3 could undermine the ability of a portfolio manager to generate active returns. Some investors could exclude even more securities based on other considerations in addition to ESG and SRI, such as climate change, leading to a further reduction in the opportunity set. Do these restrictions translate into a significant effect on credit active returns?

In the sections that follow, we first use numerical simulations with imperfect foresight to develop our intuition regarding the impact of ESG constraints on active returns. We show that ESG exclusions usually have a detrimental effect on portfolio alpha, especially when ESG scores and informative signals driving managers' decisions are negatively correlated.

We then introduce value, momentum, and sentiment systematic strategies in credit and use historical simulations to quantify the effect of ESG constraints on the performance of each of these strategies. We find that ESG exclusions have a persistently negative effect on the active returns of the systematic strategies.

When we consider the same strategies in the context of SRI-motivated exclusions, we also observe negative effects, although slightly smaller, on active returns.

Finally, we consider a realistic systematic portfolio that jointly implements the three strategies, while imposing turnover constraints and accounting for transaction costs; and analyse the effect of ESG and SRI constraints on its performance. Portfolio alpha is significantly reduced when ESG exclusions affect a large number of issuers. SRI exclusions have a modest negative effect on portfolio performance in comparison.

NUMERICAL SIMULATIONS: WHAT TO EXPECT?

Consider an active manager who selects issuers using an informative signal that is predictive of future returns with imperfect foresight.[2] In this setup, the performance of an unconstrained strategy should increase with the size of the investment universe (the opportunity set) as the manager benefits from a larger pool of names from which to select. As ESG constraints are imposed, the size of the investment universe is reduced and could impact the ability of the manager to generate alpha. We use numerical simulations to develop our intuition on the interaction between ESG constraints and portfolio performance. In our simulation setup, we assume that the portfolio manager will assemble an equally weighted portfolio of n issuers from an underlying investment universe of N issuers, for different values of n and N. The manager selects issuers according to his active views, which are modelled as 'informative signals' that are simulated to be weakly correlated with future issuer-specific returns.[3] In our simulations, we assume that the manager's signals have a correlation of 3% with future returns. This positive correlation represents 'imperfect foresight' because it gives the manager a modest advantage compared to a completely uninformed decision: the manager has a slightly higher chance to be right than to be wrong. We also assume that the manager includes names in the portfolio according to the magnitude of the informative signals. Names with higher signal values have higher expected alphas and therefore are included first. Names with negative signal values are normally avoided. In addition to the informative signals, all names in the investment universe are assigned with ESG scores, which can be positively or negatively correlated with informative signals. As we proceed with our analysis, issuers with low ESG scores will be progressively excluded from the investment

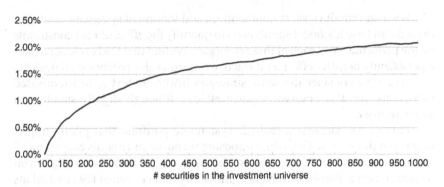

FIGURE 6.4 Portfolio alpha increases with the number of eligible issuers in the investment universe.

Note: The systematic portfolio includes 100 issuers selected according to the systematic signal. The signal predicts future issuer returns with imperfect foresight: the correlation between signal and subsequent issuer return is 3%. Results are derived from 10,000 simulated scenarios.

Source: Barclays Research.

universe. We use 10,000 simulated scenarios for all issuers in the investment universe, where we simultaneously simulate informative signals, ESG scores, and future issuer-specific returns.

In Figure 6.4, we show how the expected active return of a fixed-size portfolio of 100 names varies with the number N of available issuers in the corresponding investment universe from which they are chosen. If the investment universe is small, the portfolio includes the vast majority of the available names, and the manager's ability to generate alpha is therefore limited. As the size of the universe increases, so does the potential for differentiating among issuers, which leads to higher alpha because only the most attractive names, according to the signal, are included in the portfolio.

The relationship between portfolio alpha and the size of the investment universe is not linear. Alpha increases faster when the sizes of the portfolio and the investment universe are close to each other, and more slowly when the universe becomes significantly larger than the portfolio. We conclude that a larger investment universe should be beneficial for portfolio active returns, a conclusion that aligns well with the results in Grinold and Kahn (1999).

Next we consider the question of portfolio diversification. How large and diversified should an active portfolio be? Here, we assume a fixed universe of $N=1,000$ issuers, and vary the number of issuers included in the portfolio from 1 to 1,000. Assuming our informative signal is used to select the highest-ranked issuers available, two opposite effects are at play. On one hand, issuer-specific risk declines due to diversification as more names are added to the portfolio. This decline in active risk benefits risk-adjusted performance. On the other hand, each new name added to the portfolio contributes less alpha than the previous one, assuming that the manager includes more attractive names with stronger signal values first. As a result, portfolio alpha is gradually diluted as the portfolio becomes more diversified. At the extreme, when all issuers in the benchmark investment universe are included, portfolio alpha reduces to zero. The reduction in active risk and alpha dilution have opposite effects on portfolio risk-adjusted returns, so that the portfolio information ratio reaches its maximum at about 250 names, as illustrated in Figure 6.5.

Until now, we have not considered ESG constraints, which typically exclude names with low ESG scores (rating) from the investment universe, thereby reducing the opportunity set. Figure 6.4 shows that reducing the size of the universe has a negative impact on portfolio alpha.

This reduction in portfolio alpha should be even larger if ESG scores and systematic signals are negatively correlated. For example, low-ESG names can appear attractive from a relative value perspective if they trade at wider credit spreads than their high-ESG peers. As a result, excluding low-ESG names from the universe can reduce the ability of a relative value strategy to generate alpha.

Figure 6.6 illustrates the impact of the correlation between ESG scores and systematic signal on portfolio alpha. Here, we hold the size of the portfolio constant at 100 issuers, out of a full bond universe of 1,000 issuers, which is first subject to filtering based on ESG rankings. We vary the percentage of the universe excluded by ESG filtering and observe the effect on performance for different values of the correlation between the ESG scores and

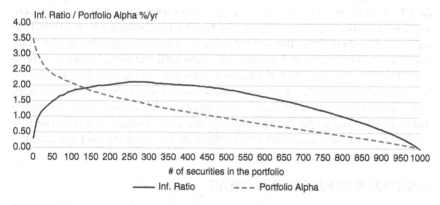

FIGURE 6.5 Portfolio alpha and information ratio as functions of portfolio size. *Note:* Portfolios include *n* issuers selected from an investment universe of 1,000 issuers according to an informative signal that predicts issuer returns with imperfect foresight: the correlation between signal and issuer return is 3%. Results are derived from 10,000 simulated scenarios.
Source: Barclays Research.

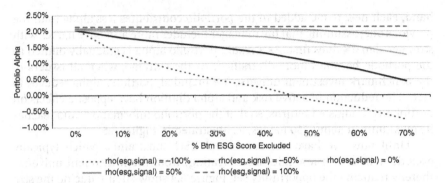

FIGURE 6.6 Effect of ESG exclusions on portfolio alpha: the role of the correlation between ESG scores and issuer signals.
Note: Portfolios includes 100 issuers selected according to systematic signals. Issuers are selected from a universe of 1,000 issuers subject to ESG exclusion constraints: a percentage of issuers with low ESG scores is excluded from the universe. Informative signals predict issuer returns with imperfect foresight. Portfolio simulated alpha is reported for different correlations between signals and ESG scores. Results are derived from 10,000 simulated scenarios.
Source: Barclays Research.

the selection signal. When ESG scores and signals are uncorrelated, portfolio alpha gradually declines as a progressively higher proportion of the investment universe is excluded. This decline is moderate: excluding 20% of the investment universe leads to only a 4% reduction in portfolio alpha (from 2.0% to 1.92%). When ESG scores and signals used for issuer selection are negatively correlated, the decline in portfolio alpha becomes steeper: excluding 20% of issuers from the universe leads to a 19% reduction in portfolio alpha (from 2.0% to 1.62%) when ESG scores and the signal have a correlation of −50%. The negative correlation between ESG scores and the signal increases the probability that ESG-related constraints exclude names with high signal values. Positive correlation between ESG scores and the signal makes the decline in portfolio alpha less dramatic because attractive issuers (with higher signal values) are less likely to be excluded by the ESG screen.

SYSTEMATIC STRATEGIES IN CREDIT

We analyse the impact of ESG constraints on three systematic strategies in the US IG corporate bond market: value, momentum, and sentiment. Detailed discussion on these and other systematic signals in credit is available in *Systematic Investing in Credit* (Ben Dor et al. 2021), so here, we only provide a short summary.

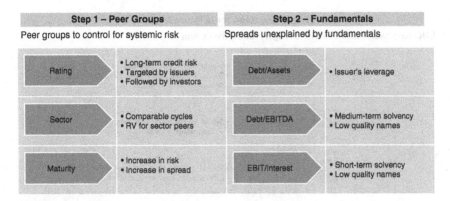

Step 1 – Peer Groups		Step 2 – Fundamentals	
Peer groups to control for systemic risk		Spreads unexplained by fundamentals	
Rating	• Long-term credit risk • Targeted by issuers • Followed by investors	Debt/Assets	• Issuer's leverage
Sector	• Comparable cycles • RV for sector peers	Debt/EBITDA	• Medium-term solvency • Low quality names
Maturity	• Increase in risk • Increase in spread	EBIT/Interest	• Short-term solvency • Low quality names

FIGURE 6.7 Relative value (Excess Spread to Peers [ESP]) model implementation. *Source:* Barclays Research.

The value strategy is based on a quantitative model called Excess Spread to Peers (ESP), which is designed to identify mispriced corporate bonds given their issuers' fundamental characteristics. The model is implemented as outlined in Figure 6.7. First, peer groups are identified based on rating, sector, and maturity to capture systematic credit risk. ESP calculates the excess spread of each bond over its peer group average. Bonds with high or low excess spreads over peers are deemed undervalued or overvalued, respectively. In a second step, the model corrects excess spreads for differences in issuer fundamentals and bond characteristics.

The approach is similar to decomposing bond spread into portions attributed to systematic credit risk, issuer fundamental characteristics, and mispricing. Securities with high positive mispricing component are assigned high ESP scores and are deemed undervalued. Issues with a negative mispricing component receive low ESP scores and are deemed overvalued.

Our momentum strategy is based on a model called Equity Momentum in Credit (EMC), which aims to differentiate issuers by their relative stock price momentum, as shown in Figure 6.8. The model is based on a positive empirical relationship between past equity returns and subsequent excess returns of corporate bonds.[4]

Our sentiment strategy is based on a model called Equity Short Interest (ESI), which is designed to identify bond issuers with significant short positions in the parent company's stock.[5]

To measure the return premium associated with each systematic signal, we build exposure-matched portfolios that either maximize or minimize the selected signal subject to allocation, exposure, and issuer concentration constraints. Table 6.1 outlines the process.

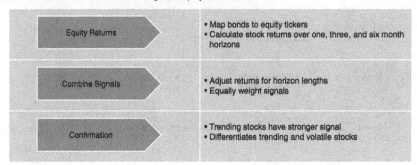

FIGURE 6.8 Momentum (Equity Momentum in Credit [EMC]) model implementation.
Source: Barclays Research.

TABLE 6.1 Building max and min exposure-matched portfolios for individual systematic signals.

Building Systematic Exposure-Matched Portfolios	Details
Objective	Maximize (minimize) portfolio systematic signal: value, momentum, or sentiment
Index Exposure Constraints	Match index aggregate exposures: ■ Portfolio OAS, DTS, OASD ■ Portfolio avg. amount outstanding ■ Portfolio avg. bond age
Allocation/Exposure Constraints by Sector	Target index exposures by sector: ■ Target index sector weights ■ Target sector DTS contributions
Rating Constraints by Sector	Target index weights by rating: A and above / Baa
Issuer / Bond Concentration Constraints	■ Limit maximum issuer overweight over index weight ■ Limit maximum bond overweight over index weight
Investment Universe	Constituents of the Bloomberg US Corporate Index
Rebalancing Frequency	Monthly: each month-end
Benchmark Index	Bloomberg US Corporate Index

Source: Barclays Research.

By selecting securities that maximize (minimize) a systematic signal at the portfolio level, we create a positive (negative) style tilt relative to the index. For example, we can create a value style portfolio by maximizing its average value (ESP) score. We then use allocation and exposure constraints relative to the index to ensure that our tilted portfolios closely track risk exposures of the index and avoid unintended systematic tracking errors. Finally, issuer and bond concentration constraints ensure that our systematic portfolios are sufficiently diversified, so that any issuer included in the portfolio has a relatively small contribution to portfolio active risk. Note that this procedure is closely related to the one we used to create Max ESG and Min ESG portfolios in Chapters 2 and 3.

Provided that our value, momentum, and sentiment signals are informative, we expect systematic portfolios with a positive signal tilt (max portfolios) to outperform the index and portfolios Insert and those to make protfolios and those with a with a negative tilt (min portfolios) to underperform. At this stage, we are interested in illustrating the economic effect of each strategy and therefore ignore practical aspects such as liquidity considerations, turnover control, and transaction costs.

Figure 6.9 reports cumulative excess returns of the systematic value, momentum, and sentiment exposure-matched portfolios, as well as those of the Bloomberg US Corporate index. As expected, portfolios with positive signal tilts persistently outperform the index, while portfolios with negative signal tilts underperform the index. The issuers included into the portfolios with negative signal tilts should be avoided by a systematic long-only strategy, or shorted if implementing a long-short strategy.

Table 6.2 summarizes the performances of value, momentum, and sentiment exposure-matched portfolios. The value strategy has demonstrated the strongest performance in the period between 2009 and 2023: the max value portfolio outperformed the index and the min value portfolio by 1.81 %/yr and 4.12 %/yr respectively, with information ratios above 2. The outperformance has been robust across sub-periods. The momentum strategy has also delivered a sizable alpha, but with asymmetric active returns across max and min exposure-matched portfolios: the max momentum portfolio outperformed the index and the min momentum portfolio by 0.82 %/yr and by 3.02 %/yr respectively. These results suggest that avoiding issuers with weak equity momentum was more important than selecting issuers with strong equity momentum. Finally, the sentiment strategy has also had positive alpha: the max sentiment portfolio outperformed the index and the min sentiment portfolio by 0.58 %/yr and by 1.59 %/yr respectively. Avoiding issuers with significant equity short interest was more important than selecting issuers with low short interest.

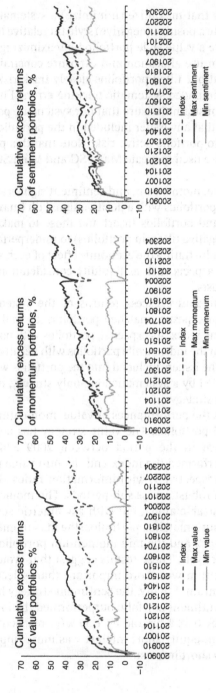

FIGURE 6.9   Cumulative excess returns of systematic exposure-matched portfolios with value, momentum, and sentiment tilts.
Source: Bloomberg, Barclays Research.

TABLE 6.2 Summary performance statistics of systematic exposure-matched value, momentum, and sentiment portfolios across sub-periods.

	Index	Systematic Value Portfolios				Systematic Momentum Portfolios				Systematic Sentiment Portfolios			
		Max	Min	Max over Index	Max over Min	Max	Min	Max over Index	Max over Min	Max	Min	Max over Index	Max over Min
Panel A: February 2009 to July 2023													
Avg. exc. return, %/y	2.68	4.49	0.37	1.81	4.12	3.50	0.48	0.82	3.02	3.27	1.68	0.58	1.59
Volatility, %/y	5.06	4.64	5.29	0.87	1.73	4.67	4.96	0.82	1.44	5.00	4.92	0.45	0.85
Inf. ratio	0.53	0.97	0.07	2.07	2.37	0.75	0.10	1.00	2.10	0.65	0.34	1.29	1.86
Panel B: February 2009 to April 2016													
Avg. exc. return, %/y	3.57	5.55	0.98	1.98	4.58	4.46	1.22	0.88	3.24	4.22	2.68	0.65	1.54
Volatility, %/y	4.88	4.37	5.01	1.04	1.87	4.25	4.63	1.03	1.37	4.70	4.35	0.54	0.70
Inf. ratio	0.73	1.27	0.20	1.91	2.45	1.05	0.26	0.86	2.36	0.90	0.62	1.19	2.18
Panel C: May 2016 to July 2023													
Avg. exc. return, %/y	1.79	3.43	−0.23	1.64	3.66	2.55	−0.26	0.75	2.81	2.32	0.67	0.52	1.64
Volatility, %/y	5.22	4.87	5.55	0.67	1.57	5.04	5.27	0.52	1.50	5.27	5.42	0.34	0.98
Inf. ratio	0.34	0.70	−0.04	2.45	2.32	0.50	−0.05	1.46	1.87	0.44	0.12	1.52	1.67

Source: Bloomberg, Barclays Research.

EFFECT OF ESG CONSTRAINTS

To understand the effect of ESG constraints on the performance of systematic strategies in credit, we progressively exclude issuers with the lowest MSCI ESG scores from the investment universe. Figure 6.2 shows that the constraints on ESG ratings typically imposed by investors can exclude a varying percentage of the index over time, most recently between 5% and 20% of the US IG universe. In this section, we use a different approach, in which the ESG screen is assumed to exclude a fixed percentage of the index universe each month (by appropriately varying the level of ESG score used as a threshold). We span a wide range of exclusion levels, and deliberately include more extreme cases as well, excluding up to 60% of the index universe. We expect to see a larger reduction in portfolio alpha when a larger portion of the investment universe is excluded.

Our exclusions affect various industry sectors differently because MSCI ESG scores are not uniformly distributed within industry sectors and because large issuers can have several outstanding bonds with the same ESG score,[6] so that excluding a large issuer can have a disproportionally large impact on the number of bonds and on market capitalization. Table 6.3 shows the effects of

TABLE 6.3 Effect of progressively excluding issues with the lowest ESG scores from the Bloomberg US corporate index on bond count by sector, 31 July 2023.

	Index	Percentage reduction in number of bonds by sector					
	Index	ex 10%	ex 20%	ex 30%	ex 40%	ex 50%	ex 60%
Index	**7658**	**9%**	**19%**	**29%**	**39%**	**49%**	**57%**
Basic	272	10%	17%	35%	44%	47%	58%
Capital Goods	505	1%	12%	23%	30%	50%	52%
Cyclical	542	7%	26%	38%	52%	67%	74%
Non-cyclical	472	4%	14%	25%	31%	35%	40%
Healthcare	661	4%	8%	14%	21%	35%	67%
Energy	550	14%	22%	31%	50%	61%	63%
Technology	636	1%	16%	25%	32%	43%	47%
Communication	468	19%	37%	57%	58%	59%	63%
Industrial Other	317	18%	18%	18%	61%	76%	90%
Utility	1127	8%	13%	26%	30%	41%	48%
Banks & Brokerage	1173	6%	9%	12%	26%	31%	36%
Insurance	442	23%	37%	48%	55%	62%	70%
Financial Other	493	18%	37%	62%	66%	75%	79%

Source: Bloomberg, Barclays Research.

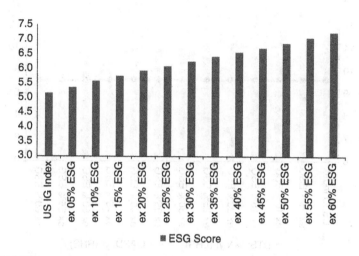

FIGURE 6.10 Average ESG score of the remaining US IG index as a function of ESG exclusions, January 2009–July 2023.
Source: Bloomberg, MSCI, Barclays Research.

various degrees of ESG exclusion across sectors as of 31 July 2023. Sectors that are affected more significantly include insurance, communication, energy, industrial other, and financial other.

ESG exclusions can also affect the characteristics of the remaining index universe, especially if ESG ratings are correlated with issuer or bond characteristics. Figure 6.10 reports the average ESG scores of the bonds remaining in the index after ESG exclusions, while Figure 6.11 shows average DTS and OASD. The first bar on the left of the two figures corresponds to the Bloomberg US IG Corporate index, when no issuer is excluded. The subsequent bars from left to right represent the remaining index universe after a certain percentage of bonds with the lowest ESG scores is excluded.

As expected, the average ESG score of the index increases as a larger proportion of issuers with low ESG scores is excluded from the universe. We also see that ESG exclusions lead to reduction in the average DTS of the remaining index because, as documented in Chapter 1, ESG and credit ratings are related: higher quality issuers tend to have higher ESG ratings. As a result, excluded issuers tend to have higher spreads and DTS than the remaining ones.

According to the results shown in Figure 6.6, the degree to which ESG constraints affect the active returns of an active strategy depends on the correlation between signals and ESG scores. Negative signal-ESG correlations would be most detrimental for portfolio active returns because excluded issuers with low ESG scores would also have the highest expected returns. Figure 6.12

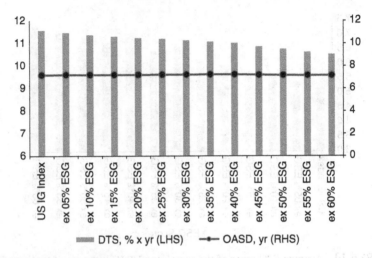

FIGURE 6.11 Average DTS and OASD of the remaining US IG index as a function of ESG exclusions, January 2009–July 2023.
Source: Bloomberg, MSCI, Barclays Research.

reports cross-sectional rank correlations between value, momentum, and sentiment signals and MSCI ESG scores.

Correlations between ESG scores and systematic signals vary over time. The correlation between ESG scores and value signals has been mostly negative, averaging to −5.4% over the whole period and declining to −10% in recent years. The negative correlation between ESG and value signals could be due to the fact that bonds issued by companies with low ESG ratings tend

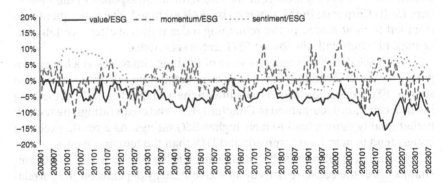

FIGURE 6.12 Cross-sectional Kendall rank correlations between systematic value, momentum, sentiment signals, and MSCI ESG scores in US IG.
Source: MSCI, Barclays Research.

to have higher spreads than their peers. This spread premium can make low-ESG bonds attractive from a relative value perspective. Correlations between ESG scores and momentum signals varied over time in a range between −12% and +12%, with the average over the whole period being −0.4%. The correlation reached −12% in July 2023. Finally, correlations between ESG scores and sentiment signals have been mostly positive, ranging between −4% and +10% and averaging to +2% over the whole period.

To analyse the effect of the ESG constraints on the active returns of value, momentum, and sentiment strategies, we construct systematic exposure-matched portfolios with positive and negative signal tilts as outlined in Table 6.1. However, we now expand the original analysis by building a series of max and min exposure-matched portfolios for each ESG exclusion scenario. The systematic portfolios are constructed to track a narrower version of the index, *after* ESG exclusions, and are allowed to include only bonds from the remaining universe of eligible bonds.

Portfolios are constructed by maximizing a positive (max) or negative (min) signal tilt over the index (which is customized to reflect ESG exclusions) subject to exposure and issuer concentration constraints. We measure the signal tilt of a systematic strategy as the difference in average signal values between max and min portfolios. Without ESG exclusions, systematic strategies achieve the largest signal tilts. As we progressively exclude issuers with low-ESG scores, the tilt between max and min portfolios is reduced. Figure 6.13 reports the average percentage reductions in signal tilts relative to the tilt of the unconstrained portfolios (with no ESG exclusions). The percentage reductions are attributed to the max and min signal portfolios. As a larger proportion of low-ESG issuers is removed from the universe, the ability of the systematic portfolios to implement style factors is reduced.

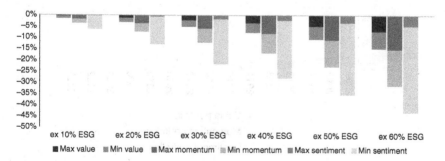

FIGURE 6.13 Average percentage reduction in signal tilts of max over min systematic portfolios resulting from ESG exclusions, 2009–2023.
Source: Barclays Research.

The reduction in signal tilt of the value and momentum portfolios are evenly distributed between max and min portfolios. For the sentiment strategy, reductions in tilts of max and min portfolios are very asymmetric: the reduction in tilt of the max sentiment portfolio constitutes only 4–12% of the overall effect, with the remaining part attributed to the reduction in tilt of the min sentiment portfolio. This asymmetry appears because there are relatively few names with significant equity short interest; these names are selected into the min sentiment portfolio that minimizes sentiment (maximizes short interest). As most index issuers have low short interest, it is easier to deviate from the index average sentiment signal value when minimizing rather than maximizing sentiment signals.

Figure 6.13 also shows that the reduction in signal tilts is much larger for the momentum and sentiment portfolios than for the value portfolios. This happens because momentum and sentiment signals are defined at the issuer level, while value signals are defined at the bond level, meaning that the opportunity set relative to portfolio size is much larger for the value strategy than for momentum and sentiment.

The effect of narrowing the index and portfolio universes varies over time. Figures 6.14 and 6.15 show the time series of reductions in signal tilt between max and min portfolios resulting from excluding the lowest-ESG 20% and 40%

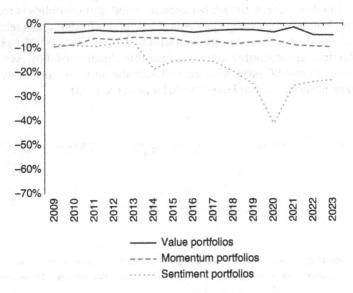

FIGURE 6.14 Percentage reduction in signal tilt of max over min systematic portfolios when 20% of issues with the lowest ESG scores are excluded.
Source: Barclays Research.

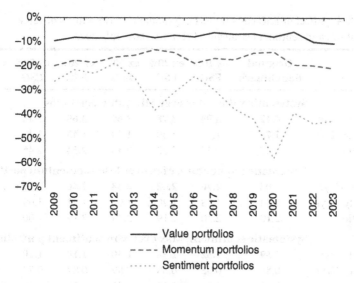

FIGURE 6.15 Percentage reduction in signal tilt of max over min systematic portfolios when 40% of issues with the lowest ESG scores are excluded.
Source: Barclays Research.

of issues, respectively. Reductions in value, momentum, and sentiment signal tilts are reported as percentages of the original tilts in the systematic portfolios *without* any ESG exclusions.

Figures 6.14 and 6.15 confirm our earlier result that ESG exclusions have a smaller effect on value tilts and larger effects on momentum and sentiment tilts. We also see that sentiment tilts are more volatile over time than those of either value or momentum. For example, excluding the 20% bottom ESG names reduces the average tilt between max and min sentiment portfolios by 13% of the original tilt (when there are no ESG constraints). However, this reduction ranged between 8% in 2012 and 41% in 2020. Such variability in the sentiment tilt over time could have resulted from changes in the number of available issuers with significant equity short interest in bullish and bearish periods.

Next, we analyse the effect of ESG exclusions on the active returns of our value, momentum, and sentiment strategies, measured as the difference in excess returns between the max and min strategy portfolios. Table 6.4 shows that excluding 20% of names with the lowest ESG scores reduces value alpha from 4.12 to 3.78%/y; momentum alpha from 3.02 to 2.62%/y; and sentiment alpha from 1.59 to 1.38%/y. Table 6.4 also shows that tracking error volatility (TEV) tends to decline as a progressively larger portion of the universe is

TABLE 6.4   Effect of ESG constraints on systematic active returns of value, momentum, and sentiment strategies, February 2009–July 2023.

	Original Benchmark	ex 10% ESG	ex 20% ESG	ex 30% ESG	ex 40% ESG	ex 50% ESG	ex 60% ESG
Systematic value: Max over Min value portfolios							
Exc. Ret. %/yr	4.12	3.90	3.78	3.69	3.65	3.45	3.12
Volatility, %/yr	1.73	1.58	1.50	1.49	1.43	1.40	1.32
Inf. Ratio	2.37	2.47	2.53	2.48	2.54	2.46	2.37
Systematic momentum: Max over Min momentum portfolios							
Exc. Ret. %/yr	3.02	2.70	2.62	2.38	2.46	2.19	1.87
Volatility, %/yr	1.44	1.28	1.20	1.04	1.12	1.09	0.99
Inf. Ratio	2.10	2.10	2.19	2.29	2.19	2.00	1.89
Systematic sentiment: Max over Min sentiment portfolios							
Exc. Ret. %/yr	1.59	1.52	1.38	1.30	1.10	1.10	0.96
Volatility, %/yr	0.85	0.92	0.88	0.89	0.87	0.79	0.58
Inf. Ratio	1.86	1.65	1.58	1.46	1.26	1.40	1.66

Source: Barclays Research.

excluded. This decline in TEV is related to the reduction of the investment universe relative to the portfolio size. As the index universe is reduced, the diversified exposure-matched portfolios become more representative of a narrower index.

The effect on active returns can also be measured in terms of the percentage reduction relative to the original active returns of the value, momentum, and sentiment strategies without ESG constraints. Figure 6.16 reports the percentage decline in active returns as a progressively larger share of bonds is excluded from the universe. The effect is split between the change in alphas of the max and min portfolios.

For the momentum and sentiment strategies, the reduction in the underperformance of min portfolios relative to the index constitutes a larger part of the percentage decline in alpha than the reduction in the outperformance of max portfolios. When 40% of low-ESG names are excluded, the reductions in underperformance of min-value, min-momentum, and min-sentiment portfolios represent respectively 6%, 16%, and 20% of the original alphas, while the reductions in outperformance of the max portfolios over index are 5.4%, 3%, and 11%. By contrast, the negative effect on the performance of the value strategy is equally split between the max and min portfolios. Why should the negative effect of the ESG constraint on the momentum and sentiment strategies be concentrated in the min portfolios? ESG constraints seem to eliminate

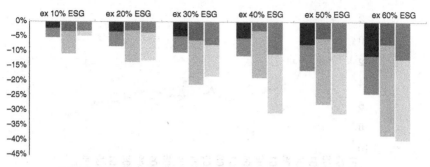

FIGURE 6.16 Percentage reduction in signal alpha as a function of ESG exclusions, February 2009–July 2023.
Source: Barclays Research.

some *unattractive* momentum and sentiment issuers from the universe and, therefore, make it harder to find bonds to avoid.

Figures 6.17 and 6.18 show that the negative effect of ESG exclusions on active returns of the systematic strategies is fairly persistent over time. Figure 6.17 measures the cumulative effect on active returns of value, momentum, and sentiment strategies, when we exclude 20% of low-ESG names from the investment universe. We measure the effect as the monthly difference in excess returns of max over min exposure-matched portfolios implemented *with* and *without* ESG constraints. In almost every period, the outperformance

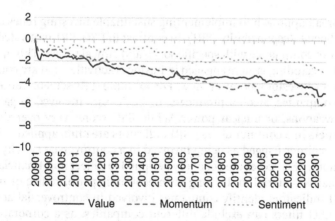

FIGURE 6.17 Cumulative effect of excluding 20% of issuers with the lowest ESG scores on active returns of value, momentum, and sentiment strategies.
Source: Barclays Research.

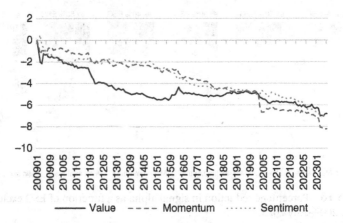

FIGURE 6.18 Cumulative effect of excluding 40% of issuers with the lowest ESG scores on active returns of value, momentum, and sentiment strategies.
Source: Barclays Research.

of max over min portfolios *without* the ESG constraint is stronger than that *with* the ESG constraint. Figure 6.18 shows that the negative effect on strategy alpha is more severe if we apply more stringent ESG restrictions and exclude 40% of names with the lowest ESG scores from the universe.

EFFECT OF SRI EXCLUSIONS

A widespread approach to implementing sustainable investing relies on indicators of Social Responsibility (SRI). In contrast to ESG, SRI-motivated exclusions ensure compliance with specific social and ethical values. This approach consists of excluding issuers engaged in business activities that are controversial from an investor's point of view. For example, SRI screens can exclude tobacco companies, alcohol producers, or businesses involved in gambling, military weapons, or nuclear power. While ESG scores vary over time and across issuers in a continuous way, SRI indicators are often applied as binary: an issuer is either flagged as being involved in a controversial activity or not. Furthermore, ESG scores are generally designed to reflect non-financial information that is material to the long term economic performance of the firm while SRI indicators identify companies involved in controversial activities. SRI and ESG filters can exclude different companies, as a corporation can score well in terms of Environment, Social, and Governance metrics while, at the same time, being involved in an activity (e.g. alcohol) deemed to be controversial. It is therefore unclear that the results shown so far, based on ESG scores, would also hold for SRI exclusions. Indeed, we showed in Chapter 5 that exclusions based on MSCI SRI indicators had a neutral effect on performance, all else equal, while in Chapter 2 we saw that maximizing portfolio average ESG score enhanced returns.

Figure 6.2 shows that SRI exclusions in the Bloomberg MSCI US Corporate SRI index reduce the eligible investment universe of the standard Bloomberg US Corporate index by 19% using bond counts as of July 2023. Figure 6.3 shows that SRI exclusions in different industry sectors are very different from exclusions based on ESG ratings.

We now measure the impact of SRI exclusions on active returns of value, momentum, and sentiment portfolios. Similar to the previous case of ESG constraints, we use exposure-matched portfolios that maximize value, momentum, and sentiment tilts to measure the impact of SRI exclusions. First, we build max and min signal portfolios in the universe of the standard US corporate index, using the methodology outlined in Table 6.1. Then we repeat the same exercise but in the SRI-filtered universe. Performance differences between the two sets of systematic portfolios can be used to measure the impact of SRI exclusions on systematic alpha.

Figure 6.19 shows the percentage reductions in achievable signal tilts that result from SRI exclusions. Signal tilts in the unconstrained universe are used as benchmarks relative to which we measure reductions in achievable tilts after SRI exclusions. Average percentage changes in signal tilts resulting from

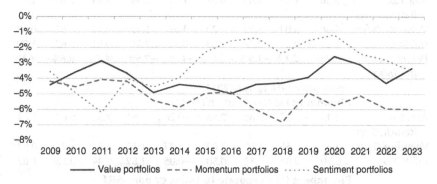

FIGURE 6.19 Percentage reductions in signal tilts of systematic strategies when an SRI screen is applied.
Note: This chart shows the percentage reduction in signal tilt of systematic value, momentum, and sentiment strategies when an SRI filter is applied to the US IG Corporate Bond Index universe. Percentage changes are calculated every month relative to the tilt achieved in max over min signal portfolios constructed without SRI exclusions and with respect to the standard bond index.
Source: Barclays Research.

SRI exclusions are relatively small compared to those resulting from ESG constraints (Figures 6.14 and 6.15): 4% for value, 5% for momentum, and 3% for sentiment. The reductions in signal tilts change over time and are more volatile for sentiment and less volatile for value and momentum.

How does a reduction in signal tilt translate to performance? Table 6.5 reports reductions in portfolio alphas resulting from SRI exclusions for each of the systematic strategies in two sub-periods: from February 2009 to April

TABLE 6.5 Reduction in value, momentum, and sentiment alphas in US IG as a result of SRI exclusions.

	Value portfolios			Momentum portfolios			Sentiment portfolios		
	Max	Min	Max–Min	Max	Min	Max–Min	Max	Min	Max–Min
From February 2009 to April 2016									
Bloomberg US Corporate IG index									
Avg. Exc. Return, %/yr	5.55	0.98	4.58	4.46	1.22	3.24	4.22	2.68	1.54
Volatility, %/yr	4.37	5.01	1.87	4.25	4.63	1.37	4.70	4.35	0.70
Inf. Ratio	1.27	0.20	2.45	1.05	0.26	2.36	0.90	0.62	2.18
Bloomberg US Corporate IG index ex non–SRI									
Avg. Exc. Return, %/yr	5.56	1.07	4.49	4.37	1.38	2.99	3.84	2.67	1.17
Volatility, %/yr	4.46	5.04	1.92	4.23	4.58	1.33	4.72	4.35	0.68
Inf. Ratio	1.25	0.21	2.34	1.03	0.30	2.25	0.81	0.62	1.70
Pct. reduction in alpha	*0.2%*	*−2.1%*	*−1.9%*	*−2.6%*	*−4.9%*	*−7.5%*	*−24.7%*	*0.6%*	*−24.1%*
From May 2016 to July 2023									
Bloomberg US Corporate IG index									
Avg. Exc. Return, %/yr	3.43	−0.23	3.66	2.55	−0.26	2.81	2.32	0.67	1.64
Volatility, %/yr	4.87	5.55	1.57	5.04	5.27	1.50	5.27	5.42	0.98
Inf. Ratio	0.70	−0.04	2.32	0.50	−0.05	1.87	0.44	0.12	1.67
Bloomberg US Corporate IG index ex non–SRI									
Avg. Exc. Return, %/yr	3.35	−0.17	3.52	2.52	−0.03	2.54	2.37	0.75	1.62
Volatility, %/yr	4.94	5.59	1.56	5.20	5.37	1.35	5.19	5.49	1.11
Inf. Ratio	0.68	−0.03	2.26	0.48	−0.01	1.89	0.46	0.14	1.46
Pct. reduction in alpha	*−2.2%*	*−1.5%*	*−3.7%*	*−1.1%*	*−8.3%*	*−9.4%*	*3.2%*	*−4.8%*	*−1.6%*

Source: Bloomberg, Barclays Research.

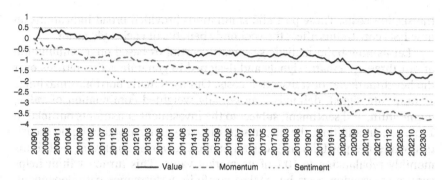

FIGURE 6.20 Cumulative effect of SRI exclusions on active returns of value, momentum, and sentiment systematic strategies in the US IG corporate bond market. *Source:* Barclays Research.

2016, and from May 2016 to July 2023. In the first sub-period, sentiment was the most affected strategy, with alpha declining by 24%, from 1.54 to 1.17%/y. Momentum was the second-worst affected strategy as its alpha declined by 7.5%: from 3.24 to 2.99%/y. Value was the least impacted as its average excess return declined only by 2%, from 4.58 to 4.49 %/yr. In the second sub-period, the most affected strategy was momentum (−9.4%), followed by value (−3.7%) and sentiment (−1.6%).

Figure 6.20 reports the cumulative effects of SRI exclusions on active returns of value, momentum, and sentiment strategies. The effect is measured monthly for each systematic strategy as the outperformance of the max over min exposure-matched portfolios implemented with and without SRI exclusions. We see that the negative effects of SRI exclusions persist over time for all three strategies, with the momentum (value) strategy affected the most (least) over the whole period.

These empirical results confirm our theoretical conclusions: restricting an investment universe by excluding low-ESG or non-SRI issuers typically leads to a reduction in the active returns of systematic strategies. The magnitude of the effect depends on the interplay between systematic signals and the exclusion rule.

IMPLEMENTING SYSTEMATIC CREDIT PORTFOLIOS WITH ESG CONSTRAINTS

So far, our analysis has focused on theoretical style portfolios, which were designed to express value, momentum, and sentiment styles in the presence of ESG or SRI constraints but did not explicitly account for turnover or transaction costs. These portfolio simulations provided broad indications on how ESG constraints affect the economic benefits of each style factor.

Let us now build realistic systematic portfolios based on a combination of our three systematic signals and designed to generate active returns over the benchmark net of transaction costs. Our systematic portfolios maximize a composite signal, defined as an equally weighted combination of value, momentum, and sentiment, subject to the investment constraints outlined in Table 6.1. In addition, the investment universe is narrowed to liquid securities, while the portfolio includes an explicit turnover constraint that limits monthly rebalancing to 10% of its market value. This turnover limit helps control transaction costs but makes portfolio performance path-dependent. This time, the effect of ESG constraints on performance reflects not only the reduction in the size of the investment universe but also the interaction of ESG or SRI exclusions with the turnover constraint. We therefore expect different results from those previously obtained for individual signals in Tables 6.4 and 6.5 and Figure 6.16.

We estimate portfolio transaction cost using Barclays Liquidity Cost Scores (LCS),[7] which are based on direct observations of bid–offer quotes provided by Barclays' trading desks for individual bonds. LCS is a conservative measure of transaction cost as it relies on the input of a single broker-dealer. Investors with access to a broader set of broker-dealers should generally be able to achieve more efficient execution than that implied by LCS.

In addition to controlling turnover and accounting for transaction costs, our realistic portfolio only invests in liquid bonds, to make an actively traded strategy feasible. To that effect, the investment universe excludes bonds with low outstanding amount and comparatively poor Trade Efficiency Score (TES). TES is part of Barclays' liquidity analytics, which ranks index bonds both on trading volume and LCS information. Like LCS, TES are available historically for all bonds in the US IG corporate bond index. The liquidity filter replaces the constraints on age and outstanding amount shown in Table 6.1. We no longer want our portfolios to have the same liquidity characteristics as the index, but to invest exclusively in liquid securities.

To measure the impact of ESG constraints, we progressively exclude issuers with low ESG ratings from the portfolio and benchmark index universes. Instead of targeting for exclusion a particular percentage of names with low ESG scores (and so letting the score threshold vary) as in the approach described in Table 6.3, we exclude issuers that fall into or below the following MSCI ESG ratings categories: CCC, B, BB, and BBB. This deviation from the previous approach is more practical, as it corresponds to typical mandate specifications that portfolio managers are likely to encounter. Such letter-based rating filters are also more stable over time than percentile ranking. However, as shown in Figure 6.2, excluding bonds based on their letter ESG ratings would disproportionately affect our historical sample, where up to 50% of bonds could have been excluded. This variation in the size of the excluded universe can significantly affect the active returns of the systematic portfolio.

Table 6.6 shows that excluding issuers rated B and below as of July 2023 has only a modest effect on the universe of eligible bonds, both in terms of market value and number of bonds. Excluding issuers rated BB and below or BBB and below reduces the index market value by 12% and 28% respectively.

There is a significant variation in how ESG exclusions at different levels affect different industry sectors. Raising the bar to exclude issuers rated BB or below reduces the capitalizations of the communications, insurance, and industrial other sectors more than those of any other industry sectors. Raising it further to excluding BBB-rated names significantly affects the capital goods, technology, communications, insurance, and financial other sectors.

In addition to simulating systematic portfolios using the ESG exclusions summarized in Table 6.6, we also repeat the exercise for MSCI SRI-motivated exclusions. Excluding non-SRI names reduces the size of the investment universe by about 16%, as shown in Figure 6.2. SRI and ESG exclusions tend to affect sectors very differently, as shown in Figure 6.3. As opposed to ESG ratings, which change over time, SRI exclusions tend to be more stable, as they relate to the activity of the firm.

Running our realistic portfolio simulations for the period from January 2009 to July 2023, we find that both ESG and SRI-motivated exclusions would have reduced the net alpha of a systematic portfolio. Table 6.7 reports average active returns before (gross) and after (net) transaction costs for different ESG-related constraints and for two different sub-periods.

Excluding issuers with MSCI ESG ratings of BB or below led to a 23% reduction in net alpha relative to the unconstrained universe. When the threshold for exclusion is set at an ESG rating of BBB, it affects close to a third of the index universe and portfolio alpha drops by 37%, from 1.07 %/yr to 0.68 %/yr. Lower thresholds (CCC or B) result in much smaller reductions (−4 or −7%/y respectively) in alpha.

Excluding non-SRI names had a relatively small effect on the active returns of the systematic portfolio: net alpha dropped by only 3–4 bp/y as a result of excluding non-SRI names from the portfolio and benchmark universes. We postulate that the smaller effect on net alpha can be explained by two characteristics of SRI compared with ESG-rating based filters. First, the companies excluded by SRI screens rarely change over time as exclusions are based on the nature of business activities, while ESG ratings are updated periodically to reflect changes in ESG policies. Second, exclusions motivated by ESG rating could be more (negatively) correlated with our composite performance signal than those motivated by SRI considerations.

TABLE 6.6 Effect of progressively excluding issuers with the low ESG ratings from the Bloomberg US corporate index on the composition of the eligible bond universe by sector, 31 July 2023.

	Percentage reduction in market value, $bn					Percentage reduction in bond counts				
	Index	ex CCC or below (%)	ex B or below (%)	ex BB or below (%)	ex BBB or below (%)	Index	ex CCC or below (%)	ex B or below (%)	ex BB or below (%)	ex BBB or below (%)
Index	**6336**	**3**	**4**	**12**	**28**	**7658**	**5**	**6**	**14**	**31**
Basic	168	4	8	15	36	272	3	5	11	33
Capital Goods	332	0	0	1	24	505	0	0	1	20
Cyclical	435	0	2	6	37	542	1	3	8	38
Non-cyclical	373	5	5	7	32	472	4	4	6	26
Healthcare	606	10	10	13	26	661	27	27	31	40
Energy	439	0	7	13	33	550	0	7	14	32
Technology	614	0	0	1	21	636	0	0	1	20
Communication	553	3	3	25	60	468	2	2	19	51
Industrial Other	171	14	15	35	35	317	23	23	40	40
Utility	548	1	1	11	24	1127	1	1	9	22
Banks & Brokerage	1560	0	0	8	11	1173	0	1	6	11
Insurance	290	3	7	22	40	442	2	8	25	48
Financial Other	246	12	13	26	55	493	12	14	30	61

Source: Bloomberg, Barclays Research.

TABLE 6.7 Effect of ESG and SRI constraints on active returns of the systematic credit portfolios based on value, momentum, and sentiment.

	Index Universe	ex CCC or below	ex B or below	ex BB or below	ex BBB or below	ex Non-SRI
	Period: from February 2009 to July 2023					
Avg. Gross Alpha, %/yr	1.98	1.92	1.89	1.72	1.54	1.94
Avg. Net Alpha, %/yr	1.07	1.03	1.00	0.83	0.68	1.04
TEV, %/yr	0.94	0.90	0.83	0.75	0.65	0.93
Inf. Ratio	1.14	1.15	1.19	1.10	1.04	1.11
% Reduction in Net Alpha	—	**−4%**	**−7%**	**−23%**	**−37%**	**−3%**
	Period: from February 2009 to April 2016					
Avg. Gross Alpha, %/yr	2.68	2.58	2.52	2.19	1.95	2.64
Avg. Alpha, %/yr	1.62	1.56	1.50	1.17	0.97	1.59
TEV, %/yr	1.17	1.10	0.98	0.87	0.74	1.16
Inf. Ratio	1.39	1.41	1.52	1.35	1.31	1.37
% Reduction in Net Alpha	—	**−4%**	**−8%**	**−28%**	**−40%**	**−2%**
	Period: from May 2016 to July 2023					
Avg. Gross Alpha, %/yr	1.29	1.27	1.25	1.24	1.13	1.25
Avg. Alpha, %/yr	0.52	0.51	0.50	0.49	0.38	0.49
TEV, %/yr	0.61	0.59	0.62	0.60	0.53	0.59
Inf. Ratio	0.86	0.86	0.80	0.81	0.72	0.83
% Reduction in Net Alpha	—	**−2%**	**−4%**	**−6%**	**−26%**	**−7%**

Source: Barclays Research.

One should also note that tracking error volatility (TEV) tends to be lower for portfolio/index combinations that are subject to high level of exclusion. As a consequence, information ratios decline less quickly than alphas when ESG related filters become more stringent. This can be partially explained by the fact that issuer-specific TEV, which is effectively the main contributor to risk, is lower when the overlap between a systematic portfolio and the index is larger.

CONCLUSION

In our analysis, we demonstrated that ESG-related constraints are likely to reduce expected active returns of corporate bond portfolios that are managed to outperform their benchmark indices.

The mechanism for alpha reduction is twofold. First, portfolio alpha declines because ESG constraints reduce the size of the investment universe, thereby restricting the process of issuer selection. Second, ESG exclusions can potentially conflict with informative signals by excluding otherwise attractive names from the eligible universe. Therefore, a negative correlation between ESG scores and informative signals can amplify the negative effect of ESG exclusions on portfolio alpha.

We use numerical simulations to illustrate the negative effect of ESG-related constraints on portfolio alpha. We then employ a combination of value, momentum and sentiment strategies to quantify the costs of ESG constraints in a realistic US IG portfolio: the percentage reduction in expected alpha over the index net of transaction costs varied between 3 and 37%, depending on the proportion of the investment universe affected by ESG constraints. While mild ESG (ex B and below) or SRI exclusions have had small effects on portfolio active returns (3–4% reduction), more restrictive constraints (BB and below or BBB and below) have reduced portfolio alpha significantly (23–37% reduction).

From a practical standpoint, institutional investors should be aware that restricting the eligible investment universe by imposing ESG constraints is likely to lower portfolio alpha. Ensuring that the proportion of affected names relative to the overall size of the investment universe is moderate should help keep the negative effect of ESG exclusions reasonably low.

REFERENCES

Ben Dor, A., Desclee, A., Dynkin, L., Hyman, J., and Polbennikov, S. (2021). *Systematic Investing in Credit*. Wiley.

Dynkin, L., Hyman, J., and Wu, W. (2000). Value of Skill in Security Selection versus Asset Allocation in Credit Markets. *Journal of Portfolio Management*, 27, pp. 20–41.

Grinold, R.C. and Kahn, R.N. (1999). *Active Portfolio Management: A Quantitative Approach for Producing Superior Returns and Selecting Superior Returns and Controlling Risk*. McGraw Hill.

Konstantinovsky, V., Ng, K.Y., and Phelps, B.D. (2016). Measuring Bond-level Liquidity. *Journal of Portfolio Management*, 42, pp. 116–128.

NOTES

1. MSCI ESG Research reports their ESG rankings in different formats. In addition to numeric rankings on a scale of 0 to 10, they produce alphabetic ESG ratings meant to correspond roughly to the scale used by credit rating agencies. Bloomberg and MSCI have adopted this alphabetic format in the definitions of their corporate bond sustainability indices.

2. Imperfect foresight (Dynkin, Hyman and Wu 2000) means that the portfolio manager is able to anticipate future returns, so that managers' active views and future returns of respective issuers are slightly positively correlated. This small positive correlation (often called the 'information coefficient') gives a portfolio manager an advantage in a probabilistic sense relative to an uninformed decision. While there is still a significant chance of making a wrong call, the probability of making the right call is slightly higher, so that, on average, the manager is able to generate positive active returns. See also the discussion on information coefficient in Grinold and Kahn (1999).

3. Alternatively, we could form an optimal portfolio that includes all issuers weighted according to the respective informative signals. While the main conclusions would remain qualitatively similar, we felt that a heavily optimized portfolio that includes thousands of names might be less practical. We therefore chose a simpler portfolio construction approach for our analysis.

4. This equity-bond momentum signal empirically has much stronger predictive power for excess returns of corporate bonds than bond momentum. Therefore, we define momentum in credit as cross-asset equity-bond momentum. The strategy is discussed in Chapter 15 of our book on *Systematic Investing in Credit* (see Ben Dor et al. 2021).

5. Chapter 21 of Ben Dor et al. (2021) documents that the level of short interest in a company's equity is associated with low subsequent corporate bond returns.

6. For the same reason, we do not have an exact correspondence between the targeted exclusion percentiles and the realized percentage of bonds excluded from the index.

7. See Konstantinovsky et al. (2016).

CHAPTER 7

Incorporating ESG Considerations in Equity Factor Construction

The previous chapter discusses the impact of incorporating ESG considerations in systematic strategies in credit. This chapter focuses on equity factor portfolios, which are stock portfolios defined by common attributes with characteristic risk and return profiles. We examine several methods of incorporating ESG considerations into the factor construction process, and compare their associated effects. As factor portfolios are basic building blocks for systematic strategies in equities, the methodologies we discuss are relevant for a broad range of investors.

Equity factors are typically constructed without any ESG considerations (ESG-agnostic). A key challenge is that there is no uniformly agreed-upon best practice for incorporating ESG considerations into factor portfolio construction, as investors can express ESG considerations in different ways. Moreover, its effects on factor performance and exposure are not well-documented. In the context of factor investing, this is of particular interest, as factors are designed to capture systematic drivers of return or 'styles'. Thus, factor portfolios should preserve a particular factor style even after incorporating ESG considerations.

We consider commonly used approaches to incorporate ESG considerations into portfolio construction and investigate their effects on the risk exposures and performance of equity factors. Those approaches include exclusionary (negative screening) and inclusionary (portfolio optimization with ESG targets) policies.

Negative screening removes stocks from the investible universe based on pre-defined criteria before factor portfolios are constructed. Typical criteria applied by investors relate to a company's activity, such as the manufacturing of controversial weapons, or a company's ESG score. We consider both in this chapter. We show that exclusionary policies can have a material impact on the universe composition, as negative screening can introduce significant sector tilts. In addition, exclusionary policies do not control for exposures to other risk characteristics that drive factor performance. As a consequence, the effect on performance, in particular return correlations with ESG-agnostic portfolios, can be substantial. Moreover, the improvement in a portfolio's average

169

ESG score from exclusionary policies varies across factors and is relatively small in magnitude. One reason for this result is that excluded activities do not necessarily have low ESG scores – a challenge we will discuss in Chapter 13.

As an alternative, portfolio optimization does not initially exclude any stocks from the investible universe. Instead, it maximizes the respective factor exposure while simultaneously preserving other key risk characteristics and targeting a particular improvement of the ESG score. In particular, we consider the improvement of a portfolio's average ESG score relative to that of the ESG-agnostic factor. Thus, portfolio optimization allows for specific ESG-tilts, unlike exclusionary policies in isolation. On the other hand, portfolio optimization does not guarantee the exclusion of specific stocks from portfolios, which may not align with an investor's objective. Overall, we find that portfolio optimization preserves factor style better than exclusionary policies, a consequence of preserving key risk exposures such as sector or market capitalization composition.

The effects of incorporating ESG considerations on factor performance can be decomposed into two channels: a higher exposure to the ESG premium, and a lower exposure to the factor premium. This finding is intuitive, as ESG-agnostic factor portfolios offer the highest possible factor exposure by construction. Introducing an ESG constraint, therefore, leads to a reduction in factor exposure. However, the ESG constraint also results in a higher exposure to the ESG premium, which has on average been positive in the US, Europe, and Japan over the previous decade. Our findings are consistent across seven popular factors in each of these geographies.

Intuitively, the lower factor exposure means that an ESG-tilted factor portfolio participates less in the characteristic factor premium, resulting in milder out- and underperformance. At the same time, its higher exposure to the ESG premium adds an uncorrelated performance component that dominates the effect of a lowered factor exposure in Europe and Japan, where the ESG premium has been more consistent and larger than in the United States.

SAMPLE AND ESG-AGNOSTIC FACTOR PORTFOLIO CONSTRUCTION

A portfolio's ESG score is one of the most commonly used metrics to quantify ESG considerations. In our analysis, we use MSCI's ESG scores. Our choice is for illustrative purposes, and the methodologies discussed in this chapter are universally applicable to other ESG metrics or datasets, such as a portfolio's carbon emissions.

For factor construction, we use *Barclays Equity Factor Scores*,[1] which measure a security's exposure to seven popular factors including Value,

Growth, Quality, Low Volatility, Yield, Momentum, and Size. As benchmarks, we construct ESG-agnostic (or generic) long-only factor portfolios. The portfolios are equal-weighted and rebalanced at monthly frequency. At each rebalancing date, we sort the stock universe into quintiles based on the respective factor score, and allocate the top quintile of highest ranking stocks within their sector into the long portfolio, without any ESG consideration. We report portfolio returns in excess of an equal-weighted portfolio comprising all stocks in the respective market.

The choice of long-only portfolios reflects most common ESG mandates. Moreover, examining the effects of ESG considerations in the context of long-short portfolios requires assumptions about how ESG considerations are treated in the short leg. For example, an investor whose investment universe is restricted by mandate cannot short the very names excluded from the universe. Therefore, we focus in this chapter on long-only portfolios and their returns in excess of market returns.

We consider three separate markets, including the United States, Europe, and Japan. In each market, we construct our samples from the largest 500 stocks for which we observe an ESG and equity factor score. The sample period spans from January 2013 to April 2023.

The ESG Premium has been Positive on Average in the United States, Europe, and Japan over the Past Decade

In Chapter 3, we showed that the US and European ESG return premia have on average been positive over the past decade. In line with our factor construction methodology in this chapter, we measure the ESG premium in a long-only portfolio using the same stock universe with available factor scores. To do so, we follow the methodology discussed in Chapter 3 by maximizing the portfolio's ESG score while matching key risk characteristics and sector weights in each respective market. The resulting return difference between the portfolio and an equal-weighted market portfolio represents the ESG return premium. Figure 7.1 shows that the ESG return premium has been positive and stable in Europe and Japan, while the ESG return premium in the United States mostly materialized in the second half of the sample period. Moreover, we find that the ESG return premium in Japan was highly correlated to the ESG return premium in Europe.

This finding has important implications in the context of factor portfolios that incorporate ESG considerations. These portfolios are expected to have an increased exposure to the ESG return premium. Given our finding that the ESG return premium has on average been positive over the past decade, the performance of an ESG-tilted factor portfolio would likely have benefited from such an increased exposure.

FIGURE 7.1   Cumulative ESG return premium.
Note: Cumulative return of an ESG-maximized portfolio in excess of an equal-weighted benchmark. Largest 500 stocks in the United States, Europe, and Japan with MSCI ESG score coverage.
Source: MSCI, Refinitiv, Barclays Research.

The Correlation Between ESG and Factor Scores is Low in Magnitude

We first inspect whether ESG and factor scores capture similar aspects of a company using a correlation analysis. In the case of high correlations, incorporating ESG considerations into factor portfolio construction might not have a large effect on factor performance and exposure, as the constituents of an ESG-tilted factor portfolio would tend to overlap with its ESG-agnostic counterpart.

However, we find that the correlations between ESG and factor scores are generally low in magnitude and vary across factors and time. Thus, the effect of incorporating ESG considerations on factor performance and exposure is not clear ex-ante, as it is unclear how ESG considerations affect each factor's portfolio compositions. Table 7.1 summarizes the average pairwise cross-sectional

TABLE 7.1   Average monthly pairwise cross-sectional rank correlations between ESG and equity factor scores, January 2013–April 2023.

	Value	Growth	Quality	Yield	LowVol	Momentum	Size
US	−0.04	−0.09	0.11	0.09	0.12	−0.01	−0.07
Europe	−0.04	−0.03	0.08	0.13	0.12	0.01	−0.11
Japan	0.06	−0.04	−0.09	0.09	0.03	0.01	−0.15

Note: Largest 500 stocks in the US, Europe, and Japan with MSCI ESG score coverage
Source: MSCI, Refinitiv, Barclays Research.

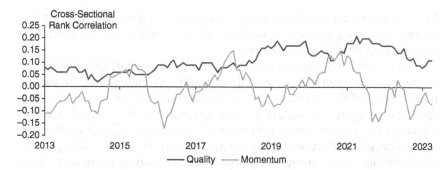

FIGURE 7.2 Monthly cross-sectional rank correlations between factor and ESG scores in the United States.
Note: Monthly cross-sectional rank correlation between ESG and Quality and Momentum scores in the United States. Largest 500 stocks in the US with MSCI ESG score coverage.
Source: MSCI, Refinitiv, Barclays Research.

rank correlations between factor and ESG scores in each market, and shows that our findings are consistent globally. More specifically, we find that the correlation between ESG scores and Quality, Yield, and Low Vol scores tends to be positive in the United States and Europe, as more mature companies tend to have higher ESG scores. On the other hand, the correlation between ESG and Growth and Size scores suggest that smaller, growing companies tend to have lower ESG scores. This may indicate that those companies dedicate fewer resources towards ESG.[2] In Japan, we find that the correlation between ESG and Value scores tends to be positive on average, and the correlation between ESG and Quality scores tends to be negative on average, albeit low in magnitude.

Correlations can vary substantially over time. Figure 7.2 highlights this time-variation and shows the monthly cross-sectional rank correlations between the Quality, respectively Momentum, and ESG scores in the United States. We find that the correlation between ESG and Quality scores has been consistently positive (albeit small in magnitude) over the sample period. On the other hand, Figure 7.2 shows that the correlation between Momentum and ESG scores varies significantly over time and even changes sign. We conclude that the effect of incorporating ESG considerations in the construction of factor portfolios on factor performance and exposure is likely to vary across factors and time.

Average ESG Scores of ESG-agnostic Factors are Close to Universe Average

Next, we investigate an ESG-agnostic factor portfolio's average ESG score, relative to the universe average, and refer to this quantity as *ESG-tilt*. This is an important consideration for investors who aim to improve a factor portfolio's average ESG score, as the ESG-tilt indicates the extent to which a portfolio is already tilted relative to the universe.

We find that ESG-agnostic factor portfolios have small ESG-tilts relative to the universe, which is in line with our previous finding that the correlations between ESG and factor scores are generally low in magnitude. More specifically, Figure 7.3 displays the average ESG score of generic factor portfolios, relative to the average ESG score of the universe in each market. The figure shows that the relative ESG-tilts are typically within +/− 4% across factors, meaning that the average ESG scores of ESG-agnostic factor portfolios is close to the universe average. Moreover, we find that the tilts tend to be stable over time and consistent across markets.

The numbers suggest that each factor's ESG score could probably have been improved significantly. However, an increase in ESG scores comes at the cost of giving up factor exposure. This tradeoff is explained by the ESG-agnostic factor portfolio offering the highest possible exposure to the respective factor by construction, and improving a factor portfolio's ESG score is an additional constraint in portfolio construction. Reducing a portfolio's exposure to the factor premium raises the question whether such a portfolio preserves the original factor style. We address this question in the next sections.

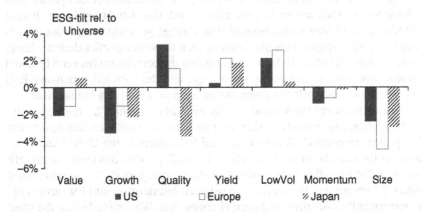

FIGURE 7.3 Average ESG score of factor portfolios relative to the universe average, January 2013–April 2023.
Note: Time-series average of monthly average ESG score of a factor portfolio relative to time-series average of monthly average ESG score of the universe, expressed as a percentage, for each factor and geography. Largest 500 stocks in the United States, Europe, and Japan with MSCI ESG score coverage.
Source: MSCI, Refinitiv, Barclays Research.

INCORPORATING ESG CONSIDERATIONS: EXCLUSIONARY POLICIES

Investors often incorporate ESG considerations through exclusionary policies or negative screening. Negative screening excludes stocks from the investible universe, based on pre-defined criteria. The factor portfolios are then constructed on the remaining (smaller) universe, following the same approach as discussed before. However, there is no best practice for how to screen the universe. For example, an investor might exclude stocks from the investible universe based on a company's revenue exposure to thermal coal, a company's activity (general business model), or ESG score. In its most restrictive form, under SFDR (Sustainable Finance Disclosure Regulation), Article 9 funds are constructed from a heavily restricted universe. To reflect different ways of screening the investible universe, we consider two different exclusionary policies in this chapter: excluding stocks based on a company's activity, and excluding stocks based on a company's ESG score.

Exclusionary policies based on a company's activity are commonly applied by investors. Edwards and Mirchandani (2023) show that exclusionary policies are becoming increasingly important to investors, with 92% (by assets under management [AUM]) of equity ESG funds employing exclusions in 2023. Exclusionary policies are often based on a company's activity, where a common approach is the exclusion of stocks that belong to a specific sub-sector, such as Tobacco. While excluding stocks based on a company's activity is common practice by investors, it involves an element of subjectivity as different investors may exclude different stocks based on their individual screening criteria. To address this ambiguity, we also investigate exclusionary policies based on a company's ESG score relative to peers, which offers a more objective approach due to the numerical nature of the ESG scores. However, the methodologies we use to examine the effects of negative screening on the universe composition or relative factor exposure apply to alternative exclusionary policies.

Universe Composition Differs with the Exclusion Criteria

The first approach we investigate screens the investible universe based on a company's activity. One example is the exclusion of companies that manufacture controversial weapons. We exclude Energy, Aerospace & Defence, Casinos and Gaming, Brewers, Distillers and Vintners, and Tobacco stocks from the investible universe before factor portfolios are constructed, with the list of excluded sub-sectors representing an approximation of the most commonly excluded company activities by investors.[3] In the United States, this approach excludes an average of 52 stocks per month, which reduces the investible universe by ~10% on average.

With the second approach, we exclude stocks based on their ESG score relative to peers.[4] In particular, we exclude the 1% to 20% (in 1% incremental steps) of stocks with the lowest ESG scores. The advantage of this approach is that it is more objective, as no decisions about which company activities to exclude need to be made, and the degree of exclusion can be varied more easily by adjusting the exclusionary thresholds.

Unfortunately, ESG scores can vary considerably across sectors. For example, Energy stocks typically have lower ESG scores than Utility stocks. As a consequence, excluding stocks with the lowest ESG scores from the universe can affect Energy stocks disproportionally compared to Utility stocks. This effect is summarized in Figure 7.4, which compares two ways of screening the universe based on a company's ESG score: excluding the 10% of the stocks from the universe with the lowest ESG scores across sectors, and within each sector. The figure shows that when we exclude stocks based on their relative ESG score across sectors, the number of Energy stocks in the remaining universe drops by ~30% relative to the unrestricted Energy sector, while the number of stocks in the IT sector only drops by ~5%. In contrast, excluding the 10% of stocks with the lowest ESG scores relative to their sector peers preserves

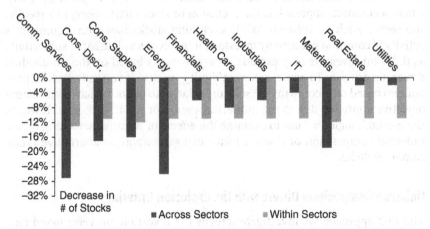

FIGURE 7.4   Sector composition after stock exclusion based on ESG scores: across and within sectors, January 2013–April 2023.
Note: Average decrease in the number of stocks in each sector after excluding the 10% of stocks from the universe with the lowest ESG scores across and within sectors, relative to the number of stocks in each sector in the unscreened universe, expressed as a percentage. Largest 500 stocks in the United States with MSCI ESG score coverage.
Source: MSCI, Refinitiv, Barclays Research.

the relative sector composition in the remaining universe. In the context of factor portfolios, preserving the relative sector composition of the investible universe is desirable, as the factors are constructed to isolate factor performance from sector effects. Therefore, we follow the sector-neutral approach to avoid undesirable sector tilts in the universe going forward.

Screening the universe based on ESG scores preserves the relative sector composition in the eligible universe. This is not the case when stocks are excluded based on a company's activity. This is to be expected as certain company activities, such as the manufacturing of controversial weapons, are only part of particular sub-sectors such as Aerospace & Defence. As a consequence, large portions of entire sectors can be excluded from the universe while the composition of other sectors remains largely unchanged, which is summarized in Figure 7.5. The overall effect is a change in relative sector composition in the remaining universe.

Closely related to the change in sector composition is the fact that neither of the two considered exclusionary policies account for exposures to other risk characteristics. Excluding stocks from the universe can introduce shifts in risk exposures, such as that to the Size factor. This poses a challenge as changes in performance or return dynamics cannot be attributed to the incorporation of ESG considerations alone.

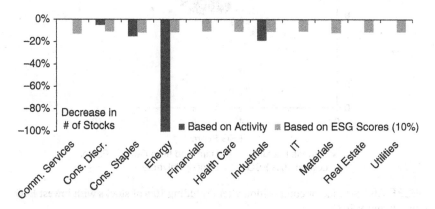

FIGURE 7.5 Sector composition after stock exclusion based on ESG scores and company activity, January 2013–April 2023.
Note: Average decrease in the number of stocks in each sector after excluding the 10% of stocks from the universe with the lowest ESG scores within sectors and based on company activity, relative to the number of stocks in each sector in the unscreened universe, expressed as a percentage. Largest 500 stocks in the United States with MSCI ESG score coverage.
Source: MSCI, Refinitiv, Barclays Research.

The Effect of Negative Screening on a Portfolio's Average ESG Score and Factor Exposure

Negative screening reduces the investible universe and, combined with the low correlations between ESG and factor scores, ultimately changes factor portfolio composition. In this section, we discuss the effects of negative screening on the factor and ESG scores of a portfolio's constituents constructed from a screened universe. In particular, we focus on an exclusionary policy that excludes stocks from the universe based on their ESG scores as it allows us to investigate the effects for targeted degrees of exclusion. We return to the results relating to negative screening based on company activity later.

The factor scores of portfolio constituents quantify a portfolio's factor exposure. Since screening the universe has an effect on portfolio composition, it also affects a portfolio's factor exposure, which we visualize in Figures 7.6 and 7.7. We exclude the 10% of stocks with lowest ESG scores from the US universe, and compare Size and Quality portfolio compositions before and after exclusion as of January 2023. In the scatter plots, each dot represents a stock that is sorted based on its ESG (x-axis) and factor score

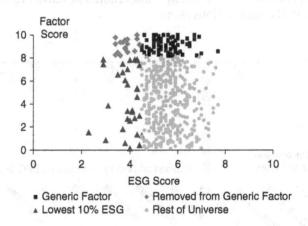

FIGURE 7.6   Size factor composition after excluding 10% of stocks with lowest ESG score, January 2023.
Note: Each dot represents a stock sorted by its ESG score (x-axis) and Size score (y-axis). The triangular dots represent stocks that are excluded from the universe based on their ESG score (lowest 10%). Similarly, the diamond-shaped dots represent stocks that are excluded based on their ESG score (lowest 10%), but that were previously included in the generic Size factor. The square dots represent stocks with the highest Size scores. Largest 500 stocks in the United States with MSCI ESG score coverage.
Source: MSCI, Refinitiv, Barclays Research.

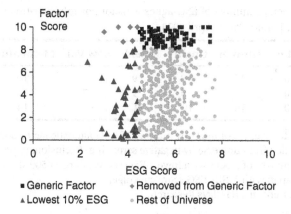

FIGURE 7.7 Quality factor composition after excluding 10% of stocks with lowest ESG score, January 2023.
Note: Each dot represents a stock sorted by its ESG score (x-axis) and Quality score (y-axis). The triangular dots represent stocks that are excluded from the universe based on their ESG score (lowest 10%). Similarly, the diamond-shaped dots represent stocks that are excluded based on their ESG score (lowest 10%), but that were previously included in the generic Quality factor. The square dots represent stocks with the highest Quality scores. Largest 500 stocks in the US with MSCI ESG score coverage.
Source: MSCI, Refinitiv, Barclays Research.

(y-axis). The diamond-shaped and square dots represent the composition of an ESG-agnostic factor portfolio. It comprises stocks with the highest ranking factor scores, which by construction represents a portfolio with the highest possible factor exposure. The triangular dots represent stocks that are excluded from the universe due to their low ESG scores, with the diamond-shaped dots representing stocks that are excluded from the universe, but that were previously constituents of the ESG-agnostic factor portfolio.

There are two key takeaways from the figures. First, the effect on factor exposures is factor-specific. Figure 7.6 shows that excluding 10% of stocks removes 17 stocks from the universe that would have otherwise been included in the ESG-agnostic Size portfolio (diamond-shaped dots). On the other hand, this screen only removes six stocks that would have otherwise been included in the generic Quality factor (diamond-shaped dots in Figure 7.7). Since the factor portfolio constructed from the screened universe has the same number of constituents as the generic portfolio, screened portfolio constituents are replaced with stocks from the remaining universe. Those stocks have, by construction, lower factor scores than the stocks removed from the generic factor portfolio. Thus, negative screening will most likely lead to a reduction in factor exposure. The magnitude depends on the factor and degree of exclusion.

TABLE 7.2 Average number of ESG-agnostic factor portfolio constituents excluded from universe, January 2013–April 2023.

	Value	Growth	Quality	Yield	Low Vol	Momentum	Size
US	10	12	8	9	6	10	11
Europe	10	12	9	9	7	11	14
Japan	10	18	19	11	12	14	14

Note: Time-series average of monthly number of ESG-agnostic factor portfolio constituents excluded from universe by negative screening. Exclusionary policy based on removing the 10% of stocks with lowest ESG scores. Largest 500 stocks in the US, Europe, and Japan with MSCI ESG score coverage.
Source: MSCI, Refinitiv, Barclays Research.

The second takeaway is that negative screening might not lead to a meaningfully higher ESG score at the portfolio level. A change in a portfolio's average ESG score depends on the ESG score distribution of the stocks that replace the stocks that were originally included in the ESG-agnostic factor portfolio. However, negative screening does not take this distribution into account. Moreover, the distribution is factor-specific and can vary over time. As a result, the magnitude of the improvement of a factor portfolio's average ESG score is hard to predict. We return to this finding later in the section.

Figures 7.6 and 7.7 show the effect on the Size and Quality factor composition in the United States in January 2023. Table 7.2 summarizes the average number of screened stocks for each generic factor portfolio for each factor and market, over the entire sample period. As in the previous analysis, the table refers to the case of excluding the 10% of stocks with the lowest ESG scores from the universe. The effect of negative screening tends to be consistent across markets and factors, a finding that is in line with our previous finding that the correlations between ESG and factor scores also tend to be consistent across markets. The table also shows that the effect varies across factors. For example, excluding stocks with the lowest ESG scores tends to have a consistently large effect on the composition of the Size factor, as ESG scores are generally lower for smaller companies.

The Effect of Negative Screening on Factor Style

While factor scores quantify a portfolio's factor exposure, they provide little information (in isolation) about the return dynamics or style of a factor portfolio. However, factor portfolios are designed to capture specific factor dynamics and, thus, incorporating ESG considerations into factor portfolio construction should ideally preserve a factor's return dynamic or style.

To quantify the effect on factor style, we turn to the return correlation between the factor portfolios constructed before and after screening the universe. The higher the correlation, the better the factor style is preserved. In addition, for each factor, we examine the improvement in a portfolio's average ESG score resulting from negative screening – relative to its ESG-agnostic counterpart – and refer to this quantity as ESG-tilt. For robustness, we vary the exclusion threshold from 1% to 20% of stocks with the lowest ESG scores from the universe (in 1% incremental steps), and report the corresponding return correlations and ESG-tilts for each factor. Figure 7.8 summarizes our findings for the United States.

There are two key takeaways. First, negative screening based on ESG scores leads to only moderate improvements in a portfolio's average ESG score. Each dot in Figure 7.8 refers to a different degree of exclusion, spreading horizontally in increasing order corresponding to excluding 1% to 20% of stocks. As expected, increasing the number of stocks excluded from the universe monotonically increases the ESG-tilt. However, even when screening 20% of stocks, the tilts remain moderate. For example, excluding 20% of stocks from the universe leads to an improvement in the Quality portfolio's average ESG score of 6%. This is visualized by the rightmost square dot (on the solid line) corresponding to the Quality factor in Figure 7.8. The average

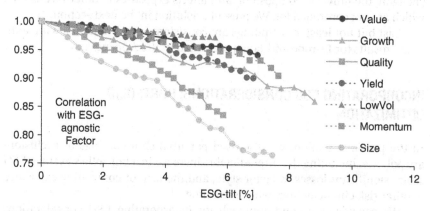

FIGURE 7.8 Effect of negative screening on ESG-tilt and factor style in the United States, January 2013–April 2023.
Note: Return correlations of ESG-tilted with ESG-agnostic factor portfolio (y-axis) and average ESG-tilt (x-axis), relative to ESG-agnostic counterpart, for different levels of stock exclusion and across factors. From left to right, each dot represents an incremental increase in stock exclusion of 1%, ranging from 0% to 20%. Largest 500 stocks in the United States with MSCI ESG score coverage.
Source: MSCI, Refinitiv, Barclays Research.

ESG-tilt across all seven factors is ~7% after excluding 20% of stocks from the universe. Moreover, the ESG-tilts are different across factors for a given level of stock exclusion. Visually, this is shown in Figure 7.8 by the fact that the dots do not align horizontally for a given level of stock exclusion. Second, the loss in factor style varies considerably across factors and can be substantial, even for moderate levels of exclusion. Figure 7.8 shows that for certain factors, such as Size or Quality, the return correlation drops significantly even for moderate levels of stock exclusion. For example, excluding 8% of stocks from the universe leads to a reduction in return correlation of about 10% for the Size factor. On the other hand, the return correlation for the Low Vol factor drops by only 3% even after excluding 20% of stocks from the universe, indicating that the factor style is largely preserved.

From these results it is not clear if a loss in factor style is necessarily detrimental for factor performance. For example, the reduction in correlation may be a result of an increased exposure to the ESG return premium, which historically could have benefited factor performance. Such a factor might outperform its ESG-agnostic counterpart and a reduction in return correlation would not necessarily be seen as negative. Therefore, we would like to decompose the drivers behind these return differences. However, one of the key challenges with negative screening is that the changes in performance cannot be attributed to ESG considerations and loss in factor exposure alone. As discussed before, changing the universe composition also affects exposures to other risk factors, which are not controlled for. We present a solution in the next section.

Last but not least, our findings are consistent across markets, with additional results for Europe and Japan presented in the Appendix.

INCORPORATING ESG CONSIDERATIONS: PORTFOLIO OPTIMIZATION

In the previous section, we discussed potential shortcomings of exclusionary policies, including the unpredictable increase in a portfolio's average ESG score, significant losses in factor style, and the lack of controlling exposures to other risk characteristics when screening.

We consider a second approach for incorporating ESG considerations that addresses these shortcomings: portfolio optimization with ESG targets. Here, we maximize a portfolio's factor exposure subject to ESG and risk exposure constraints. Regarding risk exposures, we match those to the levels (sector weights, size exposure, etc.) of the corresponding ESG-agnostic factor portfolio to allow for an 'apples-to-apples' comparison. The ESG target is measured in a percentage improvement relative to the ESG-agnostic factor portfolio's average ESG score. We consider targets (ESG-tilts) of 1% to 10% (in

TABLE 7.3   Construction details of the portfolio optimization approach.

	ESG-tilted Factor Portfolio
Objective	Maximize factor exposure
ESG Constraint	Improve ESG score relative to generic factor portfolio (e.g. + 5%)
Sector Constraints	Match sector weights of generic factor portfolio
Risk Exposure Constraints	Match risk exposures of generic factor portfolios, except the one that is maximized
	■ Size
	■ Value
	■ Growth
	■ Quality
	■ Yield
	■ Momentum
	■ Low Vol
Weight Constraint	Weights are capped at 1%
Universe	Largest 500 stocks
Rebalancing	At close of last business day each month

Source: Barclays Research.

1% incremental steps). The portfolio weight for each stock is capped at 1% to reduce idiosyncratic movements and align it with the number of stocks in the generic (quintile sort) portfolios. A detailed list of constraints is summarized in Table 7.3.

One key advantage of portfolio optimization with ESG targets is that the effect on performance should largely be driven by a) the higher ESG exposure and b) the lower factor exposure, as all other systematic sources of risk and return are neutralized. Any residual effect is then mostly driven by idiosyncratic movements in the stocks that are not part of both portfolios.

Portfolio Optimization Preserves Factor Style Better Than Negative Screening

For each factor and market, we construct factor portfolios following the portfolio optimization approach for varying degrees of ESG-tilts, ranging from 1% to 10% (in 1% incremental steps). We repeat our analysis from the previous section and examine the effects on factor style and a portfolio's average ESG score. However, the ESG-tilt is now explicitly part of the optimization, such that they are no longer random. Our findings are summarized in Figures 7.9 and 7.10. For expositional clarity, we focus our discussion on two representative examples: the Value and Quality factors in the US market. Our findings are consistent across all factors and markets.

Three findings are worth highlighting. First, across all factors and markets, we find that the portfolio optimization approach consistently preserves factor style better than exclusionary policies for given levels of ESG-tilts. Figures 7.9 and 7.10 show that the returns of (optimized) ESG-tilted portfolios have consistently higher correlations with their ESG-agnostic counterparts than those portfolios constructed after negative screening. For example, the return correlation in Quality performance drops to 0.91 after targeting a 6% ESG-tilt. A similar tilt using negative screening alone requires screening at least 20% of stocks, and reduces correlation to 0.84. The improved factor style preservation is a result of matching risk factor exposures.

Second, we find that across all factors and markets, portfolio optimization can tilt factor portfolios further towards higher ESG scores than exclusionary policies, within reasonable loss levels in factor style. For example, the figures show that the portfolio optimization approach can deliver a relative ESG-tilt of 10%. In contrast, Figure 7.8 shows that even excluding up to 20% of stocks with the lowest ESG scores results in a maximum ESG-tilt of 8.8% for the Growth factor. While the ESG-tilt could theoretically be further increased using the negative screening approach by simply excluding more stocks from the universe, it would involve excluding an unrealistically large portion of stocks from the investible universe. Therefore, we do not consider such cases.

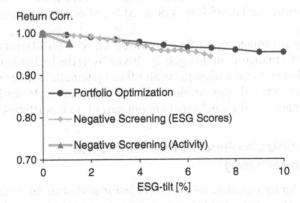

FIGURE 7.9 Effect on ESG-tilt and factor style for Value: negative screening vs portfolio optimization, January 2013–April 2023.
Note: For each approach, return correlations of ESG-tilted with ESG-agnostic factor portfolio (y-axis) and average ESG-tilt (x-axis), relative to ESG-agnostic counterpart, for different levels of stock exclusion and across factors. From left to right, each dot represents an incremental increase in stock exclusion of 1%, ranging from 0% to 20%. Largest 500 stocks in the United States with MSCI ESG score coverage.
Source: MSCI, Refinitiv, Barclays Research.

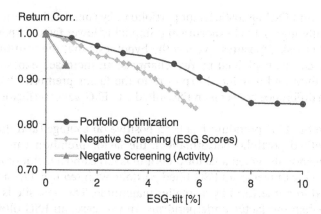

FIGURE 7.10   Effect on ESG-tilt and factor style for Quality: negative screening vs portfolio optimization, January 2013–April 2023.
Note: For each approach, return correlations of ESG-tilted with ESG-agnostic factor portfolio (y-axis) and average ESG-tilt (x-axis), relative to ESG-agnostic counterpart, for different levels of stock exclusion and across factors. From left to right, each dot represents an incremental increase in stock exclusion of 1%, ranging from 0% to 20%. Largest 500 stocks in the United States with MSCI ESG score coverage.
Source: MSCI, Refinitiv, Barclays Research.

Third, we find that excluding stocks from the universe based on corporate activity results in moderate ESG-tilts with more pronounced losses in factor style, shown in Figures 7.9 and 7.10. The moderate ESG-tilts are explained by the fact that the ESG scores of excluded companies are not necessarily low. Aerospace & Defence stocks, for example, have an average ESG score of 4.6 across our sample period, which is close to the universe average. While an investor might be more concerned about a company's activity than ESG score, the loss in factor style is still an important consideration. The exclusionary policy based on company activity excludes on average ~10% of stocks from the universe per month. Interestingly, we find a comparable loss in factor style when the 10% of stocks with the lowest ESG scores are excluded from the universe, however with a larger ESG-tilt.

DECOMPOSING THE RETURN DIFFERENCE BETWEEN ESG-TILTED AND ESG-AGNOSTIC FACTOR PORTFOLIOS

In the previous section, we discussed how careful optimization can introduce an ESG-tilt to a factor portfolio while keeping risk exposures equal to those of its ESG-agnostic counterpart. As a result, the return difference between an

ESG-tilted and ESG-agnostic factor portfolio is, by construction, driven by the intentionally higher ESG exposure and implicitly lower factor exposure, and not by other risk exposures. We test the hypothesis that the resulting return difference can be explained by two channels: an increased exposure to the ESG premium and a reduced exposure to the factor premium. We refer to the return difference between an ESG-tilted and ESG-agnostic factor portfolio as *spread*.

While the ESG premium has been positive on average (and thus would have benefited portfolio performance), the factor premium can vary over time. Conceptually, when a factor premium is large and a factor outperforms the underlying universe, an ESG-tilted portfolio with reduced factor exposure is expected to outperform by a smaller magnitude. The opposite is expected in times when the factor underperforms. In this case, an ESG-tilted portfolio with reduced factor exposure is expected to underperform by a smaller amount. In both scenarios, the higher ESG exposure translates into an additional source of return, the ESG premium. It is uncorrelated to other systematic risks by design, and therefore works as a hedge.

Figures 7.11 and 7.12 visualize this intuition. The figures display cumulative factor returns in excess of an equal-weighted benchmark portfolio comprising all stocks in the universe. Figure 7.11 shows the performance of Value portfolios: the ESG-agnostic portfolio, and two ESG-tilted portfolios with a 1% and 10% tilt. All three portfolios generate almost the same performance

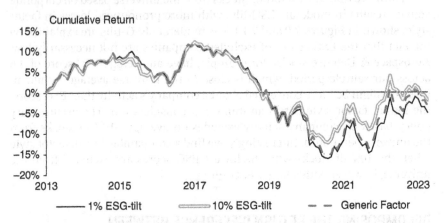

FIGURE 7.11 Cumulative excess returns of generic and ESG-tilted Value factor (United States), January 2013–April 2023.
Note: Cumulative returns in excess of an equal-weighted market portfolio, for selected ESG-tilts. Largest 500 stocks in the United States with MSCI ESG score coverage.
Source: MSCI, Refinitiv, Barclays Research.

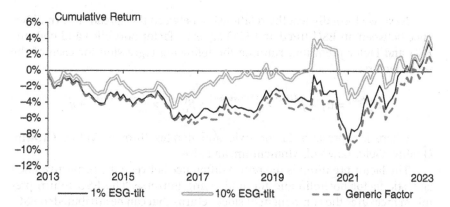

FIGURE 7.12   Cumulative excess returns of generic and ESG-tilted Quality factor (United States), January 2013–April 2023.
Note: Cumulative returns in excess of an equal-weighted market portfolio, for selected ESG-tilts. Largest 500 stocks in the US with MSCI ESG score coverage.
Source: MSCI, Refinitiv, Barclays Research.

during the first half of our sample period, and then diverge in the second half. This result is in line with our previous finding that the factor exposure of an ESG-tilted Value portfolio largely aligns with the ESG-agnostic Value portfolio. Moreover, the ESG premium in the United States mostly materializes in the second half of the sample, explaining the relative outperformance of the ESG-tilted Value factor from 2020 onwards.

For Quality, the dynamics look different, but are in line with our understanding of having two distinct channels. The ESG-tilted portfolios, shown in Figure 7.12, outperform the ESG-agnostic portfolio in the first half of the sample, to then again converge in the second half. This aligns with our previous finding, that the loss in factor exposure for ESG-tilted Quality portfolios is more pronounced. As a consequence, the ESG-tilted Quality portfolios participate less in the factor premium, meaning the ESG-tilted portfolios outperform the ESG-agnostic portfolio during its weak performance in the first half. They then underperform the ESG-agnostic factor portfolio in the second half of the sample, when the ESG-agnostic Quality portfolio mostly outperforms the universe.

Figures 7.11 and 7.12 show that an ESG-tilted factor portfolio does not necessarily outperform its ESG-agnostic counterpart. This is because the aggregate effect depends on the magnitude of the respective premium and its exposure, which is factor-specific. This is an important finding, as an investor's decision to incorporate ESG considerations into factor portfolio construction may not be motivated by performance considerations, but by improving a portfolio's ESG score – with the goal of preserving factor style.

Next, we formally test the relationship between the spread (return difference between an ESG-tilted and ESG-agnostic factor portfolio) and both the ESG and factor premium, running the following regression for each of the seven factors:

$$r_{t,k}^{(spread)} = \alpha_K + \beta_k^{(ESG)} \times r_t^{(ESG\ premium)} + \beta_k^{(factor)} \times r_{t,k}^{(factor\ premium)} + \varepsilon_{t,k}$$

where k represents factor style and iterates through Value, Growth, Quality, Yield, Low Vol, Momentum, and Size.

The factor premium is the return difference between the respective ESG-agnostic factor portfolio and the underlying universe. The ESG return premium measures the component of stock returns that can be attributed to ESG: it is the return difference between a portfolio that maximizes ESG scores while matching key risk characteristics of the underlying universe, and the underlying universe itself. Since any ESG-tilted factor portfolio matches the risk characteristics of the ESG-agnostic counterpart, the regression setup effectively estimates the contribution of the ESG and factor premium to the spread. We focus our attention on the significance of the coefficient estimates. According to our hypothesis, both the ESG and factor premium should be important contributors to the spread, at least for more material ESG-tilts.

Figures 7.13 and 7.14 display the resulting t-statistics of the two beta coefficients. The figures show that for larger ESG-tilts, the coefficients turn

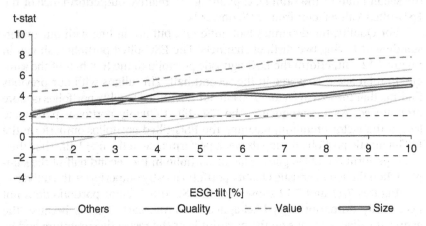

FIGURE 7.13 t-statistics for ESG premium beta per ESG-improvement, January 2013–April 2023.
Note: t-statistics of ESG premium coefficients across factors and for varying levels of ESG-tilts. Largest 500 stocks in the United States with MSCI ESG score coverage. Positive t-statistic indicates positive coefficient.
Source: MSCI, Refinitiv, Barclays Research.

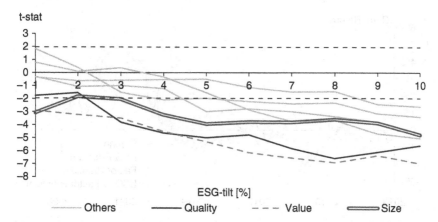

FIGURE 7.14 *t*-statistics for factor premium beta per ESG-improvement, January 2013–April 2023.
Note: *t*-statistics of factor premium coefficients across factors and for varying levels of ESG-tilts. Largest 500 stocks in the United States with MSCI ESG score coverage. Negative *t*- statistic indicates negative coefficient.
Source: MSCI, Refinitiv, Barclays Research.

statistically significant across all seven factors. Moreover, it can be seen that the ESG premium coefficient is positive, while the factor premium coefficient is negative, confirming our previously formulated intuition: a positive ESG-tilt translates to higher ESG-exposure but lower factor exposure.

We now turn to decomposing the spread with the help of the regression model. By multiplying the beta estimates with the ESG and respective factor premium, we obtain an estimate of the contribution of each premium over time (under the assumption that the beta estimate is representative across the entire sample period). Figures 7.15 and 7.16 display the decomposition. For clarity and simplicity, the figures focus on the Value and Quality factor in the United States alone. We expand this analysis to all factors and markets in the next section.

Three findings are worth highlighting. First, we find that the contributions from the ESG premium and the factor premium are comparable in magnitude. Second, the figures are aligned with our previous findings that the ESG premium in the United States mostly materialized in the second half of the past decade. Third, the decomposition does not perfectly explain the spread. However, this is expected as the regressions are estimated over the entire sample period and, therefore, capture average effects. Moreover, the regression model assumes a linear relationship between the spread and the ESG and factor premiums. Nonetheless, Figures 7.15 and 7.16 show that the combined decomposition, which is displayed by the double line, captures the return dynamics of the spread well.

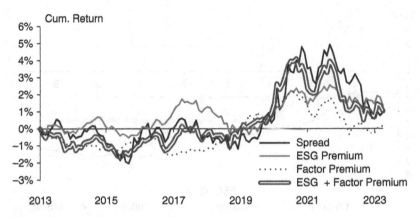

FIGURE 7.15 Decomposing the effect on Value performance for 10% ESG-tilt (United States), January 2013–April 2023.
Note: Cumulative return of the ESG Value spread, and its decomposition into the ESG premium and factor premium component. Largest 500 stocks in the United States with MSCI ESG score coverage.
Source: MSCI, Refinitiv, Barclays Research.

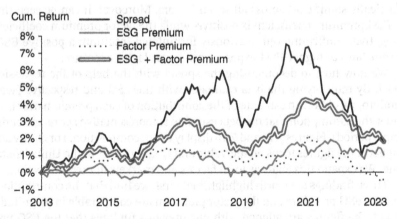

FIGURE 7.16 Decomposing the effect on Quality performance for 10% ESG-tilt (United States), January 2013–April 2023.
Note: Cumulative return of the ESG Quality spread, and its decomposition into the ESG premium and factor premium component. Largest 500 stocks in the United States with MSCI ESG score coverage.
Source: MSCI, Refinitiv, Barclays Research.

CONSISTENT RESULTS ACROSS MARKETS

We repeat the analysis from the previous section in Europe and Japan, and decompose the return difference between the ESG-tilted and ESG-agnostic factor portfolio for each factor. Our findings are consistent across all markets: the contribution from the ESG and factor premium are statistically significant, especially for larger ESG-tilts. Moreover, we confirm our previous finding that the ESG premium contributes positively to the spread, while the reduced factor exposure of the ESG-tilted factor portfolios lowers the contribution from the factor premium. This finding is intuitive, as the underlying trade-off between increasing the exposure to the ESG premium at the cost of giving up exposure to the factor premium generalizes across markets.

Most importantly, we find that the ESG return premium has been larger in Europe and Japan than in the United States. Accordingly, the contribution from the ESG return premium was larger in these two markets. At the same time, we find that the contribution from the factor premium was of similar magnitude as in the United States, indicating that incorporating ESG considerations into factor portfolio construction resulted in a comparable reduction in factor exposure across markets.

As a consequence of those two dynamics, the return difference between ESG-tilted and ESG-agnostic factor portfolios has been larger in Europe and Japan. In other words, the performance of factor portfolios in Europe and Japan was more strongly affected from incorporating ESG considerations: returns were higher on average, but correlation between ESG-tilted and ESG-agnostic factors was lower.

Figures 7.17 and 7.18 visualize this finding. For clarity and simplicity, the figures focus on the Quality factor alone and show the cumulative return of the ESG and factor premium contribution to the spread across markets. In particular, the figures summarize our findings for factor portfolios with a 10% ESG-tilt. Figure 7.17 shows that the performance of the ESG-tilted factors consistently benefited from the larger ESG premium in Europe and Japan. Aligned with our previous finding, the figure also shows that the ESG premium contributes to the spread from the beginning of the sample, whereas it materializes later in the United States. Interestingly, Figure 7.18 shows that the cumulative contribution from the factor premium over the period was close to zero in all three markets.

Looking beyond the Quality factor, Table 7.4 summarizes the annualized average return of the ESG and factor premium component in the spread decomposition across all seven factors and markets. Note that the spread includes a component that is unexplained by the ESG and factor premium,

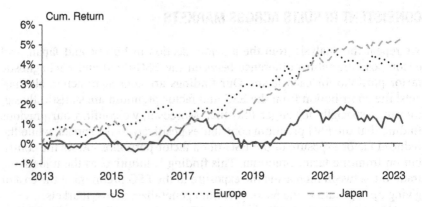

FIGURE 7.17 Cumulative return of the ESG premium contribution in the spread decomposition for the Quality factor across regions, January 2013–April 2023.
Note: Cumulative return of the ESG premium component across markets. Largest 500 stocks in the United States, Europe, and Japan with MSCI ESG score coverage.
Source: MSCI, Refinitiv, Barclays Research.

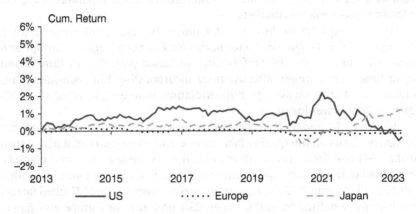

FIGURE 7.18 Cumulative return of the factor premium contribution in the spread decomposition for the Quality factor across regions, January 2013–April 2023.
Note: Cumulative return of the factor premium component across markets. Largest 500 stocks in the United States, Europe, and Japan with MSCI ESG score coverage.
Source: MSCI, Refinitiv, Barclays Research.

such that the decomposition is not additive. This is expected, as the regressions are run over the entire sample and, therefore, capture average effects. Moreover, the regression setup assumes a linear relationship between the spread and the ESG, respectively factor premium, by construction.

Table 7.4 shows that the effect from the increased exposure to the ESG premium has been positive across all factors and markets over the past decade.

TABLE 7.4   Annualized average factor returns, and their decompositions across markets, January 2013–April 2023.

	Value	Growth	Quality	Yield	Low Vol	Momentum	Size
United States							
Generic Factor	−0.16	−0.05	0.17	0.77	−0.57	0.11	−0.95
ESG Premium Component	0.13	0.13	0.10	0.12	0.08	0.07	0.10
Factor Premium Component	0.02	0.01	−0.04	−0.08	0.05	−0.01	0.24
ESG-tilted Factor (10%)	−0.06	−0.33	0.34	0.39	−0.70	0.31	−1.07
Europe							
Generic Factor	−0.78	1.30	0.43	1.09	0.50	0.67	−0.31
ESG Premium Component	0.43	0.40	0.38	0.47	0.43	0.30	0.47
Factor Premium Component	0.10	−0.16	−0.01	−0.17	−0.08	−0.08	0.06
ESG-tilted Factor (10%)	0.14	1.93	1.37	1.58	0.98	1.56	0.51
Japan							
Generic Factor	2.48	−0.14	−1.19	0.87	−1.63	0.61	−0.76
ESG Premium Component	0.47	0.69	0.49	0.62	0.75	0.64	0.40
Factor Premium Component	−0.43	0.01	0.11	−0.06	0.22	−0.08	0.17
ESG-tilted Factor (10%)	2.35	0.36	−0.09	2.03	−1.34	0.38	−0.17

Note: This table reports annualized average returns, with the generic and ESG-tilted factor returns reported in excess of an equal-weighted market portfolio. Note that the spread includes an unexplained component (residual term from the regression), such that the sum of the ESG and factor premium do not necessarily add up to the spread. Largest 500 stocks in the United States, Europe, and Japan with MSCI ESG score coverage.
Source: MSCI, Refinitiv, Barclays Research.

The table also shows that this effect has been larger in Europe and Japan than in the United States. For example, the annualized average return of the ESG premium component was 0.10% for the Quality factor in the United States, while it was 0.38%, respectively 0.49%, in Europe and Japan. On average, the annualized average return of the ESG premium component is 0.10% in the United States, and 0.41%, respectively 0.58%, in Europe and Japan.

The table also confirms our previous finding that the factor premium component tends to be smaller in magnitude than the ESG premium component. Moreover, the magnitude of the average return of the factor premium component is comparable across markets, averaging 0.03% in the United States, and −0.05%, respectively −0.01%, in Europe and Japan. Thus, the average spread in Europe and Japan is mostly driven by the ESG-premium. The table shows that the average spread is consistently larger in Europe and Japan, with the exception of the Value and Momentum factors in Japan. In Europe, the average spread is positive across all factors, while it is negative for four out of seven factors in the United States. This finding is consistent with the results in Chapter 3, which shows that the ESG return premium has historically been larger in Europe.

CONCLUSION

We address different methods of incorporating ESG considerations into factor portfolio construction and discuss their effects on factor performance and exposure. We find that the loss in factor style can be significant in factor portfolios that incorporate ESG considerations based on exclusionary policies – a consequence of a reduced investment universe and unintended exposures to other risk factors.

On the other hand, portfolio optimization enables specific ESG-tilts while also controlling for other risk exposures without initially excluding any stocks from the universe. As a result, factor style is consistently better preserved across all factors and markets compared to an exclusionary policy. In practice, negative screening and portfolio optimization are often combined as portfolio optimization can help mitigate some of the drawbacks from mandatory exclusionary policies imposed by, for example, Paris-aligned benchmarks (PAB).

We show that the return difference between an ESG-tilted and ESG-agnostic factor portfolio can be decomposed into two main channels: a higher exposure to the ESG return premium, which we find has been on average positive over the past decade in the United States, Europe, and Japan, and the reduced exposure to the factor premium. In the United States, we find that both contributed similarly in magnitude to the ESG-tilted factor performance. In Europe and Japan, we find that the ESG return premium has been larger than in the United States. Thus, the performance of factor portfolios in Europe and Japan has tended to be higher after incorporating ESG considerations, as the increased exposure to the ESG return premium dominated the effect from the lower participation in the factor premium.

Our findings suggest that incorporating ESG considerations into factor portfolio construction can result in meaningful improvements in ESG scores without a large reduction in the characteristic behaviour of the respective factor. However, investors should be mindful of controlling exposures to other risk characteristics.

APPENDIX: EFFECT OF NEGATIVE SCREENING ON ESG-TILT AND FACTOR STYLE IN EUROPE AND JAPAN

Figure 7.A1 and Figure 7.A2 show the effect of negative screening based on ESG scores on a portfolio's ESG-tilt and factor style in Europe and Japan.

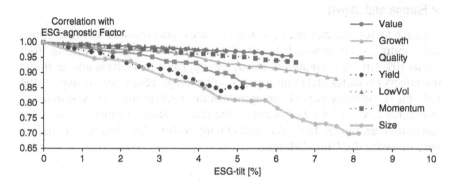

FIGURE 7.A1 Effect of negative screening on ESG-tilt and factor style in Europe, January 2013–April 2023.
Note: Return correlations of ESG-tilted with ESG-agnostic factor portfolio (y-axis) and average ESG-tilt (x-axis), relative to ESG-agnostic counterpart, for different levels of stock exclusion and across factors. From left to right, each dot represents an incremental increase in stock exclusion of 1%, ranging from 0% to 20%. Largest 500 stocks in Europe with MSCI ESG score coverage.
Source: MSCI, Refinitiv, Barclays Research.

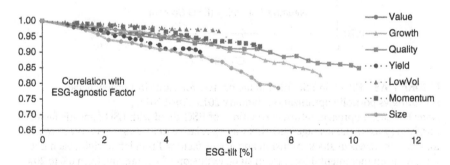

FIGURE 7.A2 Effect of negative screening on ESG-tilt and factor style in Japan, January 2013–April 2023.
Note: Return correlations of ESG-tilted with ESG-agnostic factor portfolio (y-axis) and average ESG-tilt (x-axis), relative to ESG-agnostic counterpart, for different levels of stock exclusion and across factors. From left to right, each dot represents an incremental increase in stock exclusion of 1%, ranging from 0% to 20%. Largest 500 stocks in Japan with MSCI ESG score coverage.
Source: MSCI, Refinitiv, Barclays Research.

We vary the exclusion threshold from 1% to 20% of stocks with the lowest ESG scores from the universe (in 1% incremental steps), and report the corresponding return correlations and ESG-tilts for each factor. Our findings are in line with those for the United States.

Effect of Portfolio Optimization on ESG-tilt and Factor Style in Europe and Japan

For each factor and market, we construct factor portfolios following the portfolio optimization approach for varying degrees of ESG-tilts, ranging from 1% to 10% (in 1% incremental steps). We repeat our analysis and examine the effects on factor style and a portfolio's average ESG score. However, the ESG-tilt is explicitly part of the optimization. Our findings are summarized in Figures 7.A3 to 7.A6. For clarity in the visualization, we focus on two representative examples: The Value and Quality factors. Our findings are in line with those for the United States.

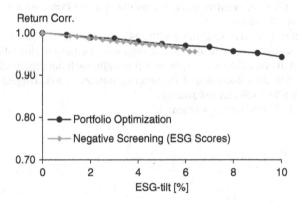

FIGURE 7.A3 Effect on ESG-tilt and factor style for Value in Europe: negative screening vs portfolio optimization, January 2013–April 2023.
Note: For each approach, return correlations of ESG-tilted with ESG-agnostic factor portfolio (y-axis) and average ESG-tilt (x-axis), relative to ESG-agnostic counterpart, for different levels of stock exclusion and across factors. From left to right, each dot represents an incremental increase in stock exclusion of 1%, ranging from 0% to 20%. Largest 500 stocks in Europe with MSCI ESG score coverage.
Source: MSCI, Refinitiv, Barclays Research.

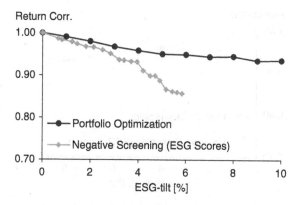

FIGURE 7.A4   Effect on ESG-tilt and factor style for Quality in Europe: negative screening vs portfolio optimization, January 2013–April 2023.
Note: For each approach, return correlations of ESG-tilted with ESG-agnostic factor portfolio (y-axis) and average ESG-tilt (x-axis), relative to ESG-agnostic counterpart, for different levels of stock exclusion and across factors. From left to right, each dot represents an incremental increase in stock exclusion of 1%, ranging from 0% to 20%. Largest 500 stocks in Europe with MSCI ESG score coverage.
Source: MSCI, Refinitiv, Barclays Research.

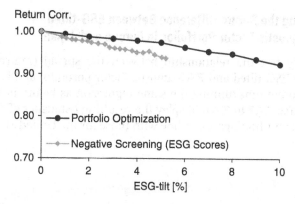

FIGURE 7.A5   Effect on ESG-tilt and factor style for Value in Japan: negative screening vs portfolio optimization, January 2013–April 2023.
Note: For each approach, return correlations of ESG-tilted with ESG-agnostic factor portfolio (y-axis) and average ESG-tilt (x-axis), relative to ESG-agnostic counterpart, for different levels of stock exclusion and across factors. From left to right, each dot represents an incremental increase in stock exclusion of 1%, ranging from 0% to 20%. Largest 500 stocks in Japan with MSCI ESG score coverage.
Source: MSCI, Refinitiv, Barclays Research.

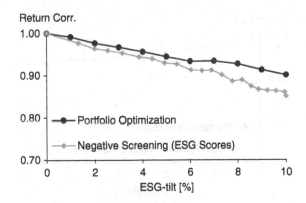

FIGURE 7.A6   Effect on ESG-tilt and factor style for Quality in Japan: negative screening vs portfolio optimization, January 2013–April 2023.
Note: For each approach, return correlations of ESG-tilted with ESG-agnostic factor portfolio (y-axis) and average ESG-tilt (x-axis), relative to ESG-agnostic counterpart, for different levels of stock exclusion and across factors. From left to right, each dot represents an incremental increase in stock exclusion of 1%, ranging from 0% to 20%. Largest 500 stocks in Japan with MSCI ESG score coverage.
Source: MSCI, Refinitiv, Barclays Research.

Decomposing the Return Difference Between ESG-tilted and ESG-agnostic Factor Portfolios in Europe and Japan

We formally test the relationship between the spread (return difference between an ESG-tilted and ESG-agnostic factor portfolio) and both the ESG and factor premium, running the same regression as before in Europe and Japan. Figures 7.A7 to 7.A10 display the resulting *t*-statistics of the two beta coefficients. Our findings are in line with those for the United States.

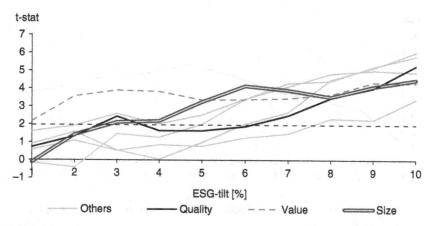

FIGURE 7.A7 *t*-statistics for ESG premium beta per ESG-improvement in Europe, January 2013–April 2023.
Note: *t*-statistics of ESG premium coefficients across factors and for varying levels of ESG-tilts. Largest 500 stocks in Europe with MSCI ESG score coverage. Positive *t*-statistic indicates positive coefficient.
Source: MSCI, Refinitiv, Barclays Research.

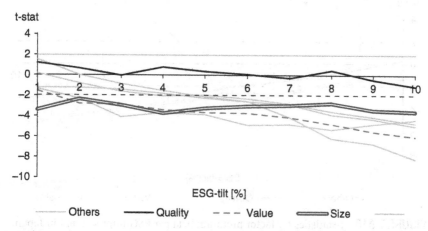

FIGURE 7.A8 *t*-statistics for factor premium beta per ESG-improvement in Europe, January 2013–April 2023.
Note: *t*-statistics of factor premium coefficients across factors and for varying levels of ESG-tilts. Largest 500 stocks in Europe with MSCI ESG score coverage. Negative *t*-statistic indicates negative coefficient.
Source: MSCI, Refinitiv, Barclays Research.

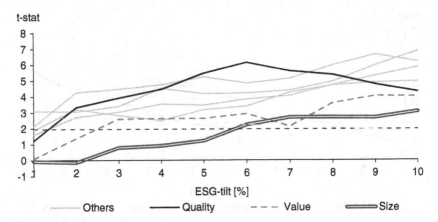

FIGURE 7.A9   *t*-statistics for ESG premium beta per ESG-improvement in Japan, January 2013–April 2023.
Note: *t*-statistics of ESG premium coefficients across factors and for varying levels of ESG-tilts. Largest 500 stocks in Japan with MSCI ESG score coverage. Positive *t*-statistic indicates positive coefficient.
Source: MSCI, Refinitiv, Barclays Research.

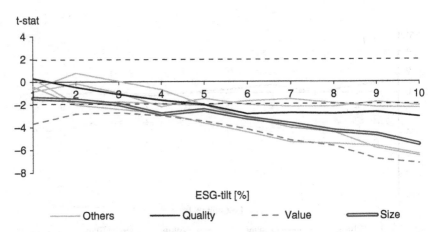

FIGURE 7.A10   *t*-statistics for factor premium beta per ESG-improvement in Japan, January 2013–April 2023.
Note: *t*-statistics of factor premium coefficients across factors and for varying levels of ESG-tilts. Largest 500 stocks in Japan with MSCI ESG score coverage. Negative *t*-statistic indicates negative coefficient.
Source: MSCI, Refinitiv, Barclays Research.

REFERENCES

Ben Dor, A. and Florig, S. (2021). Introducing Barclays Equity Factors. *Barclays Research*, 24 March.

Edwards, C., Gordon, C., and Dani, S. (2022). Getting Serious on ESG. *Barclays Research*, 7 September.

Edwards, C. and Mirchandani, D. (2023). Zones of Exclusion: Everything, Everywhere, But Not All At Once. *Barclays Research*, 22 May.

Gaspari, C., Vincenzini, J., Picagne, P., O'Neal, M., Edwards, C., and Mirchandani, D. (2023). Opportunities, Challenges and Constraints in ESG Investments. *Barclays Research*, 12 May.

NOTES

1. See Ben Dor and Florig (2021).
2. See Edwards et al. (2022), where the ESG Research Team at Barclays showed that smaller companies struggle the most with the cost of ESG disclosure requirements.
3. See, for example, Gaspari et al. (2023), which examines commonly used screens by European insurers. The exclusion of Energy stocks reflects common restrictions in Paris-aligned investment universes.
4. Note that the methodologies discussed also apply to exclusionary policies based on absolute ESG scores. For example, excluding all stocks with MSCI ESG scores < 3 (scale 0–10).

Three

Performance Implications of Companies' ESG Policies

INTRODUCTION TO PART III

We now shift our focus from the implications of ESG policy for an investor to its implications for an issuer. There is no doubt that one of the goals of ESG investing is to influence the behaviour of companies and incentivize them to move in the direction of more sustainable business practices. The companies' ability to improve their ESG profiles may differ significantly along the Environmental, Social, and Governance directions. The key question for issuers is whether the investments they make to become more sustainable are rewarded by the market in the form of better scores and improved performance and valuation of their debt and equity securities. If so, are these rewards different across the three pillars of the ESG score?

One of the arguments for the best-in-class approach to ESG investing, as opposed to the negative screening of entire industries, is that it can allow investors to provide incentive even to issuers in activities considered problematic. Another approach that some investors take is to target ESG improvers. For example, instead of a blanket exclusion on all utilities that use coal, one could choose to invest in the issuers that are doing the most to reduce their reliance on coal. In Chapter 8, we investigate the effects of such an approach.

Rather than looking at the level of ESG ratings, as in previous chapters, we focus on changes in these ratings, which we refer to as ESG momentum. We examine whether improving ESG scores have led to superior performance of the firm's debt and equity vs risk-matched peers. Was the outperformance due to ESG momentum significant, even after controlling for the level of the ESG scores?

One of the main things a company can do in order to change its ESG profile is to hire professionals into dedicated roles to create and manage its ESG policies. In Chapter 9, we investigate whether companies that invested more than their peers in ESG-related hiring were subsequently rewarded by improvement in their ESG scores. To do so, we employ a novel dataset of job postings by US firms, as well as natural language processing, to identify ESG-related openings and assess the planned ESG activities of firms in our sample. We posit that ESG job postings data can serve as a leading indicator of future changes in firms' ESG ratings, given the time lag between hiring decisions for ESG-related roles and the implications on the firms' operations and activities. We find that firms with higher 'abnormal' ESG posting intensity were more likely to experience improvements in ESG ratings and higher subsequent stock returns.

Of the three ESG pillars, it stands to reason that governance scores should be most directly connected to financial performance. We have seen some reflections of this earlier. We have demonstrated links between governance scores and credit ratings for corporates in Chapter 2 and for sovereigns in Chapter 4. In Chapter 10, we study the relationship between a company's governance scores and its profitability. We show how to accurately measure the effect of corporate governance on future earnings while accounting for other relevant firm characteristics. These methods can be extended to examine the relationship between other ESG characteristics and firm financial-performance metrics.

Answering these questions empirically, based on historical data, is important to both investors and issuers.

CHAPTER 8

ESG Rating Improvement and Subsequent Portfolio Performance

In Chapters 2 and 3, we measure the return effects from incorporating ESG considerations – using an exposure-matched approach to control for key risk characteristics and sector allocations. We find that firms with higher MSCI ESG scores indeed had higher corporate bond and stock returns in both the United States and Europe after controlling for other risk factors.

Besides a firm's ESG level, its ESG momentum (i.e. changes in ESG scores) may also matter for performance. This is because investors may take ESG momentum into consideration when making investment decisions. For example, ESG investors may not only favour companies with high current ESG scores, but also prefer companies in the process of improving their ESG scores (i.e. with positive ESG momentum). Some investors may even prefer a company with a lower ESG score but stronger ESG momentum to one that already scores high. With this in mind, we examine whether ESG momentum has a separate effect from the ESG level on returns. In other words, would two companies with the same ESG scores have different returns if their ESG momentum had been different?

While conceptually simple, isolating the effect of ESG momentum is complicated because of a number of challenges. The first challenge is the need to separate the effect of momentum from the effect of level in ESG scores, as the two are related. A company that just experienced an increase in ESG scores (positive momentum) tends to end up with higher ESG scores, leading to a positive correlation between momentum and level. Without proper control of ESG levels, any positive return effect we pick up on ESG momentum may actually be a manifestation of the positive ESG level effect documented in Chapters 2 and 3. The second challenge is the need to isolate the systematic drivers of returns so that they don't contaminate the return effect from ESG momentum. The third is the need to make sure that the effects are not driven by idiosyncratic returns from a small number of companies. In this chapter, we investigate the ESG momentum effect by building on the exposure-matched approach developed in Chapters 2 and 3. By design, the exposure-matched approach can address the second challenge by matching the risk characteristics in the portfolio pair that maximize and minimize ESG momentum respectively and the third challenge by imposing a weight cap on each individual issuer to ensure diversification. For the first challenge, we modify the portfolio construction to address the linkage between ESG level and momentum: the pair of portfolios are now required to have the same average ESG level. This additional constraint ensures that the level effect will not drive the return difference between the Max- and Min-ESG momentum portfolios. Moreover, compared to an alternative regression approach discussed in detail in Chapter 3, the exposure-matched approach not only has the ability to measure the ESG momentum effect accurately, but also offers an easy way to capture it for investors in practice.[1]

Because ESG is a firm-level attribute and the effect of ESG momentum is relevant to both equity and bond investors, we examine the ESG momentum effect in equities and bonds in parallel. A similar approach was applied in several studies, for example to evaluate the post-earnings-announcement drift phenomenon (Ben Dor et al. 2020) and the application of natural language processing to earnings call transcripts for return prediction (Ben Dor et al. 2019). Conducting such studies (which we term 'integrated studies') is challenging as it requires both detailed security-level pricing and analytics data as well as knowledge of equity and credit markets, but has several important benefits. First, the analysis will be applicable to a much larger universe of investors given the investor base in the two markets is distinct. Second, the analysis can cross-validate the existence of a certain phenomena, confirming that it is not a result of data mining. Furthermore, comparing dynamics across asset classes may also help investors better understand the core dynamics of the effect. To ensure comparability, we specifically construct the equity and credit portfolios for the same sample period and in similar ways (except having different key risk characteristics specific to each asset class).

This chapter is organized along the following outline. We first examine various dynamics related to ESG score changes – such as magnitude, updating frequency and timing – that can affect the construction of the ESG momentum portfolios. Next we describe the exposure-matched approach in detail, including the risk characteristics being matched and the over/underweight constraint for diversification. Then we examine the ESG momentum effects in equities and credit jointly by comparing their dynamics at different ESG levels and in each individual pillar. Next we compare the ESG level and momentum effects and evaluate the benefit of combining them. We then proceed to test the consistency of the ESG momentum effect in different universes (Russell 1000 and 2000, and HY bonds), using a more frequently updated score, at various diversification levels and rebalancing horizons. We conclude by discussing the versatility of the exposure-matched approach.

DATA: UNDERSTANDING ESG SCORE CHANGES

Source of ESG Scores

Our analysis relies on MSCI ESG scores, a more detailed description of which can be found in Chapter 3. MSCI has pillar level (E, S, and G) as well as composite scores, all ranging from 0 to 10, with 0 and 10 indicating the maximum and minimum level of key ESG-related risk respectively. Our analysis focuses mostly on the dynamics of the composite ESG scores since they represent a more comprehensive picture of firms' ESG practices, but we also present results for the individual pillars.

MSCI monitor companies' ESG metrics on a daily basis and also conduct in-depth full score reviews on an annual basis, based on a broad set of inputs, such as macro data at segment level, company disclosures, and government databases.[2] The full reviews are usually carried out around the same time for firms from similar industries, but the timing can differ between industries. Unlike daily monitoring, ratings from in-depth full reviews are validated by ESG analysts and hence are more thorough. In addition, as suggested by MSCI, ratings from full reviews are also less noisy. Taking into consideration the accuracy advantage, our analysis uses changes in MSCI's full review scores as a measure of ESG momentum.

Sample Construction

In equities, we focus on the universe of companies included in the S&P 500 index, but also analyse broader universes of firms constituting the Russell 1000 and 2000 Indices. MSCI has high coverage of S&P 500 and Russell 1000 (above 90%) starting in 2009, and decent coverage (above 70%) for Russell 2000 starts in 2013.

In credit, we start with the bonds in the Bloomberg US Corporate index (investment grade [IG] universe) with MSCI ESG scores, and later expand to the US High Yield (HY) index. The coverage of MSCI ESG scores is high for the US Corporate index (above 95%) and lower but reasonable for the HY Index (~80%) towards the end of the sample period in terms of both total market value and number of securities. The detailed numbers are reported in the Appendix.

To ensure that the final credit results are not driven by illiquid bonds, whose recorded prices may not reflect their actual market value, we apply a set of liquidity filters to exclude the following illiquid bonds from being added[3] to a portfolio in both IG and HY:

- Bonds with remaining time to maturity < 3 years (bonds with less than 1 year remaining maturity would have to exit the index and become less liquid)

- Bonds in bottom (illiquid) five TES (Trade Efficiency Scores) buckets (out of 10)
- Bonds with market values below the 25th percentile that have been issued more than a year prior (i.e. 'off-the-run' small bonds) are excluded as well to ensure the resulting sample is reasonably liquid.

Next we discuss various aspects of analysis formulation, including the choice of lookback window for calculating ESG momentum, magnitude of ESG momentum, and the rebalancing frequency. Since the dynamics of ESG momentum are not asset-class specific, for the interest of brevity we only present the descriptive statistics of ESG momentum for the S&P 500 universe. The subsequent performance analysis is asset-class specific, so we present it for both the equity and bond universes separately.

Length of Lookback Window

One key parameter in forming any type of momentum indicator is the length of the 'lookback' window,[4] which presents a trade-off: a shorter window would result in more observations with unchanged scores, hence uninformative, while a longer window would lead to more observations but their informational content may be stale (e.g. with a 24-month lookback window, the change could have happened 23 months ago). When the lookback window is either too short or too long, the ESG momentum measure may not reflect relevant information for many of the firms, and therefore would not be predictive of future performance. The appropriate lookback window should be aligned with ESG scores' update frequency to balance the two effects.

Panel A of Figure 8.1 reports the average number of ESG score changes per company per year, averaged across all companies. The results suggest that ESG scores were updated annually on average, consistent with the frequency described by MSCI. To get a sense of how different lookback windows affect population size, Panel B lists the percentage of firms in the universe with non-zero ESG score changes for several lookback windows (1m, 3m, 6m, 12m, and 24m), for three sub-periods with roughly equal length. For lookback windows of 1–6m, less than 50% of firms experienced a change in their ESG score, whereas for 12m and 24m windows, the majority of firms experienced changes. However, there is no substantial benefit of going from 12m to 24m, as the increase in the percentage of firms with non-zero ESG changes is limited, especially in the later part of the sample period.

Magnitude of ESG Momentum

Based on Figure 8.1, we decide to use a 12-month lookback window to calculate momentum in our main analysis. This window results in portfolios

Panel A: Average number of annual ESG score changes per issuer by year (S&P 500 universe)

Panel B: Percentage of firms with non-zero ESG score changes by length of lookback window and period (S&P 500 universe)

Sub-Period	1m (%)	Lookback Window				
		3m (%)	6m (%)	12m (%)	24m (%)	
2009–2012	6	18	36	68	81	
2013–2016	9	25	48	89	92	
2017–2021	8	23	45	82	92	

Note: Statistics represent time-series averages of individual months in the relevant period.

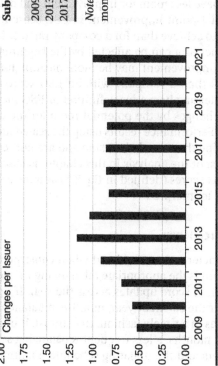

FIGURE 8.1 Summary of number of ESG score changes.
Source: Bloomberg, Compustat, MSCI, Barclays Research.

that are sufficiently populated, while still reflecting fresh information with limited delay. This window also aligns well with the full reviews, which are updated annually.

Formally, a firm i's ESG momentum at month t, termed $ESGMOM_{i,t}$, is defined as the change in its ESG score over the previous 12 months:

$$ESGMOM_{i,t} = ESG_{i,t} - ESG_{i,t-12} \qquad 8.1$$

Table 8.1 reports summary statistics on ESGMOM by time period, separately for positive and negative momentum, and the combined population. Several interesting observations emerge from the table: First, the average momentum (column 1) were small. Second, the magnitude of the positive (columns 7–8) and negative momentum (columns 10–11) were fairly similar, with no skewness in one direction. Third, the cross-sectional standard deviation of ESG momentum (column 2) decreased over time, suggesting that the ESG momentum in the sample have become more similar over time. This trend is also evidenced by the decreases in magnitude for Q1 (column 3) and Q3 (columns 5) of ESG momentum.

As ESG scores are bounded between 0 and 10, firms with high and low scores would have less room for improvement and deterioration, respectively. For example, a 1-point improvement in ESG score for a company rated 9 is more difficult to achieve than for a company rated 1. In other words, the magnitude of momentum can be affected by the beginning-of-period ESG levels, and a 1-point improvement may be more meaningful for a company with an ESG score of 9 than a company with an ESG score of 1. To correct for this bias, we consider an alternative definition of ESG momentum that scales the realized ESG changes by the potential room for the change at the beginning of the period.[5] Performance results using the scaled momentum are very similar to those using the unscaled version and are not reported in the interest of brevity. The rest of the analysis in this chapter is based on using the unscaled changes in ESG scores (defined in Eq. 8.1) as a measure of momentum since they are easier to interpret.

Rebalancing Frequency

Another parameter to be considered when constructing a portfolio based on ESG momentum is the appropriate rebalancing frequency, which depends on the distribution of score updates across the year. If updates are fairly equally spread out over the calendar year, monthly rebalancing would be best to capture the updates in a timely fashion. In contrast, if updates tend to be concentrated in a few months, a less frequent rebalancing schedule may be optimal. To better understand the updating schedule, Figure 8.2 displays the average

TABLE 8.1 ESG momentum summary statistics (S&P 500 universe, MSCI ESG scores, Scale 0–10).

Period	All ESG Momentum					Positive ESG Momentum				Negative ESG Momentum		
	Mean	Std. Dev.	Q1	Median	Q3	Avg. # of Issuers	Mean	Median		Avg. # of Issuers	Mean	Median
	(1)	(2)	(3)	(4)	(5)	(6)	(7)	(8)		(9)	(10)	(11)
2009-2012	-0.07	1.14	-0.80	-0.09	0.70	156	0.86	0.71		178	-0.90	-0.72
2013-2016	-0.07	0.69	-0.50	-0.05	0.30	209	0.50	0.38		234	-0.56	-0.45
2017-2021	0.12	0.42	-0.14	0.13	0.38	258	0.38	0.31		152	-0.30	-0.22

Note: ESG momentum is calculated as the 12m change in full-review MSCI ESG scores. All statistics are first calculated from the cross-section on a monthly basis, and the time-series averages are reported in the table. The mean, std dev, Q1, Median, and Q3 are based on the population of firms with non-zero ESG momentum.
Source: Bloomberg, Compustat, MSCI, Barclays Research.

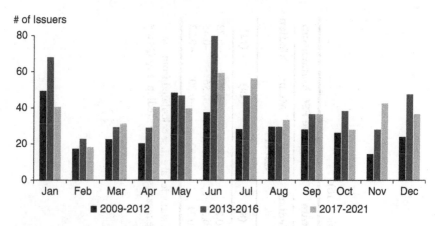

FIGURE 8.2 Average number of ESG score updates (non-zero ESG score changes) by month (S&P 500 universe).
Source: Bloomberg, Compustat, MSCI, Barclays Research.

number of companies having ESG score updates by month. The numbers suggest that updates occurred fairly uniformly throughout the year, so the portfolios based on ESGMOM should be rebalanced monthly.

METHODOLOGY: EXPOSURE-MATCHED PORTFOLIOS

Isolating the part of returns attributable to ESG momentum requires neutralizing all other systematic drivers of returns. While conceptually simple, isolating the ESG momentum effect is complicated because of a number of challenges. The first is the need to separate the effect of momentum from the level in ESG scores; the second is the need to neutralize the systematic drivers of returns, and the third is the need to make sure that the effects are not driven by idiosyncratic returns from a small number of companies. Next we elaborate on the three challenges and describe the approach we use to address them.

Challenge 1: Separating the Effect of ESG Momentum from the Effect of ESG Level

First, it is necessary to separate the effect of momentum from the level of ESG scores because the two have a mechanic correlation: issuers that experienced positive momentum will have higher end-of-period ESG scores, therefore leading to a positive correlation between the two. Figure 8.3 illustrates this relation

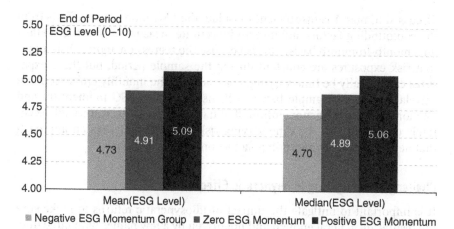

FIGURE 8.3 Time-series averages of group mean and median ESG levels (end of period) for firms with negative, positive, and zero ESG momentum (S&P 500 universe), January 2009–December 2021.
Note: ESG Momentum is defined as the 12m change in MSCI ESG Scores. All statistics are first calculated from the cross-section on a monthly basis, and the time-series averages are reported.
Source: Bloomberg, Compustat, MSCI, Barclays Research.

by reporting the average and median ESG levels at the end of each month for firms that experienced negative, zero, and positive ESG momentum during the previous 12-month window. The numbers show that the firms which have gone through positive ESG momentum indeed had higher ESG levels at the end of the period than firms with negative ESG momentum. The difference in ESG levels between the two groups was considerable at about one-third of the cross-sectional standard deviation of ESG level. Given the mechanical relation between ESG level and momentum, it is especially important to control for ESG levels in studying ESG momentum effect, because Chapters 2 and 3 show a positive return effect from ESG level. If we also find a positive return effect from ESG momentum without controlling for ESG level, it will be difficult to conclude whether such return effect is actually driven by ESG momentum or is instead a manifestation of the positive ESG level effect, given the positive correlation between the two.

Challenge 2: Neutralizing Systematic Drivers of Returns

The second challenge is to neutralize the systematic drivers of returns so that they don't confound the momentum effect, and existing approaches are not sufficient to achieve this. For example, the bucketing and regression approach discussed in note 1 is insufficient to isolate the ESG momentum effects from the confounding factors and give an inaccurate measure of the return effect on a month-to-month basis. This is because the regression approach assumes that risk exposures are constant during the sample period, but these exposures can actually be time varying. For example, the monthly cross-sectional correlations in our sample between firms' 12-month ESG momentum and 12-month equity price momentum[6] fluctuated between −0.20 and 0.20. Accurately controlling for the time varying risk exposures requires an approach that neutralizes the confounding factors on a monthly basis.

Challenge 3: Mitigating Idiosyncratic Effects

It is important to mitigate the impact of idiosyncratic returns to make sure the results are general enough and not driven by a few names with large fluctuations. To achieve this, we want to build diversified portfolios so that idiosyncratic returns are averaged out. But we also want to make sure that the portfolios do not have too many securities such that the long and short have a big composition overlap and therefore insufficient difference in their ESG momentum to shed light on the momentum return effect.

Methodology: Exposure-matched Portfolios

To address the above three challenges, we follow the exposure-matched approach introduced in Chapters 2 and 3. The approach constructs a pair of portfolios with one maximizing (Max-ESGMOM) and the other one minimizing (Min-ESGMOM) their ESG momentum and having matched exposures through an optimization process. On a monthly basis, we match the ESG level, systematic risk factor exposures, and sector allocations of the pair to make sure that the return differences captured are distinct from the ESG level effect (challenge 1) and systematic return drivers (challenge 2). We also implement a cap on each issuer's weight deviation from its index weight to ensure the right diversification level of the portfolios (challenge 3). Table 8.2 outlines the details of portfolio construction.

Specifically, the risk factors in equities are the Fama and French (2015) five factors (market beta, size, book-to-market, profitability, and investment) plus two additional factors that are widely used: price momentum (Jegadeesh and Titman 1993, Carhart 1997) and volatility (Ang et al. 2006).[7] In credit, the major key risk dimensions we match are: rating, option adjusted spread (OAS), spread duration (OASD), and duration times spread (DTS), which measures the expected volatility of a bond's excess returns (see Ben Dor et al. 2007).

The risk exposure matching guarantees that returns are not driven by unintended factor tilts, but it does not guarantee that the portfolios are sufficiently

TABLE 8.2 Construction details of exposure-matched Max- and Min-ESGMOM portfolios.

	Max-ESGMOM Portfolio	Min-ESGMOM Portfolio
Objectives	**Maximize** portfolio's weighted-average **ESG momentum**	**Minimize** portfolio's weighted-average **ESG momentum**
Sector-neutral Constraint	Matching sector weights of the index (GICS for Equity, and level 3 industry for Credit)	
Key Risk Exposure Constraints	Portfolio risk characteristics are matched with the index	

Equity Risk	**Bond Risk**
■ Size	■ DTS (relative) : +/−5% of index exposure
■ Market Beta	■ OAS (relative) : +/−1% of index exposure
■ Book to Market Value	
■ Investment Rate (% change in total assets)	
■ Operating Profit (Operating Profit/Book Equity)	■ OASD : +/−0.1yr of index
■ Price Momentum	■ Rating: +/−1% over index weight
■ Volatility	

	ESG Level	
Issuer Over-/ Underweight Constraint	Allow 0.5% issuer over-/underweight compared to index weight [An issuer also has a minimum weight of 0% and maximum weight of 10%]	
Universe	Index constituents with available ESG ratings (additional liquidity filters apply for bonds)	
Index benchmark	Corresponding Index e.g. equity: S&P 500, Russell 1000, Russell 2000; credit: Bloomberg US Corporate (HY) Indices	
Rebalance frequency	Month-end	

Source: Barclays Research.

diversified and returns are not driven by idiosyncratic risk. Therefore, in addition to matching the risk exposures, we also use a weight constraint to ensure that the portfolios are well diversified. We implement an over/underweight constraint of 0.5% for each issuer relative to its weight in the underlying index. For example, if Apple's weight in the S&P 500 is 6%, its weight in the exposure-matched portfolio has to stay within the [5.5%, 6.5%] range.[8]

We use similar sets of constraints in both equities and credit to make sure that the results from the two asset classes are comparable and any differences between them are not driven by methodological differences. The constraints have the same broad categories as in Chapter 3: 1) matching sector allocation; 2) matching risk at the index level, and 3) issuer concentration, but the exact risk characteristic differ by asset class.[9]

Table 8.3 reports the number of securities in the Max- and Min-ESGMOM portfolios at the ends of 2014, 2017, and 2021. The number of securities/issuers[10] in each portfolio was over 100, far beyond what is considered sufficient for diversification (30–40 stocks) outlined in Statman (1987).

The effect of ESG momentum on performance at time t is captured by the return difference between the exposure-matched Max- and Min-ESGMOM portfolios:

$$Return\ Effect\ of\ ESG\ Momentum_t = Ret\left(Max\text{-}ESGMOM\ Portfolio\right)_t -$$
$$Ret\left(Min\text{-}ESGMOM\ Portfolios\right)_t \qquad 8.2$$

Returns associated with ESG level and other systematic exposures cancel out because the two portfolios have identical sector allocations and key risk characteristics. To measure performance, we use total returns for equities, and excess return over duration-matched Treasury portfolios for credit to reduce the effect of yield curve changes that are unrelated to firm fundamentals.

A requirement for our approach to effectively measure the ESG momentum effect is that the ESG momentum in the Max and Min portfolios are

TABLE 8.3   Average number of securities in the Max- and Min-ESGMOM portfolios.

		Year	Index constituents with ESG Data	Max-ESGMOM	Min-ESGMOM
Equity	Number of	2014	494	132	141
(S&P 500)	Stocks	2017	495	132	135
		2021	498	126	124
Credit	Number of	2014	4,816	174	167
(Bloomberg	Bonds	2017	5,267	164	162
US Corporate		2021	6,521	165	171
Index)	Number of	2014	1,018	171	165
	Issuers	2017	1,003	162	160
		2021	1,075	163	169

Source: Bloomberg, Compustat, MSCI, Barclays Research.

Panel A: Average ESGMOM of Max- and Min-ESGMOM portfolios (S&P 500 universe)

Panel B: Average ESGMOM differences of Max-over-Min--ESGMOM portfolios

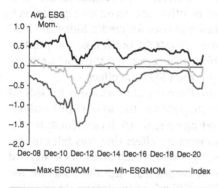

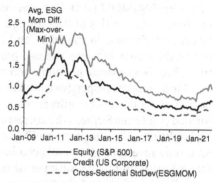

FIGURE 8.4 Average ESG momentum of the Max- and Min-ESGMOM portfolios. *Source:* Bloomberg, Compustat, MSCI, Barclays Research.

sufficiently different. Chapter 3 for example demonstrates that the exposure-matched portfolios (Max- and Min-ESG portfolios) differed considerably in terms of their ESG level despite the set of constraints they were subject to. To evaluate the difference in terms of ESG momentum between the Max- and Min-ESGMOM portfolios, Panel A of Figure 8.4 plots the average ESG momentum (scale −10 to 10) of the two portfolios in equities. Despite all the constraints imposed, the Max-ESGMOM portfolio still had considerable difference in ESG momentum compared with the Min-ESGMOM portfolio consistently over time. Panel B shows that this is also the case in credit: the magnitude of the ESG momentum difference (of Max-over-Min-ESGMOM) was constantly above one standard deviation of the ESG momentum in the cross-section in both equities and credit. Another observation is that the ESGMOM differences between the Max and Min portfolios decreased over the sample period for both equities and credit. Such decreases were driven by the consistent decreases in the cross-section dispersions of ESG momentum: when firms become more similar in their ESG momentum, it is more difficult to create a momentum spread between the Max and Min portfolios.

EFFECTS OF ESG MOMENTUM ON PERFORMANCE

This section compares the ESG momentum effects in both equities and credit to examine the consistency of the dynamics across asset classes. The analysis is first performed for the composite ESG scores at the average ESG level, then separately at different ESG levels, and for individual E, S, and G pillars.

Panel A of Figure 8.5 reports performance statistics for the effect of ESG momentum on returns. The first observation is that investing in companies with large ESG improvements had a positive effect on performance: the Max-over-Min-ESGMOM portfolios generated positive returns on average, delivering information ratios of 0.47 for equities and 0.43 for credit. Since the ESG levels are matched in the Max- and Min-ESGMOM portfolios, the positive return difference between the two portfolios suggests that the ESG momentum effect is a separate phenomenon from the ESG level effect.

Moreover, the respective contributions from the Max- and Min-ESGMOM portfolios to the return effects were both positive: the Max (Min) outperformed (underperformed) the corresponding benchmark index. These results highlight one advantage of the ESG momentum effect that was relevant for long-only investors. Often, it is challenging for long-only investors to harvest factor return premia because performance comes from the short side for the majority of factors, and shorting could be difficult to implement in practice. The ESG momentum effect was an exception: more than 60% (75% for equities and 63% for credit) of the long-short (Max-over-Min) returns came from the long side (Max-over-Index). So besides the long–short investors, long-only investors also benefited from having an ESG momentum tilt.

Beside the ESG momentum effects being positive in equities and credit, their time-series trends (Panel B of Figure 8.5) also share some similarities: in both markets, the return effects were strong from 2016 to June 2020, and weakened after that. Moreover, despite the two Max-over-Min-ESGMOM portfolios having returns from different asset classes, their return correlation was still moderately positive (0.19 for 2009–2021) and increased over the sample period (0.39 for the last five years of the sample, 2017–2021). The similarities of ESG momentum returns between the two asset classes confirm that the portfolios are picking up the same systematic return effects driven by ESG momentum. Also, the rising correlations across asset classes reflect the increasing consideration and adoption of ESG improvement as an attribute in the investment communities across asset classes.

Do ESG Momentum Effects Vary for Different ESG Levels?

We investigate whether the strength of the ESG momentum effect differs at various ESG levels. In other words, did positive ESG momentum predict stronger returns for firms with low or high ESG levels? Some may argue that an increase in ESG scores may be more meaningful for firms with low ESG scores because it represents a real improvement. On the other hand, an ESG improvement could be more predictive of returns for firms with already high ESG scores because an improvement is harder to achieve for them.

To answer this question, we set the portfolio ESG levels to low/medium/ high and examine whether the ESG momentum effects are different at each

Panel A: Performance summary, January 2009–December 2021

	Equity (S&P 500 Universe)			Credit(Bloomberg US Corporate Index)		
	Max over Min	Max over Index	Index over Min	Max over Min	Max over Index	Index over Min
Avg. (Ex.) Ret (%/Yr)	1.03	0.77	0.26	0.32	0.20	0.12
Vol (%/Yr)	2.21	1.41	1.28	0.74	0.62	0.55
Inf. Ratio (ann.)	**0.47**	**0.55**	**0.20**	**0.43**	**0.32**	**0.22**
Worst Monthly Ret (%)	−1.62	−1.14	−0.93	−0.97	−0.62	−0.66
Max. Drawdown (%)	−5.32	−3.30	−3.33	−1.15	−1.52	−1.15

Source: Bloomberg, Compustat, MSCI, Barclays Research

Panel B: Cumulative performance of ESG momentum returns in equity and credit markets (Max-over-Min-ESGMOM, S&P 500 and Bloomberg US Corporate index universes)

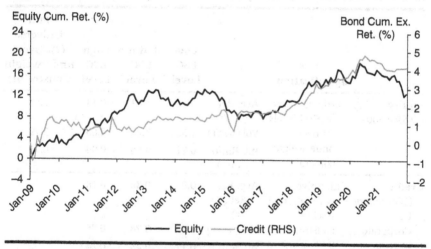

FIGURE 8.5 Effect of ESG momentum on performance.
Source: Bloomberg, MSCI, Compustat, Barclays Research.

level. The method varies slightly between equities and credit because the risk-matching constraints are more binding in credit, so we have to make modifications in credit to make sure that we can find portfolio weights that meet all the constraints. For equities, each month we divide the universe into three buckets based on their ESG levels: low, medium, and high. In each bucket, we construct a pair of Max- and Min-ESGMOM portfolios with matching risk exposures, sector allocations, and respective ESG levels.[11] Since the population in each bucket was only a third of the universe, we relax the issuer over/underweight constraint in the optimization to be 2% (instead of 0.5% in the main specification), so that it will not require too many stocks in each portfolio. There are still 50–60 names each in the Max and Min portfolios to ensure a reasonable level of diversification. In credit, because dividing the universe into three buckets makes it difficult to match all the constraints, we instead select bonds from the whole universe and vary the portfolio average ESG score constraint to low/medium/high levels respectively.[12]

Table 8.4 reports the average performance of ESG momentum returns by ESG level, and Figure 8.6 plots the time-series cumulative returns of the ESG momentum returns (Max-over-Min-ESGMOM) for the three ESG levels. The numbers suggest that ESG momentum effects were strongest for issuers around the medium ESG level in both equities and credit. For

TABLE 8.4 Performance of ESG momentum portfolios with different ESG levels (Max-over-Min-ESGMOM), January 2009–December 2021.

Specification		Low ESG Level	Medium ESG Level	High ESG Level	Full Universe (2% Over/ underweight Constraint)
Equity (S&P 500)	Partial Universe by ESG levels, 2% over/ underweight constraint	Avg. Ret (%/Yr)	0.52	**1.81**	0.13	2.85
		Vol (%/Yr)	2.53	**3.21**	2.80	3.79
		Inf. Ratio (ann.)	0.21	**0.56**	0.04	0.75
Credit (Bloomberg US Corporate Index)	Full universe with different ESG level constraint, 0.5% over/ underweight constraint	Avg. Ex. Ret (%/ Yr)	0.07	**0.32**	0.18	
		Vol (%/Yr)	0.63	**0.74**	0.75	
		Inf. Ratio (ann.)	0.11	**0.43**	0.24	

Note: Partial universe results are obtained under three ESG-level bucket constraints, 2% over-/underweight cap constraints. There are 50–60 stocks in the Max- and Min-ESGMOM portfolios. Full universe result is run with ESG-level of exposure-matched portfolios matching ESG-level of the index. For credit low, medium, and high ESG level results, Max-/Min ESGMOM portfolios' weighted average ESG scores are set to Q1, median and Q3 of cross-sectional ESG scores of US Corporate index, respectively. The ESG values in credit were set slightly differently to ensure finding feasible portfolio solutions. *Source:* Bloomberg, MSCI, Barclays Research.

example, the Max-over-Min-ESGMOM portfolios generated annualized average returns of 1.81% (equity)/0.32% (credit) at the medium ESG level versus 0.52%(e)/0.07%(c) and 0.13%(e)/0.18%(c) at the low and high ESG levels. The medium ESG level Max-over-Min- ESGMOM portfolios also had the highest information ratios among the three ESG levels.

This pattern is consistent with Giese and Nagy's (2018) finding that the ESG momentum effect was strongest among stocks with medium-level ESG scores. One possible reason for this pattern is that ESG momentum could have a more substantial effect on a company's ESG standing and market demand when its ESG score is in the medium range: momentum in its ESG score could either push the company up into the more attractive high-ESG bucket or knock it down to the less demanded low-ESG bucket. As a comparison, when a company is already in the high- or low-ESG bucket, a moderate ESG momentum would have kept the company in the same bucket and thus have limited effect on the demand of its securities. Therefore, subsequent security returns could be more sensitive to ESG momentum when the ESG levels are in the middle.

One thing worth mentioning for equity results is that, even though the ESG momentum in the medium bucket had the highest returns among the three level buckets, applying the ESG momentum strategy to the whole universe with the same 2% over/underweight constraint still generated a higher

Panel A: Equity (S&P 500 universe)

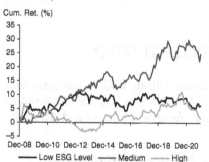

Panel B: Credit (US Corporate index universe)

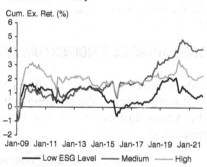

Note: Partial universe results are obtained three ESG-level bucket constraints, 2% over-/underweight cap constraints. There are 50–60 stocks in the Max- and Min-ESGMOM portfolios.

Note: For low, medium, and high ESG level results, Max-/Min ESGMOM portfolios' weighted average ESG scores are set to Q1, median and Q3 of cross-sectional ESG scores of US Corporate Index, respectively.

FIGURE 8.6 Cumulative returns of ESG momentum portfolios with different ESG levels (Max-over-Min-ESGMOM).
Source: Bloomberg, Compustat, MSCI, Barclays Research.

average return (2.85%/year) and a higher information ratio of 0.75 for the whole sample period, outperforming the ESG momentum in the medium ESG level bucket. The ESG momentum strategy generated a higher information ratio in the whole universe because it had more breadth and was applied to a larger number of stocks than the partial universe, therefore gaining efficacy.[13]

ESG Momentum Effects in Individual E, S, and G Pillars

Besides the momentum effect from the composite ESG scores discussed so far, Panel A of Figure 8.7 reports the performance statistics of Max-over-Min portfolio returns based on momentum in individual pillar scores. There are several similarities in the individual pillar momentum effects between the equity and credit markets: first, the momentum effects in all three pillars were positive; second, the E-pillar momentum effects were the strongest among the individual pillars; and third, the G-pillar momentum effects were the weakest.[14] Panel B (equities) and Panel C (credit) plot the cumulative momentum returns from the individual pillars. E-pillar momentum returns were the strongest among the three individual pillars and did not exhibit large drawdowns around 2015 unlike the other pillars and the composite ESG score momentum.

Overall, we find historically positive ESG momentum effects in both equity and credit markets, regardless of the ESG level, for the composite ESG score and for all individual E, S, and G pillars. The ESG momentum effects in both asset classes also shared several similarities, confirming the existence of the phenomenon.

COMPARING ESG MOMENTUM AND ESG LEVEL EFFECT

This section compares the effects on returns from ESG momentum and ESG level. Using a similar approach, the ESG level effects are measured as the return differences between the exposure-matched Max- and Min-ESG portfolios:

$$[Level]\,ESG\,Return\,Premium_t = Ret\big(Max\text{-}ESG\,Portfolio\big)_t$$
$$- Ret\big(Min\text{-}ESG\,Portfolio\big)_t \qquad 8.3$$

The Max- and Min-ESG portfolios are constructed using similar specifications outlined in Table 8.2, with the two portfolios maximizing and minimizing the portfolio's ESG levels, and dropping the ESG level constraint.

Table 8.5 compares the performance of the momentum and level Max-over-Min portfolios, in both equities and credit during the entire sample period as well as in sub-periods. First, the average return effects from both

Panel A: Performance statistics, January 2009–December 2021.

		E-Pillar			S-Pillar			G-Pillar			ESG		
		Max-over-Min	Max-over-Index	Index-over-Min	Max-over-Min	Max-over-Index	Index-over-Min	Max-over-Min	Max-over-Index	Index-over-Min	Max-over-Min	Max-over-Index	Index-over-Min
Equity	Avg. Ret (%/Yr)	1.19	0.90	0.29	0.62	0.56	0.06	0.54	0.47	0.08	1.03	0.77	0.26
	Vol (%/Yr)	1.97	1.27	1.25	2.00	1.21	1.14	2.32	1.34	1.38	2.21	1.41	1.28
	Inf. Ratio (ann.)	0.60	0.71	0.23	0.31	0.46	0.05	0.23	0.35	0.05	0.47	0.55	0.20
Credit (IG)	Avg. Ex. Ret (%/Yr)	0.23	0.06	0.17	0.18	-0.04	0.22	0.08	0.12	-0.04	0.32	0.20	0.12
	Vol (%/Yr)	0.78	0.68	0.52	0.78	0.61	0.55	0.76	0.62	0.61	0.74	0.62	0.55
	Inf. Ratio (ann.)	0.30	0.08	0.34	0.23	-0.07	0.40	0.11	0.19	-0.06	0.43	0.32	0.22

Panel B: Cumulative returns, Equity (S&P 500 universe)

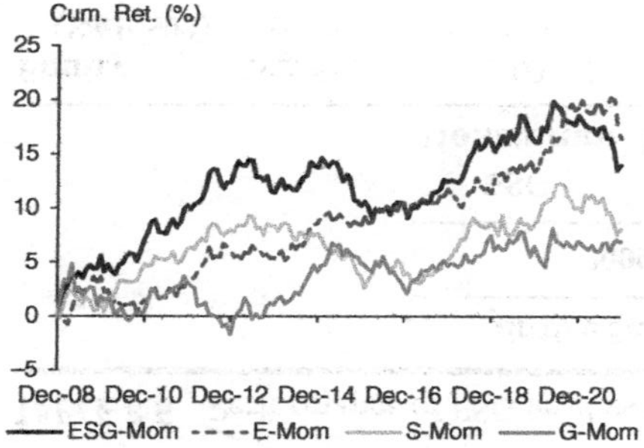

Panel C: Cumulative excess returns, Credit (Bloomberg US Corporate index)

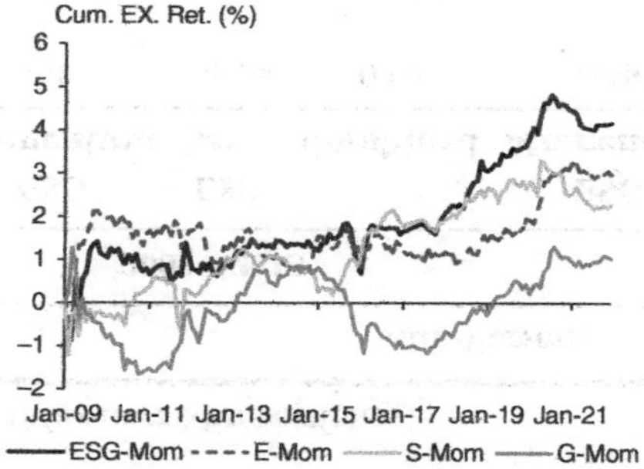

FIGURE 8.7 Momentum effects from individual E, S, and G pillars and composite ESG score (Max-over-Min portfolios).
Source: Bloomberg, Compustat, MSCI, Barclays Research.

TABLE 8.5 Performance of ESG level vs ESG momentum effects (Max-over-Min portfolios).

| | | Entire Sample Period | | | Sub-Periods | | | | | |
| | | 2009 – 2021 | | | 2009 – 2015 | | | 2016 – 2021 | | |
		ESG Momentum	ESG Level	Combined	ESG Momentum	ESG Level	Combined	ESG Momentum	ESG Level	Combined
Equity (S&P 500)	Avg. Ret (%/Yr)	1.03	0.95	0.99	1.42	−0.04	0.69	0.58	2.10	1.34
	Vol (%/Yr)	2.21	2.35	1.72	2.25	2.08	1.73	2.16	2.60	1.72
	Inf. Ratio (ann.)	0.47	0.40	0.57	0.63	−0.02	0.40	0.27	0.81	0.78
Credit (US IG)	Avg. Ex. Ret (%/Yr)	0.32	0.71	0.51	0.13	0.52	0.33	0.53	0.93	0.73
	Vol (%/Yr)	0.74	0.88	0.59	0.89	0.83	0.63	0.52	0.94	0.55
	Inf. Ratio (ann.)	0.43	0.81	0.87	0.15	0.62	0.52	1.03	1.00	1.33

Source: Bloomberg, Compustat, MSCI, Barclays Research.

ESG attributes were positive in the sample period. There was no consistent pattern on which effect was consistently stronger. In equities, the ESG momentum effect was stronger than the ESG level effect in the first half of the sample period, but weaker in the second half, due to the strong improvement in ESG level effect post 2016, a pattern also documented in Chapter 3. In Credit, the ESG level effect was stronger than the momentum effect in the first sub-period, and similar in the second sub-period based on information ratios.

Figure 8.8 compares the cumulative returns of the ESG momentum effect versus ESG level effect in equities (Panel A) and credit (Panel B). Consistent with the sub-period analysis in Table 8.5, there was no clear dominance of one effect over the other persistently over time. Moreover, the time series of the ESG momentum and level effects showed complementarity: for example, in the equity markets during 2009–2014 period, the ESG level portfolio delivered close to zero returns, and the ESG momentum portfolio delivered steady positive returns. In 2016, when the ESG momentum portfolio returns were flat, the ESG level portfolio delivered positive returns. Not only were the general trends of ESG momentum and level returns different, their month-to-month dynamics were also different. The correlations between the two ESG effects were low: 0.14 for equities and 0.07 for credit. The complementary return patterns and low correlations suggest potential diversification benefits in using both level and momentum attributes in ESG investing.

To examine the diversification benefit, we combine the two Max-over-Min portfolios constructed using ESG momentum and level with equal weights and report the performance statistics in Table 8.5. The volatilities were reduced

Panel A: Equity (S&P 500 universe)

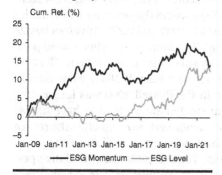

Panel B: Credit (Bloomberg US Corporate index)

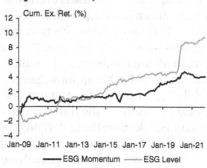

FIGURE 8.8 Cumulative performance of portfolios capturing ESG momentum and ESG level effects (Max-over-Min portfolios).
Source: Bloomberg, Compustat, MSCI, Barclays Research.

as a benefit of diversification. As shown in the table, the combined portfolios achieved improved information ratios in both equities and credit for the entire sample period, higher than the portfolios formed on each individual ESG attribute. Notice that the combined portfolio did not necessarily deliver better performance than portfolios formed on each individual attribute in all sub-periods. However, over a long period, when investors don't know ex ante which ESG attribute would have a stronger effect, the combined portfolio worked as a hedge of the two effects and thus led to lower volatility and better risk-adjusted performance. This suggests that investors could have selected companies with both strong ESG level and improvement to enhance performance.

CONSISTENCY OF ESG MOMENTUM EFFECTS

In this section, we examine the ESG momentum effects in different indices, with a more frequently updated ESG score, different diversification levels and rebalancing frequencies to make sure that the phenomenon is consistent across the board.

Different Indices

Equities: Russell 1000 and Russell 2000 Universes

In addition to the main analysis of the US large cap universe (S&P 500 index), we expand our analysis to mid- and small-cap universes in the United States (Russell 1000 and 2000). The sample periods start from January 2009 for Russell 1000 (the same as for S&P 500) and from December 2013 for Russell 2000 because of its limited coverage of ESG scores at the beginning of the sample, as shown in the Appendix. Figure 8.9 compares the performance statistics of the ESG momentum effects in the Russell 1000 and 2000 universes beside those of the S&P 500 universe. The average ESG momentum effects were positive in all three universes. In addition, the volatilities of the return effects in the large- and mid-cap universes (S&P 500 and Russell 1000) were similar, while the volatility of the return effects in the Russell 2000 was larger. One possible reason for the difference is that smaller stocks tend to have higher volatility.[15] Because the underlying constituents were more volatile, the return effect from ESG momentum in Russell 2000 was more volatile as well.

To compare the time-series dynamics, Panel B plots the cumulative performance of ESG momentum returns in the three universes. The ESG momentum returns in all showed upward trends from 2016 to 2019, and diverged afterwards. Among the three, the ESG momentum returns for the large- and mid-cap universes (S&P 500 and Russell 1000) showed very similar patterns, while those for the Russell 2000 showed a slightly different and more volatile

Panel A: Performance statistics

Universe		Max over Min	Max over Index	Index over Min
S&P 500	Avg. Ret (%/Yr)	1.03	0.77	0.26
(Jan. 2009 -	Vol (%/Yr)	2.21	1.41	1.28
Dec. 2021)	Inf. Ratio (ann.)	0.47	0.55	0.20
Russell 1000	Avg. Ret (%/Yr)	0.23	0.41	−0.19
(Jan. 2009 -	Vol (%/Yr)	2.45	1.73	1.56
Dec. 2021)	Inf. Ratio (ann.)	0.09	0.24	−0.12
Russell 2000	Avg. Ret (%/Yr)	1.95	0.52	1.43
(Jan. 2014 -	Vol (%/Yr)	4.71	3.45	2.96
Dec. 2021)	Inf. Ratio (ann.)	0.41	0.15	0.48

Panel B: Cumulative performance

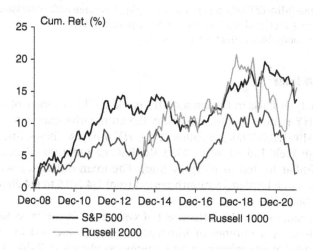

FIGURE 8.9 ESG momentum returns for S&P 500, Russell 1000, and Russell 2000. *Source:* Bloomberg, Compustat, MSCI, Barclays Research.

pattern, consistent with the ESG level effect patterns found in Chapter 3. The patterns from the cumulative returns are confirmed by the return correlations: the correlations of ESG momentum returns were relatively high among the large- and mid-cap universes (above 0.80 between S&P 500 and Russell 1000 in all periods), and low between the Russell 2000 and those in the large- and mid-cap universes (averaged at 0.09).

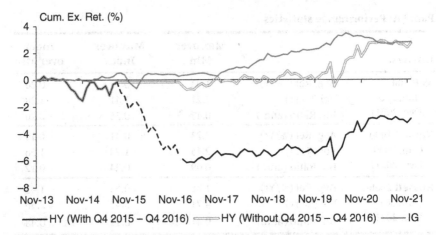

FIGURE 8.10 Cumulative excess returns of ESG momentum (Max-over-Min, US HY Index, medium ESG level).
Note: The Max-/Min-ESGMOM portfolios' weighted average ESG scores are set to median of cross-sectional ESG scores of US Corporate index.
Source: Bloomberg, MSCI, Barclays Research.

Credit: US HY Index

The HY analysis starts in December 2013 based on the coverage of MSCI ESG scores on HY issuers. Figure 8.10 plots the cumulative excess return of the Max-over-Min-ESGMOM portfolios in the HY universe (black line, Bloomberg US High Yield Index). After 2020, the ESG momentum effect in HY was positive, similar to that in IG (grey line). The main difference versus IG is concentrated in a limited 15-month period from Q4 2015 to Q4 2016 (dashed part of the black line).

The dynamics in 2015–2016 was not systematic in the cross-section but instead driven by a number of idiosyncratic names focused in two out of ten industries (communications and energy) as shown in Table 8.6.[16] If we remove this 15-month period from the time series, there is a positive momentum effect in the whole sample (double line in Figure 8.10).

Using More Frequently Updated ESG Scores

Beginning in 2014–2015, MSCI started a more frequent and dynamic updating process between the in-depth full reviews (MSCI 2016, henceforth referred to as 'raw scores'). The raw ESG scores are updated automatically based on controversies and governance events, which are monitored on a daily basis. The

TABLE 8.6 Cumulative excess returns of ESG momentum in Q4 2015–Q4 2016 period (US HY, Max-over-Min).

Sector	Cum. Ex. Ret. (%)	Sector	Cum. Ex. Ret. (%)
Communications	−2.46	Capital Goods	−0.03
Energy	−1.94	Brokerage asset managers and exchanges	0.00
Consumer non-cyclical	−1.52	REITS	0.14
Basic industry	−0.36	Industrial Other	0.18
Insurance	−0.20	Technology	0.25
Banking	−0.16	Finance Companies	0.29
Financial other	−0.15	Consumer cyclical	0.66
Transportation	−0.13	Electric	0.90

Source: Bloomberg, MSCI, Barclays Research.

raw scores are also automatically updated when there are updates in certain underlying inputs, such as number of directors, greenhouse gas emissions, clean technology revenue, etc. As shown in Figure 8.11 Panel A, raw scores were updated on average four times per year for each company starting in 2015, compared to only once per year with the full-review scores used in the main analysis. Even though the full review scores have the advantage of being more accurate and thorough as they are validated by senior ESG analysts, the raw scores may provide a stronger ESG momentum effect because their changes may capture more timely information with their frequent updating.

Figure 8.11 Panel B compares the performance of the Max-over-Min ESGMOM portfolios using the two types of scores following the same exposure-matched approach. Since MSCI started the frequent updating in 2015, the comparison period starts in 2016 (it takes one year of data to calculate the 12m change). The numbers show that the ESG momentum effects were actually stronger using the full-review scores: the Max-over-Min-ESGMOM portfolios using the full review scores earned 23 bp/year more (58-35 bp/year) than using the raw scores in S&P 500 universe.

Another potential benefit of using raw scores is that one can use a shorter lookback window, which captures more timely information and would still have enough observations with non-zero changes. The last column of Panel B shows the portfolio performance using a 3m lookback window on raw scores to calculate the momentum. The numbers show that the momentum effect was still stronger using the full-review scores.

Panel A: Average number of ESG score changes per issuer per year, by score type and year

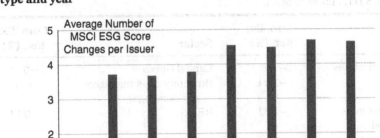

Note: The number of changes were first calculated for each company in the S&P500 over a one-year horizon, and then averaged in the cross-section for each year.
Source: Bloomberg, Compustat, MSCI, Barclays Research.

Panel B: Performance summary (Max-over-Min-ESGMOM, S&P 500), January 2016–December 2021

	Full-Review Scores (Original, 12m Lookback Window)	Raw Scores	
		12-m Lookback Window	3-m Lookback Window
Avg. Ret (%/Yr)	0.58	0.35	0.34
Vol (%/Yr)	2.16	2.01	2.11
Inf. Ratio (ann.)	0.27	0.18	0.16

FIGURE 8.11 ESG momentum effect by ESG score type (S&P 500 universe).
Source: Bloomberg, Compustat, MSCI, Barclays Research.

These results suggest that the momentum in the full-review scores contained more price-relevant information than the momentum in raw scores. The raw scores may reflect more timely information, but could also introduce more noises through their current updating models (there could be future improvement in the process that makes momentum in raw scores more informative). To sum up, in the case of ESG momentum, the accuracy from full reviews was more important than the updating speed gained in raw scores.

ALTERNATIVE SPECIFICATIONS FOR PORTFOLIO CONSTRUCTION

Diversification Level

To make sure that the return effect from ESG momentum is not specific to the choice of the over/underweight constraints (which governs the portfolio diversification level), we repeat the equity analysis with different over/underweight limits and display the results in Panel A of Table 8.7. When the over/

TABLE 8.7 ESG momentum returns by different over/underweight constraints and rebalancing frequencies (Max-over-Min-ESGMOM returns, S&P 500 universe), January 2009–December 2021.

	Panel A: By Over/ Underweight Constraint			Panel B: By Rebalancing Frequency			
	0.5% (Original)	1.0%	2.0%	Monthly (Original)	Quarterly	Semi-Annual	Annual
Avg. Ret (%/Yr)	1.03	1.59	2.85	1.03	0.71	0.49	0.42
Vol. (%/Yr)	2.21	2.77	3.79	2.21	1.94	1.69	1.25
Inf. Ratio (ann.)	**0.47**	**0.58**	**0.75**	**0.47**	**0.36**	**0.29**	**0.34**
Avg. number of Stocks in Max- or Min-ESGMOM	132	86	53				

Note: the 'Avg. number of Stocks' numbers were first calculated each month as the average number of stocks in the max and min portfolios ((N_max+N_min)/2), then averaged across the time series. For quarterly, semi-annual, and annual rebalancing, the returns each month are calculated as the averages of the monthly returns from rebalancing at different months to smooth out the effect of the rebalancing month. For example, the return in Dec. 2010 for the quarterly rebalancing is from the average of the returns in Dec. 2010 from three strategies rebalancing in {Jan., Apr., Jul., and Oct}, {Feb., May, Aug., Nov.}, and {Mar., Jun., Sep., Dec.}.
Source: Bloomberg, Compustat, MSCI, Barclays Research.

underweight constraints were relaxed, the portfolio is concentrated in fewer names with higher ESG momentum, which led to larger ESG momentum effects (higher returns) but also higher risk (more idiosyncratic risk). Overall, the ESG momentum effect was present regardless of how restrictive the over/ underweight constraint was.

Rebalancing Frequency

We also examine how the ESG momentum effects change with alternative rebalancing frequencies. Table 8.7 Panel B shows that the average ESG momentum returns remained positive with all rebalancing frequencies, but the monthly frequency generated the highest average return and information ratio. These results suggest that ESG momentum metrics contain timely information valuable for predicting security returns. When rebalanced less frequently, the portfolios did not incorporate the updated information fast enough and therefore performed worse.

CONCLUSION

Besides the positive ESG level effects documented in Chapters 2 and 3 following an exposure-matched approach, we find that ESG momentum also had a distinctly positive return effect, evident in both equities and credit, at different ESG levels, and with different portfolio construction specifications. The ESG momentum effects shared several similar patterns across asset classes, validating the consistency of the phenomenon. Moreover, the ESG level and momentum effects were complementary to each other. Investors who believe that these historical patterns will continue can combine exposures to ESG level and momentum effects to gain a diversified exposure to ESG-related returns.

The exposure-matched approach used in this and previous chapters is very versatile. The approach is agnostic to the source of the ESG score data, but the results may vary if scores from a different provider are used. Besides capturing ESG level and momentum returns, it can also be applied to identify effects of other ESG attributes, such as the dispersion among ESG scores from different providers (Chapter 13), or to combine several ESG attributes to enhance the ESG returns. It can be used by long–short investors to maximize absolute returns, and also by long-only investors to boost risk-adjusted returns relative to a benchmark while controlling tracking error volatility.

APPENDIX: COVERAGE OF MSCI ESG SCORES

TABLE 8.A1   MSCI ESG score coverage of US equity and credit indices.

	Coverage (Number of Stocks)					Coverage (Market Cap)				
	Equity			Credit		Equity			Credit	
	S&P 500 (%)	RS1000 (%)	RS2000 (%)	IG (%)	HY (%)	S&P 500 (%)	RS1000 (%)	RS2000 (%)	IG (%)	HY (%)
2009	87	56	1	84	30	96	89	2	89	35
2013	99	95	74	91	59	100	99	88	93	62
2017	100	98	72	95	76	100	99	91	96	79
2020	100	96	66	96	78	100	99	87	96	80

Note: All coverage ratios reported are as of the end of December each year.
Source: Bloomberg, Compustat, MSCI, Barclays Research.

REFERENCES

Ang, A., Hodrick, R., Xing, Y., and Zhang, X. (2006). The Cross-section of Volatility and Expected Returns. *The Journal of Finance*, 61 (1), pp. 259–299.

Asness, C., Frazzini, A., and Pedersen, L. (2018). Quality Minus Junk. *Review of Accounting Studies*, 24, pp. 34–112.

Ben Dor, A., Dynkin, L., Hyman, J., Houweling, P., van Leeuwen, E., and Penninga, O. (2007). DTS^{SM} (Duration Times Spread). *Journal of Portfolio Management*, 33 (2), pp. 77–100.

Ben Dor, A., Guan, J., and Zeng, X. (2019). Is Information Extracted from Earnings Call Transcripts Using Natural Language Procession (NLP) Predictive of Bond Returns? *Barclays Research*, 5 June 2019.

Ben Dor, A., Guan, J., and Zeng X. (2020). Does Post-Earnings Announcement Drift (PEAD) Extend to Credit Markets? *Barclays Research*, 4 February 2020.

Carhart, M. (1997). On Persistence in Mutual Fund Performance. *Journal of Financial Economics*, 52 (1), pp. 57–82.

Fama, E.F. and French, K.R. (2015). A Five-factor Asset Pricing Model. *Journal of Financial Economics*, 116 (1), pp. 1–22.

Giese, G. and Nagy, Z. (2018). How Markets Price ESG. *MSCI Research Insights*, November 2018.

Grinold, R.C. (1989). The Fundamental Law of Active Management. *The Journal of Portfolio Management*, 15 (3), pp. 30–38.

Jegadeesh, N. and Titman, S. (1993). Returns to Buying Winners and Selling Losers. Implications for Stock Market Efficiency. *Journal of Finance, pp.* 48 (1): 65–91.

MSCI (2016). MSCI ESG Ratings Methodology. *MSCI ESG Research*, April 2016

MSCI (2020). MSCI ESG Ratings Methodology. *MSCI ESG Research*, December 2020

Statman, M. (1987). How Many Stocks Make a Diversified Portfolio? *Journal of Financial and Quantitative Analysis*, 22 (3), pp. 353–363.

NOTES

1. This approach involves forming a top-over-bottom long–short portfolio sorted on ESG momentum, and regressing the time series of return differences on a host of factor returns to remove the systematic return components. The intercept is then used as a measure of alpha. However, this will not give an accurate measure of the return effect on a month-to-month basis because while the regression assumes risk exposures are constant, they are actually time varying. For example, in Chapter 3 we show that firms with higher ESG scores had lower profitability than the broad universe mostly before 2016, but had higher profitability after 2016. In any month, the realized factor exposures could have large deviations from those captured by the coefficients in the regression and make the estimate of monthly ESG momentum effect inaccurate. Another approach is to estimate a cross-sectional regression of security returns against ESG attributes, while controlling for other firm risk exposures and fixed effects. This approach generates monthly estimates, but is sensitive to the formulation of the regression models, similar to the time-series case. In addition to the sensitivity to model specifications, neither technique allows investors to harvest the ESG related returns.

2. In-depth full reviews can also be triggered by significant events, such as new severe or very severe controversy or upgrade/downgrade of severe/very severe controversy, significant change in Corporate Governance Score, new information provided by a company, and a significant corporate action (MSCI 2020).

3. Bonds already in the portfolio are not affected by the liquidity filters, i.e. they are not automatically sold if their liquidity worsens.

4. For a lookback window of s-month, the momentum at month t would be calculated as the change of ESG score during the lookback window $(ESG_t - ESG_{t-s})$

5. For example, for a firm with a starting ESG score of 1, any positive change is divided by the maximum possible improvement of 9 (10–1), and any negative ESG change is divided by the maximum possible deterioration, which equals 1.

6. The lookback window of the price momentum skips the most recent month to follow the standard momentum specification.

7. Market beta is the slope estimate from a trailing five-year regression of monthly stock excess returns (over 1m Libor) on the market excess returns (S&P 500 return over 1m Libor). Size is measured as the market capitalization of each company. B/M is a company's most recent book equity over its current month market cap. Operating profit is defined as a company's annualized revenues minus cost of goods sold, interest expense, and selling, general, and administrative expenses divided by book equity from the previous year. Investment rate is measured as the change in a firm's most recent total assets from the previous year. Price momentum is a stock's cumulative returns over the past 12 months, excluding the most recent month. Volatility is the total volatility using daily returns from the past 3-month window. The investment and profitability factors are similar in concept to the QMJ (quality-minus-junk) factor proposed by

Asness et al. (2018). The QMJ factor captures three components: profitability, growth, and safety. The operating profitability in Fama and French (2015) captures a concept similar to the profitability component in QMJ, although the latter includes several profitability measures, instead of just one as in Fama and French (2015). The investment factor in Fama and French (2015) is similar to the safety factor in QMJ: it finds that firms expanding too quickly have lower returns, on average. The safety factor measures this aspect from another angle by focusing on firms' betas (already captured in our beta factor), leverage (taking on too much debt to expand) and volatility.

8. An alternative to ensure diversification is to implement an absolute weight cap. This approach will produce a portfolio that is more similar to equal weighting and deviate further from existing index weights. We choose the current approach because it represents more of a tilt from the index within some reasonable range and is closer to what is done in practice. Portfolios generated using the relative weight caps are also more scalable.

9. As a result of aligning with the equity constraints from Chapter 3, our credit constraints are less stringent compared to those in Chapter 2. For example, we match sector allocation and OAS at the index level, but don't match OAS at the sector level as in Chapter 2. However, we find that the ESG effects using the less stringent constraints have similar time-series dynamics as the more stringent constraints.

10. The number of bonds is roughly equal to the number of issuers, indicating that the portfolios are diversified at issuer level as well. In general, the linear optimization algorithm picks one bond from each issuer that best fits the constraints.

11. For equities, we set the ESG levels of the Max- and Min-ESGMOM portfolio in the low/medium/high ESG level buckets equal to index_avg_ESG-1stdev/ index_avg_ESG/ index_avg_ESG+1stdev, where stdev=cross-sectional standard deviation of ESG scores in the universe at each month. The max- and min-ESGMOM portfolios match the risk characteristics and sector allocations to those of the S&P500 index to ensure that the different results in each bucket were not driven by different risk characteristics or sector representation. Occasionally, we need to supplement a small number of stocks from outside of the buckets to match the index risk characteristics, but the overall weight in these out-of-bucket stocks was very limited and did not affect the general results.

12. For credit low, medium, and high ESG level results, Max-/Min-ESGMOM portfolios' weighted average ESG scores are set to Q1, median and Q3 of cross-sectional ESG scores of US Corporate index, respectively.

13. According to Grinold (1989), IR = IC*$\sqrt{N}$, where IR is the information ratio of a strategy, IC is the information coefficient, and N is the breadth of the strategy.

14. In constructing the pillar level Max- and Min- portfolios, the two were required to have the same ESG level, risk characteristics, and sector allocation constraints as in the main specification. The only difference is that they now maximize and minimize the respective pillar score momentum, instead of the momentum in the composite ESG score.

15. The annualized volatility of the S&P 500 and Russell 1000 indices were similar at about 15%/year from January 2009 to December 2021, whereas the volatility of the Russell 2000 index was 20%/year for the same period.

16. For example, one company from the communications sector experienced some negative returns due to downgrades by Moody's for non-ESG related reasons, but happened to have improvements in its ESG scores right before the event, which put it in the Max-ESGMOM portfolio.

CHAPTER 9

Predicting Companies' ESG Rating Changes Using Job-posting Data

A s ESG-related investing grew in popularity, an increasing number of studies examined the performance implications of incorporating ESG considerations in investment processes. These studies focus on issues such as the relation between firms' ESG ratings, valuation, and performance (in equity or credit markets), and how to properly incorporate ESG considerations in portfolio construction.[1] Almost no research, however, was undertaken to systematically analyse firms' ESG-related activities (e.g. community involvement, setting workforce diversity goals, and green energy adoption) based on empirical data, despite the fact that identifying and measuring ESG-related activities and actions taken by corporations can offer important insights to different market participants. Policymakers and regulators, for example, would be able to better understand how the ESG landscape is evolving among firms and the impact ESG investing is making on firms. Asset managers may use the information to design better ESG-related products, by distinguishing among companies and sectors based on various 'ESG friendliness' metrics, while asset owners would be able to monitor the activities of companies they invest in and ensure they operate in line with their expectations.

The limited attention given so far to empirically analysing firms' activities in the ESG space reflects the considerable challenges related to data availability. Unlike various financial aspects of firms' operations, there are no standard reporting requirements pertaining to ESG-related activities. As a result, information disclosure is partial and varies greatly across companies and time. Furthermore, the lack of a uniformly accepted definition for what constitutes ESG-related activities results in inconsistent reporting across sectors/firms, and even when similar actions are taken, companies may use different terms to describe them. Another reason is the fact that most corporations started to pay attention to the subject only in late 2010s, and as a result the historical data is limited in length. Taken together, most relevant data is incomplete, not standardized, and relatively short, which make it difficult to systematically examine ESG-related efforts across firms' and their implications.

To address some of these challenges, in this chapter we employ a novel data set of corporate job postings scraped from the internet to identify and measure firms' planned ESG-related activities. Each job posting in the data set provides detailed information, including the employer's name, job title, job location, wage, and job requirements, such as skills, experience, and education level. Based on the job description, we identify ESG-related openings, and use them to measure firms' ESG-related hiring efforts as a proxy for firms' overall efforts towards improving their ESG credentials. The data set offers two important advantages when examining firms' ESG-related efforts systematically: first, it is comprehensive, as almost all job openings are now posted online[2]; second, the ESG job vacancy rate relative to the overall job vacancy rate can be easily standardized and compared across different firms. The unique nature of the data allows us to measure the scope of firms' planned ESG-related efforts based on firms' actions rather than announcements in a timely manner, and examine the relationship between the scope of corporates' planned ESG-related activities and subsequent changes in their ESG ratings and security performance.

Unlike traditional financial data, job postings are in text form and require additional processing before use. We leverage natural language processing techniques to sift through more than 200 mn job posts to construct a sample of those related to ESG hiring for S&P 500 firms. The ESG-related job-posting data set provides several advantages in capturing corporates' ESG-related efforts. First, firms' labour demand is intrinsically forward-looking. Current job openings are associated with future hires in ESG, which are further associated with future business actions in ESG. Second, the job-posting data is at the micro-level. It includes all types of ESG-related jobs. It covers not only positions such as the head of corporate social responsibility but also includes less highly ranked jobs such as ESG analysts and field environmental engineers. The detailed job-level data captures ESG-related actions from the very bottom of firms' corporate ladders. Last but not least, the labour cost is a significant portion of firms' operating cost, and workforce planning is usually driven by business need. Hence, job openings usually match firms' real actions more closely than their high-level ESG commitments and strategies.

Using the job-posting data, we find that ESG job vacancies for S&P 500 firms have increased more than other types of job vacancies since 2014. This highlights that firms indeed started investing more resources to improve their ESG practices. Second, we find that the majority of tagged ESG-related jobs are related to the 'E' pillar. As a result, we focus on firms that are most sensitive to environmental issues. By tracking their subsequent rating changes since 2015, we find that firms with high 'abnormal' (i.e. relative to their own histories) ESG hiring interest were more likely to experience subsequent rating improvements in the 'E' pillar compared to peers with low abnormal

ESG hiring interest. Thus, timely information related to firms' ESG activities can serve as a leading indicator of upcoming changes in firms' ESG ratings and allow investors a way to potentially exploit this lead-lag effect to identify firms that are more likely to experience future improvement in their ESG ratings. Furthermore, firms with higher 'abnormal' ESG posting intensity also enjoyed significantly better subsequent stock performance relative to other firms, after accounting for exposures to common risk factors. This subsequent outperformance only became evident a few years after the increase in ESG hiring interests, consistent with the gradual incorporation of the 'ESG' hiring impact on stock performance.

The rest of the chapter is organized as follows. We start by describing the job-posting data and how we identify ESG-related job posts. Next, we examine the overall ESG hiring trend since 2014 and the trend across different sectors. We then investigate the relationship between firms' ESG hiring and their subsequent rating changes and stock performances.

DATA AND METHODOLOGY

Job-posting Data

The job-posting data are sourced from Burning Glass Technologies (BGT), an analytics software company that scrapes online job postings from recruiting websites and company career websites in real time. The data set goes back to January 2014 and is updated daily with newly posted job openings. It hosts more than 200 mn job postings in total for the period between January 2014 and December 2020 and adds about between 10,000 and 100,000 postings per day. For each job posting, BGT extracted detailed information from the job description text, such as job title, employer name, and required skills. The data set contains 56 data fields for each posting. Table 9.1 details some of the data fields extracted by BGT. As the same job could be posted on multiple sites, BGT has also actively tried to remove duplicate postings.[3]

Another commonly used data source for job openings is the Job Opening and Labor Turnover Survey (JOLTS) data produced by the US Bureau of Labor Statistics. While the JOLTS has a much longer history and is regarded as an important measure of macroeconomic activity, the BGT data set offers more granular information at the posting level. The JOLTS data are based on aggregated survey results and are updated monthly with a significant lag between data collection and reporting. The BGT job data instead are updated on a real-time, daily basis. However, as BGT data only consists of online job postings, it could have a bias against job openings that are often posted offline (such as restaurant workers). Figure 9.1 shows the percentage of job openings grouped by

TABLE 9.1 Selected data fields in the job posting data from Burning Glass Technologies.

Data Field	Description
JobTitle	The posted job title after removing any extraneous text and/or noise from posted job title
JobDate	Date the posting was acquired
JobText	The text of the job posting
JobDomain	Domain from which the posting was acquired
Employer	A standardized version of employer names so that variants of an employer name are grouped together
RequiredDegrees	Required degree level specified in the job posting
YearsOfExperience	The amount of experience required for a job, as specified in the job posting
Standard Major	The standardized form of majors extracted from the job posting. The standard forms are based on Classification of Instructional Programs (CIP) taxonomy
Skills	Skills specified in the job posting
Metropolitan Statistical Area (MSA)	Defined by the Office of Management and Budget 2009 MSA lookup, listed with Area Type

Source: Burning Glass Technologies.

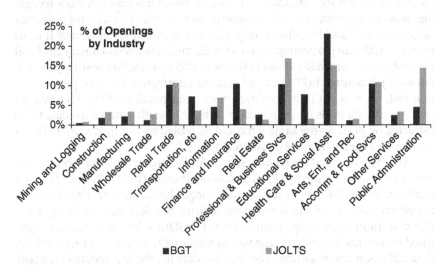

FIGURE 9.1 Percentage of openings grouped by NAICS for Burning Glass sample and JOLTS sample.
Source: Burning Glass Technologies, US Bureau of Statistics, Barclays Research.

sectors based on the North American Industry Classification System (NAICS) industry code for JOLTS and BGT respectively. The sector composition is similar between the two data sources; the difference is generally in line with the sector's tendency of posting jobs online. For example, financial firms are usually more likely to post jobs online than firms in the hospitality industry. One notable difference between the two samples is the percentages of jobs from the Educational Services and the Public Administration industries. However, the difference is mainly driven by the fact that JOLTS data reclassify Educational Services openings from publicly owned establishments under the Public Administration industry while BGT does not. Overall, Figure 9.1 suggests that postings collected by the BGT are largely representative of the US labour market.

An important advantage of the detailed posting-specific information is that it allows us to glean a deeper insight of the labour market than what can be gleaned solely from the national count of job openings. In this chapter, we use text analysis techniques to identify ESG-related openings, which is only made possible by having posting-level data. The posting-level information also allows us to better capture the implied level of hiring efforts made by the hiring firm. For example, an ESG-related job that requires a higher level of education or more years of experience is usually costlier to the firm and therefore indicates more commitment from the employer. By delving into firms' ESG hiring dynamics, we aim to understand firms' 'real' actions in improving ESG and its implication on their subsequent ESG rating and performance.

Sample Construction

We use US job openings posted by firms in the S&P 500 index for our analysis. By narrowing the universe to S&P 500 companies, we are able to examine the hiring dynamics for one of the most representative US equity market indices while keeping the data-cleaning work manageable. Although using the micro-level job posting data set is appealing, it poses many challenges due to its data size and unstructured nature. One of the main challenges is to map job posting data to firms' ESG ratings and financial data. The BGT data set lacks a unique security identifier such as CUSIP and SEDOL.[4] Therefore, extracted employer names are used to match job posting data to firm identifiers which is an inexact science. Name of the employer listed in job postings is often different to the official one or is sometimes misrecorded. To address these challenges, we use 'fuzzy matching' to map extracted employer names with firms' official names as listed in commercial data vendors. We further improve the coverage by manually mapping names that are not matched by 'fuzzy matching'.

The sample contains 16.4 mn posts in total between January 2014 and December 2020. Figure 9.2 reports the sample's coverage of the S&P 500 universe. On average, the sample covers 78% of firms in the index and the ratio

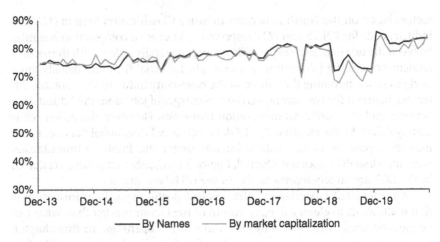

FIGURE 9.2   Sample coverage of the S&P 500 index.
Source: Burning Glass Technologies, Compustat, Barclays Research.

is similar in terms of market capitalization. In addition, the coverage ratio is relatively stable across time, suggesting that our sample is also relatively stable over time. The second and third columns in Table 9.2 report the percentage of firms in each Global Industry Classification Standard (GICS) sector in the index versus in the sample. The sectoral composition is very similar, suggesting that the incomplete coverage is not significantly biased toward any specific industry. The fourth column in Table 9.2 further shows the percentage of postings in the sample for each sector. Given labour intensity and employee turnover varies across sector, postings by sector will invariably differ to the percentage of firms. The last column of Table 9.2 report the percentage of total number of employees in each GICS sector in the index based on financial statements released by firms as of 2020. The percentage is closer to the percentage of postings in the sample. Note that the number of employees does not account for the turnover, which also affects the number of openings. In sum, Figure 9.2 and Table 9.2 show that the sample is largely representative of the index in terms of sectoral composition and labour-market activity.

Apart from mapping the BGT data to other types of firm-level data, Table 9.3 summarizes three additional data challenges: messiness, magnitude, and measurement. In the interests of space, we only review in detail the last challenge: how to identify ESG-related job posts.

Identifying ESG-related Jobs

Identifying these openings is not straightforward. Companies do not self-identify whether an opening is ESG-related. To process a large quantity of

TABLE 9.2 Sectoral breakdown of Burning Glass versus S&P 500.

Sector	Number of Firms (%, S&P 500)	Number of Firms (%, Sample)	Number of Postings (%, Sample)	Number of Employees (%, S&P 500)
Energy	7.3	4.8	1.2	1.8
Materials	5.7	5.1	1.8	2.6
Industrials	14.2	17.3	15.3	14.4
Consumer Discretionary	14.0	15.7	35.4	23.1
Consumer Staples	7.4	5.9	6.6	16.8
Health Care	12.3	15.7	13.0	11.2
Financials	13.6	13.8	14.7	10.3
Information Technology	13.0	12.7	9.7	12.1
Communication Services	2.4	1.7	0.9	5.8
Utilities	6.0	4.8	1.0	1.3
Real Estate	4.1	2.6	0.4	0.7

Source: Bloomberg, Burning Glass Technologies, Compustat, Barclays Research.

TABLE 9.3 Handling messiness, magnitude, mapping, and measurement.

Issue	Problem	Solution
Mapping	Company names are inconsistently recorded E.g. Walmart: 'walamart,' 'wallmart,' 'wamart'	Fuzzy match issuer names to Burning Glass, analyst correctly tags company names. Result: **78% coverage** of S&P 500, by names and market cap
Messiness	Data are in XML (Unstructured text)	Write parser convert to Parquet DataFrame
Magnitude	200 million observations 10,000–100,000 new postings/day	Use Pyspark to manipulate data Create **SQL** API
Measurement	Defining ESG jobs	Data Science approach to developing text search rules (see text)

Source: Barclays Research.

postings, we first generate a list of search terms that are ESG-related, such as 'environment', 'corporate social responsibility', and 'sustainability'. The list is further expanded by including terms from a set of real ESG-related postings. These terms are subsequently lowercased and stemmed in order to allow for more possible matches. For example, the stem for the word 'sustainable' is 'sustainab', which can be matched to other words sharing the same stem such as 'sustainability', assuming 'sustainability' is not in the original search term list. The stems are then used to query job posting in order to identify whether the post is ESG-related or not.

The stem list and other technical parameters used in the identification process are validated with a sample that is first tagged by the algorithm and then manually checked for accuracy. The initial run had a precision of 0.86 and 0.93 respectively based on checks by two Barclays analysts. This implies 86% or 93% of posts in the sample that are tagged as ESG-related by the algorithm are confirmed as indeed ESG-related by each analyst.[5] After thus confirming its accuracy on the test sample, we applied the identification process to our entire dataset.

We find 47,315 ESG-related job postings out of 16.4 mn total postings in the sample. Table 9.4 lists a few examples of ESG-related posts that cover a variety of jobs. Some are for junior analysts while some are for a director of corporate social responsibility. Some are more related to environmental issues while others focus more on firms' social responsibility. The posts may also vary by their required education levels. In addition, the posts are scraped from different sites, including company websites, recruiting portals, and websites dedicated to sustainability issues. The richness of different ESG-jobs in our sample demonstrates the coverage of our data is broad. The Appendix also provides a sample job post for an ESG-related role.

To better understand the tagged ESG-related posts, we slice and dice them in different ways. First, Figure 9.3 shows how the posts can be categorized based on the related pillar subject. Specifically, if a job's title contains the word 'environment', 'environmental', 'ehs', or 'environments', it is classified as 'E' pillar. The 'S' pillar looks for words such as 'social', 'sustainability', and 'responsibility' while the 'G' pillar uses words such as 'governance' and 'compliance'. Since the categorization is done separately for each subject, a job posting may be classified as matching more than one pillar, and the sum of the three percentages might be different from one. Figure 9.3 is not meant to offer a complete and precise classification, which would require additional natural language processing. Rather, it aims to help us understand the relative composition of different types of ESG-related jobs. The results reported in Figure 9.3 indicate that the majority of openings (over 50%) are related to the 'E' pillar, while almost 40% are linked to the 'G' pillar. In contrast, only a minority of the roles (about 10%) can be considered as related to the 'S' pillar.

Second, jobs are grouped into different levels of seniority based on the required years of experience mentioned in the job posts. Figure 9.4 shows that about 30% of the posts require at least of six years of experience. We also find that the percentage is much higher compared to that for non-ESG jobs,

TABLE 9.4 Examples of ESG-related job posts identified by the algorithm.

Job Title	Job Date	Domain	Preferred Degree	Required Degree
Director, Corporate Social Responsibility	23/04/2015	www.sustainablebusiness.com	Master of Business Administration |Master's	
Manager, Global Supplier Relations Social Responsibility Strategy	03/08/2017	my.jobs		
Environmental Toxicologist/ Entomologist	27/03/2017	jobs.monsanto.com		Doctor of Philosophy
Environmental Compliance Specialist	11/10/2018	jacobs.taleo.net		Bachelor's
Supply Chain Sustainability Analyst	19/03/2018	jobs.cisco.com	Bachelor's	Bachelor's
Finance Governance Manager	27/10/2016	www.postjobfree.com		

Note: Field values are reported as listed in Burning Glass Technologies' data.
Source: Burning Glass Technologies, Barclays Research.

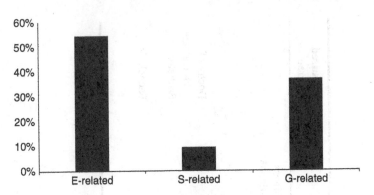

FIGURE 9.3 Percentage of postings by ESG pillar.
Source: Burning Glass Technologies, Barclays Research.

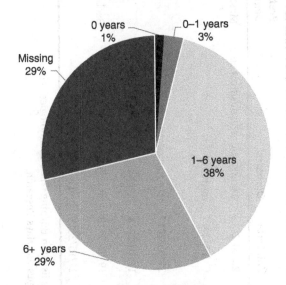

FIGURE 9.4 Required years of experience for ESG roles.
Source: Burning Glass Technologies, Barclays Research.

suggesting that ESG-related jobs are usually more demanding and require more hiring efforts from firms. An alternative way to group job openings by their level of seniority is to use job titles. Specifically, we search for jobs that contain words from the list 'head', 'chief', 'director', and 'president' (which would capture vice-presidents as well). Figure 9.5 shows that approximately 7% of jobs are deemed as senior based on this approach. Finally, we also compare the required education levels for ESG-jobs. The ratio of jobs requiring a Bachelor degree versus advanced degrees higher than a Bachelor is 2:1.

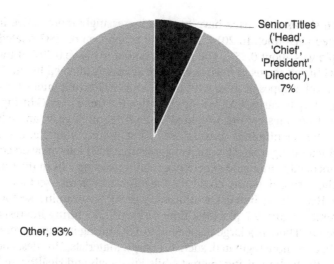

FIGURE 9.5 Seniority of ESG roles based on title search.
Source: Burning Glass Technologies, Barclays Research.

MEASURING ESG HIRING INTEREST

Overall ESG Hiring Trend

As hiring is costly for firms, ESG-related hiring should partly reflect firms' efforts in improving their ESG performance. Like capital budget planning, human capital planning also indicates firms' business strategies. Therefore, we use firms' hiring activities in ESG to try to capture their planned ESG activities. We define the overall ESG hiring interest (HI) in our sample as the percentage of ESG-related vacancies relative to the overall vacancies. Specifically, the ESG HI for month t is defined as

$$ESG\ HI = \frac{\sum \text{Weighted ESG-related job openings}_t}{\sum \text{Weighted job openings}_t} \tag{9.1}$$

where the summing operators are aggregated across firms. The weight used for each posting is based on the role's required level of education and experience. This is motivated by the fact that senior and more experienced jobs usually represent more demanding hiring efforts from employers and are therefore more informative of firms' interest in the ESG space. To account for such type of job heterogeneity, we weight each posting by its required level of education and experience. In particular, we take the average of the required number of years of education and the required number of years of experience and each job is multiplied by that average before being summed up in Equation (9.1).[6]

Figure 9.6 shows that firms have become increasingly more active in hiring ESG-related personnel. In 2014, the overall proportion of ESG-related jobs in our sample was about 0.35%. The ratio increased to above 0.50% at the end of 2019. ESG hiring seems to have been more adversely affected by the Covid-19 crisis than other types of jobs, with the overall ESG-hiring interest experiencing a large drop in early 2020. We also find that the trend in ESG hiring interest is similar if postings are not weighted by their required years and education. However, the magnitude of unweighted hiring interest is smaller compared to the weighted hiring interest, which suggests that ESG jobs on average require more years of education and experience than remaining jobs in the sample.

As the hiring dynamic could vary significantly across sectors, we compute the ESG hiring interest within each sector to examine sector-specific hiring trends. Figure 9.7 plots the time series of ESG hiring interests for different sectors. There is a large dispersion in ESG hiring interest across sectors. Sectors that are more regulated, such as Energy, Materials, Utilities, and Financials, have the highest hiring interest while Financials and Healthcare have the most evident increasing trend in ESG hiring. Table 9.2 shows that Financials and Healthcare have the third and fourth most job postings in the sample only after Consumer Discretionary and Industrials. This raises the concern that the increasing trend in Figure 9.6 could be entirely driven by the two sectors. Figure 9.8 plots the average ESG hiring interest across sectors. We apply Equation (9.1) to firms in each sector separately and then aggregate the sector-level ESG hiring interests across sectors. Therefore, the ratio is less affected by a trend in any particular sector. The figure suggests that the increasing trend in the overall ESG efforts is robust to alternative specifications.

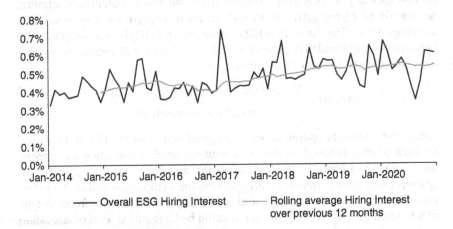

FIGURE 9.6   Overall ESG hiring interest in the sample.
Source: Burning Glass Technologies, Compustat, Barclays Research.

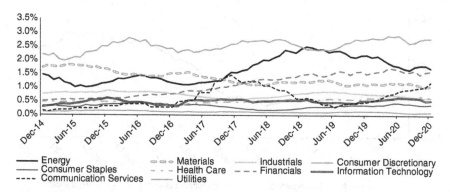

FIGURE 9.7 Rolling 12 month weighted ESG hiring interest, by GICS sectors.
Source: Burning Glass Technologies, Compustat, Barclays Research.

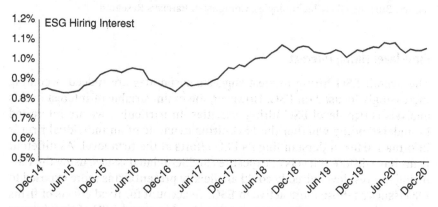

FIGURE 9.8 Average ESG hiring interest across sectors.
Source: Burning Glass Technologies, Compustat, Barclays Research

The job opening data suggest that Financials has one of the highest ESG hiring interest and one of the most evident increasing trend in ESG hiring. Another unique feature about Financials is that ESG-related jobs are not necessarily used to help firms improve their own ESG performance. Instead, some are hired to carry out ESG research on other firms. Figure 9.9 plots the weighted ESG hiring interest for different sub-industries within Financials. The figure shows that sell-side firms seem to have started to hire in ESG earlier than the buy-side firms. One caveat is that since our sample only started in 2014, it might be possible that the hiring dynamic was different before then. However, it's quite evident that asset management firms have been more active in hiring ESG-related analysts since 2017 than sell-side firms.

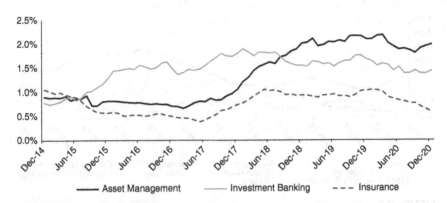

FIGURE 9.9   Rolling 12 month weighted ESG hiring interest within financial sub industries.
Source: Burning Glass Technologies, Compustat, Barclays Research.

Firm-level Hiring Interest

The overall ESG hiring interest suggests corporates are indeed becoming increasingly focused on ESG. However, the main variable of interest in this analysis is firm-level ESG hiring activities. In particular, we are interested in understanding whether the ESG hiring dynamic of an individual firm is informative for understanding its ESG efforts at the firm level. As different firms have different levels of exposures to ESG-related issues, using the ESG hiring interest level directly could artificially present firms more exposed to ESG issues as those more active in ESG. To account for fixed effects of firms such as the nature of business, we use the *Abnormal ESG Hiring Interest* (HI) to measure a firm's ESG hiring dynamic. To calculate the abnormal ESG HI, we first compute annual ESG hiring interest (ESG HI) for firm i in year j

$$\text{Annual ESG HI}_{i,j} = \frac{\text{Weighted sum of ESG-related job posts}_{i,j}}{\text{Weighted sum of all job posts}_{i,j}}$$

where posts are weighted by experience/education to account for job heterogeneity. Abnormal ESG HI is then defined as the difference between the annual ESG HI in year j and the average of annual ESG HI from all the previous years. If a firm has zero ESG-related job posts in a year, the annual ESG HI for that year is set as zero. The abnormal ESG HI is then calculated accordingly. However, if a firm has no ESG-related job posts in year j and all the previous years, the abnormal ESG HI is set as missing for year j.

We use average ESG HI from all previous years as the benchmark in order to smooth out years in which no ESG job were tagged as being posted. This does not necessarily mean that firms were not hiring in the ESG space in those years; it could mean we have been unable to capture those jobs from the data. Using historical ESG HI from just one year, say, the previous year, would lead to a noisier abnormal ESG HI due to some ESG-related jobs not being tagged.

Take a firm at the end of 2015 as an example. Its abnormal ESG HI is essentially the difference between its annual ESG HI in 2015 and in 2014 since the sample starts from 2014. If there are no ESG-related jobs in 2015, then the abnormal ESG HI would be −1 times the HI in 2014. If there are no ESG-related jobs in 2014, then the abnormal ESG-related interest is set as the annual ESG HI in 2015. Figure 9.10 plots the histograms of abnormal ESG HI for firms in 2015. Overall, the abnormal ESG HI is bell shape distributed and resembles a normal distribution. However, there are a few firms with very positive or negative abnormal HI, exhibiting a fat tail. In the subsequent analysis, we exploit the information from HI in a non-parametric way. Specifically, we group firms into different buckets based on the ranking of their abnormal ESG HI. This alleviates issues in statistical inference driven by fat tails.

To understand the characteristics of firms with different levels of abnormal ESG HI, at the end of each year, we rank firms into terciles based on their abnormal ESG HI within sectors. Table 9.5 reports the average characteristics for firms in each bucket across different years. The figure shows that different abnormal ESG HI groups show little systematic bias in their characteristics such as market beta, book-to-market ratio, and investment rates. However, firms with missing abnormal ESG HI tend to be smaller in size but also have higher investment rates.

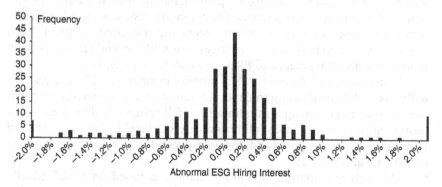

FIGURE 9.10 Histogram of abnormal ESG HI for firms at the end of 2015.
Source: Burning Glass Technologies, Barclays Research.

TABLE 9.5   Average firm characteristics of terciles ranked by abnormal ESG HI.

Abnormal ESG Hiring Interest Rank	# of Stocks	Abnormal ESG Hiring Interest (%)	Equity Market Cap (USD bn)	Beta (Trailing 60 months)	Book to market ratios	Earnings to price ratios	Investment rate (%, annual growth rate in total assets)
High	117	0.7	51	0.93	0.41	0.040	11
Medium	119	0.0	51	1.02	0.38	0.044	8
Low	114	−0.7	40	0.98	0.40	0.028	8
Missing	71		34	0.91	0.39	0.042	15

Source: Burning Glass Technologies, Compustat, Barclays Research.

ESG HIRING AND SUBSEQUENT ESG RATING CHANGES

If increasing ESG hiring interest is indicative of firms' greater focus on ESG, we would expect this to translate into actions that have a material impact on how they are rated on their ESG practices. In this section, we examine whether such a relationship exists and focus on ESG ratings from MSCI.

MSCI rates firms on individual ESG pillars, E, S, and G, separately, on a scale of 0–10. A weighted sum of scores for individual pillars forms the composite ESG score, which, by construction, also has a scale of 0–10. The pillar weights used in the composite score vary across industrials and depend on firms' exposure to Environmental, Social, and Governance risks. For example, firms that are more sensitive to environmental issues usually have a higher weight for the 'E' pillar, making their performance on the E front more prominent in their composite ESG scores. The composite ESG score is subsequently normalized against scores of industry peers and converted to one of seven notches. In order to look at rating changes across different pillars, we focus on scores for individual pillars and ESG, which all have a scale of 0–10.

As discussed in Chapter 8, MSCI monitor companies' ESG metrics on a daily basis while conducting in-depth full rating reviews on an annual basis. Our analysis tracks changes in ratings from full reviews. Unlike daily monitoring, ratings from in-depth full reviews are validated by ESG analysts and hence are more thorough. In addition, as suggested by MSCI, ratings from full reviews are also less noisy.

Although our analysis on rating changes is based on MSCI, ideally we would also like to examine the relationship between hiring and rating changes with ratings from other vendors in order to see whether the results are robust. In fact, as there is no consensus on the definition, scope, and measurement for ESG, the ESG ratings for the same firm from different rating agencies can vary significantly. In Chapter 13, we show that there is large dispersion in ratings from three ESG rating providers, MSCI, Sustainalytics, and Vigeo Eiris. However, Sustainalytics changed its methodology in 2018, which makes it difficult to track rating changes, and Vigeo Eiris only starts to provide annual rating updates in 2020. Therefore, our analysis focuses on ratings from MSCI.

Before we examine how hiring dynamics might be associated with subsequent rating changes, we first address a challenge brought by the bounded rating scale. Given scores are reported on a scale from 0 to 10, firms that have a high current rating have less room for improvement. Similarly, for firms with a low current rating, there is less space to deteriorate. Intuitively, a 1-point score improvement for a company rated 8 is more difficult to achieve than for a company with a rating of 3. Therefore, comparison based on raw score changes directly will be biased by the current rating level. The issue is not unique to ESG ratings but has general implications for comparing ratings with bounds.

To address this challenge, we adjust the rating change by the space of change. Specifically, we look at the change percent in the rating score:

$$\text{Change Percent} = \begin{cases} \dfrac{\Delta\text{Rating}}{10 - \text{Current Rating}}, & \text{if } \Delta\text{Rating} > 0 \\[2ex] \dfrac{\Delta\text{Rating}}{\text{Current Rating}}, & \text{if } \Delta\text{Rating} \leq 0 \end{cases}$$

For example, if the firm is currently rated at 6, then any subsequent rating improvement will be normalized by the maximum possible improvement, which equals $4 (= 10 - 6)$ whereas any rating deterioration will be normalized by the largest possible deterioration of $6 (= 6 - 0)$.

Methodology

Another challenge in examining the relationship between hiring and subsequent rating changes is the limited sample period. The job-posting data from BGT starts from 2014. Constructing the abnormal ESG hiring interest requires at least one historical annual hiring interest, which effectively only allows us to track rating changes starting from the end of 2015. What exacerbates the sample size issue is that the impact from hiring on subsequent rating, if there is any, takes time to materialize. Therefore, for hiring observed in recent years, we may still not have sufficient data to examine potential rating changes.

To address the issue, we put our focus on the cohort that gives us the longest sample to track subsequent changes. In particular, we zoom in on the firms in our sample at the end of 2015 and then track their rating changes over the subsequent one-, two-, three-, four-, and five-year windows. Besides this approach, we also look at an alternative approach, in which we fix the rating tracking window instead of the cohorts. For each cohort, we look at the rating changes over the window and then average the changes.

The Cohort of 2015

Our main analysis is built on the cohort of 2015, i.e. firms included in our sample at the end of 2015. The cohort provides the longest tracking window for analysis in our sample.

Table 9.6 reports the rating distributions of firms at the end of different years. For example, at the end of 2015, which is also the beginning of the tracking window, the cohort has a median rating of 5.6, 4.1, 4.9, and 4.5 for the 'E' pillar, 'S' pillar, 'G' pillar, and overall ESG respectively (out of a scale 0–10). The figure shows that scores for the individual pillars and ESG generally improve between 2015 and 2020, but the overall changes are very small. Take the 'E' pillar as an example. The median only increases by 0.1 while the 10th and 95th percentiles both increase by 0.3.

Despite the small change in overall rating distribution, rating changes do vary across individual firms. Figure 9.11 shows histograms of rating change percent in E, S, G, and ESG. The figure focuses on rating changes till the end of 2020. Results for other tracking windows are similar. The histogram for all the rating changes have a bell shape distribution and are relatively spread out between [−1,1], the support of rating change percent. Compared to individual pillars, changes in ESG seems to be the most concentrated, suggesting smaller variation in ESG changes across firms. However, since the ESG score is the weighted sum of individual pillar scores, it is unsurprising that its variation is smaller.

Subsequent Rating Changes

Next, we examine whether the variation of rating changes across firms is associated with their hiring activities. We rank firms into terciles based on their abnormal ESG HI. The ranking is done within sectors to remove systematic effects driven by sector dynamics. Then we track the average rating changes for firms in each bucket. If more active hiring leads to improved ESG ratings, we expect the bucket of high abnormal ESG HI to have more positive average rating changes compared to the bucket with low abnormal ESG HI. We first look at the results for the entire cohort. As the challenges firms face in ESG

TABLE 9.6 MSCI ESG rating (scale: 0–10) percentiles for the 2015 cohort.

Rating as the end of Year	E			S			G			ESG		
	10th	50th (Median)	90th	10th	50th (Median)	90th	10th	50th (Median)	90th	10th	50th (Median)	90th
2015	2.6	5.6	9.7	2.1	4.1	6.5	3.2	4.9	6.3	3.2	4.5	6.2
2016	2.6	5.6	8.9	2.3	4.2	6.4	3.2	5.0	6.5	3.2	4.6	6.2
2017	2.8	5.6	9.7	2.5	4.3	6.5	3.4	5.0	6.7	3.6	4.7	6.1
2018	2.8	5.7	10.0	2.6	4.4	6.3	4.3	5.7	7.1	3.7	4.9	6.2
2019	2.8	5.5	10.0	2.8	4.6	6.5	4.4	5.8	7.3	3.9	5.1	6.2
2020	2.9	5.7	10.0	2.9	4.5	6.5	3.9	5.7	7.1	3.9	5.0	6.3

Source: Burning Glass Technologies, Compustat, MSCI, Barclays Research.

Panel A: E pillar

Panel B: S pillar

Panel C: G pillar

Panel D: ESG

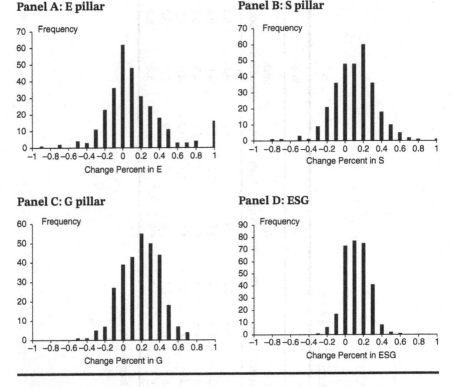

FIGURE 9.11 Histograms of rating change percent till 2020 for the 2015 cohort. *Source:* Burning Glass Technologies, Compustat, MSCI, Barclays Research.

differ, we also look at a sub-sample of firms that are more sensitive to certain issues and see how their rating changes vary across different pillars.

Table 9.7 reports the difference in rating change percent between firms with top abnormal ESG HI and firms with bottom abnormal ESG HI. The rating change is tracked since the end of year 2015 for all firms, while the end of the tracking window varies across different years between 2016 and 2020. For example, in 2016, the difference in the average change percent for the 'E' pillar is roughly 4.8%, which is approximately equivalent to a difference of 0.21 (= 4.8%*(10-5.6)) in scores out of a scale of 0–10. In Table 9.7, we also normalize the rating change percent by its sector mean and standard deviation and then report the difference in the average standardized rating change percent between top and bottom abnormal ESG HI firms. The normalization accounts for the fact that firms from different industries are rated by different items under each pillar and therefore their rating change percent might not be directly comparable.

TABLE 9.7 Difference in rating change percent between firms with top and bottom abnormal ESG HI in the 2015 cohort.

End of Tracking Window (in Year)	Sector Neutral Difference in Change Percent				Sector Neutral Difference relative to its Cross–sectional Standard Deviation			
	E (%)	S (%)	G (%)	ESG (%)	E	S	G	ESG
2016	4.8	−1.9	4.8	0.1	0.17	−0.16	0.22	−0.01
2017	2.9	0.1	2.0	0.7	0.08	0.00	0.10	0.04
2018	3.1	−1.2	1.9	0.8	0.10	−0.09	0.09	0.04
2019	4.6	−1.7	1.1	1.5	0.12	−0.10	0.04	0.10
2020	6.5	−2.7	1.1	0.5	0.17	−0.17	0.04	0.00

Source: Burning Glass Technologies, Compustat, MSCI, Barclays Research.

Table 9.7 shows that differences in rating changes are positive for 'E' and 'G' pillars but are insignificant. In addition, they fluctuate from year to year, lacking a gradually increasing trend. Overall, we do not find consistent predictability of the abnormal ESG HI for subsequent rating changes.

As the nature of businesses varies across different firms, some might be more sensitive to environmental issues while some might be more exposed to governance issues. Therefore, when we look at rating changes in individual pillars, we would expect firms that are more sensitive to issues of that pillar would have more meaningful changes. For example, for the 'E' pillar, as financial firms are less exposed to environmental issues, their rating changes in the 'E' pillar are usually less meaningful, hence noisier than those for energy companies. To address this dynamic, we look at a subset of firms that are particularly sensitive to issues of individual pillars. Given most of the jobs are environment-related, we focus on the 'E' pillar first.

We rely on the pillar weight from MSCI to identify firms that are sensitive to environmental issues. Specifically, we exclude firms that have an 'E'-pillar weight below the sample median. In addition, we remove three sectors – financial, healthcare, and consumer discretionary. The additional filter has minimal impact on the sample: only a few firms from these three industries remain once the 'E' pillar weight filter is applied. For example, none of the firms from the healthcare industry have an 'E' pillar weight higher than the sample median. However, all the firms from Energy and Materials industries survived the 'E' pillar weight filter. This indicates that the filter appears consistent with the general nature of different industries.

Table 9.8 reports changes in the 'E' pillar ratings for the E-sensitive subsample. The figure shows that within the E-sensitive sample, the difference in

TABLE 9.8 Differences in E-rating change percent between firms with top and bottom abnormal ESG HI in the 2015 cohort.

End of Tracking Window (in Year)	Sector Neutral Difference in E-pillar Rating Change Percent (relative to the standard deviation of full sample difference)	
	Full Sample	E-sensitive Subsample
2016	0.17	0.12
2017	0.08	0.17
2018	0.10	0.29*
2019	0.12	0.25*
2020	0.17	0.29*

Note: * represents significance at the level of 0.1. Statistical significance is based on the null hypothesis that the bucket assignment is completely random.
Source: Burning Glass Technologies, Compustat, MSCI, Barclays Research.

the E-rating between top and bottom abnormal ESG HI gradually increases and becomes significant after three years. In addition, the difference seems to become stable and does not revert subsequently. Comparing the results with those from the full-sample, the difference also has a much larger magnitude for the E-sensitive sample. The result highlights that the effects from hiring dynamics are mostly concentrated among those firms most sensitive to the underlying ESG pillar.

We repeat the analysis for the 'S' and 'G' pillars. Similar to the E-sensitive firms, we identify S-sensitive and G-sensitive firms based on the S-pillar and G-pillar weights from MSCI. Table 9.9 shows the rating changes in the S-pillar and G-pillar for the S-sensitive and G-sensitive firms respectively. However, we do not see the same improvement as in the E-pillar. The results for the S-sensitive and G-sensitive firms remain insignificant and inconsistent. This could in part be because most of the ESG-related job openings are environmental related, offering less information for the other two pillars.

The main analysis is based on the 2015 cohort. We also examine the rating changes for multiple cohorts after fixing the rating change tracking window. We focus on four cohorts, 2015, 2016, 2017, and 2018. This allows us to examine two rating change tracking windows – one-year and two-year. Figure 9.12 reports the changes in the 'E' pillar ratings for the full sample and the E-sensitive subsample. Similar to previous findings, the effects of abnormal ESG HI in predicting subsequent rating changes seem to be stronger for the E-sensitive firms. The difference is much bigger for the E-sensitive firms in the two-year window. Unlike the full-sample, the difference in

TABLE 9.9 Differences in S- and G-rating change percent between firms with top and bottom abnormal ESG HI in the 2015 cohort.

End of Tracking Window (in Year)	Sector Neutral S-Rating Difference (relative to the standard deviation of full sample difference)		Sector Neutral G-Rating Difference (relative to the standard deviation of full sample difference)	
	Full Sample	S-sensitive Subsample	Full Sample	G-sensitive Subsample
2016	−0.16	−0.25	0.22	0.14
2017	0.00	−0.24	0.10	0.17
2018	−0.09	−0.13	0.09	0.07
2019	−0.10	0.07	0.04	0.14
2020	−0.17	0.05	0.04	−0.04

Source: Burning Glass Technologies, Compustat, MSCI, Barclays Research.

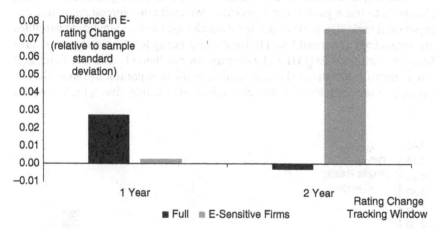

FIGURE 9.12 Average differences in E-rating change percent between firms with top and bottom abnormal ESG HI across 2015, 2016, 2017, and 2018 cohorts. *Source:* Burning Glass Technologies, Compustat, MSCI, Barclays Research.

the two-year window is higher than that in the one-year window for the E-sensitive subsample.

In sum, our analysis suggests that an increasing interest in ESG hiring seems to be associated with subsequent rating improvements. However, the effects seem to be concentrated in the 'E' pillar for firms that are most sensitive to environmental issues.

Alternative Rating Change Measure

As a robustness check, we use alternative ways to model the rating changes. Specifically, instead of using the rating change percent, we focus on the simple rating change, which is the difference between the new rating and the current rating. The rating change percent allows us to address the issue that the simple rating change could be biased by the current rating level given the room of improvement (deterioration) is more limited when the current rating is high (low). However, the simple rating change is easier to interpret and understand. Figure 9.13 reports the average difference in simple rating change in the 'E' pillar between firms with top and bottom abnormal ESG hiring interests. We track the differences for the full 2015 cohort and its E-sensitive sub-sample. The dynamics are very similar to Table 9.8 where differences based on rating change percent are reported. First, for the E-sensitive sample, the difference in simple rating change gradually increases when the ranking window lengthens and does not revert. In addition, differences in the E-sensitive sample are larger than the full sample except in the first year.

One way to control for the current rating while using the simple rating change is to use a parametric regression. We estimate regressions where the dependent variables are the simple rating changes and independent variables are winsorized abnormal ESG HI, the current rating level, an interaction term between abnormal ESG HI and a dummy for not being E-sensitive firms and other controls. Results are broadly similar to the non-parametric analysis. For example, the coefficient for the interaction term is negative, which suggests

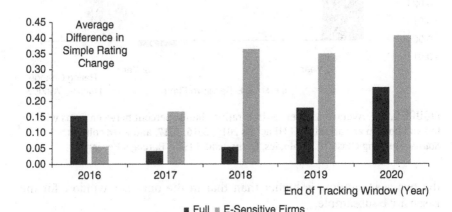

FIGURE 9.13 Differences in E-rating change between firms with top and bottom abnormal ESG HI in the 2015 cohort.
Source: Burning Glass Technologies, Compustat, MSCI, Barclays Research.

the E-rating changes of E-sensitive firms are relatively more sensitive to ESG hiring activities. The parametric regression also allows us to control for intermediary hiring activity. When we include hiring activity between 2016 and 2018 as one of the independent variables for regressing the rating change between 2015 and 2019, the intermediary hiring activities do not yield significant coefficients while the abnormal ESG HI in 2015 does. This confirms that it takes time for hiring activity to have an effect on the ESG ratings.

ESG HIRING AND SUBSEQUENT PERFORMANCE

In the previous section, we show that for firms that are sensitive to environmental issues, their rating changes in the 'E' pillar appear partly associated with their prior ESG hiring activity. Given improving ESG performance usually creates value for firms, we examine whether hiring activity is also correlated with subsequent stock performance.

To examine the question, we again focus on the firms from the 2015 cohort that are sensitive to environmental issues. Stocks are ranked into tercile portfolios based on firms' abnormal ESG HI at the end of 2015. Stocks in each tercile are either equally weighted or weighted by market capitalization. The ranking is done within sectors to eliminate sector biases across portfolios. Portfolios are rebalanced annually to maintain the respective weighting scheme after price changes while the constituents of each tercile are unchanged. If ESG hiring indeed has an effect on subsequent equity performance, we should expect to see the portfolios generate significantly different returns in subsequent periods.

Table 9.10 summarizes the performance of each tercile portfolio between January 2016 and December 2020. Regardless of the weighting scheme, the high abnormal ESG HI portfolio outperforms the other two portfolios with either medium or low abnormal ESG HI. The high abnormal ESG HI portfolio also has lower volatility and better tail risk than the other two portfolios. As a result, the high abnormal ESG HI portfolio had the best risk-adjusted performance. In addition, the average returns and risk-adjusted performances are monotonic in the abnormal ESG HI level. Most importantly, a long–short portfolio between the high and low abnormal ESG HI buckets delivered an annualized information ratio of 0.59 in equal weighting and 0.65 in value weighting, suggesting that the performance difference is significant. Finally, we also investigate the possibility that the outperformance associated with high abnormal ESG HI is not ESG specific and instead is related to a more active overall hiring. It is worth noting that the ESG HI is scaled by the total number of ESG and non-ESG-related job postings. Therefore, firms with high abnormal ESG HI are not necessarily those with more overall job postings. Still,

TABLE 9.10 Portfolio performance of firms sensitive to environmental issues, ranked by abnormal ESG HI, January 2016–December 2020.

	Equally Weighted, Sector Neutral, Annual Rebalancing				Value Weighted, Sector Neutral, Annual Rebalancing				Equally Weighted, Sector Neutral, Annual Rebalancing			
		High Abn ESG				High Abn ESG				High Overall		
	H-L	HI	Medium	Low	H-L	HI	Medium	Low	H-L	Openings	Medium	Low
Avg. Ret (%/Yr)	4.17	15.67	13.54	11.50	5.06	15.94	13.09	10.88	1.05	14.95	11.88	13.90
Vol (%/Yr)	7.09	16.94	17.11	21.52	7.78	14.75	15.85	18.80	7.31	16.20	19.30	19.48
Sharpe (Inf.) Ratio (ann.)	0.59	0.85	0.71	0.47	0.65	0.99	0.74	0.51	0.14	0.84	0.55	0.64
Worst Monthly Ret (%)	−3.96	−16.19	−17.71	−22.40	−5.11	−13.41	−14.86	−18.45	−4.45	−16.67	−19.63	−18.88
Max Drawdown (%)	−9.94	−25.85	−27.43	−36.93	−8.43	−20.29	−22.19	−30.60	−12.37	−26.34	−31.93	−30.58

Source: Burning Glass Technologies, Compustat, MSCI, Barclays Research.

we examine this possibility by ranking firms directly on their overall hiring activity. Specifically, we formulate tercile portfolios in the same way as the abnormal ESG HI portfolios except that firms are ranked by their total number of postings in 2014 and 2015 divided by the average number of employees in the same period.[7] The last four columns in Table 9.10 show performances of these tercile portfolios. Unlike abnormal ESG HI portfolios, these portfolios' performances are not monotonic in the overall hiring activities and the L–S portfolio delivered much smaller average returns (1.05% vs 4.17%) and smaller information ratio (0.14 vs 0.59).[8] Therefore, the outperformance seems to be more related to ESG-specific hiring rather than overall hiring.

Although we've shown that firms in different abnormal ESG HI buckets have little systematic biases in their characteristics, the outperformance could still be driven by other well-known risk factors rather than the differences in firms ESG hiring activities. To address this possibility, we run factor regressions on the Fama–French three-factors and Fama–French five-factors (Fama and French 1993, 2015). Table 9.11 shows that the long–short portfolio between the high and low abnormal ESG HI firms generated significant alphas after controlling for the common risk factors. The annualized alpha is between 4.7% and 5.6%, depending on the factor specification and weighting scheme. The positive and significant alphas suggest that the outperformance is not driven by common risk exposures but is more likely due to the ESG hiring activity.

To further understand the performance dynamic, Figure 9.14 plots the cumulative return of the long–short portfolio. As it takes time for the hiring

TABLE 9.11 Factor regression estimates, January 2016–December 2020.

	Sector Neutral, Top Tercile – Bottom Tercile Ranked by Abnormal ESG HI			
	Equal Weighting		**Value Weighting**	
Alpha (%/Yr)	4.7**	5.2***	4.9*	5.6***
Mkt-Rf	−0.14***	−0.17***	−0.09*	−0.14***
SMB	−0.26***	−0.26***	−0.40***	−0.38***
HML	−0.23***	−0.10	−0.23***	−0.03
RMW		0.02		0.07
CMA		−0.32***		−0.48***
Adjusted R-squared	55%	58%	52%	59%

Note: *, **, *** represent significance at the level of 0.1, 0.05, and 0.01 respectively.
Source: Burning Glass Technologies, Compustat, Ken French Data Library, MSCI, Barclays Research.

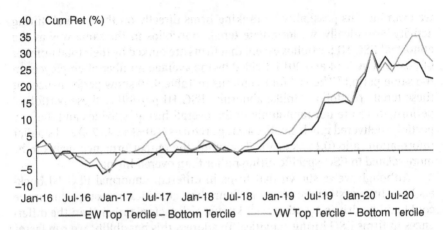

FIGURE 9.14 Cumulative return difference between high and low abnormal ESG HI firms from E-sensitive sample.
Source: Burning Glass Technologies, Compustat, MSCI, Barclays Research.

activity to have an effect on performance, we expect the outperformance would only emerge sometime after 2015. Figure 9.14 shows that the outperformance largely started to materialize in late 2018, consistent with our expectation. The time series dynamic lends further support to the hypothesis that the outperformance of high abnormal ESG HI firms over otherwise similar low abnormal ESG HI ones is associated with firms' ESG hiring activities.

As shown earlier, firms with high abnormal ESG HI had better subsequent rating changes in the 'E' pillar, which in turn could partly explain the outperformance seen in Tables 9.10 and 9.11 and Figure 9.14. To examine this possibility, we formulate four portfolios by intersecting the E-sensitive sample into two by two buckets based on firms' rating changes (see Chapter 8 for ESG rating momentum) and ESG hiring dynamic. Specifically, firms are ranked into two buckets based on their median rating change percent in the 'E' pillar between the end of 2015 and the end of 2018. Independently, they are sorted into two buckets based on their median abnormal ESG HI in 2015. Both rankings are done within sectors. Table 9.12 reports the performance between January 2019 and December 2020 for the two by two portfolios. The choice of the breakup point for the sample period is based on the emergence of outperformance in Table 9.12. Several key observations emerge from the table. First, there are more stocks in the buckets where abnormal ESG HI and rating change percent are either both high or low, which confirms a positive relation between ESG hiring and subsequent rating changes (note the hiring window and rating change window are not overlapping). Second,

TABLE 9.12 Portfolio performance from a double sort between ESG hiring and rating change.

	Performance between 2019 and 2020				Risk-adjusted Abnormal Performance between 2019 and 2020			
Abnormal ESG HI	Low	Low	High	High	Low	Low	High	High
Rating Change Percent between 2015 and 2018	Low	High	Low	High	Low	High	Low	High
Avg Ret (%/Yr)	13.23	18.75	17.03	20.91	−8.23	−1.83	−7.02	1.51
Vol. (%/Yr)	27.12	28.34	23.74	22.86	6.35	13.32	7.32	6.24
Inf. (Sharpe) Ratio	0.43	0.61	0.65	0.85	−1.30	−0.14	−0.96	0.24
Worst Month Ret (%/mo)	−21.51	−19.14	−18.46	−16.26	−3.70	−6.75	−4.60	−3.20
Max Drawdown (%)	−34.89	−31.53	−28.36	−25.79	−20.32	−16.48	−15.31	−5.38
Number of Stocks	33	29	27	39				

Source: Burning Glass Technologies, Compustat, MSCI, Barclays Research.

improved rating changes are associated with improved stock performances. Within each hiring bucket, stocks with better rating changes between 2015 and 2018 experienced better performances subsequently (18.75% vs 13.23% within low ESG hiring firms and 20.91% vs. 17.03% within high ESG hiring firms). The outperformance is still present after taking out the returns driven by exposures to Fama–French five factors (−1.83% vs −8.23% within low ESG hiring and 1.51% vs −7.02% within high ESG hiring).[9] This suggests that better rating changes seem to lead to better stock performances. Since more ESG hiring appears to lead to positive rating changes, part of the outperformance associated with ESG hiring could be related to improvement in ESG ratings. Nevertheless, within each rating change bucket, stocks with high abnormal ESG HI still delivered higher performance than those with low abnormal ESG hiring interest, which shows that not all the outperformance is driven by rating change improvements. The result is not surprising given that ESG ratings are far from perfect to capture firms' ESG practices hence rating momentum does not reflect the full picture of firms with increasing ESG efforts (see Chapter 13 for the large ESG rating dispersions from different providers). In sum, the results suggest that rating changes and hiring dynamics might be complementary in identifying future outperformers.

CONCLUSION

Interest in ESG investing has grown significantly over the past decade, leading many studies to try to understand the effect of ESG ratings on security performance and how best to construct portfolios with ESG ratings in mind. Yet, there is very limited analysis examining actions from corporates to address ESG-related challenges, especially in a systematic way. For example, while there are many studies reporting the increasing size of assets related to ESG investing, very few reports show whether the increasing trend in AUM is accompanied by increasing efforts from corporates to address ESG-related challenges.

In this chapter, we use a novel data set on job postings to capture individual firms' ESG-related hiring activities, through which we systematically examine the efforts firms make to improve their ESG performance. As workforce planning is often based on business need and is usually associated with concrete business actions, the data set allows us to capture firms' concrete ESG efforts that would otherwise be missing from firms' ESG reports or announced commitments.

We find that overall ESG job hiring interest for S&P 500 firms has increased more than other types of job vacancies since 2014. This highlights that firms are indeed investing more resources to improve their ESG performance, in line with the growing trend in ESG assets. Second, as most of the tagged ESG-related jobs are related to the 'E' pillar, we zoom in on firms that are most sensitive to environmental issues. By tracking their subsequent rating changes since 2015, we find that firms with high abnormal ESG hiring interest had more subsequent rating improvements in the 'E' pillar than peers with low abnormal ESG hiring interest. In addition, the former outperformed the latter in subsequent stock returns. The outperformance cannot be explained by common risk factors and only emerged a few years later, consistent with the gradual incorporation of hiring impact on stock performance. The results suggest that hiring activity in ESG may reflect future actions taken by firms that could lead to improved ESG ratings.

Since the job-posting data only start from 2014 and it takes time for any impact from hiring to materialize, the effective data sample we can use is very limited. Hence, the results should be interpreted with caution. However, our analysis highlights a possible positive relationship between ESG hiring and subsequent ESG rating changes and performance. It would be interesting to revisit the relationship when more data become available.

APPENDIX: A SAMPLE JOB POST

Environmental Policy and ESG Manager

Dummy Company, Detroit, MI

Full-time Estimated: $81,000 – $110,000 a year

Dummy Company is seeking an environmental/ESG manager who is passionate about the impact company behavior has on society, the environment and on corporate performance and has experience integrating ESG considerations into the corporations operations. This includes development and management of our global sustainability strategy, as well as managing Dummy Company's responses to third-party disclosure requests and supporting content development for our Global Sustainability Report, providing benchmarking and research on industry ESG-related trends and issues, and internal engagement across multiple key business functions such as Investor Relations, Legal (Governance), Global Manufacturing, GPSC, Fleet & Commercial, and Communications.

An ideal Environmental/ESG manager will bring subject matter expertise on governance topics and environmental and social issues, along with an understanding of how these issues can be leveraged beneficially in the corporation's operations. We are particularly interested in candidates with a background/interest in the environmental or transportation sectors. The candidate will be able to communicate views clearly, will be credible with company management teams as well as internal and external stakeholders, will enjoy acting as an individual contributor within a highly collaborative culture, and will thrive by building strong relationships with colleagues.

Key areas of responsibility will include:

- Build and maintain data which reflect our materiality matrix for the purpose of evaluating how to differentiate our ESG program and performance. This includes identifying ESG key performance indicators that have proven to be most impactful and enhance integration into program framework
- Use information from data vendors and our own research to analyse, score, rate, and rank our ESG performance

■ Seek and evaluate sources of information regarding the environmental, social, and governance policies (including science-based targets) and performance of corporations and other issuers of securities

■ Develop expertise within industry sectors and relevant peer groups of companies

■ Engage with external stakeholder to help develop a strong ESG program

■ Contribute to our team's knowledge of ESG factors and materiality

■ Identify strengths, weaknesses, opportunities, and threats to Dummy Company's ESG programs and concisely communicate to our leadership

■ Assist in creating a productive, collaborative, and innovative team culture

■ Lead our response development for third-party disclosure requests

■ Benchmark corporate peers, competitors, and auto industry on key ESG trends, and best practices in areas such as sustainability reporting and third-party disclosure

Basic Required Skills:
■ 3–10 years of professional experience
■ A Bachelors' Degree is required, preferably in engineering, public policy, communications, or business; advanced degree such as a MBA or MPA is highly desirable
■ Project management experience, strong cross-functional knowledge and project management leadership required (including managing of multiple projects simultaneously)
■ Work well both independently and in teams
■ Highly developed oral and written communications skills
■ High level of interpersonal skills to work effectively with others, motivate team members, and elicit work output
■ Very high level of analytical problem solving skills where problems are very complex
■ Experience with financial tools and databases (e.g. Bloomberg, FactSet, MSCI)

Additional Required Qualifications:
■ Experience and strong skills in group/team facilitation
■ High level of enthusiasm, persistence, leadership ability, initiative, and experienced judgment to identify priorities, initiate projects, and complete activities in a timely fashion

- Experience working externally with policy makers and regulators on complex rulemakings
- Prior work experience in automotive engineering, finance, marketing &/or planning
- Proficiency in Excel and PowerPoint
- Media/PR experience
- Experience in interacting directly with a broad group of external stakeholders, policymakers and investors.

Source: Burning Glass Technologies, Barclays Research

REFERENCES

Albuquerque, R., Koskinen Y., and Zhang, C. (2019). Corporate Social Responsibility and Firm Risk: Theory and Empirical Evidence. *Management Science*, 65, pp. 4451–4469.

Fama, E. and French, K. (1993). Common Risk Factors in the Returns on Stocks and Bonds. *Journal of Financial Economics*, 33 (1), pp. 3–56.

Fama, E. and French, K. (2015). A Five-factor Asset Pricing Model. *Journal of Financial Economics*, 116 (1), pp. 1–22.

Luo, H.A. and Balvers, R.J. (2017). Social Screens and Systematic Investor Boycott Risk. *Journal of Financial and Quantitative Analysis*, 52 (1), pp. 365–399.

NOTES

1. See, for example Albuquerque et al. (2019), Luo and Balvers (2017); and other chapters of the book and references therein.
2. See, for example, Connecting talent with opportunity in the digital age, McKinsey, 1 June 2015.
3. See the note from Burning Glass Technologies https://www.burning-glass.com/about/faq/, accessed on 27 May 2021. Our examination of the data also confirms that very few job postings share the same job title, employer, and location.
4. The data set has a stock ticker field. However, the field is incomplete and therefore inappropriate for mapping.
5. Precision measures the percentage of posts that are tagged as ESG-related by the algorithm that are confirmed to be correctly classified. Another important measure of accuracy, which is not calculated here, is recall, which would report the percentage of all ESG-related job posts that are correctly identified.
6. The field of required experience has three possible non-missing values: 0–1, 1–6 and 6+. Each value is converted to a numeric value of 1, 2, and 3 respectively. The field of minimum level of education is converted to numeric values as follows: less than or equal to 14 years of education is converted to 1; 15–16 years of education is converted to 2; 17 and 20 years of education is converted to 3 and 21+ years of education is converted to 4. The job posting weight is computed as the average of

the coded numeric values for experience and education. If the posting has missing value for the required years of education, the weight is the numeric value for the required years of experience and vice versa. If the posting misses both required years of education and experience, the weight is based on the median years of education and experience.

7. The average number of employees is computed by averaging the number of employees reported in the most recent two annual statements before the end of 2015.

8. In the interest of space, we only report equally weighted portfolios for overall hiring in Table 9.10. Value-weighted portfolios have slightly better performance but the L–S portfolio does not generate significant alphas. In addition, we also looked at overall hiring portfolios in the full sample rather than the E-sensitive sample. The portfolio still does not produce significant alpha after controlling for Fama–French five factors (Fama and French 2015).

9. For each stock, the risk-adjusted abnormal return for each month is computed by subtracting the sum of products between a stock's factor exposure and contemporaneous factor returns from the stock's return. The factor exposure is estimated by running factor regression using a fixed window between January 2016 and December 2020.

CHAPTER 10

The Relationship Between Corporate Governance and Profitability

ESG practices are being widely adopted by companies to address societal concerns and regulatory pressures. Not only might these practices benefit society as a whole, but many components in these practices are also believed to positively affect a company's financial performance by reducing risks and enhancing reputation. Given the growing importance of ESG considerations, regulators, investors, and company management are interested in quantifying the relation between ESG attributes and company profitability. The challenge is to measure this relationship accurately, given many other confounding factors.

In this chapter, we examine the relationship between governance (the G-pillar of ESG) and profitability while accounting for other relevant firm-specific characteristics that might also affect profitability. The G-pillar is thought to be particularly relevant to companies' profitability, because effective corporate governance can mitigate risks, increase accountability and transparency, and ultimately promote value creation. Our methodology can be easily extended to investigate the association between other ESG attributes and a variety of financial performance metrics of companies.

We use the exposure-matched approach and the regression approach. The former was introduced in Chapter 2 and Chapter 3. It constructs a pair of diversified portfolios that maximize and minimize governance scores while matching other key firm characteristics that are relevant to profitability. The difference in the subsequent average profitability of the two portfolios thus is purely driven by governance, as their exposures to other relevant characteristics are neutralized by construction. The exposure-matched approach makes it easy to explicitly control for time-varying key attributes (other than G) and is less susceptible to mis-specifications. However, it only provides the estimates while holding the other firm characteristics at a specific point (e.g. index average) and can only estimate the effect from one variable of interest, and cannot be used to measure the relationships between several governance metrics and profitability simultaneously.

Given the limitation of the exposure-matched approach, we also consider the regression approach, in which we regress the future profitability of individual companies against their governance scores while controlling for the other key attributes that are relevant to profitability to validate the results from the exposure-matched approach. This approach provides estimates for a more general relationship between the governance metric and profitability (i.e., not requiring all other characteristics to be at a specific level). It is easier to implement and interpret; however, the results can be sensitive to the specifications. Comparing the results from both approaches can provide valuable insights and help ensure the validity of the findings. Another advantage of the regression approach is that it can be used to analyse the relationship between several granular governance metrics (such as accounting, board structure, pay) and profitability jointly, accounting for the correlations among the governance metrics.

With both approaches, we use companies' return on equity (ROE) for the year following the ESG rating as the measure of profitability. ROE calculations scale company earnings by their book value of equity and therefore facilitate a fair comparison among companies of varying size. The relationships between governance scores and ROEs can be directly translated into other earnings metrics. For example, the expected change in earnings-per-share (EPS) by 1-point improvement in G-score can be easily derived using our results.[1]

The rest of the chapter first describes the governance scores used. Next, it explains the detailed construction steps of the exposure-matched approach, followed by results. Then it presents the results from the regression approach, which demonstrates the consistency between the two approaches.

OVERVIEW OF MSCI GOVERNANCE SCORE DATA

We use MSCI G-pillar scores and sub-pillar scores as measures of companies' governance practices. The MSCI governance scores are structured as follows: the composite G score captures the overall governance practice of a company. This comprises two theme scores: Corporate Governance and Corporate Behaviour, each containing several key issue scores. The key issue scores further break down into key metrics, which are evaluated directly based on raw data.

Figure 10.1 illustrates the structure of the MSCI G-score, including the composite scores at the pillar level and various scores at granular levels. The Corporate Governance theme evaluates the degree to which a company adheres to good core corporate governance. This encompasses aspects

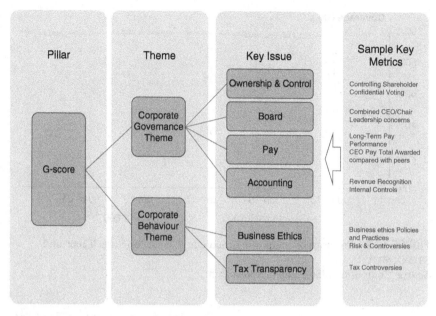

FIGURE 10.1 MSCI Governance scores structure.
Source: MSCI, Barclays Research.

including the composition and independence of the board of directors, executive compensation practices, shareholder rights, and accounting quality. In simple terms, it looks at how well a company follows good governance rules. It is believed that following good governance practices would boost performance of the company and safeguard the interests of its shareholders. The Corporate Behaviour theme, meanwhile, assesses a company's commitment to ethical and responsible practices in areas such as fraud, corrupt practices, and tax controversies. Scoring high in this indicates the company has good practices in keeping a good reputation and mitigating risks. The theme scores are presented on a scale of 1 to 10, with higher scores indicating better governance practices.

Universe and Coverage

We focus our analysis on stocks in the Russell 1000 index universe for US stocks and the STOXX 600 index universe for European stocks.[2] Figures 10.2 and 10.3 report the coverage of the MSCI governance scores and two theme scores on both universes. The composite G-score and the Corporate Governance theme scores cover almost all stocks in the Russell 1000 universe since

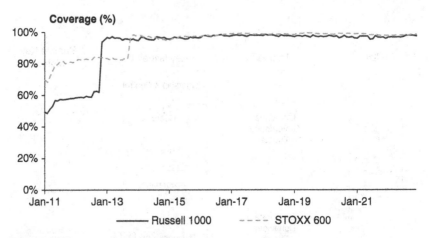

FIGURE 10.2 Coverage of composite G-Score in # of stocks (Russell 1000 and STOXX 600).
Source: Compustat, MSCI, Barclays Research.

2013 and almost all STOXX 600 stocks since 2014. Given this, our sample period starts in January 2014. It ends in December 2021 for the G scores, as we examine the relation between these and the subsequent year's ROEs (the last observation covers the earnings period ending in December 2022). The Corporate Behaviour theme score, however, has much lower coverage in earlier years. MSCI has changed their methodology on this theme score several times, and the current definition covers close to 100% of the Russell 1000 and STOXX 600 universe starting in January 2021, but less than half of either universe before that (Figure 10.3).

    Besides the composite G-score, we also assess the relationship between the Corporate Governance theme score with profitability. This is because the composite G-score contains both the Corporate Governance theme score and the Corporate Behaviour theme score, each of which captures a different aspect of a firm's governance (e.g. the Corporate Governance theme focuses more on internal controls that affect the shareholders, and the Corporate Behaviour theme captures business ethics that are more external and relevant to the rest of society). The Corporate Governance theme score may have a stronger relationship with profitability than the Corporate Behaviour theme, as the latter is more relevant for the benefit of society as a whole, not shareholders of the company. In addition, the Corporate Behaviour theme score has a very short history of full universe coverage. For these reasons, our main analysis focuses on the composite G-score and the Corporate Governance theme score.

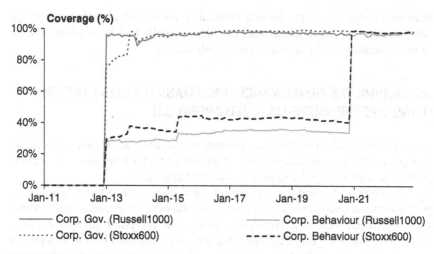

FIGURE 10.3 Coverage of theme scores in # of stocks (Russell 1000 and STOXX 600).
Source: Compustat MSCI, Barclays Research.

TABLE 10.1 Distribution of MSCI composite G-score and theme score.

| | | Russell 1000 | | | | STOXX 600 | | | |
| | | | Std. | | | | | Std. | | | |
	Year	Mean	Dev	Q1	Median	Q3	Mean	Dev	Q1	Median	Q3
Composite	2015	4.7	1.4	3.8	4.8	5.7	6.3	1.5	5.3	6.4	7.4
G-Score(0–10)	2018	5.6	1.2	4.9	5.8	6.5	6.3	1.5	5.3	6.4	7.5
	2021	5.2	1.1	4.6	5.4	6.0	6.0	1.2	5.3	6.1	6.8
Corp. Gov.	2015	4.6	1.5	3.8	4.7	5.7	6.8	1.4	6.0	6.9	7.7
Theme(0–10)	2018	5.9	1.2	5.3	6.0	6.7	6.8	1.3	6.1	7.1	7.8
	2021	5.8	1.2	5.2	6.0	6.7	7.0	1.3	6.3	7.3	7.9

Note: Numbers are calculated for the end of 2015, 2018, and 2021.
Source: Compustat, MSCI, Barclays Research.

Distribution of MSCI Governance Scores

Table 10.1 reports the distributions of the MSCI composite G-score and the Corporate Governance theme scores. Their averages are relatively stable, with a decreasing standard deviation over the sample period. European companies show higher average scores than the US companies,[3] which is not surprising because European companies and investors have played a leading role in the development and adoption of ESG practices globally and have a long history of incorporating ESG practices and considerations.

MEASURING THE GOVERNANCE–PROFITABILITY RELATIONSHIP USING THE EXPOSURE-MATCHED APPROACH

To measure the effect of company governance on ROE accurately, it is crucial to separate the influence from other relevant firm characteristics. To accomplish this, we leverage the exposure-matched approach.

The key idea behind the exposure-matched approach is building a pair of portfolios with one maximizing (Max-) and the other one minimizing (Min-) the governance score (e.g. composite G- score or sub-pillar governance metrics), while matching other relevant characteristics that may lead to differences in profitability. Since both portfolios have the same exposures to other firm characteristics that are related to profitability, the future profitability differences of the two portfolios can be attributed to the differences in their governance scores. The two portfolios are re-balanced at the end of each month for close characteristic matching. The differences in profitability each month leads to a time series of the measured relations, which help us understand the stability of the relationship between governance and profitability over time.

Table 10.2 illustrates the construction details of this approach, using STOXX 600 as an example. We make sure the two portfolios have the same characteristics that are relevant to profitability: equity market capitalization, beta, book-to-market ratio, investment rate, leverage, sector exposure, historical profitability (trailing 5-year ROE), and the environment and social pillar scores. In addition, we set an issuer over-/underweight constraint so that the Max- and Min- portfolios are well diversified. We then measure the differences in the average 1-year forward ROE of the two portfolios. The relationship between governance and profitability can be measured by:

$$
ROE\ Difference\ per\ 1pt\ of\ G\text{-}Score \\
= \frac{\left(avg.1yr\ fwd\ ROE\ of\ MaxG\text{-}avg.1yr\ fwd\ ROE\ of\ MinG\right)}{\left(Avg.\ G\ of\ MaxG\text{-}Avg.\ G\ of\ MinG\right)}
$$

We have carried out this analysis four times, using two different governance metrics and applied to two stock universes. Table 10.3 reports the average *ROE Difference per 1pt of G-Score,* by metric and universe, with performance summarized over different time periods. Figures 10.4 and 10.5 show the time series of this quantity for the Russell 1000 and STOXX 600 stock universes,

TABLE 10.2 Construction details of the exposure-matched approach.

	MaxG Portfolio	MinG Portfolio
Objectives	**Maximize** portfolio's weighted-average G-score	**Minimize** portfolio's weighted-average G-score
Sector Neutral Constraint	Matching sector weights of the index	
Key Risk Exposure Constraints	Portfolio risk characteristics are matched with the index - Size - Beta - Value (B/M) - Investment Rate (% change in total assets) - Leverage - E-score and S-score - Historical ROE (Trailing 5yr Avg.)	
Issuer Over-/ Underweight Constraint	Allow 0.5% stock over-/underweight compared to index weight [a stock has a minimum weight of 0% and maximum weight of 10%]	
Profitability Measure	Weighted Avg. 1yr_fwd_ ROE of MaxG	Weighted Avg. 1yr_fwd_ ROE of MinG
Universe	Index constituent stocks with available G-ratings	
Index benchmark	STOXX 600 index	
Rebalance frequency	Month end	

Source: Barclays Research.

respectively. Over the entire sample period, both metrics considered – the MSCI Composite G-score and the Corporate Governance theme score – show very similar relationships with ROE. The average relationship shown in Table 10.3 can be interpreted as follows: a 1-point improvement of the composite G-score (0–10) is associated with a 0.75% increase in ROE for Russell 1000 stocks (e.g. from 10% to 10.75%) and a 0.45% increase for the STOXX 600 universe. Table 10.3 shows that both types of governance scores have consistently positive relationships with ROE across different periods and for both the United States and Europe. The fact that the respective relations with profitability have similar magnitude for both types of G scores suggests that the Corporate Behaviour theme scores would have a very insignificant relation with profitability, since the composite G score comprises the Corporate Governance and Corporate Behaviour theme scores.

There are several observations worth noting. First, the measured relationships have a larger mean and standard deviation for the Russell 1000 universe than the STOXX 600 universe. Second, while the relationships of both

TABLE 10.3 Summary statistics of the Governance–Future ROE relation by the exposure-matched approach (Russell 1000, STOXX 600, 2014–2021).

		Russell 1000			STOXX 600		
	Stats	**Whole Period (2014–2021)**	**2014–2017**	**2018–2021**	**Whole Period (2014–2021)**	**2014–2017**	**2018–2021**
Composite G-score	Average Effect	0.75	0.63	0.86	0.45	0.70	0.20
	Std. Err.	0.21	0.19	0.33	0.14	0.07	0.13
	t-stat	3.6	3.3	2.6	3.3	10.5	1.6
	% positive months	82	83	81	82	100	65
Corp. Gov. Theme	Average Effect	0.78	0.46	1.10	0.42	0.42	0.42
	Std. Err.	0.24	0.06	0.36	0.07	0.12	0.06
	t-stat	3.3	7.8	3.1	6.4	3.5	7.5
	% positive months	86	85	88	95	94	96

Note: ROE in %. Standard error and t-stat are robust estimations, adjusted for serial correlation.
Source: Refinitiv, World Scope, Compustat, MSCI, Barclays Research

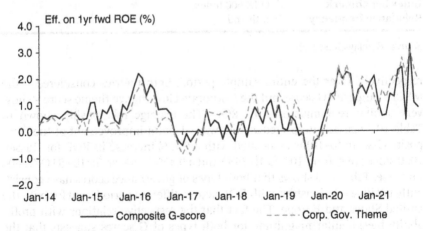

FIGURE 10.4 Time series of the Governance-Future ROE relation by exposure-matched approach for Russell 1000.
Source: Refinitiv, World Scope, Compustat, MSCI, Barclays Research.

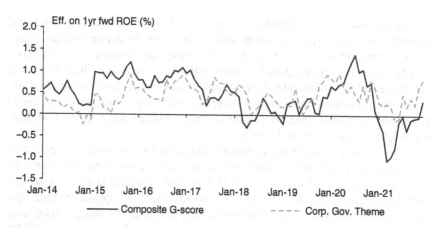

FIGURE 10.5 Time series of the Governance-Future ROE relation by exposure-matched approach for STOXX 600.
Source: Refinitiv, World Scope, Compustat, MSCI, Barclays Research.

governance metrics are similar for the US stocks, those using the Corporate Governance theme for the European stocks are more stable over time: its average relationship with profitability remains similar across the two sub-periods, and the measured relationships are positive in more than 94% of the sample months. The average measured by the composite G-score for European stocks, on the other hand, dropped by more than 50% in the second sub-period, even though in the entire period it was similar to that of the Corporate Governance theme scores. Moreover, the relationships measured by the Corporate Governance theme are stronger than the composite G-scores after 2018 for both universes.

MEASURING GOVERNANCE–PROFITABILITY RELATIONSHIPS USING REGRESSIONS

Even though the exposure-matched approach is able to measure the relationship between governance scores and profitability accurately, it measures the relationship holding the other firm characteristic at a specific point (i.e. equal to the index average). In order to estimate a more general relationship, we therefore turn to the regression approach, which accounts for the correlations between all independent variables and does not hold the control variables at a specific value. The results will help validate those using the exposure-matched approach.

In particular, we perform a cross-sectional regression each quarter and average the beta coefficients across time to estimate the average relationship. For independent variables, we include the composite G-score and the Corporate Governance theme score in separate models. We also include the same set of control variables as in the exposure-matched approach, which include sector dummies and firm characteristics relevant to profitability (beta, book-to-market ratio, size, investment rate, leverage, E-score and S-score, and trailing 5-year average historical ROE).

Table 10.4 shows the regression results using the composite G-score and the Corporate Governance theme scores as independent variables (two separate models). The relationships shown in Table 10.4 are largely consistent with those from Table 10.3 using the exposure-matched approach. First, the relationships are positive for both universes, although the Russell 1000 universe shows a stronger relationship. Second, the relationships measured by Corporate Governance theme scores are either similar to (Russell 1000) or larger than (STOXX 600) the composite G-score between 2018 and 2021. In particular, the corporate governance relationships with profitability are more

TABLE 10.4 Summary statistics of the Governance-Future ROE relation using the regression approach (Russell 1000, STOXX 600, 2014–2021).

		Russell 1000			STOXX 600		
	Stats	**Whole Period (2014–2021)**	**2014–2017**	**2018–2021**	**Whole Period (2014–2021)**	**2014–2017**	**2018–2021**
Composite G-score	Average Effect	0.71	0.34	1.07	0.32	0.57	0.07
	Std. Err.	0.27	0.06	0.33	0.16	0.04	0.05
	t-stat	2.62	5.37	3.24	1.95	13.90	1.42
	% positive quarters	88	88	88	84	100	69
	Avg. Adj. Rsq (%)	30	35	25	41	45	38
Corp. Gov. Theme	Average Effect	0.60	0.12	1.09	0.26	0.29	0.23
	Std. Err.	0.35	0.03	0.39	0.03	0.10	0.08
	t-stat	1.70	4.54	2.83	8.34	2.93	2.91
	% positive quarters	72	63	81	88	88	88
	Avg. Adj. Rsq (%)	30	34	25	41	44	38

Note: ROE in %. A regression using log G-score instead of raw G-score shows similar adjusted R-squared. The relations are measured by the β in the regression equation $1yr\_fwd\_ROE \sim intercept + \beta * (G\_score$ or Corp. Gov. Theme$) + controls$. Standard errors and t-stat are robust estimations, adjusted for serial correlation.
Source: Refinitiv, World Scope, Compustat, MSCI, Barclays Research.

stable for the European stocks across the sample period.[4] These results are consistent with our findings using the exposure-matched approach.

Other Applications of the Regression Approach

The regression approach also allows us to analyse the relationship between more granular governance metrics (such as the key issue scores shown under the Corporate Governance theme in Figure 10.1) and ROE, while controlling for their correlations. We tested a multivariate regression model that regresses ROE on the four key issue scores and control variables. This model could help investors understand each individual key issue's relationship with ROE. However, we found that the more granular metrics jointly did not explain more variation in the ROE than the Corporate Governance theme score. One possible reason is that the granular scores are more sensitive to the specifics of how the scores are constructed and may contain some noise from the measurement process, whereas the coarser measure, such as the theme scores, aggregates granular-level measures and will dampen some noise in the aggregation process. Therefore, combining the benefit (capturing separate aspects of governance) and cost (high noise level) of the granular scores, they serve as a similar representation as the general governance score.

In addition, the governance–profitability relationship for specific sectors can be easily measured using the regression approach by adding interaction terms between governance and the sector dummies.[5] For example, for consumer staples stocks, we find that a 1-point improvement in G-score has been associated with a 1.17% increase in ROE for the Russell 1000 universe and a 0.24% increase for STOXX 600 stocks.

CONCLUSION

In this chapter, we introduce two approaches (exposure-matched and regression) that can be used to measure the relationships between ESG attributes and company profitability accurately. We illustrate these approaches by analysing the effect of companies' governance G- scores on ROE. Our findings suggest that companies with good governance practices also have higher future ROE. Specifically, a one-point improvement in the composite MSCI G-score is estimated to have led to an increase in ROE of about 0.7% (e.g. from 10% to 10.7%) for Russell 1000 stocks and 0.32-0.45% for STOXX 600 stocks, depending on the approach used. We also find that for STOXX 600 stocks, the MSCI Corporate Governance theme, which evaluates key corporate governance factors including board composition, executive pay, shareholder rights, and accounting quality, shows a more consistent relationship with profitability than the composite G-score, across the sample period for both approaches. The methodology can be applied to assess the relationships between other pillars of ESG attributes and a range of firm financial performance metrics.

NOTES

1. EPS = ROE * Book Equity/# of shares. Percentage changes in ROE ($ROE_{t+1}/ROE_t - 1$) equals the percentage changes in EPS, assuming book equity and number of shares do not change between t to t+1.
2. The index constituents' identifiers and fundamental data are from World Scope and Compustat. All fundamental data are winsorized to mitigate the effect of outliers.
3. The MSCI methodology makes G-score comparable for stocks in the entire coverage universe.
4. The adjusted R-squared of a model that uses key issue level governance scores is similar to that of the model using theme-level scores, suggesting granular key issue scores do not offer additional benefits in measuring the relationship between governance and profitability.
5. The relation between governance and profitability for any particular sector i can be measured by $\beta + \beta\_sec_i$ in regression of $1yr\_fwd\_ROE \sim intercept + \beta*G\_score + \beta\_sec_1*G\_score *Sec_1\_Dummy + \beta\_sec_2*G\_score *Sec_2\_Dummy +...+\beta\_sec_i*G\_score *Sec_i\_Dummy + controls$

Four

The Lack of Uniformity in ESG Definitions– Investment Implications

INTRODUCTION TO PART IV

Regulation, particularly in Europe, is driving increased integration of ESG considerations into portfolio construction. New rules are also driving an increase in products that aim to demonstrate specific social and environmental characteristics and/or outcomes. One of the challenges for investors looking to create portfolios with an ESG lens is the lack of consensus on where to draw acceptable parameters around what, and what not, to hold; many investors are also debating what constitutes a truly sustainable investment.

In the absence of clear definitions from regulators, investors have to form their own views on how to embed ESG considerations within their products. In practice, exclusions often play a key role in how investors embed ESG considerations into portfolio construction. While this makes sense from a practical perspective, excluding certain sectors (e.g. controversial weapons, thermal coal, tobacco) can have an effect on portfolio performance and valuations.

In Chapter 11, we investigate the use of ESG labels on US equity mutual funds. Using two decades of security holdings data from US equity funds, we find that ESG-labelled funds have not necessarily provided more ESG exposure than conventional ones. Our analysis shows that ESG funds have

283

had higher, but not significantly different, ESG scores than those of non-ESG funds. Furthermore, while ESG-labelled funds have attracted a higher percentage of inflows than other equity funds, the growth in assets under management has been driven by interest in sustainable investing, rather than superior performance. The risk-adjusted returns and factor loadings of ESG funds have been similar to those of conventional funds.

Lack of definitions is one part of the puzzle that investors need to address when incorporating ESG considerations into their portfolios; another challenge is the availability of the data. Regulations requiring greater corporate disclosures, such as the EU's Corporate Sustainability Reporting Directive and California's climate disclosure law (SB-253) will, over time, contribute to more data being available to investors. In the meantime, gaps in corporate reporting have caused investors to use ESG scores to assess the attributes of companies. ESG ratings can vary by provider due to differences in methodology. This can pose challenges to investors looking to combine scores from a number of providers. We approach this issue from two different points of view. In Chapter 12, we present a methodology for combining ESG information from multiple providers to form a consensus score. The scores need to first be normalized such that they express information in comparable terms; combining the normalized scores then yields a consensus score. In Chapter 13, we examine whether the dispersion in firms' ESG rankings among providers is informative in its own right, beyond what is reflected in the average level of their ESG ratings. We find that firms with higher dispersion in their ESG rankings have tended to experience larger rating revisions in the following year. We also document that dispersion is negatively related to future performance in both stock and bond portfolios.

CHAPTER 11

ESG Equity Funds: Looking Beyond the Label

ESG (Environmental, Social, and Governance) investing has grown considerably since 2010, encompassing various aspects of the investment landscape, such as issuance of securities (e.g. 'green' bonds) and creation of new products (e.g. mutual funds and exchange-traded funds [ETFs]). For instance, in the United States, one in four dollars of professionally managed assets is placed in socially responsible investments (US SIF 2018), and mutual and exchange-traded US equity funds with a focus on sustainability had more than $240bn of assets under management in early 2020, according to data compiled by EPFR Global (in short, EPFR).

There is as yet no consensus on how to define an ESG fund, or the attributes that it may or may not have. While a fund's asset class or geographical focus is relatively easy to determine, other characteristics, such as establishing whether it qualifies as an ESG fund, are more difficult to assess. In fact, regulators have sought guidance on ways to identify ESG products systematically. The Securities and Exchange Commission (SEC 2020) has asked for public comments on whether ESG products should follow existing rules that require a fund's name to broadly match what it invests in.[1] Besides the fund name, the SEC also asked whether there should be specific requirements to which funds must adhere in order to call their investments ESG or sustainable. Many regulators around the world (e.g. the EU Commission in Europe, the Financial Conduct Authority in the United Kingdom, the Autorité des Marchés Financiers in France, and the Financial Services Agency in Japan) have raised similar questions on how to define ESG funds.

For the purpose of this analysis, we categorize a fund as ESG-focused by relying on the fund name or other self-reported information, such as the wording used in the fund prospectus.[2]

This chapter provides a systematic study of ESG-focused US equity funds and contributes to the literature along two dimensions. First, we examine whether ESG portfolios differ from those of conventional funds in terms of the ESG scores of their holdings and factor exposures. Second, we investigate the economic consequences of labelling a fund as ESG by comparing fund flows of ESG and conventional funds.

We find that portfolios of ESG funds have higher, but not significantly different, ESG scores than those of non-ESG funds. Holdings data provide an accurate, de facto, description of mutual fund investment strategies (Lettau et al. 2018). For this reason, we use data on actual portfolio holdings to compute a fund-level ESG score, which is constructed by averaging ESG scores of individual securities in fund portfolios.

In addition to our comparison of ESG vs non-ESG funds, we perform an event-study analysis of those non-ESG funds that switched to an ESG investment objective. When doing so, we control for various fund characteristics, such as size, strategy type, and age, as in an experimental setting. Do we see a significant difference between the ESG scores of such funds before and after the change in their stated objective? Our conclusions depend on the source of ESG scores; this highlights the challenges in unambiguously quantifying the ESG nature of a fund.

An alternative way to compare ESG and non-ESG funds is to look at factor exposures estimated from regressions of fund returns on factor portfolios. We find that risk-adjusted returns and factor loadings of ESG funds are similar to those of conventional funds. Therefore, ESG funds do not add significant diversification benefits to investors who already invest in conventional funds. In addition, we show that a change from non-ESG to ESG is not a consequence of poor past abnormal performance.

In the mutual fund industry, the predominant contract between investors and funds is one in which fees are proportional to assets under management. Furthermore, fund managers' pay is closely related to the fund's revenues, rather than being directly tied to return performance (Ibert et al. 2018). Previous research examines the effects of name changes on fund flows. For instance, Cooper et al. (2005) document that those funds that change their name to reflect 'hot' investment styles (e.g. by adding 'growth' or 'value' to the fund name) earn significantly positive abnormal fund flows, that is, in excess of the flows earned by funds in a matched peer group.

This chapter extends the literature by exploring the economic consequences of labelling a fund as ESG. To do so, we compare the determinants of fund flows between ESG and conventional funds. We find that, on average, ESG funds had about 0.7% more monthly inflows than non-ESG funds. The relation between past performance and fund flows was, however, not different for ESG funds. Therefore, the effect was mostly a level shift, rather than a change in the sensitivity to previous performance.

This chapter highlights the challenges of defining investments as ESG or sustainable, for portfolio managers and investors alike. Although labelling a fund as ESG has been beneficial for fund managers in terms of significantly increasing fund inflows and, thus, represents a salient fund characteristic, the results of this chapter highlight the challenges of identifying and investing in ESG products. For instance, at the fund level, the ESG attribute is better measured on a continuous scale ranging between 0 and 1, rather than a binary (presence/absence) variable.

Moreover, the ESG aspect is inherently multidimensional and encompasses a number of different types (e.g. ESG, SRI, environmentally friendly, religiously responsible, etc.). At the company level, there is a lack of consensus on how to measure the various ESG aspects. The measurement problems are exacerbated further by the availability of many, and imperfectly correlated, ESG indicators. In addition, there is a large dispersion of ESG scores among different data providers, as we will discuss further in the following chapters.

The rest of the chapter is organized as follows. We start by describing the data, the fund universe, and ESG measures. Then, we provide a comprehensive analysis of portfolios of ESG mutual funds and ETFs, and examine the extent to which the holdings of ESG funds exhibit higher ESG scores than those of conventional funds. We proceed by analysing whether the performance and factor loadings of ESG funds are systematically different from non-ESG funds. Next, we explore the economic consequences of classifying a fund as ESG by comparing the determinants of fund flows for ESG and conventional funds. We conclude with a discussion of the challenges of ESG classification.

DATA

Mutual Funds: Data Set and ESG Classification

We consider all equity funds, both mutual funds and ETFs, domiciled in the United States and with a US geographical focus. The data on fund-level pricing, fund flows and characteristics are provided by EPFR and cover 2006–2020 at a monthly frequency. The EPFR data set comprises the name of the fund, monthly net returns, total net assets under management, investment objectives, and the names of the fund managers. A key feature of the EPFR database is the granularity of their fund classifications, which are based on prospectuses, annual reports, fact sheets, and other available resources. In particular, funds are classified by type, geographic focus, domicile, and numerous other filters, including whether the fund is active or passive and whether it is an ETF.

EPFR's analysts aggregate fund data from various sources, including fund managers' data reporting and accounting departments, custodians and third party fund administrators, stock exchanges, and designated third-party intermediaries. EPFR does not delete or artificially perpetuate data for funds that close, so the dataset is robust to survivorship bias due to disappearing funds.[3] Both retail and institutional funds are included, and different share classes of the same fund are aggregated at the fund level.

A salient variable of the EPFR dataset is a dummy that specifies whether the fund has an Environmental, Social, and Governance/Socially Responsible Investment (ESG/SRI) investment focus. EPFR analysts use a systematic approach to identify those funds that invest in companies compliant with ESG criteria. Specifically, a fund is marked as ESG/SRI if any of the following conditions applies: i) it has 'ESG', 'SRI', 'Sustainable', or similar wording in the fund name; ii) it is benchmarked to an ESG/SRI benchmark; iii) its factsheet or prospectus has wording that indicates one of its main objectives is investing in ESG/SRI securities; or iv) it is offered by a fund manager whose entire business is built on ESG investing principles.

We obtain quarterly security-level holdings information using the Center for Research in Security Prices (CRSP) Mutual Fund holdings database (Lipper). Mutual funds and ETFs are subject to Investment Company Act reporting requirements, and they have to disclose their portfolio holdings at the end of each fiscal quarter. We establish the link between holdings data from CRSP and funds data from EPFR by combining multiple identifiers and funds' information (e.g. CUSIPs, funds' names, prices, NAVs) at the share class level.

ESG funds have experienced rapid growth over the 2010–2020 period, with the number soaring and assets under management increasing at a fast rate. Table 11.1 shows some descriptive statistics of the fund dataset for January

TABLE 11.1 US equity funds summary statistics by type of ESG and non-ESG funds.

			2006	2011	2016	2020
Non-ESG	Active	Mutual Funds	934	1,523	2,403	2,577
		ETFs		6	33	83
	Passive	Mutual Funds	55	124	208	257
		ETFs	48	335	573	775
ESG	Active	Mutual Funds	1	11	30	96
		ETFs			1	5
	Passive	Mutual Funds	1	3	6	12
		ETFs		9	6	39
Number of Funds			1,039	2,011	3,260	3,844
of which ESG Funds			2	23	43	152
Number of Share Classes			3,204	6,181	8,834	9,638

Note: The table shows summary statistics for ESG and non-ESG US equity funds by fund type and over time. The results are reported as of January of each year.
Source: EPFR, Barclays Research.

TABLE 11.2 Percentiles of AUM of ESG and non-ESG US equity funds.

	Non-ESG			ESG		
	10%	Median	90%	10%	Median	90%
2006	40	519	4,417		435	
2011	22	338	3,335	1	125	1,150
2016	17	304	3,302	5	99	1,699
2020	15	297	4,371	11	128	2,105

Note: The table reports the 10%-, 50%- (median), and 90%-tile of AUM (in $mn) for ESG and non-ESG funds. The results are reported as of January of each year.
Source: EPFR, Barclays Research.

2006, 2011, 2016, and 2020, by breaking down ESG and non-ESG funds based on their investment strategies (active or passive) and fund type (mutual fund or ETF). The last two rows report the total number of funds and share classes.

The number of funds nearly quadrupled, from 1,039 in 2006 to 3,844 in 2020, while the number of share classes per fund decreased slightly from, on average, 3.1 to 2.5 per fund. The most interesting aspect is the sharp rise in ESG funds, from 2 in 2006 to 152 in 2020, with most of the increase happening between 2016 and 2020. The number of ESG funds is displayed in the highlighted row, and corresponds to the sum of ESG-focused active and passive mutual funds and ETFs rows. The table also shows, for both ESG and non-ESG, a decrease in the share of actively managed funds and an increase in the share of ETFs, which are mostly passive.

Table 11.2 displays the 10th, 50th (median), and 90th percentiles of AUM (in $mn) of ESG and non-ESG funds. ESG funds are smaller than non-ESG ones not only on average, but also for every time period and for all percentiles reported in the table. This finding may suggest that this investment style has not reached its full maturity.

In terms of overall size of the universe of funds considered in our sample, Table 11.3 displays the total AUM (in $bn) of non-ESG and ESG-focused US equity funds, both for all funds and for a subset based only on those benchmarked to the S&P 500 index. To provide some perspective on size compared with the overall stock market, the last two columns report the market capitalization of the total US equity market and the S&P 500 index. The key finding is the rapid growth in recent years of ESG funds, most of which (at least in terms of AUM) are benchmarked to the S&P 500. In early 2020, sustainable mutual funds and ETFs focused on US equities had more than $240bn of assets under management, corresponding to 2.3% of overall US equity fund AUM and about 0.7% of the total US equity market capitalization.

TABLE 11.3   Total AUM by fund type and total market capitalization of S&P 500 and US equity market.

Benchmark:	Non-ESG		ESG		US Stock	S&P 500
	Any	S&P 500	Any	S&P 500	Market	Index
2006	2,435	845	1	NA	16,166	11,819
2011	3,531	1,245	8	1	15,796	11,997
2016	6,304	2,097	18	6	21,430	17,252
2020	10,459	3,497	241	174	34,937	27,795

Note: This table displays the total AUM (in $bn) of non-ESG and ESG US equity funds, both for all funds (i.e. with any benchmark) and for those funds benchmarked to the S&P 500 index. The last two columns report the market capitalization of the total US equity market (Bloomberg ticker: WCAUUS Index) and the S&P 500 index. The results are reported as of January of each year.
Source: Bloomberg, EPFR, Barclays Research.

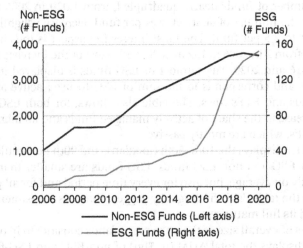

FIGURE 11.1   Number of non-ESG and ESG US equity funds.
Note: This figure displays the number of non-ESG (left axis) and ESG (right axis) US equity funds by year. The results are reported as of January of each year.
Source: EPFR, Barclays Research.

Figures 11.1 and 11.2 display more granular information on the number and total AUM of non-ESG and ESG US equity funds over time. While ESG and non-ESG funds have increased over time, the number of ESG funds has increased more rapidly since 2016. The increase in total AUM is even more pronounced.

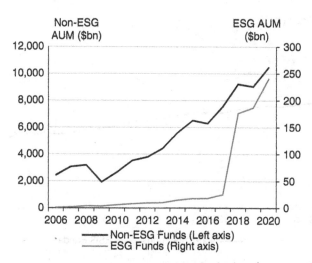

FIGURE 11.2 Total AUM by non-ESG and ESG US equity funds.
Note: This figure displays the total AUM (in $bn) of non-ESG (left axis) and ESG (right axis) US equity funds by year. The results are reported as of January of each year.
Source: EPFR, Bloomberg, Barclays Research.

Are investors paying a premium for investing in ESG funds? Figure 11.3 shows the average expense ratios by fund type. We start in 2013 to include enough ESG funds in the sample. Instead of treating all share classes equally we compute asset-weighted averages, in which the weight of each share class is proportional to its size, thus better reflecting what investors are actually paying. We find that conventional funds charged lower fees than ESG-focused funds. The figure also illustrates a downward trend in fees, highlighting the ongoing compression in fund fees. Figure 11.3 displays averages, rather than measuring how cheap or expensive a fund is relative to its peers by properly controlling for fund characteristics, such as size, investment style, and age (Cooper et al. 2020). Therefore, the evidence that ESG-focused funds have been able to charge higher fees compared with conventional funds is suggestive rather than conclusive.

To shed some light on the benchmarks used by ESG funds, Table 11.4 lists all benchmarks of ESG US equity funds in the EPFR database during 2006–2020. About two-thirds of those ESG funds use standard equity, rather than ESG-specific, benchmarks.[4] The remaining 62 funds use 60 different ESG benchmarks. This finding indicates a large heterogeneity in ESG investing and the absence of a generally accepted yardstick. Of note, the great majority (95%) of ESG funds with non-ESG benchmarks are active, leaving to the fund manager's discretion the selection of individual securities with a high ESG score. In contrast, ESG funds with ESG benchmarks are mostly passive (94%).

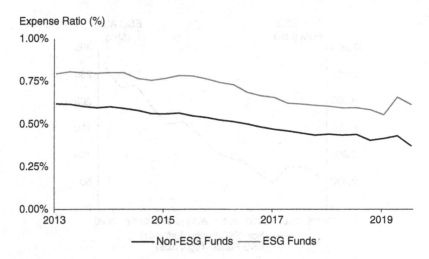

FIGURE 11.3   Expense ratios by fund type.
Note: The sample period is January 2013 to September 2019, and comprises all ESG and non-ESG US equity funds. The figure displays expense ratios by fund type. ESG funds with AUM larger than $10mn and at least two years of data are included in the sample.
Source: EPFR, CRSP, Barclays Research.

TABLE 11.4   Benchmarks of ESG US equity funds.

Benchmark	# ESG Funds
S&P 500	39
Russell 1000	25
Russell 2000	12
ESG benchmarks	62
Others	32
Unassigned	16
Total	**186**

Note: The sample is January 2006 to February 2020. The table reports the benchmarks used by ESG US equity funds.
Source: EPFR, Barclays Research.

Mutual Funds: Coverage

Is our sample of funds representative of the universe of US mutual funds? We address this issue by benchmarking EPFR data to what we think reliably tracks the universe of US funds. Specifically, to gauge the coverage of EPFR funds' data, we look at the number of funds available in CRSP. Table 11.5

TABLE 11.5 Coverage of US equity funds.

		2006	2011	2016	2020
Panel A: EPFR					
Number of Funds		1,039	2,011	3,260	3,844
Of which:	Passive	104	471	793	1,083
	ETFs	48	350	613	902
Number of Share Classes		3,204	6,181	8,834	9,638
Panel B: CRSP (CRSP fund objective)					
Number of Funds		2,826	4,377	4,502	4,401
Of which:	Passive	240	633	796	967
	ETFs	137	555	767	1,015
Number of Share Classes		7,430	11,146	11,614	10,911
Panel C: CRSP (Lipper Class)					
Number of Funds		2,297	3,287	3,152	3,061
Of which:	Passive	137	312	412	527
	ETFs	73	192	302	476
Number of Share Classes		6,122	8,823	8,731	8,236

Note: Panel A relies on EPFR data, while Panels B and C rely on CRSP data using CRSP fund objective and Lipper Class to identify US equity funds. The results are reported as of January of each year.
Source: EPFR, CRSP, Barclays Research.

displays the coverage of US equity funds relying on EPFR (in Panel A) and CRSP, using CRSP Style Codes (in Panel B) and Lipper prospectus objective codes (in Panel C), respectively.[5] Since the CRSP Mutual Fund database stores data for each mutual fund share class separately, we calculate statistics at the fund level by aggregating share classes with the same portfolio holdings. The figures in Panel C are always lower than the corresponding values in Panel B, suggesting that the Lipper filters we apply are stricter than those based on CRSP objectives. One reason is that Panel C may exclude some alternative fund strategies, such as dedicated short bias or long–short equity funds, that are included in Panel B. In terms of the number of funds, EPFR covered between 37% (Panel B) and 45% (Panel C) of CRSP data in 2006, and over 72% in 2016. Given that ESG funds have become popular since 2016, this finding indicates that sample selection issues are unlikely to drive our results.

Given the centrality of ESG/SRI definition, we conducted additional analysis to validate the ESG classification and cross-check the coverage of ESG funds. Specifically, we compared the February 2020 EPFR list of ESG US equity funds with a) the Forum for Sustainable and Responsible

Investment (also known as US Social Investment Forum, in short US SIF) and b) Bloomberg.[6] We find that the number and the identity of ESG funds available in US SIF and Bloomberg are broadly consistent with each other and with the list provided by EPFR.

ESG Scores

We rely on two sources for ESG scores, MSCI and Vigeo Eiris, which are among the most commonly used in the industry, and cover the sample period January 2007 to September 2019. The first source is MSCI ESG Ratings (MSCI 2019), and aims at identifying the most significant ESG risks and opportunities that a company faces, the exposure to those key risks and opportunities, and how well they are managed. MSCI scores 37 ESG key issues, which are in turn grouped into three pillars (environment, social, and governance) and further aggregated to an overall score, which ranges from 0 to 10.

The second source of ESG scores is Vigeo Eiris.[7] It analyses and rates the performance of companies across 38 sustainability criteria, the selection of which is based on international normative standards. In turn, these criteria are grouped into E, S, and G pillars, as well as an overall ESG score which ranges from 0 to 100.[8]

For both MSCI and Vigeo Eiris, the ESG score for a stock corresponds to a weighted average of the E, S, and G aspects (i.e. $ESG_{j,t} = w\_E_{j,t} \times E_{j,t} + w\_S_{j,t} \times S_{j,t} + w\_G_{j,t} \times G_{j,t}$, where $w\_X_{j,t}$ is the weight of pillar X for stock j in period t). We multiply MSCI scores by 10 to convert them from a [0,10] scale to a [0,100] scale, so both providers have scores ranging between 0 (minimum ESG level) and 100 (maximum). However, the scores are not comparable across providers, as the underlying score distribution and construction methodologies are different. An ESG score of 50 from Vigeo Eiris and an ESG score of 50 from MSCI mean different things. (See Chapter 12 for more details on comparing scores between providers.)

An important issue with any ESG provider is the number of companies it rates. To shed some light on the size of the ESG universe, Figure 11.4 displays the percentage of ESG-rated companies in the S&P 500 index, while Figure 11.5 reports the numbers of all US stocks covered over time. We concentrate on the S&P 500 constituents not only because the S&P 500 represents the most popular US stock market index, but also because later on we investigate funds that use it as their benchmark.

In terms of number of companies, MSCI covered most stocks in the S&P 500 index throughout the study period, starting at about 90% in the early part of the sample and reaching close to 100% since 2012. In contrast, the coverage of Vigeo Eiris was only 10% until 2008, and reached full coverage in 2018. More generally, MSCI has covered between 500 and 800 stocks until 2012, when it increased the coverage to about 3,000 stocks. Vigeo Eiris

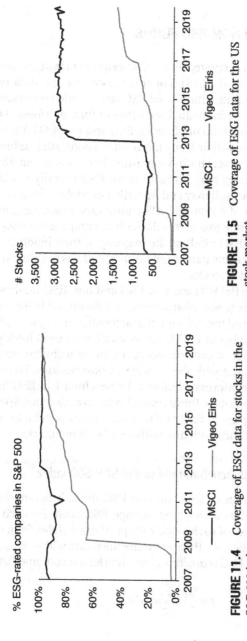

FIGURE 11.4 Coverage of ESG data for stocks in the S&P 500 index.

FIGURE 11.5 Coverage of ESG data for the US stock market.

Note: The sample period is January 2007 to September 2019. Figure 11.4 displays the percentage of ESG-rated companies in the S&P 500 index, while Figure 11.5 displays the number of stocks covered of the overall US stock market by MSCI and Vigeo Eiris.

Source: Bloomberg, MSCI, Vigeo Eiris, Barclays Research.

expanded its coverage in 2009 and by the end of 2019 rated about 1,500 stocks. Our results indicate that ESG providers prioritized rating provisions for larger companies and expanded coverage to smaller ones over time.

COMPARING ESG AND NON-ESG FUNDS

Holdings data provide an accurate, de facto, description of mutual fund investment strategies (Lettau et al. 2018). For this reason, we use data on actual portfolio holdings to compute a fund-level ESG score, which is constructed by averaging ESG scores of the individual securities in fund portfolios. However, directly comparing the portfolio holdings of ESG and non-ESG funds is challenging since mutual funds differ along many dimensions, such as investment style, age, size, active/passive, and risk exposure. For instance, an ESG sector fund that focuses on energy may invest in more ESG-friendly stocks than a non-ESG energy fund, but still may end up with a portfolio with a lower average ESG score than that of a non-ESG US equity fund closely aligned to the S&P 500 index. By the same token, it is difficult to compare the ESG score of small-cap ESG and non-ESG funds as the majority of their holdings may not be ESG-rated, at least for some part of the sample, and it is not clear what ESG score to assign to non-rated stocks.

One way to evaluate the ESG score of ESG and non-ESG funds would be to control for the various funds' characteristics. Leaving aside for a moment the difficulty in identifying the relevant characteristics, a major implementation issue is that the number of ESG funds is small, with most having a short history. Thus, the number of controls necessary to form similar peer groups is relatively large compared with the number of observations. To tackle this challenge, we exploit the information about the benchmark of ESG funds and restrict the analysis to subsets of funds most similar to each other. Specifically, we employ two subsamples: 1) ESG and non-ESG funds benchmarked to the S&P 500 index; 2) ESG funds with and without ESG benchmarks.

ESG and Non-ESG Funds Benchmarked to the S&P 500 Index

To compare the ESG scores of ESG and non-ESG funds benchmarked to the S&P 500, we first calculate a weighted average ESG score for each fund by combining the ESG scores of each stock with portfolio weights from quarterly reported fund holdings data. We then aggregate the scores within ESG and non-ESG funds. A fund-level ESG score for a given quarter q is computed as follows:

$$ESG_q^{(i)} = \sum_{s=1}^{N_q^{(i)}} w_{s,q}^{(i)} ESG_{s,q}$$

where $w_{s,q}^{(i)}$ is the portfolio weight of stock s held in fund i in quarter q, $ESG_{s,q}$ is the ESG score for stock s in quarter q, and $N_q^{(i)}$ is the number of ESG-rated stocks held in fund i in quarter q. We use value weights, where each weight, $w_{s,q}^{(i)}$, represents the stock's percentage of the total net assets of ESG-rated stocks in that fund's portfolio. Note that non-rated ESG stocks are not included in the calculation of the ESG average, so those weights equal 0. By construction, the sum of the weights is normalized to equal 1, i.e. $\sum_{s=1}^{N_q^{(i)}} w_{s,q}^{(i)} = 1$.

Having obtained fund-level average ESG scores, we proceed to compute the average ESG scores of ESG and non-ESG funds.[9] To assess the magnitude of those portfolio average ESG scores, we also report ESG scores for two indices: 1) the standard S&P 500 stock index, since both ESG and non-ESG funds are benchmarked to it; and 2) a customized S&P 500 index that excludes companies in the lowest 5% ESG score bucket, indicated as 'S&P 500 [excluding 5%]'. The latter represents an ESG-tilted version of the index, constructed using a negative screening approach based on ESG scores. We carry out the analysis separately using ESG scores from each of our two providers. Figures 11.6 and 11.7 display the average ESG scores for ESG and non-ESG funds benchmarked to the S&P 500 together with the 95% confidence bands in shaded areas, using MSCI and Vigeo Eiris ESG scores respectively. They also report the average ESG scores of the standard and customized S&P500 indices.

The sample of ESG funds benchmarked to the S&P 500 index includes about 10 funds from 2012 to 2016, 20 funds in 2017 and up to 30 funds in 2019. When using MSCI data, we find that the average ESG score for ESG funds has been consistently higher than that for the S&P 500 since 2013, which in turn has been higher than the ESG score for non-ESG funds. ESG funds have, on average, an ESG score of one point higher (on a scale of 0 to 100) than that of the S&P 500 index. This is similar to the score of the customized S&P 500 [excluding 5%]. The large confidence bands suggest considerable heterogeneity among ESG funds. Therefore, we cannot reject the hypothesis that the average ESG score for ESG funds is the same as that of non-ESG funds.

Figure 11.6 also shows that conventional funds had a lower average ESG score than that of the S&P 500. Two dynamics could explain this. First, although the aggregate AUM of the non-ESG funds is much larger than that of the ESG-focused funds ($3.5trn vs $0.2trn in early 2020 as shown in Table 11.3), it still constitutes a small fraction of the total AUM of the S&P500 stocks (roughly $28trn in the same period). Second, about half of the non-ESG funds are active, and therefore can hold stocks outside their benchmark, which tend to have lower ESG scores than those in the S&P500.

The pattern of ESG funds having a higher average ESG score than non-ESG funds is similar when using Vigeo Eiris ESG data. The main difference

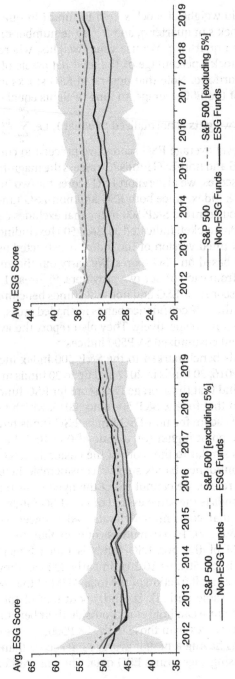

FIGURE 11.6   Average MSCI ESG score for ESG and non-ESG funds benchmarked to the S&P 500.

FIGURE 11.7   Average Vigeo Eiris ESG score for ESG and non-ESG funds benchmarked to the S&P 500.

Note: The sample period is March 2012 to September 2019 and comprises ESG and non-ESG US equity funds benchmarked to the S&P 500 index. The lines plot average ESG scores over time for ESG and non-ESG US equity funds, compared to standard and ESG-tilted versions of the S&P 500 index, using MSCI (Figure 11.6) and Vigeo Eiris (Figure 11.7) as the ESG score data provider. The shaded area is the 95% confidence interval around the average ESG scores for ESG funds. The S&P 500 [excluding 5%] represents a customized S&P 500 index that excludes companies in the lowest 5% ESG score bucket.
Source: EPFR, CRSP, MSCI, Vigeo Eiris, Bloomberg, Barclays Research.

is that for the period considered, the S&P 500 index had a higher ESG score, although not statistically different, than the average ESG scores of both ESG and non-ESG funds.

Figures 11.6 and 11.7 highlight the large dispersion of ESG scores for ESG-focused funds. One explanation of this finding is that the ESG score is a noisy measure of ESG characteristics of the funds. EPFR analysts use the same ESG flag to classify different types of ESG funds, even if these funds pursue different investment strategies, as shown in Table 11.6.

A major difference between the results in Figures 11.6 and 11.7 is that the average ESG score of the S&P 500 is higher than the ESG score of ESG-labelled funds when using Vigeo Eiris, but not when using MSCI data. Therefore, according to Vigeo Eiris, an investor would have achieved a higher ESG score by simply investing in the S&P 500 instead of buying an ESG-focused fund. A potential explanation may be related to size. For instance, in Chapter 13 we look at the relationship between ESG scores and companies' characteristics and document that in the S&P 500 universe, highly rated ESG companies tend to be larger. To better understand the relationship between the size of a company and its ESG score, we contrast the score for both the value-weighted (VW) and equally weighted (EW) S&P 500 index, and display

TABLE 11.6　Types of ESG funds.

Type	Description
ESG	Funds focus on investing in securities of companies meeting socially conscious and environmental standards
Environmentally Friendly	Funds invest in securities of companies contributing to improving the quality of the environment
Clean Energy	Funds invest in securities of companies contributing to less carbon-intensive energy production and consumption. Clean Energy investment strategies can include investing in companies that construct, build, or research solar energy, wind energy, and hydro energy among others
Socially Responsible	Funds invest in securities of companies meeting socially responsible standards, such as environmental stewardship, consumer protection, human rights, and diversity
Religiously Responsible	Funds invest in securities of companies that do not violate the core beliefs of a particular religion
Impact	Funds that are aligned with any of the 17 United Nations Sustainable Development Goals (SDGs), e.g. water, climate change, health and education, but with a mention of the SDGs

Source: Bloomberg, Barclays Research.

the results in Figure 11.8 (MSCI ESG scores) and Figure 11.9 (Vigeo Eiris). If the level of the ESG score is positively associated with the size of the company, we expect the score of the standard S&P 500 (VW) to be higher than the EW one. According to MSCI, the VW S&P 500 has a slightly higher ESG score than the EW S&P 500. Since 2016, the ESG scores of the two indices have been similar to each other. In contrast, according to Vigeo Eiris, the ESG score of the VW S&P 500 has been higher than the EW one, and the difference between the two scores has been stable over time.[10]

Since the size of companies may be a confounding effect when assessing the ESG exposure of a fund, we compare the average size of holdings by fund type, as shown in Figure 11.10. For each fund, we compute the average market capitalization of the stocks it holds. Then, we take averages across funds' type. We find that the average size of the companies held by ESG and conventional funds are fairly similar. However, the average market capitalization of the S&P 500 index is between 1.5 and 2 times larger than that of stocks held in ESG or conventional funds. Even if the conventional and ESG-focused funds are benchmarked to the S&P 500, they tend to hold smaller companies than the S&P 500, explaining at least in part why the ESG score of their benchmark tends to be higher.[11]

In sum, our findings illustrate three key takeaways. First, using the average ESG score of the underlying portfolio provides a noisy estimate of a fund's ESG characteristics given the many various types of ESG funds. Second, to properly compare the ESG score of a fund, it is important to control for stock characteristics, especially because some of those characteristics are related to ESG scores (see, among others, Giese et al. 2019, for a similar point). Third, the conclusions of the analysis may vary depending on which ESG data provider is employed (Li and Polychronopoulos 2020).

ESG Funds With and Without ESG Benchmarks

Instead of comparing ESG and non-ESG funds benchmarked to the same index, another way to control for funds' characteristics is to contrast ESG funds with and without ESG benchmarks. We do this using either MSCI (Figure 11.11) or Vigeo Eiris (Figure 11.12) as ESG data providers. The shaded areas in the two figures represent the 95% confidence interval and are constructed around funds with ESG benchmarks. The number of ESG funds in the two categories is 53 funds with non-ESG and 9 ESG funds with ESG benchmarks. According to MSCI, funds with an ESG benchmark have higher ESG scores than those without an ESG benchmark. However, there is significant uncertainty about the central tendency, and we cannot draw firm conclusions on whether those average scores are significantly different from one another. The results based on Vigeo Eiris are similar, especially as regards

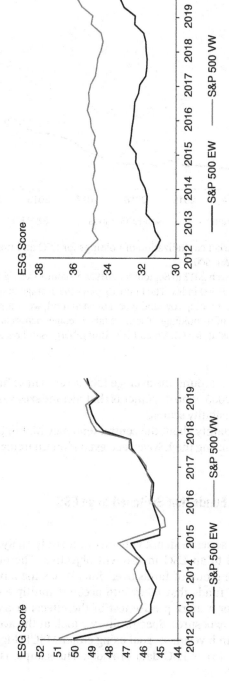

FIGURE 11.8 MSCI ESG score for S&P 500 index.

FIGURE 11.9 Vigeo Eiris ESG score for S&P 500 index.

Note: The sample period is March 2012 to September 2019. The figure displays the ESG score for the S&P 500 using MSCI (Figure 11.8) and Vigeo Eiris (Figure 11.9) as ESG score data provider. 'EW' and 'VW' stand for equally weighted and value-weighted.
Source: EPFR, CRSP, Compustat, MSCI, Vigeo Eiris, Bloomberg, Barclays Research.

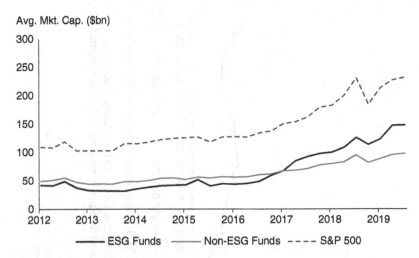

FIGURE 11.10   Average market capitalization of holdings for ESG and non-ESG funds benchmarked to the S&P 500.
Note: The sample period is March 2012 to September 2019, and comprises US equity funds benchmarked to the S&P 500 index. The figure displays the average market capitalization (in $bn) of stock holdings by fund type. For each fund, we compute the average market capitalization of its holdings. Then, we take averages across funds.
Source: EPFR, CRSP, Compustat, MSCI, Vigeo Eiris, Bloomberg, Barclays Research.

the considerable dispersion around the average ESG score. These findings are consistent with Statman 2006, who documents that SRI indexes vary in composition and social responsibility scores.

The significant uncertainty about the central tendency highlights the difficulty in objectively measuring the ESG aspect, even if an unambiguous metric of ESG is used.

Event-Study of Non-ESG Funds that Switched to an ESG Investment Objective

We complement the time-series evidence with an event-study analysis of non-ESG funds that switched to an ESG investment objective. The event-study approach tracks the same group of funds over time. It has the advantage of using a control group of funds that takes into account multiple characteristics, thereby allowing for a more precise test of the effects of a change in investment goals on ESG exposures. Specifically, we look at the average ESG score around the change in investment goal using either MSCI (Figure 11.13) or Vigeo Eiris (Figure 11.14) as ESG data provider. The sample is based on

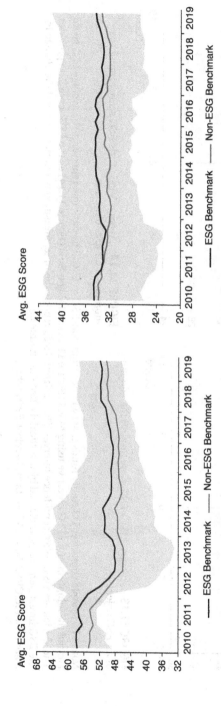

FIGURE 11.11 Average MSCI ESG score for ESG funds with and without ESG benchmarks.

FIGURE 11.12 Average Vigeo Eiris ESG score for ESG funds with and without ESG benchmarks.

Note: The sample period is January 2010 to September 2019. ESG funds with AUM larger than $10mn and at least two years of data are included in the sample. The lines report the average ESG score across funds using MSCI (Figure 11.11) and Vigeo Eiris (Figure 11.12) as the ESG score data provider. The shaded area is the 95% confidence interval and is constructed around funds with ESG benchmarks.

Source: EPFR, CRSP, MSCI, Vigeo Eiris, Bloomberg, Barclays Research.

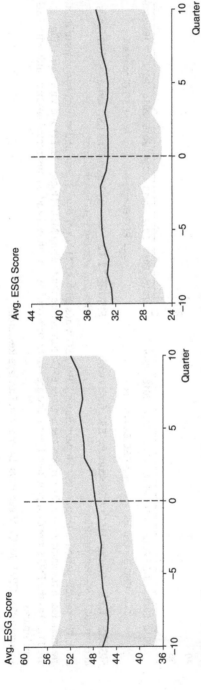

FIGURE 11.13   Average MSCI ESG score around the adoption of an ESG objective.

FIGURE 11.14   Average Vigeo Eiris ESG score around the adoption of an ESG objective.

Note: The sample comprises US equity funds that switched from non-ESG to ESG. The dark line represents the average ESG score around the adoption of an ESG objective using MSCI (Figure 11.13) and Vigeo Eiris (Figure 11.14) as the ESG score data provider. The shaded area is the 95% confidence interval. The horizontal axis reports the time, measured in quarters, around the change in the ESG investment focus, indicated by a vertical dashed line at time 0.

Source: EPFR, CRSP, MSCI, Vigeo Eiris, Barclays Research.

about 30 funds. The horizontal axis reports the time, measured in quarters, around the change in the ESG investment focus which is indicated by a vertical dashed line at time 0. We find a gradual increase in ESG score using MSCI data. The rise is economically significant, growing from 46 to about 50 in the four years around the event. As in previous exercises, the uncertainty about these numbers is large, and does not allow us to draw sharp conclusions. The results based on Vigeo Eiris show a nearly flat ESG score, suggesting no discernible change in ESG exposure.

RISK-ADJUSTED RETURNS AND FACTOR LOADINGS OF ESG AND NON-ESG FUNDS

Are ESG-labelled funds exposed to different risk factors than conventional funds? There are several reasons factor exposures may give a more accurate description of mutual fund strategies than holdings.[12] First, returns are measured objectively and precisely. Second, they are observed at higher frequency, monthly rather than quarterly. Third, there is a consensus in using Fama–French factors to evaluate the risk exposures of equity portfolios. However, factor exposures are estimated quantities and thus subject to estimation error. Moreover, factor loadings are more difficult to interpret than holdings. We view the analysis of loadings as a complementary way to test whether systematic differences exist between ESG and conventional funds.

To investigate whether factor loadings of non-ESG funds are similar to those of ESG funds, we estimate the following factor models (Nofsinger and Varma 2014):

$$r_{i,t} = \alpha_1 + \beta'F_t + \left(\alpha_2 + \gamma'F_t\right) \times D\_ESG_{i,t} + \varepsilon_{i,t}$$

where $r_{i,t}$ is the monthly return of fund i in month t, F_t are Fama–French factors, and $D\_ESG_{i,t}$ is a dummy variable that takes the value of 1 for ESG funds and 0 otherwise. We consider four risk models. The first model controls for the market factor (CAPM). The second, third, and fourth models control, respectively, for the Fama and French 1993 three-factor model (FF3), Carhart (1997) four-factor model (FF3+MOM), and Fama and French (2015) five-factor model (FF5).[13] The coefficient α_1 is the alpha for conventional funds. The coefficient α_2 is the incremental alpha for ESG funds. An insignificant α_2 indicates that an investor already exposed to the Fama–French factors would not have seen incremental return from investing in an ESG fund.[14] The coefficients β represent the factor loadings on the risk factors. The coefficients γ measure the extent to which the risk exposures of ESG funds differ from those of non-ESG funds.

Table 11.7 reports the estimation results for the sample period 2006–2020, with the column headers indicating the different risk models. As before, to control for funds' heterogeneity and limit confounding effects we focus on two subsets of funds: 1) ESG and non-ESG funds benchmarked to the S&P 500 (left panel) and 2) Non-ESG funds that switched to ESG (right panel). The top part displays the factor loadings for conventional funds, while the bottom part, shaded in grey, displays the coefficients for ESG funds, as indicated by the interaction dummy D_ESG. The R^2 coefficients, a measure of the quality of fit, are about 85%, and do not vary across different risk models. This means that most of the time series variation of fund returns is explained by the exposure to the market factor. The alpha of funds benchmarked to the S&P 500 is small but significantly negative. The magnitude of 7 basis points per month corresponds to a yearly value of about 1% and is in line with the typical expense ratio of those funds. The coefficient on the market excess return is close to one. The coefficients α_2 are not significantly different from zero, suggesting that ESG funds do not add benefits to investors already exposed to Fama–French factors. The coefficients of ESG funds (γ) on the risk factors are close to zero and not significantly different from zero, except for the SMB factor. Therefore, we cannot reject the hypothesis that alphas and most risk exposures of ESG funds are similar to those of non-ESG funds.

The right panel focuses on funds that switched over time from non-ESG to ESG. As for S&P500 benchmarked funds, we control for their characteristics and their inherent heterogeneity. Although the coefficients α_1 are negative and α_2 are positive, both sets are close to, and insignificantly different from, zero. In addition, we find that no factor loading for ESG-transitioned funds is significantly different from zero at the 1% level. Together these two pieces of evidence suggest that ESG funds have loadings on Fama–French risk factors similar to those of conventional funds.

Next, we examine whether funds that switched from non-ESG to ESG experienced abnormal performance around the months of the change. We proceed in three steps.[15] First, we create a peer group of non-ESG funds by controlling for style and size. Style consists of nine groups obtained by combining large/mid/small cap with value/growth/blend. Size requires further partitioning between small and large funds. Each fund is assigned to one category depending on style and whether its AUM is above or below the median fund AUM in that month. Second, we compute abnormal returns as the difference between the fund return and that of the benchmark, one of the 18 peer groups. Finally, we look at the abnormal cumulative return around the adoption of an ESG objective, from two years before to two after the event. Figure 11.15 displays the results, with the dashed vertical line indicating the time of change of the ESG objective. The cumulative return line is fairly flat both before and after the adoption of an ESG objective: this suggests that change in the investment

TABLE 11.7 Factor loadings of US equity funds in two subsamples.

Sample:	Funds Benchmarked to S&P 500					Funds Switching From Non-ESG to ESG				
Factor Model:	Raw Returns	CAPM	FF3	FF3+MOM	FF5	Raw Returns	CAPM	FF3	FF3+MOM	FF5
Alpha	0.69***	−0.05***	−0.07***	−0.07***	−0.06***	0.71***	−0.05	−0.06	−0.05	−0.06
Mkt_Rf		0.95***	0.96***	0.96***	0.96***		1.00***	0.98***	0.97***	0.97***
SMB			−0.05***	−0.05***	−0.06***			0.16***	0.16***	0.16***
HML			−0.01***	−0.02***	−0.02***			−0.06***	−0.09***	−0.05**
MOM				−0.01***					−0.03**	
CMA					0.01					−0.03
RMW					−0.03***					0.01
Alpha x D_ESG	0.07	−0.01	0.01	0.01	0.01	0.03	0.07	0.13	0.11	0.11
Mkt_Rf x D_ESG		0.01	−0.01	−0.01	−0.01		−0.03	−0.03	−0.04*	−0.01
SMB x D_ESG			0.10***	0.10***	0.10***			−0.06	−0.07***	−0.08**
HML x D_ESG			−0.01	−0.01	−0.01			0.05*	0.03	0.02
MOM x D_ESG				−0.01					−0.03	
CMA x D_ESG					0.01					0.13**
RMW x D_ESG					0.00					−0.12
R²	0.00	0.85	0.85	0.85	0.85	0.00	0.81	0.82	0.82	0.82
Funds	729	729	729	729	729	31	31	31	31	31
Observations	51,956	51,956	51,956	51,956	51,956	3,945	3,945	3,945	3,945	3,945

Note: The sample is January 2006 to February 2020. The table reports alphas and factor loadings of regressing US equity funds monthly returns on the Fama–French factors. The fund universe in the left panel consists of funds benchmarked to the S&P 500 index and have AUM larger than $100mn. The fund universe in the right panel consists of funds that have become ESG and have AUM larger than $10mn. Mkt_Rf stands for the market return in excess of the risk-free rate. SMB is the size factor (the return spread of small minus large stocks). HML is the value factor (the return spread of cheap minus expensive stocks). MOM is the momentum factor (the return spread of buying last year's winners and selling last year's losers). CMA is the investment factor (the return spread of firms that invest conservatively minus aggressively). RMW is the profitability factor (the return spread of the most profitable firms minus the least profitable). D_ESG is a dummy variable that equals one when the fund is classified ESG and zero otherwise. The superscripts ***, **, and * indicate statistical significance at the 1%, 5%, and 10% level, respectively, and are based on robust standard errors.
Source: EPFR, Ken French data library, Barclays Research.

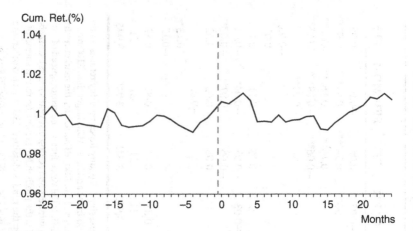

FIGURE 11.15   Abnormal cumulative return around the adoption of an ESG objective.
Note: The sample comprises US equity funds that switched from non-ESG to ESG.
The solid dark line represents the abnormal cumulative return according to the adoption of an ESG objective. The abnormal return is the difference between the fund and the benchmark return. The benchmark return controls for the fund's style and size. Style is the combination between large/mid/small cap and value/growth/blend. Size is above or below the median fund AUM. The dashed vertical line is set at the time of change of the ESG objective.
Source: EPFR, Barclays Research.

objective does not follow a period of under-performance. It also confirms, non-parametrically, the results reported in Table 11.7.

Despite the fact that ESG considerations might constrain the investable universe, we find that ESG funds have risk-adjusted performance and factor loadings similar to conventional funds. In addition, we show that a change from non-ESG to ESG has not been associated with underperformance relative to peers.

ECONOMIC CONSEQUENCES OF LABELLING A FUND AS ESG

Funds that market themselves under an ESG label may attract more investor money compared with conventional funds. Indeed, Figure 11.16 shows that ESG-focused US equity funds have had more inflows than non-ESG ones. In particular, the dashed lines indicate that ESG-focused funds had, on average, inflows of about 6.5% per year from 2013 through 2020, while non-ESG funds had about a net 2.6% of outflows. In addition, ESG funds have, as a group, attracted a higher percentage of investors' money, as a proportion of AUM, in every year since 2013, while their non-ESG counterparts suffered outflows every year since 2015 despite the robust performance of the US equity market during this period. However, the rise in inflows appears not to be driven by performance. Figure 11.17 displays that ESG funds have delivered roughly similar returns to other equity funds since 2013, with ESG funds only slightly outperforming in the last two years of the sample period.

Previous research has documented that a fund name (or label) is a key driver of inflows. For instance, Cooper et al. (2005) exploit changes in the fund name to investigate its effect on fund flows. The authors document that those funds that change their name to reflect a 'hot' investment style (e.g. by adding 'growth' or 'value' to the fund name) earn significantly positive abnormal fund flows, i.e. in excess of the flows earned by funds in a matched peer group. In this section, we extend the literature by exploring the economic consequences of labelling a fund as ESG. To do so, we compare the determinants of fund flows between ESG and conventional funds. Although there are many studies on the relation between fund flows and returns for mutual funds in general, starting with Carhart (1997) and Sirri and Tufano (1998), this issue has received little attention in the ESG market. To examine the flow–performance relationship, we estimate the following panel regression in which fund flows are modelled as a function of past returns and a number of controls. A dummy variable is included for ESG funds to assess differences between conventional and ESG funds (Benson and Humphrey 2008). Specifically, the flow-performance relationship is modelled as follows:

$$Flow_{i,t} = \alpha + \beta' Q_{i,t-1} + \gamma' Q_{i,t-1} \times D\_ESG_{i,t-1} + Controls + \varepsilon_{i,t}$$

The variable $Flow_{i,t}$ stands for the flows (in percentage of the beginning-of-month AUM) of fund i in month t.[16] Since we are interested in asymmetric responses to low and high historical performance, we follow Sirri and Tufano (1998) and posit a piecewise linear relationship between lagged returns and flows. To accomplish this, the funds are first ranked into quintiles by their prior month performance, where Q1 comprises the funds with the poorest performance in the past month and Q5 the best. The factor loadings for each fund are defined such that each fund has a full loading of 0.2 to all lower-ranked quintiles and a proportional loading to the quintile it is in, based on its relative rank within its quintile. This allows us to estimate separately the sensitivity of flows to performance in each of the five performance quintiles.[17] The equation is written in vector form, in which $\beta' Q_{i,t-1} = \beta_1 Q1_{i,t-1} + \beta_2 Q2_{i,t-1} + \beta_3 Q3_{i,t-1} + \beta_4 Q4_{i,t-1} + \beta_5 Q5_{i,t-1}$, and similarly for $\gamma' Q_{i,t-1}$. $D\_ESG_{i,t-1}$ is a dummy variable that equals one when the fund i is classified ESG in period $t-1$, and zero otherwise. *Controls* stand for a number of control

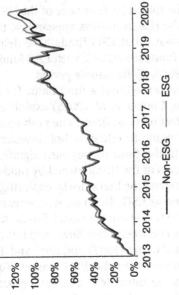

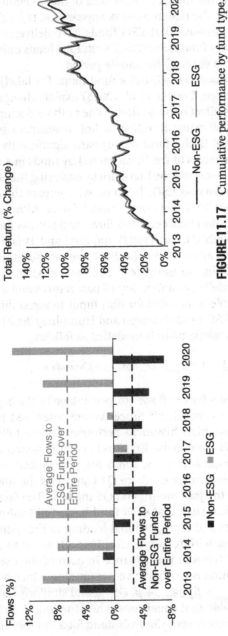

FIGURE 11.16 Fund flows by fund type.

Note: The sample is January 2013 to February 2020. Flows (in %) are averaged by month and fund type, and then averaged by year and annualized by multiplying by 12. Funds with AUM larger than $100mn are included in the sample. Flows are truncated at the 2nd and 98th percentiles.

Source: EPFR, Barclays Research.

FIGURE 11.17 Cumulative performance by fund type.

Note: The sample is January 2013 to February 2020. The figure displays total returns (net of fees), where returns are averaged by month and fund type. Funds with AUM larger than $100mn are included in the sample. Flows are truncated at the 2nd and 98th percentiles.

Source: EPFR, Barclays Research.

variables, such as size (measured by the logarithm of the beginning-of-month fund AUM), age (years between month t and the fund's inception date), the fund's expense ratio, and investor sentiment, broadly defined as optimism or pessimism about stocks (Baker and Wurgler 2006). The variable $\varepsilon_{i,t}$ stands for the error term. The coefficient α is the intercept. The coefficients β measure the sensitivity of flows to past returns, while the coefficients γ measure the additional sensitivity of ESG funds compared with conventional funds.

Table 11.8 reports the regression results for four specifications for the period January 2006 to February 2020 (or determined by data availability).[18] Each regression is estimated using Ordinary Least Squares (OLS) with robust standard errors. The last row indicates what type of fixed effects are included. As standard in the literature, several filters are applied to the sample. We consider funds with AUM larger than $100mn and at least 12 months of data. We also truncate fund flows at the 2nd and 98th percentiles.

The first column reports the results for the baseline specification based on the full sample. There are about 300,000 fund-month observations, and 3,727 unique funds. As expected, all of the β coefficients are positive, indicating that within each quintile, funds with better past performance have higher (or at least less negative) flows. Furthermore, the flow-performance relation is convex. The worst performing funds have a significant coefficient of 3.2 associated with the performance variable (worse performers have significantly greater outflows), while the top funds have a coefficient of 4.6 (the best performers get the greatest inflows). Funds in the intermediate quintiles have small, but significant, positive coefficients.

Next, we allow the flow-performance relationship to change for ESG funds. The coefficients γ are insignificant, indicating that the relationship is similar to those of conventional funds. The third and fourth columns include additional control variables. The convex relationship between past performance and flows becomes more pronounced, with the difference between the top and bottom quintile coefficients roughly doubling from 1.4 (i.e. 4.59−3.16) to 2.4 (i.e. 4.87−2.5). Of note, the incremental coefficient of the bottom quintile for ESG funds is positive and significantly different from zero. This result suggests that ESG funds have experienced, on average, more inflows than non-ESG funds. The control variables do not change the conclusions above, and their signs are intuitive. For instance, higher expense ratios and older funds are associated with lower flows, and periods with stronger sentiment are associated with higher flows.

To flesh out these results, Figure 11.18 plots the piecewise linear functions for the dependence of fund flows on performance estimated based on the regression results from column 3 of Table 11.8, for both ESG and non-ESG funds. We see clearly that the slope of this function is steepest in the

TABLE 11.8 Flow–performance relationship.

	1	2	3	4
Constant	−1.00***	−1.01***	−0.26***	−0.12**
Bottom Quintile	3.16***	3.15***	2.50***	2.42***
2nd Quintile	0.23*	0.23*	0.38***	0.45***
3rd Quintile	0.74***	0.73***	0.77***	0.74***
4th Quintile	0.29**	0.29**	0.40***	0.37**
Top Quintile	4.59***	4.60***	4.87***	5.34***
Bottom Quintile x D_ESG		1.55	3.03***	2.25***
2nd Quintile x D_ESG		0.53	0.79	0.62
3rd Quintile x D_ESG		0.13	−0.13	−0.67
4th Quintile x D_ESG		0.07	0.38	0.04
Top Quintile x D_ESG		−0.95	−1.14	−1.78
Log(Size)			0.05***	0.04***
Age			−0.03***	−0.03***
Expense Ratio			−0.49***	−0.51***
Sentiment				0.15***
R²	0.17	0.17	0.05	0.04
Number of Funds	3,727	3,727	3,073	2,998
Number of Periods	169	169	169	155
Observations	298,683	298,683	252,458	223,350
Fixed Effects	Time and Fund	Time and Fund	Time	No

Note: The sample period is January 2006 to February 2020. The dependent variable is monthly fund flows in percentage. Within a given month, the returns of each fund are ordered from low to high and assigned a percentile, $Percentile_{i,t}$, which ranges from 0 (poorest performance) to 1 (best performance), in increments of 0.01. The loading for the bottom quintile, or $Q1_{i,t}$, is defined as min($Percentile_{i,t}$, 0.2). For the 2nd quintile, $Q2_{i,t}$, is defined as min($Percentile_{i,t} - Q1_{i,t}$, 0.2). Thus, for funds in quintile Q2, the loading will be between 0 and 0.2, proportional to the fund's relative performance rank within the quintile; this loading will be 0 for all funds in Q1 and 0.2 for all funds in Q3 through Q5. Similarly for $Q3_{i,t}$ and $Q4_{i,t}$, and $Q5_{i,t}$, which is defined as min($Percentile_{i,t} - Q1_{i,t} - Q2_{i,t} - Q3_{i,t} - Q4_{i,t}$, 0.2). D_ESG is a dummy variable that equals one when the fund is classified ESG and zero otherwise. Age is expressed in years since the fund inception date. Funds with AUM larger than $100mn and at least 12-month of data are included in the sample. Flows are truncated at the 2nd and 98th percentiles. The econometric method is Ordinary Least Squares. The superscripts ***, **, and * indicate statistical significance at the 1%, 5%, and 10% level, respectively, and are based on robust standard errors.
Source: EPFR, Bloomberg, Jeff Wurgler data library, Barclays Research.

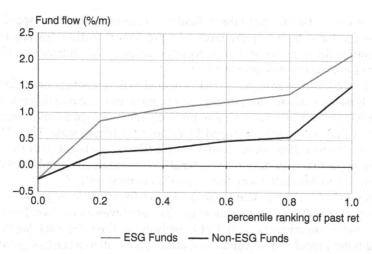

FIGURE 11.18   Piecewise linear dependence of fund flows on past performance.
Note: The sample period is January 2006 to February 2020. The results are based on the regression results from Column 3 of Table 11.8, ignoring the effect of the control variables.
Source: EPFR, Bloomberg, Jeff Wurgler data library, Barclays Research.

two extreme quintiles. In addition, we see that during the study period, flows into ESG funds were greater than those into non-ESG funds at all performance levels.

We examine the robustness of these results along several dimensions. First, we consider a shorter sample period, starting in 2013 instead of 2006. Second, we apply stricter fund filters by including funds with AUM larger than $500mn and at least 24 months of data, rather than AUM larger than $100mn and at least 12 months of data. Third, we define performance by using the cumulative returns over the past three months, instead of the most recent month.[19] The main results are robust to changes in the sample or the measure of past performance.

CHALLENGES OF ESG CLASSIFICATION

Although labelling a fund as ESG is beneficial for fund managers in terms of significantly increasing fund inflows, and thus represents a salient fund characteristic, the results of this chapter highlight the challenges in investing in

ESG products. This is due to the difficulty in measuring the ESG aspect, both at the fund and the company level. The problem is further exacerbated by the availability of many, and imperfectly correlated, ESG indicators and ESG scores from various data providers.

We start by discussing some issues related to the classification of funds as ESG. First, an ESG investing strategy can be pursued to varying degrees. Thus, the ESG attribute of a fund is more precisely measured on a continuous (i.e. taking values in the interval 0 and 1), rather than binary scale. The EU Sustainable Finance Disclosure Regulation (SFDR) is consistent with this idea, in the sense that they have three categories for sustainable funds (Article 6, Article 8, and Article 9, going from non-ESG to most ESG).[20]

Second, ESG funds may have a distinct focus, such as pursuing religiously responsible or environmentally friendly investments (see Table 11.6 for a more comprehensive list). EPFR analysts use the same ESG flag to classify different types of ESG funds, and although useful as a starting point, the partition of ESG and non-ESG is too coarse given the large variation in SRI investment strategies. A related point, underscored by the availability of many ESG benchmarks, is that an ESG strategy can be implemented in many forms (Davies et al. 2020). An ESG criterion can be used either as a positive filter (increasing exposure to best-in-class companies to raise the overall ESG quality of investments) or as negative screening, excluding certain sectors or companies from a portfolio based on specific ESG criteria.

More generally, ESG can also be added as an additional constraint in a portfolio optimization problem as discussed in Chapters 6 and 7. In addition, many ESG products and securities have been created over the past decade, especially in credit. This includes green bonds and loans, social and sustainability bonds, transition bonds, ESG-linked bonds and loans.

Third, ESG combines three dimensions – Environmental, Social, and Governance, into one score. However, the 'right' weights to aggregate those individual scores are not clear. More fundamentally, there is a lack of consensus on how many and what aspects of E, S, and G should be assessed in each relevant dimension.

Even if an agreement is reached on the methodology used to classify ESG funds, many challenges remain in assessing ESG characteristics at the stock level. First, alternative ESG data providers measure differing E, S, and G aspects, and the ESG scores may not be comparable among each other (see Chapter 12).[21] Furthermore, to measure the relative value of a given ESG metric, ESG data providers rely on both publicly available data (e.g. 10-K's, Corporate Social Responsibility [CSR] reports, and news) and non-publicly available data (e.g. survey responses). However, the relative importance of the two sources may differ from provider to provider.

To make things worse, some asset managers may use internal rating systems (Edwards et al. 2020), which may be difficult to access and understand for outsiders. Second, ESG providers may change their rating methodology over time, making comparison over time particularly challenging. Third, a separate, although related, issue focuses on gauging a company's effort and transparency in providing ESG information to the public. In this respect, ESG disclosure scores, as opposed to ESG scores, measure the amount of ESG data a company reports publicly, rather than the company's performance on ESG aspects, with the score tailored to different industry sectors.

An important aspect of the ESG rating, as with any ranking system, is how to evaluate non-rated companies. For instance, Chen et al. (2021) provide evidence that mutual fund managers may misclassify their holdings by reporting non-rated bonds held in their portfolios as investment grade assets. By claiming to hold safer bonds, those funds tend to outperform the actual low-risk funds in their peer groups. When the authors correctly classify the bonds based on their actual risk, these funds are mediocre performers. Although the amount of non-ESG-rated stocks has steadily decreased over time, many stocks, especially small caps, are not ESG-rated yet (Figures 11.4 and 11.5). What score to assign to these companies is an open issue and may affect the classification of ESG funds.

Our findings illustrate a number of key issues in measuring the ESG dimension of a fund. First, the results about the success of a fund in assembling an ESG-friendly portfolio may depend on the ESG score providers used in the analysis. In particular, a conclusion reached using one ESG data provider may not agree with that based on another ESG provider. Second, although the overall ESG score is, by construction, related to the individual E, S, and G scores, the correlation between those dimensions is well below one. For instance, a fund may have a high environmental impact score (e.g. by overweighting stocks having low carbon emissions), but a low social impact score (e.g. by underweighting stocks with high employee satisfaction), ending up with an average ESG score. This is especially the case for specialized funds. Third, even if the ESG dimension at the fund level can be objectively and precisely measured, the problem of spelling out the trade-off between fund performance and ESG goals remains.[22] The prospectus is usually silent on what is the expected incremental performance needed to accommodate a temporary deviation from the ESG objectives, and how fast the fund portfolio should return to the 'ideal' ESG portfolio.

The challenges inherent in measuring the ESG dimension of a fund have attracted attention from regulators around the world, including the EU Commission in Europe, the Securities and Exchange Commission in the United States, the Financial Conduct Authority in the United Kingdom, the Autorité des Marchés Financiers in France and the Financial Services Agency in Japan. While ESG disclosure policies are at different stages of development in all of these countries, they have all raised questions on how to categorize ESG funds.

We believe that it is of paramount importance to enhance ESG data communication and transparency. This is likely to happen over time, based on a combination of regulatory action and natural market evolution in response to stakeholders' demands.

CONCLUSIONS

Since 2015, many ESG-labelled securities and funds have been created (Edwards et al. 2020). While there are clear metrics to assess some fund characteristics (e.g. the size of the tracking error volatility with respect to the benchmark indicates whether a fund is successful in tracking an index), it remains more ambiguous how to assess whether a fund is ESG.

We identify ESG funds by relying on the fund name and prospectus. Then we go beyond the label and test whether ESG-focused funds are different from non-ESG funds by looking at their holding data and factor loadings to standard risk factors.

We find that portfolios of ESG funds have higher, but not significantly different, ESG scores than those of non-ESG funds. In addition, we find that risk-adjusted returns and factor loadings of ESG funds are similar to those of conventional funds.

Although ESG funds are not that different from non-ESG funds, we show that labelling a fund as ESG is beneficial for fund managers in terms of significantly increasing fund inflows.[23]

Our findings have important implications for portfolio managers, investors and regulators about measuring, using and investing in ESG. Portfolio managers need to be transparent about the characteristics of their products to qualify them as sustainable.

Investors must do more due diligence to ensure potential investments correspond to their ESG prerequisites.

Finally, market participants would appreciate greater clarity and transparency in the labeling of funds' ESG policies. This could be achieved by a combination of evolving industry conventions and regulatory action.

REFERENCES

Baker, M. and Wurgler, B. (2006). Investor Sentiment and the Cross-Section of Stock Returns. *Journal of Finance*, 61 (4), pp. 1645–1680.

Benson, K.L. and Humphrey, J.E. (2008). Socially Responsible Investment Funds: Investor Reaction to Current and Past Returns. *Journal of Banking & Finance*, 32 (9), pp. 1850–1859.

Carhart, M. (1997). On Persistence in Mutual Fund Performance. *Journal of Finance*, 52 (1), pp. 57–82.

Chen, H., Cohen, L., and Gurun, U. (2021). Don't Take Their Word For It: The Misclassification of Bond Mutual Funds. *Journal of Finance*, 76 (4), pp. 1699–1730.

Cooper, M.J., Gulen, H., and Rau, P.R. (2005). Changing Names with Style: Mutual Fund Name Changes and their Effects on Fund Flows. *Journal of Finance*, 60 (6), pp. 2825–2858.

Cooper, M.J., Halling, M., and Yang, W. (2020). The Persistence of Fee Dispersion among Mutual Funds. *Review of Finance*, 25 (2), pp. 365–402.

Davies, Z., Edwards, C., O'Neal, M., Dynkin, L., Hyman, J., Desclee, A., Polbennikov, S., Dubois, M., Patel, H., Morrison, E., Challawala, A., and Ogundiya, K. (2020). Fundamental ESG Research: Introducing Our Integrated Approach. *Barclays Research*, 24 March 2020.

Dynkin, L., Desclée, A., Dubois, M., Hyman, J., and Polbennikov, S. (2018). ESG Investing in Credit: A Broader and Deeper Look. *Barclays Research*, 22 October 2018.

Dynkin, L., Desclée, A., Hyman, J., and Polbennikov, S. (2016). ESG Investing in Credit Markets. *Barclays Research*, 17 November 2016.

Edwards, C., O'Neal, M., Davies, Z., and Patel, H. (2020). Fundamental ESG Themes for 2020. *Barclays Research*, 2 April 2020.

Fama, E. and French, K. (1993). Common Risk Factors in the Returns on Stocks and Bonds. *Journal of Financial Economics*, 33 (1), pp. 3–56.

Fama, E. and French, K. (2015). A Five-factor Asset Pricing Model. *Journal of Financial Economics*, 116 (1), pp. 1–22.

Giese, G., Lee, L.E., Melas, D., Nagy, Z., and Nishikawa, L. (2019). Foundations of ESG Investing: How ESG Affects Equity Valuation, Risk, and Performance. *Journal of Portfolio Management*, 45 (5), pp. 69–83.

Ibert, M., Kaniel, R., Van Nieuwerburgh, S., and Vestman, R. (2018). Are Mutual Fund Managers Paid for Investment Skill? *Review of Financial Studies*, 31 (2), pp. 715–772.

Kim, S. and Yoon, A.S. (2023). Analyzing Active Mutual Fund Managers' Commitment to ESG: Evidence from the United Nations Principles for Responsible Investment. *Management Science*, 69 (2), pp. 741–758.

Lettau, M., Ludvigson, S.C., and Manoel, P. (2018). Characteristics of Mutual Fund Portfolios: Where are the Value Funds? *National Bureau of Economic Research* working paper 25381.

Li, F. and Polychronopoulos, A. (2020). What a Difference an ESG Ratings Provider Makes! *Research Affiliates*, January 2020.

MSCI (2019). MSCI ESG Ratings and Methodology. *MSCI ESG Research*, September 2019.

Nofsinger, J. and Varma, A. (2014). Socially Responsible Funds and Market Crises. *Journal of Banking & Finance*, 48, pp. 180–193.

Rohleder, M., Scholz, H., and Wilkens, M. (2011). Survivorship Bias and Mutual Fund Performance: Relevance, Significance, and Methodical Differences. *Review of Finance*, 15 (2), pp. 441–474.

SEC (2020). Request for Comments on Fund Names. Release Nos. IC–33809; File No. S7-04-20. www.sec.gov/rules/other/2020/ic-33809.pdf

Sirri, E.R. and Tufano, P. (1998). Costly Search and Mutual Fund Flows. *Journal of Finance*, 53 (5), pp. 1589–1622.

Spiegel, M. and Zhang, H. (2013). Mutual Fund Risk and Market Share-Adjusted Fund Flows. *Journal of Financial Economics*, 108, pp. 506–528.

Statman, M. (2006). Socially Responsible Indexes. *Journal of Portfolio Management*, 32 (3), pp. 100–109.

US SIF (2018). Report on Responsible Investing Trends in the US. www.ussif.org

Zhu, Q. (2020). The Missing New Funds. *Management Science*, 66 (3), pp. 1193–1204.

NOTES

1. One of the rules in the Investment Company Act of 1940 requires registered investment companies to invest at least 80% of their assets in the type of investments suggested by their names.
2. The ESG classification is provided by EPFR, a third-party data provider.
3. Survivorship bias is an important issue that needs to be taken into account in studies of mutual fund performance. In general, survivorship bias overestimates fund performance, as the predominant reason for closing a fund is inferior performance (Rohleder et al. 2011).
4. The total number of ESG funds (186) is higher than the number of ESG funds reported in Table 11.1 at the end of the sample period in February 2020 (152) because some funds ceased operation (or were over time merged or taken over).
5. To identify US equity mutual funds, a fund share class must have a CRSP fund objective code of domestic equity (ED) or one of the following Lipper classification codes: EIEI, G, LCCE, LCGE, LCVE, MCCE, MCGE, MCVE, MLCE, MLGE, MLVE, SCCE, SCGE, or SCVE (Zhu 2020). Lipper assigns its objective code, thus determining market cap and style versus a benchmark, by looking at the actual holdings of the fund and how it invests.
6. US SIF and Bloomberg provide only the most recent (point-in-time rather than time series) list of ESG funds. The data for US SIF are available at the Sustainable, Responsible, and Impact Mutual Fund and ETF Chart web page, while those for Bloomberg are available through the fund screening tool (FSRC function) using as attributes ESG or Socially Responsible.
7. Moody's Corporation acquired a majority stake in Vigeo Eiris in 2019, and it has started to include non-credit evaluations in its credit rating analysis.
8. Note that the Vigeo Eiris methodology has not changed since 2002, so the historical data are comparable. In particular, it did not change around or after Moody's

acquisition of Vigeo Eiris, which involved only an expansion of coverage, rather than a revision of the rating methodology.

9. As a robustness check, we compute the simple (equal-weighted) average in the first step. We also consider the median, instead of the mean, ESG score in the second step. The results are robust to these changes in the measures of central tendency for ESG and non-ESG funds.

10. In a similar vein, we construct 10 deciles based on market capitalization within the S&P 500 universe. Then, we compute the average ESG scores in the top (largest, D1) and bottom (smallest, D10) decile. We find that, irrespective of using EW or VW aggregation within the decile, the difference in ESG scores between D1 and D10 is limited for MSCI. In contrast, for Vigeo Eiris, the difference between D1 and D10 is larger and remains fairly consistent over time.

11. For instance, many stocks, especially small caps, are not yet ESG-rated. What score to assign to these companies is an open issue and may affect the classification of ESG funds. There is also a lack of consensus on how many and what aspects of E, S, and G should be assessed in each relevant dimension. We note that the ESG scores of MSCI and Vigeo Eiris are imperfectly correlated with each other and our finding illustrates that being a virtuous ESG fund according to one ESG provider may not reflect on the other provider's average ESG score. Furthermore, many investors create their own proprietary ESG scores and by these alternate measures, the funds might be more highly rated than the S&P500.

12. A portfolio's factor 'loading', or beta to a specific factor represents a proxy for some unobserved systematic risk.

13. The data on Fama–French five factors are provided by the Kenneth French data library (http://mba.tuck.dartmouth.edu/pages/faculty/ken.french/data_library.html). We thank Professor French for making available a rich data library containing the time-series data for various risk portfolios.

14. Investors may invest in ESG funds to pursue and foster ESG goals, rather than achieving higher Sharpe ratios. Furthermore, we acknowledge that if the investor's objective is to obtain ex-post mean-variance efficient portfolios, the one-month holding horizon may be too short. For instance, MSCI ESG analysts explain that ESG ratings reflect an anticipation of changes of business models that result from negative externalities being regulated away or that lead to changes in consumer behavior. These types of changes typically take place over long horizons.

15. A change in the fund description may be followed by a thorough restructuring of all positions and therefore the new portfolio may be based on freshly formed signals. In turn, this change should be associated with incremental portfolio turnover around the change of objective. We leave this analysis to future research.

16. In turn, fund flows, provided by EPFR, are defined as

$$Flow_{i,t} = (AUM_{i,t} - AUM_{i,t-1} (1 + r_{i,t})) / AUM_{i,t-1}$$

where $AUM_{i,t}$ is the AUM of fund i on month t, and $r_{i,t}$ is the net return of fund i between period $t-1$ and t.

17. Several papers use a fractional specification (i.e. net inflows/assets under management as dependent variable) to document a convex relation between fund flows

and past performance. Spiegel and Zhang (2013) argue that a market share model provides a better description since empirically aggregate flows are not linked to the cross-sectional distribution of fund returns, and in particular to the performance of the largest funds in the industry. This chapter tests whether ESG-focused funds have incremental inflows compared with non-ESG funds, rather than corroborating that current fund flows are convex in past returns. Hence, we use the more standard fractional specification, and we leave to future research to explore the relationship employing the market share-adjusted fund flows model.

18. The fund's inception date and expense ratios are not available for all funds. The Sentiment data ends in December 2018.

19. An alternative way (left for future research) could be to use past risk-adjusted returns, instead of raw returns.

20. Article 8 funds are those that 'promote environmental and social characteristics'. A definition designed to be broadest of all, and to apply to most ESG strategies. Article 9 funds are those that have 'sustainable investment as its objective'. Article 6 funds are those that do not claim to promote any kind of ESG objective and will encompass all funds not classified as 8 or 9.

21. MSCI's and Vigeo Eiris' methodologies differ not only in terms of the industry treatment (including the use of a different industry classification; with the ESG scores being absolute for Vigeo Eiris and intra-industry for MSCI), but also in many other aspects, such as the universe of ESG-rated companies, the E, S, and G dimensions that are scored, the weights of each E, S, and G dimension, and the range, distribution, and meaning of ESG scores.

22. A proposal by the Labor Department requires retirement-plan fiduciaries to choose investments with an unwavering focus on financial returns, rather than furthering ESG goals (https://www.dol.gov/newsroom/releases/ebsa/ebsa20200623).

23. Kim and Yoon (2023) examine whether ESG funds that adopted the United Nations Principles for Responsible Investment (PRI) increase the ESG scores of their holdings around the adoption. The authors find that neither fund-level ESG score nor risk-adjusted returns increase after the adoption, even if fund flows significantly rise. Although our conclusions are similar to theirs, a few differences remain. First, we consider different sets of funds and ESG score providers. Second, we use a narrower peer group to better control for funds' characteristics. Third, we employ many risk models, rather than just the CAPM.

CHAPTER 12

Combining Scores from Multiple ESG Ratings Providers

Investors wishing to take a 'positive screening' approach to ESG investing need to measure the ESG characteristics of companies, and to grade them appropriately. There is currently no standard for how this should be done, resulting in a plethora of ESG scores derived from a panoply of data. When we need a broad measure of what multiple score providers are saying in aggregate, the lack of standardization is a challenge, as scores are not readily comparable across providers. In this chapter we present a methodology for aggregating E, S, and G pillar scores from different providers despite their disparate scoring methodologies and score distributions.

THE CHALLENGE OF ESG SCORING

Among the broad approaches we discussed in earlier chapters to integrate ESG considerations into portfolio construction, positive screening[1] in particular presents a number of challenges to effective implementation.

When investors seek to rank or score issuers based on defined ESG metrics with positive screening, they need to decide:

- Which ESG characteristics are important to their investment goals;
- How to quantitatively measure those characteristics; and
- How to combine the chosen measures into a score or a rating.

For example, a portfolio manager seeking to reduce the carbon emissions of its investments would need to source reliable data on CO_2 emissions, as well as on carbon-offsetting measures undertaken by the company and any other data relevant to measuring net carbon emissions. Then the investor would need to decide how to combine and evaluate that data to determine which companies have displayed better or worse behaviour relative to their peers or other (potential) investments.

We believe that the objective processing of available ESG data is an inherently complex task, both practically and philosophically. How can investors construct reliable, robust, independent, and credible measures of a company's ESG characteristics? The difficulty of this task is evident in the plethora of ESG data and score providers that have sprung up to meet the challenge, as well as the widespread construction of in-house ESG scores by leading investment firms. The preference for bespoke scoring reflects an underlying lack of agreement regarding how ESG attributes should be evaluated, creating a desire for tailored and customized solutions.

Given the lack of market or regulatory standards, focusing on a single score or data provider could provide limited insight into the general perception of a company's ESG position by investors as a whole. Instead, it might be more appropriate to focus on company fundamentals (which should be a constant in the discussion) and to pair this with a high-level overview of how issuers are perceived by leading ESG score providers.[2]

BENEFIT OF CONSTRUCTING A CONSENSUS ESG SCORE

One way to aggregate the ESG scores from multiple providers is to compute a consensus ESG score, for example an average, based on market-leading ESG scores, with the aim of providing a fair representation of how companies are viewed in an ESG context. Over time, we expect significantly more standardization of how companies report ESG data, along with greater transparency in how that data is converted into scores by score providers, essentially emulating the credit rating agency model. However, this move towards greater standardization and transparency could take years and we need an indication of how investors view the ESG metrics of security issuers today.

By constructing consensus scores that are a robust and reliable reflection of aggregated ESG scores, we aim to track investor and score-provider perceptions of companies. For investors that directly use the scores of leading score providers, changes in scores are likely to lead to the buying or selling of stocks and bonds. Even when investors build in-house ESG scores, the majority of the underlying ESG data is likely to come from one or more of the external score providers. Hence, the deterioration (or improvement) in a company's ESG behaviour should not only filter into the scores generated by score providers, but also into the bespoke scores being constructed in-house by financial investors.

Thus, we believe that the consensus ESG score constructed from our methodology could give a broad view of how companies are perceived by market participants, regardless of an investor's specific approach to ESG score construction. Juxtaposed with investors' fundamental views, the consensus scores will serve as a benchmark that highlights where the ESG opinions of an investor differ from those of score providers, from which actionable investment insights would flow.

SOLVING ONE PROBLEM, CREATES SEVERAL MORE

In this chapter we use commercially available ESG scores from different providers. However, these scores are conceptually and quantitatively different. We therefore provide a methodology to form consensus ESG scores that seek to:

- Reflect a company's E, S, and G profiles in both a relative and absolute sense, as defined by an average of scores from leading providers;
- Evolve in tandem with developments in the scores of said providers; and
- Are constructed in such a way that we can add and/or substitute score providers as the available ESG data and scoring methodologies evolve over time.

Averaging Disparate Scores

The first challenge is that there is little to no agreement over what should be measured, how it should be measured, or how what is measured then feeds into an ESG score.

Many ESG data providers simplify the task by ranking companies versus a peer group on a range of metrics. There are significant limitations to this approach. First, it imposes a uniform distribution on ESG characteristics (see Figure 12.1) which is unlikely to reflect the true distribution, much in the way that ranking people by height would not fairly represent the distribution of heights. Second, ranks cannot be used to compare the qualities of names across peer groups. Third, ranks cannot track drifts in aggregate quality over time: if all companies get better equally, then their ranks stay the same.

For this reason, we focus on score providers that produce 'absolute' scores, which give more information regarding the complete distribution of scores, and the significance of differences in scores among issuers. Figure 12.2 shows the distributions of ESG scores from two ESG providers. Not only are these far from uniform, but they differ markedly from each other in terms of location and shape. The providers design these 'absolute' scores such that they can be meaningfully compared across industries and geographies, and not just within narrowly defined peer groups. However, even 'absolute' ESG score providers show little agreement over what to measure or how to construct ESG scores. We run the risk of mixing data that measures very different characteristics when constructing an aggregate ESG score.

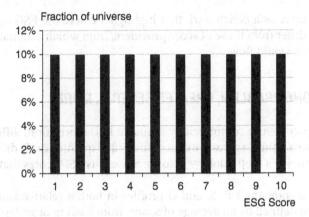

FIGURE 12.1   ESG ranking imposes a uniform distribution on the ESG characteristics of companies.
Source: Barclays Research.

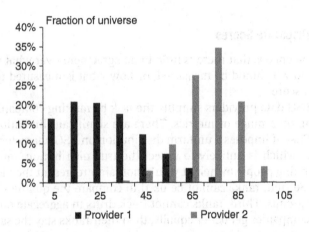

FIGURE 12.2   In reality, the ESG characteristics of companies are thought to be clustered due to market and regulatory standards.
Source: Barclays Research.

We propose a solution to the mathematical problem of aggregating scores from very different distributions, which we will illustrate using Environmental scores from two providers. Figures 12.3 and 12.4 show the distribution of E pillar scores for companies in the coverage universes of Vigeo Eiris and Sustainalytics (note that Sustainalytics scores are transformed; see the section on Transformed Sustainalytics Scores in the Appendix to this chapter).

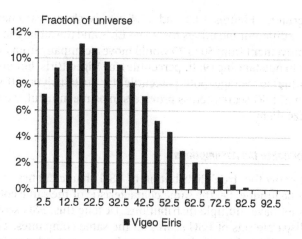

FIGURE 12.3 Distribution of E pillar scores from Vigeo Eiris.
Source: Vigeo Eiris.

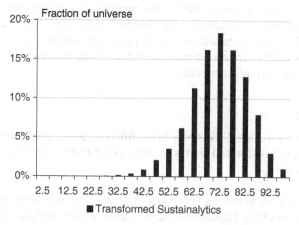

FIGURE 12.4 Transformed E pillar scores from Sustainalytics.
Source: Sustainalytics.

In these charts, 0 is the worst possible score and 100 is the best. Clearly, the scores supplied by the two providers are not comparable: the distributions have wildly different means and dispersions. Further, the distribution of scores from Sustainalytics has a heavy left tail (most names score well, but there is a tail of low performers), while the distribution of scores from Vigeo Eiris has a heavy right tail (most names score poorly but there is a tail of high performers). In short, it is clear that an E score of 40 from Vigeo Eiris and an E score of 40 from Sustainalytics mean very different things.

Furthermore, Figures 12.3 and 12.4 clearly show that changes in the E score have different meanings for Vigeo Eiris and Sustainalytics. For example, an improvement from 50 to 70 would move a company from average (50th percentile) to outstanding (95th percentile) for Vigeo Eiris, but only from bad (5th percentile) to average (50th percentile) for Sustainalytics. If we want the aggregation of ESG scores across providers to be meaningful, we first need to re-normalize them.

Solution: Normalize the Assumptions

We do not know the 'true' distribution of ESG characteristics of companies, but it must be unique, i.e. the same characteristic of the same cohort of companies cannot have multiple distributions. Despite this, ESG score providers generate disparate sets of ESG scores on the same companies. This happens because many ESG characteristics are qualitative and substantial variations exists in methodologies for score construction. That is, the ESG score distributions we observe largely derive from the assumptions of the ESG score providers. Each score provider makes its own set of assumptions, resulting in very different scores which are not directly comparable. The challenge is to transform ESG scores based on a uniform set of assumptions regarding the distribution of ESG characteristics. In our analysis, we assume that the characteristics are normally distributed.

Methodology

We seek to normalize ESG scores from different providers at the sector level such that the transformed scores become comparable. Therefore, our objective is three-fold:

- First, we seek to normalize scores from different providers in such a way that the resulting transformed scores have similar marginal distributions.
- Second, the transformation should leave broadly unchanged the ESG rankings of individual companies by each provider. If company A had a higher environmental score than company B, it should retain its higher rank post-transformation.
- Finally, the transformation should retain the broad variation of the original ESG scores across industry sectors.

We achieve this using a 3-step approach:

1. *Normalizing scores at the provider-sector level:* for each ESG score provider, we partition the universe of rated companies into sectors based on their

GICS/BICS classification. For each provider, in each sector, we estimate the cross-sectional mean and standard deviation of the distribution of scores. This is done for the E, S, and G pillar scores independently. Company pillar scores are normalized within each provider-sector pair.[3]

2. *Re-scaling scores to restore sector differences on a common scale:* For each sector, we compute the desired mean and standard deviation of the final post-algorithm scores by taking the average of the sector-averaged statistics (from step 1) across providers. We use these to map the normalized company scores from step 1 into post-algorithm scores by re-scaling by the sector standard deviation and shifting by the sector mean. The post-algorithm scores from each provider for companies in a given sector should be approximately normally distributed with the same mean and standard deviation.

3. *Aggregating scores across providers:* The new, re-scaled scores from different providers now have very similar distributions, and can easily be aggregated by averaging company scores across providers.

This methodology is illustrated in Figures 12.5 to 12.10. Throughout the sequence, we contrast a specific sector (Commodity) relative to all other sectors to illustrate how intra-sector relationships embedded in the underlying scores are preserved. Figures 12.5 and 12.6 show the original distributions of E scores from the two providers.[4] We can see clear differences in the distributions, both between the two providers and between the Commodity sector and others. Figure 12.7 and 12.8 show the effect of the normalization step,

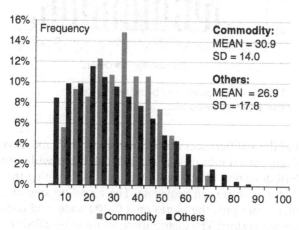

FIGURE 12.5 Distribution of Vigeo Eiris E scores.
Source: Vigeo Eiris, Barclays Research.

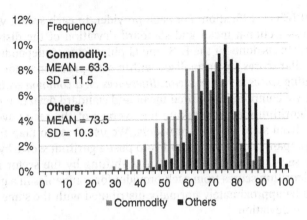

FIGURE 12.6 Partitioning of (transformed) Sustainalytics E scores.
Source: Sustainalytics, Barclays Research.

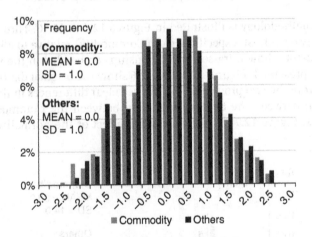

FIGURE 12.7 Vigeo Eiris E scores after being normalized.
Source: Vigeo Eiris, Barclays Research.

in which all of these differences are temporarily erased, and all of the ratings distributions are forced into near-normal distributions with a mean of zero and a standard deviation of one (although still maintaining the meaning of relative rankings within each provider). The rescaling step of Figures 12.9 and 12.10 once again puts the scores on a 0–100 scale, and restores the distinctions between sectors. The distributions of these rescaled scores are now similar between the two providers, enabling us to average them together to form composite E scores. A detailed mathematical presentation of this algorithm can be found in the Appendix.

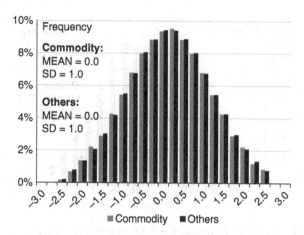

FIGURE 12.8 Sustainalytics E scores after being normalized.
Source: Sustainalytics, Barclays Research.

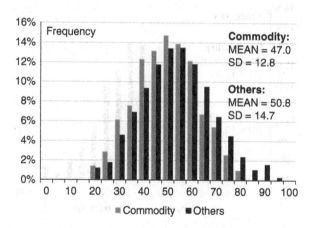

FIGURE 12.9 Re-scaled Vigeo Eiris E scores post-algorithm.
Source: Vigeo Eiris, Barclays Research.

The final output is shown in Figure 12.11: a single distribution of Environmental scores that reflects the 'average' Environmental quality of issuers based on the assessments of the two providers considered. This is then repeated for the Social and Governance scores.

While this process is relatively simple, we believe it has the following advantages:

- *It is mathematically defensible:* While taking a simple average of the scores as supplied by the providers would be problematic based on

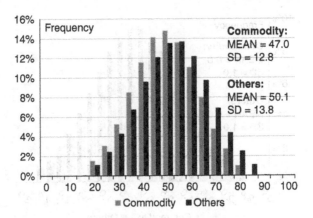

FIGURE 12.10 Re-scaled Sustainalytics E scores post-algorithm.
Source: Sustainalytics, Barclays Research.

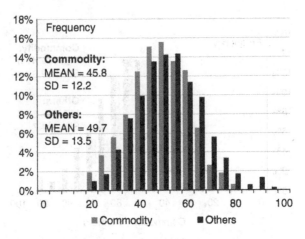

FIGURE 12.11 Final distribution of averaged Environmental scores.
Source: Vigeo Eiris, Sustainalytics, Barclays Research.

the distributions in Figures 12.3 and 12.4, our approach averages two distributions that appear comparable. Our methodology is also general enough that it should allow more ESG score providers to be added over time, even if the scores from each provider had their own distribution.

- *It preserves information:* Our methodology preserves the broad structure of the data (means and variances across industry categories), making it richer than basic ESG ranks. It also preserves the ranking of

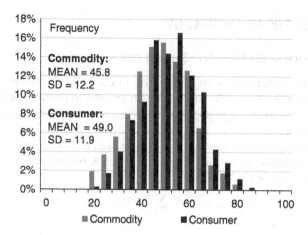

FIGURE 12.12 Distribution of averaged Environmental scores for Consumer and Commodity companies.
Source: Vigeo Eiris, Sustainalytics, Barclays Research.

company scores within and across sectors. This means that, for example, Figure 12.12 compares the distributions of Environmental scores between the Commodity and Consumer sectors, and shows that the E scores for Commodity companies tend to be lower and more widely dispersed.

- *Scores can evolve over time:* By preserving the mean scores of each sector the overall score of a sector (and indeed the entire data set) can drift over time. Thus, we can track not only relative movements in the ESG profile of companies, but also absolute shifts (higher or lower) in the ESG quality of the entire cohort or population of firms.

Dispersion of Views

As discussed earlier in this chapter, ESG scores from different providers are only loosely comparable. Our methodology attempts to resolve this issue, but we still have the problem of company scores (and even rankings) that simply do not align across providers. In simple terms, if an issuer is scored highly by some providers and poorly by others, then our algorithm will average those opinions and generate a 'middle of the road' consensus score that does not correspond well to any of the individual provider scores. This obscures the divergent views of the score providers. In fact, the existence of a dispersion of views on a company can be significant in and of itself. We investigate the usefulness of this information in Chapter 13.

APPENDIX: THE METHODOLOGY

Normalization at the Provider–Sector Level

We partition companies using high-level GICS/BICS classification. Specifically, we map the 14 GICS/ BICS to seven groups, to ensure each sector category has a relatively large population. We exclude any names mapped to the government sector.

For each score provider and sector pair, we calculate the cross-sectional mean and standard deviation (dispersion) of each pillar score across all companies in the sector (indexed by i):

$$\mu_{Sector,Pillar,Provider} = \sum_{i \in Sector} Score_{Pillar,Provider,i} / N_{Sector}$$

$$\sigma^2_{Sector,Pillar,Provider} = \sum_{i \in Sector} \left(Score_{Pillar,Provider,i} - \mu_{Sector,Pillar,Provider} \right)^2 / \left(N_{Sector} - 1 \right)$$

The scores in each sector category (cohort) are then normalized using a standard normal distribution truncated at 1 and 99 percentiles:

$$x_{Pillar,i,Provider,Sector} = \text{Scale} \times \Phi^{-1} \left(NRnk_{Pillar,i,Provider,Sector} \right)$$

where Φ is the standard normal cumulative distribution function (CDF), and Scale is the scaling factor applied to offset the truncation effect on the distribution's standard deviation,[5] and

TABLE 12.A1   Company GICS/ BICS classifications are mapped to seven sector categories.

GICS/ BICS	Map	GICS/ BICS	Map
Communication Services	Communications	Industrials	Non-commodity Industrial
Communications	Communications	Information Technology	Technology
Consumer Discretionary	Consumer	Government	Government
Consumer Staples	Consumer	Materials	Commodity
Energy	Commodity	Real Estate	Non-commodity Industrial
Financials	Finance	Technology	Technology
Health Care	Non-commodity Industrial	Utilities	Utilities

Source: Barclays Research.

$$NRnk_{Pillar,i,Provider,Sector} = 0.98 \times \frac{Rank_{Pillar,i,Provider,Sector}}{N_{Sector}} + 0.01$$

is the normalized rank of a company's score in a particular sector category mapped into the interval from 0.01 to 0.99. Companies are ranked by their scores in a given category in ascending order (a higher rank is a higher score).

Aggregation across providers

Equipped with:

- Normalized ranks for each company, for each ESG pillar;
- The mean of each group, for each pillar, for each score provider; and
- The standard deviation for each group, for each pillar, for each score provider,

we define average group means and average group standard deviations as follows:

$$\bar{\mu}_{Sector,Pillar} = \sum_{Provider} \mu_{Sector,Pillar,Provider}/N\left(Providers\right)$$

$$\bar{\sigma}_{Sector,Pillar} = \sum_{Provider} \sigma_{Sector,Pillar,Provider}/N\left(Providers\right)$$

where N(Providers) is the number of ESG score providers being considered.

Standardized scores are mapped to post-algorithm scores by re-scaling by sector standard deviations and shifting the result by sector average means:

$$\bar{x}_{Pillar,i,Provider} = x_{Pillar,i,Provider} \times \bar{\sigma}_{Sector,Pillar} + \bar{\mu}_{Sector,Pillar}$$

The resulting re-scaled scores from different providers have very similar distributions, which makes them directly comparable. In the final step, we average re-scaled scores of each company across providers:

$$\hat{x}_{Factor,i} = \sum_{Provider} \bar{x}_{Pillar,i,Provider}/N\left(Providers\right)$$

The dispersion metric used to categorize the alignment of the scores being used to construct our average scores is defined as:

$$Disp_{Pillar,i} = \sum_{Provider} \left|\left(\bar{x}_{Pillar,i,Provider} - \hat{x}_{Pillar,i}\right)\right|/\bar{\sigma}_{Group,Pillar}$$

Transformed Sustainalytics Scores

Our understanding is that Sustainalytics ESG methodology differs from those of other providers in two key ways. First, most providers score companies based on their ESG quality (high scores indicate better characteristics). In contrast, Sustainalytics' scores represent unmanaged ESG risk: lower scores indicate that a company is less exposed to ESG risks, while higher scores indicate companies have more exposure to ESG risks.

Further, where Sustainalytics decomposes its ESG scores into E, S, and G 'cluster' scores, the relationship between a company's overall ESG score and individual cluster score is defined as:

$$ESG_{Sustainalytics} = Cluster_E + Cluster_S + Cluster_G$$

In contrast, other providers usually relate a high-level ESG score to E, S, and G pillar scores using a weighted average:

$$ESG_{Score} = \sum_{i \in \{E,S,G\}} PillarScore_i \times Weight_i$$

To adjust for this, we transform Sustainalytics scores in the following way:

$$TransformedPillarScore_i = 100 - Cluster_i / Exposure_i$$

Where the *Cluster* is the unmanaged risk for each cluster score of a company *i*, and *Exposure* is the Exposure score of pillar *i* as a percentage of overall ESG risk exposure. Both Cluster and Exposure are determined by Sustainalytics. Under this transformation, the resulting scores are capped at 100 and higher scores indicate better ESG characteristics.

$$ESG_{Score} = 100 - ESG_{Sustainalytics} = \sum_{i \in \{E,S,G\}} TransformedPillarScore_i \times Exposure_i$$

Effectively we redefine the Sustainalytics ESG score as the weighted average of the transformed E, S, and G pillar scores, transposed such that higher transformed pillar scores represent higher ESG quality.

REFERENCE

Davies, Z., Edwards, C., O'Neal, M., Dynkin, L., Hyman, J., Desclee, A., Polbennikov, S., Dubois, M., Patel, H., Morrison, E., Challawala, A., and Ogundiya, K. (2020). Fundamental ESG Research: Introducing Our Integrated Approach. *Barclays Research*, 24 March 2020.

NOTES

1. Positive screening dynamically reduces exposure to worst-in-class companies and increases exposure to best-in-class companies on a sector or portfolio level, in order to raise the overall ESG quality of investments.
2. Barclays Research has used this methodology to provide a point of reference that their fundamental analysts can use when discussing ESG aspects of the companies they cover. See Davies et al (2020) for details.
3. Here we effectively force the empirical distributions of transformed ESG scores to follow a normal distribution in each sector category. As we saw, the distributions of original ESG scores can differ significantly across providers due to inherent differences in their interpretation of ESG-related information available in the market. Our approach mechanistically makes the interpretations of the ESG scale similar across providers. However, company rankings from different providers can still be very different. Please see the Appendix for details.
4. The Sustainalytics scores have been transformed as described in the Appendix to ensure that higher scores correspond to better rankings.
5. Normalized scores should have a standard deviation close to 1. We, therefore, scale them by 1.075 to offset the truncation effect. Without scaling, truncation reduces the standard deviation of the normalized scores below 1.

CHAPTER 13

The Informational Content of Dispersion in Firms' ESG Ratings across Providers

In the previous chapter, we highlighted a challenge faced by ESG investors: ESG scores from different sources vary substantially, as there is no uniform definition of the underlying measures (see also Berg et al. 2022; Li and Poly-chronopoulos 2020). We then introduced a methodology to standardize the scores from different providers in order to extract a consensus score. In this chapter, we look at the plethora of ESG scores from another angle – not as a challenge but more as an opportunity: we examine whether there is any value embedded in the cross-provider score dispersion that can be utilized by investors. Or to put it differently, after selecting a provider or coming up with a consensus score, should investors still care about the dispersion in ESG scores among different providers?

One reason that investors may care about ESG score dispersion is that it might be relevant to security performance. Previous studies have shown that the dispersion among investors' beliefs in firm valuation is closely related to subsequent stock performance. One notable example is that the disagreement in analysts' earnings forecasts leads to lower stock returns (e.g. Ackert and Athanassakos 1997; Diether et al. 2002; Dische 2002). The most cited explanation of the negative relationship between analyst forecast dispersion and subsequent stock returns comes from Miller (1977). The idea is that pessimistic investors are often less capable of influencing stock prices than optimistic investors because of shorting costs and restrictions. As a result, stock prices tend to get pushed up temporarily by the latter in the presence of disagreement. Over the long run, prices will revert back to fair value, exhibiting a negative relationship between the level of dispersion in a stock's valuation and its subsequent returns. There might be a similar relationship between the dispersion in ESG scores and subsequent stock performance, as ESG considerations have been playing a heavier role in investment decisions, and have a growing impact on firm valuation, as many studies have suggested. For example, the ESG score of a firm often reflects regulatory and reputational risks, and its scrutiny of a firm's corporate governance could protect the interests of shareholders. In fact, Giese et al. (2019) found a positive link between ESG scores and firm valuation: firms with higher ESG scores also tend to have lower book-to-market ratios and lower predicted-earnings-to-price ratios. Therefore, the dispersion in ESG scores among providers could be related to divergence in investors' beliefs about firm valuation, and thus could be used to predict future stock returns.

However, unlike disagreements in earnings forecasts, the dispersion in ESG scores is multifaceted and reflects more than divergent beliefs about one particular well-defined metric, such as earnings. As summarized by Berg et al. (2022), there are at least three sources of disagreement among ESG scores from different providers: scope – what firm aspects should be considered as relevant to ESG; measurement – how a firm performs in a particular aspect; and weight – how the various aspects are weighted to form a single or low-dimensional score. The first and third issues are usually absent in the formation of disagreement in earnings forecasts. It is possible that these extra layers of disagreement in ESG scores would add noise and thus dampen the predictive power of ESG score dispersion on future performance.

In this chapter, we empirically test the link between ESG dispersion and future stock performance. We examine whether firms with higher ESG dispersion on average have different subsequent performance than firms with lower ESG dispersion while controlling for firm characteristics. We also verify whether the link between ESG dispersion, firm valuation, and future performance is consistent with the hypothesis in Miller (1977).

As scores from different providers have different scales and underlying distributions, we first normalize the ESG scores from MSCI, Sustainalytics, and Vigeo Eiris following the methodology introduced in Chapter 12. We then construct a measure of ESG score dispersion as the average absolute deviation of each provider's normalized score from their mean. We find that the degree of dispersion can be substantial in magnitude compared to ESG levels and it exhibits systematic variation across sectors and various firms' characteristics. Firms with higher ESG dispersion also experience larger rating revisions in the following year. Next, to test the empirical link between ESG dispersion and future performance, we form a pair of index-tracking portfolios with the same risk characteristics as the index and control for the ESG level while maximizing and minimizing ESG dispersion respectively. We find that the portfolio with high ESG dispersion underperforms the portfolio with low ESG dispersion. The underperformance is especially pronounced after 2013, when the growth of ESG investing has greatly accelerated and ESG scores have become more relevant in the investment process.[1] In addition, the results hold under alternative portfolio specifications and out-of-sample after one provider made a major change to its methodology.

Although this research focuses primarily on stock performance, we also extend the analysis to corporate bonds. Since ESG is a firm-level characteristic, we expect that its reflection of regulatory and reputational risks as well as stakeholder protection also matters to credit valuations.[2] We find that the results from equities broadly hold up in the credit market. In particular, a bond portfolio of the S&P 500 firms with high ESG dispersion has underperformed an otherwise similar portfolio with low ESG dispersion since 2013 after controlling for ESG levels and various risk characteristics such as duration, spread, and sector composition. This result provides another out-of-sample validation of our main findings in a different asset class.

Our findings can benefit investors in at least three areas. First, for investors who have access to multiple ESG providers including in-house ESG research, our findings show that incorporating dispersion can potentially improve portfolio performance. All else being equal, a portfolio with lower ESG dispersion have historically outperformed a portfolio with higher ESG dispersion. Second, our results offer insights on how investors can allocate their ESG research resources more effectively. For example, we find that ESG score dispersion is more prevalent in firms in the communication and commodities sectors. A deeper in-house analysis or a second opinion of these firms from additional providers might be beneficial. Third, our results suggest that monitoring ESG dispersion can help anticipate future changes in ESG score as the two were historically related. For example, for portfolios that are subject to limits on average or minimum ESG levels, tracking ESG dispersion can help reduce turnover caused by unexpected score changes.

The rest of the chapter is organized as follows. We start by describing the ESG score data and how we measure the score dispersion. We then show how ESG dispersion varies in the cross-section. We proceed by examining the stability of ESG dispersion and how they are related to future ESG score changes. Before concluding, we investigate the relation between ESG dispersion and future stock and bond performances.

UNDERSTANDING DISPERSION OF ESG SCORES

Data and Measure of Dispersion

Sample Construction

In this chapter, we evaluate the dispersion of ESG scores on US stocks using three providers: MSCI, Sustainalytics, and Vigeo Eiris.[3] Our sample starts in August 2009, when a reasonably good coverage of US stocks from all three providers became available, and ends in April 2018, when Sustainalytics changed its rating methodology. The methodological change represents a good opportunity to test our results out-of-sample, from 2018 to 2019.

Table 13.1 presents the number of US stocks rated by each provider and their score coverage of major stock indices at the end of 2009, 2013, and 2017. In terms of market value, all three providers have decent coverage of the S&P 500 index throughout the sample. The common sample, in which stocks have ESG scores from all three providers, covers 87% of S&P 500 market's value in 2009, and almost the entire S&P 500 index at the end of 2017 (99%). In contrast, the common sample's coverage of the Russell 1000 index experienced a bigger increase (from 77% to 94%) due to a lower coverage of the index at the beginning of the sample period, and its coverage of the Russell 2000 index remained close to zero. The coverage varied across indices mostly because ESG providers usually prioritize score provision for larger companies and only expand coverage over time to smaller ones. The statistics in Table 13.1 suggest that the coverage expansion was mostly for mid-cap names and has not fully reached small-cap ones yet in our sample period. It is important for our analysis to have a stable sample comprised of similar stocks over time. Otherwise, we would not know whether results are due to dispersion dynamics or sample expansion. For this reason, we restrict our universe to S&P 500 constituents with scores from all three ESG providers.

Measuring ESG Score Dispersion

As discussed in detail in Chapter 12, ESG scores from providers are not directly comparable as they differ in several aspects, such as scale, meaning, cross-sectional variation, and distribution characteristics. It is critical to address these differences before measuring the dispersion in scores because they are mechanical and usually do not reflect the dispersion in opinions. The normalization method proposed in Chapter 12 allows us to transform and normalize each provider's scores to ensure comparability across providers and over time while preserving important information contained in the scores, such as the within-industry ranking and the inter-industry relative position for each provider. Therefore, our first step is to construct normalized ESG scores from each provider following the methodology introduced in Chapter 12.

We then define the score dispersion for company i as the average absolute deviation of each provider's normalized score from their average:

$$ESG\,Dispersion_i = \left(\begin{array}{l} |Normalized\_ESG_{i,MSCI} - AverageESG_i| + \\ |Normalized\_ESG_{i,Sustainalytics} - AverageESG_i| + \\ |Normalized\_ESG_{i,Vigeo\ Eiris} - AverageESG_i| \end{array} \right) / 3,$$

TABLE 13.1 Coverage of ESG data for US stock indices.

Year End	Subsample	Number of Stocks	By Number of Stocks			By Market Value		
			% of S&P500	% of Russell 1000	% of Russell 2000	% of S&P500	% of Russell 1000	% of Russell 2000
2009	MSCI	645	87	56	1	96	89	2
	Sustainalytics	681	90	61	0	97	90	1
	Vigeo-Eiris	388	64	35	0	91	81	0
	Extended Universe	774	96	67	1	99	93	2
	Common Sample	351	60	32	0	87	77	0
2013	MSCI	2924	99	95	74	100	99	88
	Sustainalytics	1235	96	85	5	98	95	8
	Vigeo-Eiris	542	82	46	0	94	83	0
	Extended Universe	2963	100	96	75	100	99	89
	Common Sample	511	79	44	0	92	82	0
2017	MSCI	2827	100	98	72	100	99	91
	Sustainalytics	1290	100	97	3	100	99	4
	Vigeo-Eiris	1151	98	74	8	99	94	13
	Extended Universe	2880	100	99	73	100	100	91
	Common Sample	963	97	73	1	99	94	2

Note: The Extended Universe represents the sample of stocks that are covered by any one of the three providers while the Common Sample includes stocks that are covered by all three providers.

Source: Compustat, MSCI, Sustainalytics, Vigeo Eiris, Barclays Research.

where *AverageESG$_i$* is company *i*'s average normalized ESG scores from the three providers.[4]

AverageESG$_i$ is the consensus ESG score designed to capture the broad ESG assessment of the company. In the rest of the analysis, we will use this measure to control for the level of a company's ESG score, since it is representative of the opinions from all three providers. By using the equally weighted average, we avoid bias toward any particular provider.

Another commonly used approach to analyse the dispersion between two providers is to look at the correlations between their ESG scores, either in the cross-section for a particular month, or over multiple time periods for one particular company. The drawback of the correlation approach is that it is unable to provide an accurate measure of dispersion in the ESG scores of a particular company at a particular point in time, whereas our dispersion measure can pinpoint the firm-level dispersion at any point without relying on historical data.

Unlike Chapter 12, which illustrates the methodology using individual pillar scores, this chapter focuses on dispersion in the composite ESG scores rather than in each individual pillar. There are two reasons for this. First, ESG investors focus mostly on the composite ESG score instead of individual scores in their final investment process. For example, most ESG-themed funds have mandates tied to ESG composite scores rather than individual pillars. As a result, composite ESG scores are more likely to be relevant to valuation. The second reason is that different providers might disagree on how firms' ESG attributes should be categorized into the different pillars. For example, 'product safety' can be mapped to either the S (Social) pillar, or to the G (Governance) pillar. Therefore, we expect a lot of noise in the dispersion among individual pillars due to categorizing differences, but less so at the composite level.

How Large Are the Dispersions?

We find that there are substantial disagreements among individual providers. Panel A of Figure 13.1 lists the time-series average of the monthly cross-sectional mean, first quartile, median, third quartile, and standard deviation of the ESG dispersions of individual firms. It also reports the same statistics for the average ESG score level (averaged across the three providers) and the average relative dispersion (i.e. the dispersion of each firm scaled by the firm's average ESG level). All ESG dispersions and levels are based on scores of a 0–100 scale.

Panel A of Figure 13.1 shows that the average ESG score dispersion is 3.9, which is about 9% of the average ESG score. The normalized dispersion, the ratio between the average dispersion (3.9) and the cross-sectional standard deviation in average ESG levels (6.9), is 56%. This suggests that the average dispersion is substantial, more than half of the cross-sectional standard

Panel A: Summary statistics of ESG scores and dispersions

	Average	Q1	Median	Q3	Standard Deviation
ESG Dispersion (0–100)	3.9	2.2	3.6	5.2	2.2
Avg. ESG (0–100)	46.2	41.3	46.2	51.0	6.9
% Dispersion (Dispersion/ Level, %)	8.7	5	7.8	12	5
Credit Rating Dispersion (increment of 1=1 notch)	0.7	0.4	0.6	1.0	0.5
Credit Rating (1=Aaa+, 2=Aaa, .., 9=Baa1,...)	9.0	7.4	9.0	10.2	2.3

Note: All statistics are averaged at the cross-section level each month (equally weighted) and then averaged across the time series.

Panel B: Monthly distribution of ESG dispersions

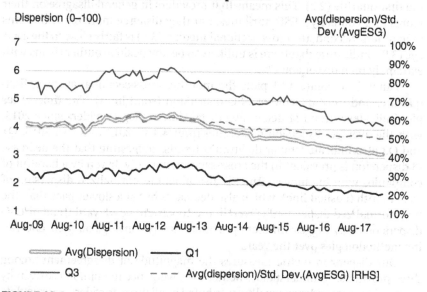

FIGURE 13.1 Descriptive statistics of ESG score and dispersion.
Note: The statistics are averaged (equal-weight) across the cross-section on a monthly basis. The time series are from Aug. 2009 to Apr. 2018.
Source: Compustat, MSCI, Sustainalytics, Vigeo Eiris, Barclays Research.

deviation of ESG levels.[5] For example, if a company is ranked in the 80th percentile based on the average ESG score, on average the more pessimistic and the more optimistic ESG providers would have ranked the same company very differently, in the 61st and the 92nd percentile respectively.[6]

The magnitude of ESG dispersion is also larger compared to dispersion in other scores such as credit rating. The last two rows of Panel A provide similar statistics for credit ratings among three major rating agencies (Moody's, S&P, and Fitch).[7] On average, the credit rating dispersion among the three providers is 0.7 notch.[8] As the cross-sectional standard deviation of average credit rating is 2.3, the normalized dispersion in credit rating is 32% (0.7/2.3), smaller than that of ESG dispersion (56%). A larger dispersion in ESG scores is not surprising given that ESG is a less well defined attribute than credit quality and the lack of a unified framework for assessing ESG.[9]

There are two more observations worth noting in Panel A. First, there is some cross-sectional variation of ESG dispersion among companies. The third quartile of dispersion in the cross-section is 5.2, more than twice as large as the first-quartile (2.2). This means that providers in general disagree on their scores of a company's ESG attributes, but they disagree more on some firms than others. Second, the cross-sectional median (3.6) is fairly close to the average (3.9), indicating that there is unlikely to be any positive outlier (firms with extremely high dispersion).[10]

Panel B of Figure 13.1 plots the monthly cross-sectional average, first-quartile, and third-quartile of ESG dispersion (solid lines). The time-series plot indicates a trend of decreasing dispersion among providers since 2013, with the average dispersion decreasing from 4.4 in 2013 to 3.1 in 2018. Q1 and Q3 also indicate similar downward trends, suggesting that the decrease in dispersion is prevalent in the cross-section, not only driven by a handful of companies with big moves. Panel B also plots the normalized dispersion of each month (dashed line), which also decreases but at a slower pace than the non-normalized dispersion.[11] Overall, the consistent downward trend of ESG dispersions may suggest different providers slowly converge on their ESG rating methodologies over the years.

Our dispersion metric measures the magnitude of disagreement among three providers. To understand whether the divergence in opinion is driven by one particular provider or equally contributed by all three providers, we calculate pair-wise dispersions and examine the correlations between the original three-provider dispersion and the pair-wise dispersion. The pair-wise dispersions are calculated for each provider pair in a similar way as our original dispersion measure.[12] The correlations are shown in Table 13.2 Panel A. The correlations between the three-provider dispersion and the two pairwise dispersions involving MSCI (i.e. MSCI–Sustainalytics and MSCI–Vigeo) are fairly high (0.78 and 0.85 respectively). The Sustainalytics–Vigeo pair-wise dispersion has the lowest

TABLE 13.2 Correlations of different ESG score dispersions.

Panel A: Correlations between the 3-provider dispersion measure with pair-wise dispersion measures

Correlation	Pair-wise Dispersion Measures		
	MSCI-Sustainalytics	MSCI-Vigeo	Sustainalytics-Vigeo
3-Provider Dispersion (original)	0.78	0.85	0.44

Panel B: Correlations between ESG scores from different providers

	Sustainalytics	Vigeo
MSCI	0.48	0.38
Sustainalytics	1	0.74

Note: Correlations are calculated in the cross-section each month and then averaged over the time-series. Correlations reported in Panel B are calculated from normalized ESG scores for each provider. The correlations using the original ESG scores from each provider are similar.

Source: Compustat, MSCI, Sustainalytics, Vigeo Eiris, Barclays Research.

correlation with the three-provider dispersion measure (0.44). To understand why this is the case, Table 13.2 Panel B reports the correlations among the ESG scores from the three providers. The correlations suggest that MSCI scores are very different from both Sustainalytics and Vigeo (correlation = 0.48 and 0.38 respectively), while the latter two are much more similar with a relatively high correlation of 0.74. As MSCI is more likely to rate a company differently from the other two providers, it contributes the most to the dispersion.

In this chapter, we use scores from three providers to illustrate the concept of dispersion and its associated investment implications. The framework is not specific to the number of providers used and can easily be expanded to include more or fewer providers. For example, we find that using pair-wise dispersions produces qualitatively similar results in the performance analysis as using the three-provider dispersion measure. This suggests that the usefulness of the dispersion measure is unlikely to be driven by any specific provider in the sample.

What Kind of Firms Have High ESG Dispersion?

Across Industries

Figure 13.2 presents the average dispersion by sector, and the numbers do show some inter-sector variation. On average, the Utilities sector has the

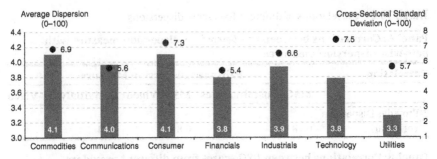

FIGURE 13.2 Average ESG dispersion across sectors.

Note: The sectors are based on GICS 2-digit sector and certain sectors with similar ESG concerns are combined to make sure that all sectors have a decent number of observations. Commodities = energy + materials. Consumer = consumer discretionary + consumer staples. Financials = financials + real estate. Industrials = industrials + health care. The other sectors are the original GICS sector classification. The statistics are EW within each sector bucket on a monthly basis then averaged in the time series. The time series are from August 2009 to April 2018.

Source: Compustat, MSCI, Sustainalytics, Vigeo Eiris, Barclays Research.

least dispersion (3.3), and the Commodities and Consumer sectors have the highest dispersion (4.1). The biggest inter-industry difference in dispersion is 0.8 (4.1 – 3.3), about a third of the cross-sectional standard deviation of firm-level dispersion (2.2 from Figure 13.1 Panel A). The results imply that sector may be an important factor affecting a firm's dispersion, but it doesn't explain the majority of the variation in dispersion. Figure 13.2 also shows the cross-sectional standard deviation of the average ESG scores within each sector, which are larger than the average provider-dispersions in each sector. There is a moderate correlation (0.46) between the sector level cross-sectional standard deviations in ESG levels and average dispersions, suggesting that sectors in which firms are very different in their ESG practices may also be difficult for ESG providers to agree on their scores.

Is ESG Dispersion Related to ESG Levels?

Apart from sector effects, ESG dispersion might also be closely related to ESG levels. Do firms with better ESG scores also get higher dispersion among providers? To answer this question, each month we sort all firms within each sector into quintiles based on their ESG level, with the low-ESG firms in Q1 and the high-ESG firms in Q5. For each quintile, we first calculate the average dispersion on a monthly basis and then average across all the months. The average dispersions by ESG quintiles are reported in Table 13.3. The results suggest that better rated ESG firms on average have lower dispersion than worse rated ones (3.68 vs 3.97). The difference in dispersion between the highest and lowest ESG quintiles is 0.30 (3.97 – 3.68), which is 14% of the magnitude of the cross-sectional standard deviation of dispersion among different firms (2.2 from Figure 13.1 Panel A). One explanation is that poorly rated ESG firms may lag behind in different aspects of their ESG practices and thus have high dispersion among providers since each provider may be looking at different aspects.

Another possible explanation could be attributed to the presence of firms with limited ESG disclosures. ESG score providers often penalize firms with low levels of ESG disclosure. In addition, a firm that is less willing to communicate its ESG activities may also spend less efforts on improving their ESG practices, leading to low level scores. In the meantime, these firms are also more likely to have high ESG dispersions because less transparency leaves room for different interpretations. Furthermore, ESG providers usually have different treatments for non-disclosed items, leading to high score dispersion. Some providers assign the worst possible score if no information is available, while other providers only rate them slightly worse than the industry average. We indeed find that in our sample firms with more ESG non-disclosures on average have lower ESG scores and higher ESG dispersion. However, the overall impact of ESG non-disclosures on ESG dispersion is very small. The ESG non-disclosures can only explain an additional 0.04% of the cross-sectional variation in ESG dispersion while controlling for other firm characteristics. Therefore, the different treatments of non-disclosures, though artificially increase ESG dispersion among providers, do not drive the dispersion measures in the cross-section.

There are two important implications from the observation that ESG dispersion seems to decrease in higher ESG levels:

- When examining the relations between ESG dispersion and other metrics, such as future performance or ESG score changes, it is important to control for the level of current ESG score to isolate the effect of dispersion;
- Because of the negative relation, it makes more sense to use the raw dispersion instead of the relative dispersion (dispersion scaled by ESG level). The latter would artificially deflate the dispersion measure for high ESG firms.

Other Firm Characteristics

To inspect any other tilt that ESG scores might have, Table 13.3 also reports the average size, beta, volatilities, quality (investment rate and operating profitability), and credit ratings by ESG quintiles.[13] Consistent with prior findings

TABLE 13.3 Characteristic differences of Q5 (high)–Q1 (low) sorted on ESG level.

ESG Score Quintiles	Dispersion	Market Cap ($bl)	Beta	Total Vol. (%/day)	Idiosyncratic Vol. (%/day)	Investment rate (%)	Operating Profitability (%)	Credit Rating
Q1 (Low ESG)	3.97	23	1.07	1.84	1.36	11	29	9.98
Q2	4.21	29	1.06	1.77	1.31	9	31	9.33
Q3	3.95	36	1.11	1.74	1.27	7	32	8.90
Q4	3.70	41	1.12	1.73	1.24	6	32	8.74
Q5 (High ESG)	3.68	54	1.08	1.59	1.14	5	35	8.17
Q5–Q1	−0.30	31	0.01	−0.25	−0.23	−6	6	−1.81

Note: The statistics are first averaged across stocks within each bucket on a monthly basis and are then averaged over time. Each month all firms are sorted into five quintiles on their ESG levels within sectors. The time series are from August 2009 to April 2018. For detailed definitions of characteristics, see note 13.

Source: Compustat, MSCI, Sustainalytics, Vigeo Eiris, Barclays Research (see, e.g. Breedt et al 2019, Giese et al 2019), highly rated ESG companies tend to be bigger in market capitalization, even in our large cap universe. We also find that ESG scores have limited tilt on the systematic market risk (market beta), but companies with higher ESG scores tend to have smaller idiosyncratic volatilities and total volatilities. This is consistent with findings from Chapter 2 that higher ESG scores are associated with lower downside risks, as evidenced by their lower intensity of credit rating downgrades. Better-rated ESG companies also demonstrate higher quality based on firm fundamental characteristics (lower investment rate and higher operating profits), which could generate a positive risk premium according to the Fama and French (2015) five-factor model. Another measure of quality is credit rating. Consistent with the findings in Chapter 1, firms with higher ESG scores also have better credit ratings.

The next step is to understand whether ESG dispersion is related to certain firm characteristics. Insights to this question could help guide in-house ESG analysts to more efficiently direct their resources to firms whose ESG attributes might be hard to assess. However, the relation between dispersion and ESG level as well as the various factor tilts of ESG levels creates a challenge on identifying which firm characteristics are related to ESG dispersion. To control for the interaction between ESG dispersion and all these variables, we run cross-sectional regressions: each year, we regress individual firm's ESG dispersion on a host of firm characteristics, such as size, risk measures (market beta, total and idiosyncratic volatilities), qualities (investment rate and operating profitability), credit ratings, and dispersion in credit ratings, while controlling for the firm's average ESG score level and sector dummies (Intercept = Commodities Sector). Since ESG scores are updated infrequently and some of the characteristics require data from the previous year to measure, and to avoid problems associated with overlapping data, we run the cross-sectional regressions annually at the end of each April (our data set ends in April).[14] All independent variables besides the sector dummies have been standardized within each sector for easy interpretation of the coefficients. Table 13.4 reports the coefficient on each independent variable averaged across time. To see if the relationship is consistent over time, we also calculate the Fama–MacBeth t-statistics for each coefficient and denote the significance with asterisks (***/**/* denotes significance at the 1%-/5%-/10%-level).[15] The second column reports the percentage of periods that the coefficients are significant in the cross-section. There are several observations worth noting in Table 13.4.

First, in terms of sectors, the estimates suggest that Commodities and Communications sectors have the highest dispersion while the Utilities sector has the lowest dispersion, consistent with the results in Figure 13.2.

Second, both ESG and credit ratings have a significantly negative relation with dispersion. Note that unlike ESG scores, a worse credit quality rating is associated with a higher numeric number. The negative relation between ESG

TABLE 13.4   Average coefficients of monthly cross-sectional regressions of ESG dispersion on firm characteristics.

	Avg. Coef	% of periods with coefficient being significant at 10%-level	Avg. Coef in Sub-Periods	
			2010–2013	2014–2018
Intercept (Commodities)	3.45***	100	3.70	3.24
Communications	0.01	11	−0.20	0.17
Consumer	−0.19	11	−0.08	−0.28
Financials	−0.28*	11	−0.25	−0.30
Industrials	−0.27	22	−0.55	−0.05
Technology	−0.65***	22	−0.76	−0.56
Utilities	−0.88***	67	−0.97	−0.80
ESG Score	**−0.16***	33	−0.13	−0.19
Credit Rating	**0.07***	33	0.09	0.05
Dispersion in Credit Rating	−0.02	11	−0.05	0.01
Market Cap	**0.37***	67	0.33	0.41
Systematic Vol. (trailing 1yr)	−0.06	11	0.04	−0.15
Idiosyncratic Vol (trailing 1yr)	0.04	11	−0.07	0.12
Investment rate	−0.01	0	−0.06	0.02
Operating Profitability	−0.04	22	−0.02	−0.06
Adj. R²	4%			

Note: All independent variables except for industry dummies have been z-scored within its respective industries for easy interpretation of the coefficients. The time period is April 2010 to April 2018.
Source: Compustat, MSCI, Sustainalytics, Vigeo Eiris, Barclays Research.

level and dispersion is consistent with the ESG quintile results in Table 13.3. The negative relation between credit rating and ESG dispersion is not surprising. Firms with lower credit quality are more likely to be resource constrained and lag behind in their ESG practices. These firms may have poor ESG practices in different areas and thus makes it difficult for ESG providers to assess.[16] Dispersion in credit ratings, on the other hand, is not significantly related to ESG dispersion, which suggests that ESG score providers might face different challenges from credit rating agencies. Therefore, firms for which the credit rating agencies have a problem agreeing on (high credit rating dispersion) are not necessarily the firms that the ESG providers have a problem agreeing on.

Third, in terms of other firm characteristics, ESG dispersion has a significant loading on the market cap. A one-standard deviation increase in market cap is related to an increase of 0.37 in dispersion (on a scale of 0 to 100). Some may find this relation counterintuitive since smaller firms usually lag behind in their ESG practices or have fewer disclosures and therefore are regarded as more difficult to assess. However, both effects are also related to ESG levels, which are explicitly controlled for in the regression analysis. The relation therefore should be interpreted as, for two firms with similar ESG scores, providers tend to disagree more on the bigger firm. One possible reason for this relation is that larger firms might be more complex in terms of their products, industries of operations, geographical locations, numbers of subsidiaries and layers of organizational structures, which make them harder to evaluate.

Coefficients on all other characteristics are fairly small and statistically insignificant, suggesting that ESG dispersions do not have a strong factor tilt as ESG levels do. The last two columns of Table 13.4 show the average regression coefficients in the first half and second half of the sample period. The coefficients that were significant in the whole sample (utilities sector dummy, ESG score, credit rating, and market cap) have the same signs and are fairly stable across the two time periods, suggesting that their effects are not driven by a specific sub-period.

Overall, our results suggest that the following types of firms are more likely to have high dispersion among providers:

- In commodities and communications sector;
- With lower average ESG scores;
- With worse credit ratings;
- With larger market cap.

High dispersion in these firms indicate that ESG score providers agree less often on the scores of these companies and suggest that these companies may have an extra layer of complexity in the ESG dimension. In addition, all the firm characteristics listed in Table 13.4 jointly explain only about 4% of the total cross-sectional variation in dispersion, which suggests that dispersion in ESG scores may be largely firm-specific. These high ESG dispersion firms may be challenging for providers to evaluate, but challenges provide opportunities. The high dispersion ESG firms may be an area where in-house ESG expertise could leverage their deep understanding of the firm and the industry to add value beyond the standard scores from external providers.

ESG DISPERSION STABILITY AND RELATION WITH FUTURE ESG SCORE CHANGES

In this section we examine the stability of ESG dispersions and how they are related to subsequent changes in ESG score. A good understanding of the ESG score dynamics would help investors monitor their portfolios' ESG scores. For example, frequent and significant upgrades and downgrades in ESG scores could lead to excess turnover in portfolios and unintended risk exposures. Could investors identify companies who are likely to experience a change in ESG by looking at ESG dispersion?

Stability

Table 13.5 reports the transition matrix of the ESG levels and dispersions. It shows the transition frequencies of ESG dispersion terciles over a 12-month horizon. Next to it, we provide the transition matrix of ESG level terciles as a comparison. The analysis reveals that ESG dispersion is somewhat persistent: 57% of low dispersion stocks still have low dispersion after one year, while 64% of high dispersion stocks still have high dispersion. The percentage staying in the same bucket is higher for the high dispersion one, indicating that providers are slightly more likely to switch from agreement to disagreement than the other way around. In addition, ESG dispersion is much less persistent than ESG levels. Indeed, the frequency for the low and high ESG stocks to stay in the same bucket is over 80%. This indicates that ESG dispersion may be more dynamic than ESG levels and may benefit from frequent monitoring.

ESG Dispersion and Future Score Changes

This section examines how ESG dispersion is related to changes in ESG score in the next 12-month while controlling for firm characteristics. Since all ESG scores are within a 0–100 range, the magnitude of a firm's ESG score changes are limited by their score levels. For example, for a firm with an ESG score of 75, the maximum possible score increase is 25 (from 75 to 100), and its

TABLE 13.5   Transition frequencies across ESG level and dispersion terciles on a one-year horizon.

			ESG Dispersion Terciles			ESG Level Terciles		
			At end of 12m			At end of 12m		
			Low	Medium	High	Low	Medium	High
Respective	At start of	Low	57	32	11	81	18	1
Terciles	period	Medium	30	45	25	13	70	17
		High	11	26	64	1	13	86

Note: The number in the ith-row jth-column represents the percentage of stocks in tercile i at the end of current year that are ranked in tercile j after 12 months. Terciles are sorted within sectors. The time period is from August 2009 to April 2018.
Source: Compustat, MSCI, Sustainalytics, Vigeo Eiris, Barclays Research.

maximum possible score decrease is 75 (from 75 to 0). Therefore, we scale a firm's score change by its maximum possible score change in the respective direction, and denote it as relative ESG score change. Any score increase in the previous example would be scaled by 25, and any score decrease would be scaled by 75. We look at whether ESG dispersion is related to net change and absolute magnitude of the change separately. The former relation would tell us whether higher dispersion is related to more upgrades or downgrades in future ESG scores, whereas the latter relation would indicate whether higher dispersion is related to larger ESG score revisions regardless of the direction.

Since other firm characteristics, such as size or the level of ESG scores, might be also related to future ESG score changes, we examine the impact of all these factors in a multivariate regression framework. We follow a Fama–MacBeth regression setting as in Table 13.4. Specifically, we run a cross-sectional multivariate regression for each April and assess the consistency of the regression coefficients across years. The dependent variables are firm-level relative ESG score change and the absolute value of the relative ESG score change. The independent variables include ESG dispersion as well as the same set of characteristics we included in the earlier regression for ESG dispersion. All independent variables are standardized for easy interpretation of the results.

Overall, we find that stocks with higher ESG dispersion are more likely to experience larger changes in their ESG scores in the next 12 months, but not necessarily in any particular direction. Panel A in Table 13.6 reports the average coefficients from annual cross-sectional regressions. When the dependent variable is the relative ESG score change, the coefficient on ESG dispersion is statistically insignificant, around 0.17%. In contrast, the coefficient on ESG dispersion is 0.32% and becomes significant at 1% level when explaining the absolute relative ESG score change. To put the coefficients in context, Table 13.6 Panel B reports the averages and cross-sectional standard deviations of the two dependent variables. A one standard deviation increase in the ESG dispersion is on average related to a 0.03 (0.17%/5.03%) standard deviation increase in the ESG score change and a 0.09 (0.32%/3.38%) standard deviation increase in the magnitude of ESG score changes. The impact of ESG dispersion on the magnitude of absolute ESG score change is almost 200% larger than the impact on the net ESG score change. Average ESG scores, on the other hand, are significantly linked to both the magnitude of future ESG changes and the directions of changes. Firms with lower average ESG scores are more likely to experience upgrades and bigger revisions in the ESG scores in the next 12-month period. The relationships between ESG level and future score changes are also of a larger magnitude than those between ESG dispersions and future score changes, suggesting that ESG dispersion may be a second order effect to ESG level in explaining future score changes. A one standard deviation decrease in ESG level is related to a 0.16 standard deviation

TABLE 13.6   ESG dispersion and subsequent ESG score changes.

Panel A: Regression of future 12-month relative ESG score changes on ESG dispersion and firm characteristics

Variable	Dependent Variable	
	relative ESG score change (%)	absolute relative ESG score change (%)
Intercept (Commodities)	1.2	2.74***
Communications	−0.13	−0.73
Consumer	−0.42	−0.17
Financials	0.34	−0.01
Industrials	−0.24	−0.33
Technology	−0.39	−0.4
Utilities	0.93	−0.36
Avg. ESG Score	−0.81***	−0.35%***
ESG Dispersion	0.17	0.32%***
Market Cap	−0.2	0.14
Systematic Vol. (trailing 1yr)	0.12	−0.05
Idiosyncratic Vol. (trailing 1yr)	−0.15	0.04
Investment rate	−0.26*	−0.03
Operating profitability	0.17	−0.09
Index Credit Rating	−0.1	0.16**
Dispersion of Index Credit Rating	−0.16	0.04
Adj R²	10.6	6

Panel B: Distribution of future 12-month relative ESG score changes

Relative ESG score change		Absolute relative ESG score change	
Average	Standard Deviation	Average	Standard Deviation
0.10%	5.03%	3.93%	3.38%

Note: The averages and standard deviations are first calculated from the cross-section in each April (one month per year to avoid overlapping observations) and then averaged across the time-series.
Source: Compustat, MSCI, Sustainalytics, Vigeo Eiris, Barclays Research.

increase in future ESG score change and a 0.10 standard deviation increase in the magnitude of future ESG score change.

One possible explanation for the positive relation between ESG dispersion and magnitude of future score changes is that high ESG dispersion is usually an indication of uncertainties and challenges in assessing firm ESG practices, which in turn leaves more room and possibilities for bigger revisions. These results suggest that investors may benefit from taking ESG dispersion into consideration.

ESG DISPERSION AND FUTURE STOCK PERFORMANCE

We now examine whether ESG dispersion is related to future stock performance. To isolate the effect attributable to ESG dispersion, we construct two portfolios, one with maximum ESG dispersion and one with minimum dispersion. We carefully construct the two portfolios such that they have the same ESG levels and other risk characteristics. We also look at alternative ways to control for risk and examine whether the same results hold in an out-of-sample period. Then we repeat the exercise with corporate bonds to evaluate whether the same dynamics hold in the credit market.

Methodology

To measure the effect of ESG dispersion on stock performance, it is important to separate the dispersion effect from the effect of ESG levels documented in Chapter 3 as well as other possible sources of performance. To achieve this objective, we follow the same methodology as in Chapters 2 and 3 to construct a pair of index-tracking portfolios with matching ESG levels and characteristics but that differ considerably in their ESG dispersions. We then compare the performance of these two portfolios to measure the effect of ESG dispersion.

In particular, we build a pair of portfolios that closely track the S&P 500 index in terms of key risk characteristics (beta, size, valuation, quality) and sector allocations on a monthly basis. We control for sector allocations to make sure that our results are not driven by any unintended sector tilt.[17] We also make sure that the two portfolios have identical average ESG levels, while having the largest possible difference in their ESG dispersion. We construct three pairs of portfolios for ESG scores with low/medium/high levels respectively to make sure that any dispersion effect we find is not specific to a particular ESG level.[18] Note that we still use the entire universe to track the index as the ESG level constraint is imposed at the portfolio level. An alternative way would be to divide the stock universe into three subsamples – high, medium, and low ESG subsamples – based on individual stock's ESG score, and then formulate separate tracking portfolios within each subsample. One drawback of this approach is that the subsample could be too small to meet all the other constraints. Therefore, we keep the entire universe and vary the constraint on the ESG level. Specifically, the portfolio-pairs are constructed with the objectives and constraints listed in Table 13.7.

TABLE 13.7   Construction details of ESG-dispersion-tilted stock portfolios.

	Max-Dispersion Portfolio	Min-Dispersion Portfolio
Objectives	Maximize portfolio average ESG dispersion	Minimize portfolio average ESG dispersion
Constraints	Matching ESG level (set equal to low, medium, or high respectively) Matching index sector weights Matching index risk characteristics Portfolio average market beta = 1 Portfolio average size beta = Index size beta Portfolio average B/M = Index average B/M Portfolio average investment rate = Index average investment rate Portfolio average operating profit = Index average operating profit Stock weight cap of 5%	
Universe	S&P 500 constituent stocks with ESG scores from all three providers	
Index benchmark	S&P 500 index	
Rebalance frequency	Month end	

Note: All averages are weighted averages using % allocation as weights for the portfolio and market cap as weights for the index.
Source: Barclays Research.

An alternative approach to study the effects on future returns is to create quintile or decile stock portfolios based on the variable of interest. For example, one can construct a long–short portfolio by buying the high-dispersion stocks and selling short the low-dispersion stocks. The returns of the long–short portfolio would then be regressed on a host of equity risk factors to remove the exposures to other risk factors (e.g. the Fama–French 5 factors, Fama and French 2015). The intercept from the regression would measure the unique explanatory power coming from the variable of interest, i.e. ESG score dispersion. This is a popular approach in equity research because of its simplicity. However, we prefer the exposure-matched approach because it is practical, investable, and provides estimates of the return effects on a monthly basis (see Chapter 3 for a more detailed discussion of the two approaches).

Relation Between ESG Dispersion and Future Stock Returns

Table 13.8 reports the performance statistics of the max- and min-dispersion portfolios with index-matching characteristics for low/medium/high ESG

TABLE 13.8 Performance of index-replicating portfolio with Max- and Min-ESG dispersion.

ESG Level		Max Dispersion	Min Dispersion	Index	Max over Index	Min over Index	Max-over-Min
Low	Avg Ret (%/Yr)	12.10	14.92	13.99	−1.89	0.92	−2.81
	Vol (%/Yr)	12.49	13.37	11.89	4.56	4.53	6.18
	Sharpe (Inf.) Ratio (ann.)	**0.94**	**1.08**	**1.14**	**−0.42**	**0.20**	**−0.46**
	Correlation with Index	0.93	0.94		−0.06	0.16	−0.16
Medium	Avg Ret (%/Yr)	12.44	15.19		−1.55	1.19	−2.74
	Vol (%/Yr)	12.53	12.82		4.37	4.05	6.14
	Sharpe (Inf.) Ratio (ann.)	**0.96**	**1.15**		**−0.36**	**0.29**	**−0.45**
	Correlation with Index	0.94	0.95		−0.03	0.07	−0.07
High	Avg Ret (%/Yr)	12.32	13.96		−1.67	−0.04	−1.64
	Vol (%/Yr)	12.03	11.92		3.45	3.63	4.80
	Sharpe (Inf.) Ratio (ann.)	**0.99**	**1.14**		**−0.48**	**−0.01**	**−0.34**
	Correlation with Index	0.96	0.95		−0.10	−0.14	0.03

Note: Low/medium/high ESG level corresponds to scores of 41/46/51, which were set as the time series average of cross-sectional Q1/Mean/Q3 each month. The returns are from September 2009 to May 2018.
Source: Compustat, MSCI, Sustainalytics, Vigeo Eiris, Barclays Research.

levels respectively. The performances are between September 2009 and May 2018. Each portfolio has high correlations with the index (all above 0.93) and modest tracking errors, indicating that the replication methodology is tracking the index relatively well. In this period, the max-dispersion portfolio underperformed the min-dispersion portfolio consistently at the low, medium, and high ESG levels. The magnitude of the overall underperformance of the max-over-min-dispersion portfolios is moderate, ranging from 1.64% to 2.81%/ year depending on the ESG level, with information ratios ranging from −0.34 to −0.46.[19] The moderate magnitude of the underperformance is in line with our expectation. Because ESG dispersion is a second moment of the variable of interest (ESG scores), we don't expect it to have a prominent effect, especially given that the ESG score itself has only started to be incorporated into invest-ment processes in the latter part of the sample period. Another observation worth noting is that the max-dispersion portfolios have lower Sharpe ratios than the min-dispersion portfolios after matching exposures to common risk factors, indicating that the underperformance of max-dispersion portfolios is still present on a risk-adjusted basis.

Figure 13.3 Panel A reports the cumulative return difference of the max-over-min dispersion portfolios for each of the three ESG levels for the whole sample period. One noticeable pattern is that the return differences hover around zero before 2012, and only start to steadily decrease in 2013, regardless of the ESG level. Because the return patterns seem to be stronger and more consistent post-2013, we report the average performance statistics of the max-over-min-dispersion portfolios in the two sub-periods in Panel B of Figure 13.3. The reported numbers indicate a consistent underperformance from the max-ESG-dispersion portfolios since 2013, but no consistent pattern before then. Since 2013, the max-dispersion portfolio underperformed the min-dispersion portfolios by more than 3%/year with information ratios over −0.55 regardless of the ESG levels. Pre-2013, there is no consistent under-/over-performance patterns between the max- and min-dispersion portfolios across the three ESG levels. It would be useful to understand what drives the change pre- and post-2013. Perhaps more fundamentally, why is there any return difference between max- and min-dispersion portfolios to begin with?

A Possible Explanation for Underperformance of the Max-dispersion Portfolios

One possible explanation for the underperformance of max-ESG-dispersion portfolio might be that the market temporarily overvalues stocks with high ESG dispersion, and later adjusts price down to their long-term fair value, creating the subsequent lower return pattern. Miller (1977) proposes a theory linking general divergence in opinions among investors and future stock returns. The market tends to temporarily overvalue stocks with a high level of divergence in opinion because the optimistic investors can bid up the price relatively easily while the pessimistic investors are less able to express their views given short-sell constraints and costs. However, over time, one would observe negative returns of the high-opinion-divergence stocks as their prices revert back to their fair value. To test this theory, Diether et al. (2002) use dispersion in analysts' earnings forecast as a proxy for divergence in opinions and find that stocks with high dispersion in analyst forecasts indeed have more negative subsequent returns.

One way to test the hypothesis in the context of ESG dispersion is to examine whether there is a positive relation between a stock's ESG dispersion and its contemporaneous valuation. Based on the hypothesis, firms with higher

Panel A: Cumulative return difference of max-over-min dispersion replicating portfolio controlling for ESG level (September 2009–May 2018)

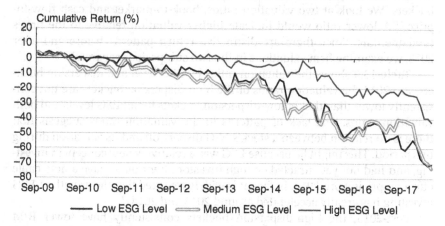

Panel B: Sub-period performance of the max-over-min ESG dispersion portfolios controlling for ESG levels

		Low ESG Level	Medium	High ESG Level
Pre-2013	Avg Ret (%/Yr)	−1.69	−2.00	1.41
(Sep 2009–	Vol (%/Yr)	5.93	6.88	5.06
Dec 2012)	Inf. Ratio (ann.)	−0.28	−0.29	0.28
	Correlation with Index	−0.20	−0.01	0.07
Post-2013	Avg Ret (%/Yr)	−3.51	−3.20	−3.51
(Jan 2013–	Vol (%/Yr)	6.36	5.69	4.58
May 2018)	Inf. Ratio (ann.)	−0.55	−0.56	−0.77
	Correlation with Index	−0.13	−0.13	0.00

FIGURE 13.3 Time series and sub-period performances of Max-over-Min replicating portfolios.
Note: Low/medium/high ESG level corresponds to scores of 41/46/51, which were set as the time series average of cross-sectional Q1/Mean/Q3 each month. The return time series are from September 2009 to May 2018.
Source: Compustat, MSCI, Sustainalytics, Vigeo Eiris, Barclays Research.

ESG dispersion should have higher valuation compared to otherwise similar firms with lower ESG dispersion, because the more optimistic investors would bid up the price while more pessimistic investors might not be able to short because of short-sell constraints. We sort stocks into two buckets based on their ESG dispersion within their respective sectors. To control for effects of the ESG levels, we also did an independent double sort based on ESG levels. The sample is therefore divided into 4 (2-ESG-level x 2-ESG-dispersion) buckets. We look at two valuation ratios, book-to-market and cash flow-to-price.[20] A lower ratio would indicate higher valuation relative to the firm's fundamentals. Since there are distinctive return patterns before and after 2013, we examine firm valuations in the two sub-periods separately.

Table 13.9 shows the valuation ratios by ESG level and dispersion buckets. Pre-2013 the valuation ratios of the high-dispersion buckets are not consistently lower than that of low-dispersion buckets for all ESG levels and both valuation ratios. The lack of patterns in the valuation ratios suggests that there is no relation between a stock's ESG dispersion and its valuation during this period. This might be because ESG was a relatively new concept in investing, and had not yet attracted enough investor attention to have a noticeable effect on pricing pre-2013. In fact, it is widely reported that the growth of ESG investing has greatly accelerated around 2013 and 2014.[21]

Post-2013, the high-dispersion buckets consistently have lower B/M and CF/P ratios regardless of the ESG level. The lower B/M and CF/P ratios indicate that the market prices of the stocks (denominators in the ratios) are higher compared to their fundamentals in the high-dispersion group, consistent with the hypothesis. Because of high-dispersion stocks' overvaluation post-2013, they subsequently exhibit lower returns as observed in Figure 13.3 when their prices adjust down to the long-term fair level.

TABLE 13.9 Valuation ratios with independent double sorts on ESG levels and dispersion.

ESG Level	ESG Dispersion	Pre-2013(August 2009–December 2012)		Post-2013(January 2013–April 2018)	
		B/M	Cash Flow / Price	B/M	Cash Flow / Price
Low	Low	0.561	0.096	0.495	0.084
	High	0.552	0.097	0.442	0.083
	High − Low	−0.009	0.001	−0.053	−0.001
High	Low	0.561	0.107	0.432	0.085
	High	0.586	0.103	0.416	0.079
	High − Low	0.025	−0.004	−0.016	−0.007

Note: The statistics are EW within each bucket on a monthly basis then averaged in the time series. Each month all firms are sorted independently on their ESG level and dispersion within sectors.
Source: Compustat, MSCI, Sustainalytics, Vigeo Eiris, Barclays Research.

TABLE 13.10 Performance of max-over-min-ESG-dispersion portfolio in original specification with additional matching constraint for CF/P.

		Original + additional matching constraint for CF/P			Original		
		Low ESG Level	Medium	High ESG Level	Low ESG Level	Medium	High ESG Level
Pre-2013	Avg Ret (%/Yr)	−0.24	−1.75	−1.22	−1.69	−2.00	1.41
(Sep 2009–	Vol (%/Yr)	5.79	6.40	5.29	5.93	6.88	5.06
Dec 2012)	Inf. Ratio (ann.)	−0.04	−0.27	−0.23	−0.28	−0.29	0.28
	Correlation with Index	−0.11	0.04	0.07	−0.20	−0.01	0.07
Post-2013	Avg Ret (%/Yr)	−3.35	−3.33	−2.55	−3.51	−3.20	−3.51
(Jan 2013–	Vol (%/Yr)	6.19	5.74	4.08	6.36	5.69	4.58
May 2018)	**Inf. Ratio (ann.)**	**−0.54**	**−0.58**	**−0.63**	**−0.55**	**−0.56**	**−0.77**
	Correlation with Index	−0.07	−0.07	0.01	−0.13	−0.13	0.00

Source: Compustat, MSCI, Sustainalytics, Vigeo Eiris, Barclays Research.

It is worth noting that the underperformance of max-dispersion portfolios is still present even when we control for the initial differences in B/M ratios between the max- and min-dispersion portfolios (see Table 13.8). This observation may seem in contradiction to the argument that max-dispersion portfolios' subsequent underperformance are associated with them being overvalued. We believe that is not the case here as firms are difficult to value and book-to-market ratio only captures one aspect of firm valuation. For example, cash-flow-to-price ratio, earnings-to-price ratio, or dividend-to-price ratios could also be used to measure valuation, and they are not always aligned. In fact, when we control for additional valuation measure in the replication portfolios (matching CF/P in addition to all the existing constraints), the magnitude of the max-over-min-dispersion portfolio returns and I.R. decreased slightly for the low and high ESG levels (see Table 13.10), but the pattern still remains the same. The results suggest that there could still be a large proportion of valuation effect not captured in B/M and CF/P ratios associated with dispersion in ESG. Our findings are consistent with Diether et al. (2002), which also find that stocks of high dispersion in analysts' forecasts still have negative future returns when controlling for the B/M factor.

ALTERNATIVE PORTFOLIO SPECIFICATIONS

In this section we look at some alternative specifications in constructing the tracking portfolios to make sure that the results we find are robust and not specific to the choice of our original constraints. In the first specification, we control for individual stock's risk exposures by looking at its abnormal returns over a size and book-to-market matched benchmark[22] instead of raw returns (Daniel and Titman 1997). Because the major risk characteristics are controlled through benchmark returns instead of matching characteristics, we drop the constraints on matching risk characteristics (size, B/M, investment rate, and operation profit), but still keep the constraints on matching ESG level, sector weights, market beta, and the weight cap. One advantage of the abnormal-return approach is that it is completely nonparametric and therefore can account for nonlinear relations between characteristics and returns.[23] In the second specification, we restrict the weight cap on an individual name to 2% (instead of the 5% in the original specification) to further limit the potential effect of a few outliers.

Table 13.11 presents the performance of the max-over-min-dispersion portfolios for the low/medium/high ESG levels under each specification, separately for the whole sample period and the pre-2013 and post-2013 sub-periods. Regardless of the specification and ESG level, the max-dispersion portfolio underperforms the min-dispersion portfolio in the whole sample period, with more pronounced differences post-2013. The magnitude of the return differences is smaller with the 2% weight cap. This is most likely because it is harder to get a big spread in dispersion between the max- and the min-dispersion portfolios when there is a tight weight cap on individual names. In other words, the signal efficacy may be diluted when we are forced to have more stocks in the portfolio.

Results from Extended Sample

Our analysis so far stopped in April 2018 because one of the providers, Sustainalytics, changed their rating methodology during 2018. Mixing the old and new data would create unintended dynamics. From a methodological standpoint, the legacy and the new Sustainalytics ESG scores can be thought of as from two different providers. It offers a unique opportunity to test the robustness of the results out of sample. If the general relation between ESG dispersion and subsequent performance holds, then higher dispersion in a firm's ESG scores should be related to future underperformance regardless of the providers. We have historical ESG scores from Sustainalytics' current methodology

TABLE 13.11 Performance of max-dispersion over min-dispersion portfolios controlling for characteristics.

		Using Abnormal returns			Using 2% weight cap		
		ESG Level			ESG Level		
		Low-	Medium-	High	Low-	Medium-	High
Whole	Avg Ret (%/Yr)	−2.72	−2.68	−1.98	−2.07	−1.06	−0.23
Sample	Vol (%/Yr)	6.67	6.89	5.96	4.27	4.11	3.34
(Sep. 2009–	**Inf. Ratio**	**−0.41**	**−0.39**	**−0.33**	**−0.49**	**−0.26**	**−0.07**
May 2018)	**(ann.)**						
	Correlation with Index	−0.22	−0.04	−0.01	−0.02	0.05	0.08
Pre-2013	Avg Ret (%/Yr)	−0.85	0.10	−0.49	−2.40	−1.00	0.74
(Sep 2009–	Vol (%/Yr)	6.57	7.08	5.69	3.94	4.19	3.38
Dec 2012)	**Inf. Ratio**	**−0.13**	**0.01**	**−0.09**	**−0.61**	**−0.24**	**0.22**
	(ann.)						
	Correlation with Index	−0.31	0.04	0.12	0.02	0.09	0.05
Post-2013	Avg Ret (%/Yr)	−3.87	−4.40	−2.90	−1.87	−1.10	−0.83
(Jan 2013–	Vol (%/Yr)	6.76	6.78	6.15	4.49	4.09	3.33
May 2018)	**Inf. Ratio**	**−0.57**	**−0.65**	**−0.47**	**−0.42**	**−0.27**	**−0.25**
	(ann.)						
	Correlation with Index	−0.14	−0.12	−0.11	−0.05	0.03	0.12

Source: Compustat, MSCI, Sustainalytics, Vigeo Eiris, Barclays Research.

starting from December. 2018, and our ESG scores from MSCI ends in September 2019.[24] This offers us a 10-month period to test the relation. However, the results should be treated with caution as the extended sample is very short.

Table 13.12 shows the performance of the max-over-min-ESG-dispersion portfolios in the extended sample, following the same aggregation and portfolio construction methodology as in the original analysis. We find that regardless of the ESG level, the general relation is the same: higher-dispersion firms underperform lower-dispersion firms regardless of the ESG level. The magnitude of the underperformance is smaller. However, it shouldn't be interpreted as a sign that the relation between ESG dispersion and future performance is decaying, because the sample period is too short and the decrease in magnitude could very likely be temporary.

TABLE 13.12 Performance of max-over-min-ESG-dispersion portfolios in extended sample (January 2019–October 2019, with new Sustainalytics scores).

	Low ESG Level	Medium	High ESG Level
Avg Ret (%/Yr)	−0.76	−0.52	−2.59
Vol (%/Yr)	6.40	5.88	9.55
Inf. Ratio (ann.)	−0.12	−0.09	−0.27
Correlation with Index	−0.62	−0.10	−0.32

Source: Compustat, MSCI, Sustainalytics, Vigeo Eiris, Barclays.

Effect of ESG Dispersion on Corporate Bonds

Another interesting question is whether the relation between dispersion and future performance extends to corporate bond markets. In Chapter 2, we show that a positive ESG tilt leads to a small but steady performance gain in corporate bonds in both investment grade and high yield as well as across US and European markets. As bond investors may have started to pay attention to firm's ESG attributes, ESG dispersion may also start to show a relation with future bond performance. To examine the effect of dispersion, we follow a similar tracking-portfolio methodology used in our equity analysis with some fine-tuning to adjust for important risk characteristics in corporate bonds.

Methodology

We start with our equity universe (S&P 500 constituents with ESG scores from all three providers) and find their mapped bonds, using a bond-to-equity mapping algorithm developed by Ben Dor and Xu (2015). For all the corporate bonds mapped to a stock, we only include the bonds that are included in the Bloomberg US Corporate and High Yield indices.[25]

To build tracking portfolios, we follow a two-step approach. The first step is to choose the most liquid bonds from each company as candidates for index tracking. We follow an approach similar to the one used in Ben Dor et al. (2020) to build our tracking universe.[26] The universe consists of one liquid bond for each company in the S&P 500 with ESG scores from all three providers. Index tracking also requires a benchmark index. In this particular exercise, because of our customized universe, we define the benchmark index to be the value-weighted (using bond market value) portfolio of all bonds in our tracking universe. To be clear, we are not proposing an index for actual investment, but simply constructing an anchor point to control for risk characteristics and accurately measure the effect of dispersion on corporate bond returns.

In the second step, we build pairs of bond portfolios to track the benchmark. We constrain the max- (min-) dispersion tracking portfolio to match the risk profiles of the benchmark while tilting the portfolio towards issuers with higher (lower) ESG dispersion by maximizing (minimizing) a portfolio's weighted average ESG dispersion. In particular, we implement the following constraints on the tracking portfolios. First, to match the risk profile of the benchmark and eliminate unintended risk exposures, we require the tracking portfolio to have the same characteristics as the benchmark across the following risk dimensions: sector weights, option adjusted spread, DTS, and ESP.[27] Second, we cap the weight of each bond in the portfolio at 2% to ensure that the tracking portfolios are not too concentrated and that idiosyncratic risk is sufficiently diversified. Furthermore, we constrain the max- and min-dispersion portfolios to have the same ESG levels (set to low/medium/high levels respectively). The details of the portfolio construction are listed in Table 13.13.[28]

TABLE 13.13 Construction details of ESG-dispersion-tilted corporate bond portfolios.

	Max-Dispersion Portfolio	Min-Dispersion Portfolio
Objectives	Maximize portfolio average ESG dispersion	Minimize portfolio average ESG dispersion
Constraints	Portfolio average ESG level is set equal to low, medium, or high respectively	
	Matching universe sector weights	
	Portfolio average OAS = universe value-weighted average OAS	
	Portfolio average DTS = universe value-weighted average DTS	
	Portfolio average ESP = universe value-weighted average ESP	
	Issuer weight cap of 2%	
Universe	Bonds of S&P 500 constituents with ESG scores from all three providers and also included in the Bloomberg US IG or HY Corporate indices (one representative bond per company)	
Benchmark	A portfolio of all bonds in our universe (weighted using bond market value)	
Rebalance frequency	Month end	

Note: All portfolio averages are weighted averages using % of portfolio allocation as weights.
Source: Barclays Research.

We examine the excess returns of the corporate bonds to exclude the rates component and focus on the credit component of returns.[29] We construct pairs of max- and min-dispersion portfolios at the end of each month and track the portfolios' excess returns over the following month.

Findings

Table 13.14 reports the performance of the max-over-min-ESG-dispersion corporate bond portfolios from September 2009 to May 2018. Because of the distinctive time-series return patterns in equities, we also separate the sample period into pre-2013 and post-2013 sub-periods. Overall, the results are qualitatively similar to the pattern we find in equities. Post-2013, there is a clear consistent pattern of the max-ESG-dispersion portfolios underperforming the min-ESG-dispersion portfolios at each ESG levels while matching benchmark risk characteristics. Pre-2013, similar to equities, we do not observe a consistent underperformance of the max-dispersion portfolios across all ESG levels. The differences in the two samples could be related to the fact that the growth of ESG investing has greatly accelerated in 2013.

Overall, we find that the max-ESG-dispersion portfolios consistently underperform the min-dispersion portfolios post-2013 in both equities and corporate bonds at all ESG score levels while matching risk characteristics. These results suggest that ESG dispersion among providers might be a useful input for ESG investors to consider in their portfolio construction.

TABLE 13.14 Corporate bond excess return differences in max-over-min ESG dispersion portfolios while controlling for ESG level and characteristics.

		Low ESG Level	Medium	High ESG Level
Whole Period	Avg Ex. Ret (%/Yr)	0.05	−0.08	−0.12
(Sep 2009–	Vol (%/Yr)	0.78	0.82	0.81
May 2018)	**Inf. Ratio (ann.)**	**0.06**	**−0.10**	**−0.15**
Pre-2013	Avg Ex. Ret (%/Yr)	0.29	0.38	0.11
(Sep 2009–	Vol (%/Yr)	0.95	1.07	1.10
Dec 2012)	**Inf. Ratio (ann.)**	**0.31**	**0.36**	**0.10**
Post-2013	Avg Ex. Ret (%/Yr)	−0.10	−0.36	−0.26
(Jan 2013–	Vol (%/Yr)	0.67	0.61	0.58
May 2018)	**Inf. Ratio (ann.)**	**−0.15**	**−0.60**	**−0.45**

Note: Benchmark and portfolio construction details are defined in Table 13.13. The sample period is from September 2009 to May 2018. Excess returns over duration matched treasury returns are reported.
Source: Bloomberg, Compustat, MSCI, Sustainalytics, Vigeo Eiris, Barclays Research.

CONCLUSIONS

Scores from ESG providers disagree substantially. As ESG attributes have become more central in investors' investment processes, understanding the nature, the degree, and the implications of the score dispersion among providers is becoming increasingly important. In this chapter, we standardize ESG scores from three market-leading providers and provide a systematic characterization of ESG dispersion based on the standardized, comparable scores. Furthermore, we investigate whether dispersion is related to firms' future ESG score and performance. We find that dispersion is higher among firms with lower ESG scores, worse credit ratings, larger market capitalization, and in the commodities and communications sectors. In addition, firms with high ESG dispersion have experienced larger score revisions over the following year. Finally, we find that dispersion is negatively related to future performances. A portfolio of S&P 500 stocks with high ESG dispersion underperforms an otherwise similar portfolio with low dispersion after controlling for ESG level and common risk exposures. The underperformance is especially pronounced after 2013 when the growth of ESG investing has greatly accelerated. The results also broadly hold up in corporate bonds. Overall, our results suggest that, in addition to ESG score levels, incorporating ESG score dispersion into the investment processes have historically been beneficial for performance.

REFERENCES

Ackert, L.F. and Athanassakos, G. (1997). Prior Uncertainty, Analyst Bias, and Subsequent Abnormal Returns. *The Journal of Financial Research*, 20 (2), pp. 263–273.

Ben Dor, A., Dynkin L., Hyman J., Houweling P., van Leeuwen E., and Penninga, O. (2007). DTS^{SM} (Duration Times Spread). *Journal of Portfolio Management*, 33 (2): 77–100.

Ben Dor, A., Guan, J., and Zeng, X. (2020). How Do Credit Markets React to Earnings Releases? Empirical Analysis and Implications for Investors. *Journal of Fixed Income*, 30 (3), pp. 47–65.

Ben Dor, A. and Xu, Z. (2015). Should Equity Investors Care About Corporate Bond Prices? Using Bond Prices to Construct Equity Momentum Strategies. *The Journal of Portfolio Management*, 41 (4), pp. 35–49.

Berg, F., Kölbel, J., and Rigobon, R. (2022). Aggregate Confusion: The Divergence of ESG Ratings. *Review of Finance*, 26 (6), pp. 1315–1344.

Breedt, A., Ciliberti, S., Gualdi, S., and Seager, P. (2019). Is ESG an Equity Factor or Just an Investment Guide? *The Journal of Investing*, 28 (2), pp. 32–42.

Daniel, K. and Titman, S. (1997). Evidence on the Characteristics of Cross-sectional Variation in Stock Returns. *The Journal of Finance*, 52 (1), pp. 1–33.

Desclée, A., Maitra, A., and Polbennikov, S. (2016). Relative Value Investing in Credit. *Barclays Research*, 9 May 2016.

Diether, K.B., Malloy, C.J., and Scherbina, A. (2002). Differences of Opinion and the Cross Section of Stock Returns. *The Journal of Finance*, 57 (5), pp. 2113–2141.

Dische, A. (2002). Dispersion in Analyst Forecasts and the Profitability of Earnings Momentum Strategies. *European Financial Management*, 8 (2), pp. 211–228.

Fama, E.F. and French, K.R. (2015). A Five-Factor Asset Pricing Model. *Journal of Financial Economics*, 116 (1), pp. 1–22.

Fama, E.F. and MacBeth, J.D. (1973). Risk, Return and Equilibrium: Empirical Tests. *Journal of Political Economy*, 81, pp. 607–636.

Giese, G., Lee, L.E., Melas, D., Nagy, Z., and Nishikawa, L. (2019). Foundations of ESG Investing: How ESG Affects Equity Valuation, Risk, and Performance. *The Journal of Portfolio Management*, 45 (5), pp. 69–83.

Li, F. and Polychronopoulos, A. (2020). What a Difference an ESG Ratings Provider Makes! *Research Affiliates*. https://www.researchaffiliates.com/content/dam/ra/publications/pdf/770-what-a-difference-an-esg-ratings-provider-makes.pdf

Miller, E.M. (1977). Risk, Uncertainty, and Divergence of Opinion. *The Journal of Finance*, 32 (4), pp. 1151–1168.

NOTES

1. See, for example, https://www.forbes.com/sites/georgkell/2018/07/11/the-remarkable-rise-of-esg/, accessed 3 August 2020.
2. For a more comprehensive discussion of the ESG rating and bond performances, see Chapter 2.
3. There are over 120 ESG data providers. Most providers focus on a particular dimension of ESG characteristics, such as carbon emission. These kinds of scores are usually more relevant for certain industries but are less applicable to a broader universe. Only a handful of ESG providers produce comprehensive scores to evaluate firms' overall ESG characteristics. We only use scores from three of them because the focus of the chapter is to illustrate the performance implication of ESG dispersion rather than examine ESG dispersion across all providers.
4. $AverageESG_i = (Normalized\_ESG_{i,MSCI} + Normalized\_ESG_{i,Sustainalytics} + Normalized\_ESG_{i,Vigeo Eiris})/3$
5. The cross-sectional standard deviation in this sample may seem to be small. This is because the transformation of scores from each provider is done on the entire population to preserve the distribution properties of each provider and make sure that there are enough observations in each provider-sector bucket. Our final sample is only a subset of the overall sample and has a tilt toward large caps, as we include only stocks in the S&P 500 index with ESG scores from all three providers. This can make the cross-sectional standard deviation in the sub-sample much smaller than the standard deviation in the broader sample.
6. An 80-percentile ranking in a normal (0, 1) distribution is equal to a z-score of 0.84. A 0.56 standard deviation around this z-score corresponds to z-scores of .28 and 1.41 respectively, which translates into a cumulative probability (conceptually

equivalent to percentile ranking) of 61% and 92%. One caveat of this interpretation is that the percentile difference of the more optimistic and pessimistic provider is dependent on the average ESG. If we assume the average ESG is ranked in the 50%-percentile, then following a similar calculation, the more optimistic and the more pessimist provider would have, on average, rated the company in the 29- and 71-percentile.

7. For each company, instead of taking the average of the numerical ratings from all three rating agencies, we convert the letter rating of each bond used by the Bloomberg Corporate and High Yield indices (index credit rating) into the numerical rating and then aggregate to the issuer level as the representative credit rating for each firm. The index rating that the Bloomberg indices use is the median rating of the three agencies. We take this approach because a large number of bond investors use the Bloomberg indices as benchmarks and follow the index ratings closely.

8. Credit ratings are transformed from letters to numerical scores where an increment of 1 represents one notch difference in rating. Higher numbers indicate worse ratings. For example, AAA+ translates into 1; A3 (worst of A ratings) translates into a numerical score of 8, and Baa1 (best of Baa ratings) translates into 9. Every month, for each firm, we calculate the credit rating dispersion among the three rating agencies in the same way as for ESG score dispersion.

9. It's interesting to mention that credit rating agencies have now become PRI signatories and have committed to including ESG considerations into their credit ratings. For example, Moody's, S&P, and Fitch's all had discussions on their effort.

10. In general, a close median and mean may not necessarily indicate lack of outliers, but in this case, since the dispersions have a lower bound of zero, which rules out negative outliers, a close median and mean suggests that there should not be big outliers on the positive side.

11. It may be difficult to compare the magnitudes of the drops directly on the graph since they are plotted on different scales. From Jan. 2013 to Apr. 2018, the average ESG dispersion (double line, left axis) decreases by 29%, from about 4.5 to just over 3. Over that period, the average ESG dispersion scaled by the cross-sectional standard deviation of ESG levels (dashed line, right axis) decreases by 16%.

12. Dispersion is calculated as the average of each provider score's distance from the mean, which in the two-provider case reduces to (max_ESG-min_ESG)/2.

13. Beta is CAPM beta calculated using trailing 36m data and requiring at least 18 months of observations. Volatilities include total volatilities and idiosyncratic volatilities. Total volatility is calculated as the volatility of daily returns in the trailing one-year window. Idiosyncratic volatility is calculated as the volatility of the residuals in the regression of daily returns of the stock on the daily returns of the Fama–French 5 factors in the past one-year window. Investment rate and operating profitability follow Fama and French's (2015) guidelines. Investment rate is the change in total assets from 1 year ago, scaled by the previous year's total assets. Operating profitability is calculated as the past 12-month operating profit (sales – costs of goods sold – sales and administrative expenses – interest expense) divided by the previous year's book equity. The investment rate and operating profitability are winsorized at 1% and 99%-tile in the original Compustat North American universe to avoid outliers.

14. For example, total and idiosyncratic vol. are from trailing 1 year's daily data. Investment rate and operating profits are also evaluated using the past 1-year's horizon.

15. The Fama–MacBeth t-statistics are calculated as the average annual coefficients over all years divided by the standard deviation of annual coefficients multiplied by the square root of number of annual regressions we run. For details, see Fama and MacBeth (1973).

16. One may argue that ESG levels should have captured this effect. However, it could be that ESG ratings are an imperfect measure of a firm's ESG practices, and credit quality may still be able to capture part of a firm's ESG effort even controlling for their average ESG ratings.

17. Size beta is calculated from a regression of monthly stock returns on the Fama–French 5 factor (Mkt_Rf, SMB, HML, RMW, CMA) using trailing 60m data requiring at least 36m of data. Valuation is controlled for by a firm's book-to-market ratio, calculated monthly. All financial statement variables are used with a two-month lag from its fiscal year/quarter end to make sure that the data would have been made available to public.

18. The low/medium/high levels are determined as the time series average of the monthly cross-sectional Q1/mean/Q3 of ESG levels in our sample. Each company's ESG level is based on the average of the normalized ESG score across the three providers.

19. Normally a negative information ratio would not make much sense in the context of a long–short strategy. In this specific case, the alternative way to look at it is that the min-dispersion portfolio outperforms the max-dispersion portfolio, with an information ratio being the negative of the reported information ratio (from 0.34 to 0.46).

20. Both B/M and CF/P ratios are calculated monthly using the most recent financial statement and current month's market price. Both ratios are winsorized at the 1%- and 99%-tile in the Compustat database of North American financial statement each month. All financial statement variables are included with a two-month lag from its fiscal year/quarter end to make sure that the data would have been made available to the public.

21. See, for example, https://www.forbes.com/sites/georgkell/2018/07/11/the-remarkable-rise-of-esg/, accessed 3 August 2020.

22. We use the 25 portfolios formed on size and book-to-market from Ken French's data library as our benchmarks. The breakpoints for the size and B/M buckets are based on NYSE market equity and B/M quintiles. The breakpoints are also available from Ken French's website. Each month, the abnormal return of a firm would be its raw return over the return of the FF portfolio with matched size and B/M.

23. In the original exercise, by matching weighted average of characteristics, we implicitly assume that there is a linear relation between each of the risk characteristics and their risk premiums (for example, the same increase of B/M from 0 to 0.1 and from 0.3 to 0.4 would be associated with the same difference in subsequent returns). In reality, the relation may be non-linear and will be accounted for more accurately using size and book-to-market buckets.

24. Sustainalytics ESG scores with the new methodology represent unmanaged ESG risk (higher scores indicate higher ESG risk exposures) while the legacy scores

used in the previous section represent ESG quality (higher scores indicate better characteristics). In order to align the new Sustainalytics ESG scores with the scores from other providers (which also represents quality), we transform the new Sustainalytics ESG scores as (100 – New Sustainalytics ESG risk).

25. Compared to the equity index like S&P 500, the Bloomberg corporate bond indices are more inclusive, as they cover the vast majority of the entire population of US publicly traded corporate bonds with a few technical rules to exclude extremely small bonds and bonds with less than one year to maturity.

26. In particular, we follow a three-step process: 1) For each issuer, we only keep senior bonds with maturity greater than 3 years and amount outstanding greater than the 25th-percentile of the notional amounts of all bonds in the corresponding Bloomberg US index. If none of the bonds satisfy these criteria, we keep all of them. 2) Among the remaining bonds, we select the ones that have age less than 2 years. If none of the bonds satisfy this criterion, we keep all of them. 3) Among the remaining bonds, we select the one that has duration closest to the industry average.

27. DTS, Duration Times Spread, is a popular metric for measuring the return volatility of a corporate bond (Ben Dor et al. 2007). ESP (Excess Spread to Peers) measures how cheap or expensive a corporate bond is relative to its peers while controlling for issuer characteristics and fundamentals (Desclée et al. 2016).

28. Our formulation of tracking portfolio is slightly different from the approach used in Chapter 2. For example, we do not control for maturity and sector DTS contributions. We leave out these constraints because our universe is much more limited.

29. The excess return of a bond is calculated as its total return over the return of a duration-matched treasury portfolio.

30. See, for example, https://www.forbes.com/sites/georgkell/2018/07/11/the-remarkable-rise-of-esg/, accessed 3 August 2020.

Index

Page numbers followed by *f and t* refer to figures and tables, respectively.